THE DEVELOPMENT OF INDUSTRY IN BURTON UPON TRENT

The Development of Industry in BURTON upon TRENT

by

C. C. OWEN

PHILLIMORE

1978

Published by
PHILLIMORE & CO. LTD.,
Shopwyke Hall, Chichester, Sussex

ISBN 0 85033 218 4

Printed in Great Britain by
UNWIN BROTHERS LIMITED
at the Gresham Press, Old Woking, Surrey

CONTENTS

	Preface	*xi*
	Acknowledgments	*xv*
I	Physical Environment	1
II	Historical Summary	8
III	The Development of Communications and Transport	13
IV	The Brewing Industry prior to 1807	28
V	The Brewing Industry during the 19th century	72
VI	The Iron-Working, Hardware and Engineering Industries	107
VII	The Textile Industries	127
VIII	The Hat Industry	155
IX	Miscellaneous Industries	161
X	Conclusion	175
	Bibliography	182
	List of Appendices	191
	Index	260

LIST OF PLATES

(between pages 48 and 49)

1. East Prospect of Burton upon Trent, 1732, by S. and N. Buck
2. View of Burton upon Trent from the east, 1753, by White
3. Plan of Burton upon Trent, 1757-60, by William Wyatt
4. View of Burton upon Trent from the north, 1779, by Wilson
5. View of Burton upon Trent from the east, *c.* 1840, by K. Thomas
6. Advertisement for the Opening of the Trent Navigation, 1712
7. Warehouses in Bond Lane, Burton upon Trent, 1800
8. Will of Benjamin Printon, 1728
9. Portrait of Henry Evans
10. Extract from Benjamin Wilson's day book, 1791
11. Extract from John Walker Wilson's day book, 1778
12. Portrait of Michael Bass
13. Robert Peel's first Cotton Mill (1780) and Burton Corn Mill
14. Design of Steam Engine installed in Peel & Co.'s Cotton Mill, 1792
15. Burton Forge Mills, *c.* 1900
16. A Feltmaker at work

LIST OF LINE DRAWINGS

(between pages 190 and 191)

1. Section across the Trent Valley at Burton upon Trent
2. Boreholes under Burton upon Trent (listed in Appendix 3)
3. Main Boreholes and Wells in Burton
4. Simplified Urban Growth Map of Burton upon Trent
5. Communications in and around Burton in 1800
6. Railway Network, Burton upon Trent, 1900
7. Benjamin Wilson's Ale Exports in 1789
8. Location of Industry in Burton, 1790
9. Distribution of Ale from Allsopp's Brewery, 1807-11 and 1822-26
10. Location of Industry in Burton 1880
11. East Anglian Centres supplying workers to Bass & Co., 1890-91
12. The Burton Breweries, 1700-1900 (listed in Appendix 52)
13. The Iron Industry and Trade, 1700-1850
14. Plan of Thornewill's works, Burton upon Trent, 1856
15. The Burton Lower Mills, 1760
16. The Peel Cotton Mills at Burton, 1820

PREFACE

The world-wide reputation of Burton upon Trent as a brewing centre has tended to divert attention from the great industrial variety that it has possessed at certain stages in its history. This diversity was particularly evident during the second half of the 18th century when industrial and commercial enterprise showed a marked expansion.

Despite the intriguing development of the town and its industries Burton has been largely ignored by economic historians. Early writers, such as R. Plot (*Natural History of Staffordshire*, 1686) and S. Shaw (*History of Staffordshire*, 1798) and the early directories, commencing with Bailey's *Western Directory* of 1784, referred only briefly to the town's main industries. Shaw's comments were the most detailed and accurate and many later writers were indebted to him. The great expansion of the town's brewing industry after 1840 attracted considerable attention and helped to bring forth *Burton and its Bitter Beer* by J. S. Bushnan in 1853, *Burton-on-Trent: its History, its Waters and its Breweries* by W. Molyneux in 1869 and *The Noted Breweries of Great Britain and Ireland* by A. Barnard in 1889, which contained extensive sections on Burton's breweries.

From them until 1941, when C. H. Underhill published his general history of the town, little attention was paid to it. In recent years the only significant relevant works produced have been A. J. Halliday's 'The Development of Burton-on-Trent – A Study in Urban Geography' (unpublished M.A. Thesis, University of London, 1956), which deals particularly with the expansion of the town during the 19th century, and Professor P. Matthias' *The Brewing Industry in England, 1700–1830*, which contains an excellent account of the Baltic ale trade during the 18th century.

While reading Molyneux's work in 1965 I became aware of the enormous scope that Burton had to offer to the student of industrial history. Many problems concerning the town's early development remained unanswered, although Molyneux's writings were both accurate and well-informed. It was clear from the work of Professor Matthias, however, that the Allsopp Records were especially illuminating in respect of 18th-century brewing, while the recently deposited and uncatalogued Paget MSS in the Staffordshire County Record Office promised solutions to many problems. These, together with the complete set of *The Derby Mercury* in Derby Reference Library and the extensive collection of Burton Wills in Lichfield Library, provided a basis for much of my early research in 1965 and 1966.

Exhaustion of the main local sources led to a search for further material elsewhere in 1967 and 1968. The most rewarding discoveries were the Lothian MSS at Melbourne Hall, which provided much detailed information on the early history of the Trent Navigation; the Wyatt, Boulton & Watt and Lloyd MSS in Birmingham Reference Library and the Hull Port Books in the Public Record Office. The quantity of material available was remarkable although the total lack of business records for the Peel Cotton Mills and the paucity of information concerning the shipping and mercantile business in Hull was disappointing.

The industrial historian cannot be content with merely reconstructing the development and progress of the various industries within a single town or area. He must analyse the possible reasons for the emergence, growth and decline of those industries and their relationship with regional and national patterns. This necessitates a thorough knowledge of their technical characteristics and of regional and national economic trends. In the ensuing chapters it will be noted that an attempt has been made to fulfil these requirements and it is hoped, therefore, that they will have general as well as local interest. The great variety of industrial activities practised in Burton during the past three centuries inevitably added to the complexity as well as the interest of the task. One extractive industry, namely agriculture, was deliberately omitted as it was felt that this was too distinct and extensive an activity to be included. There is clearly great scope for further research in this direction.

An attempt has been made to limit the detailed research to Burton and its immediate neighbourhood wherever possible. In the case of brewing this was an easy task for the industry has been largely confined to Burton itself and, except in its domestic phase, has not spread to the surrounding areas. When studying the cotton industry this was far more difficult, for the Burton mills formed part of a broad regional complex extending to Tutbury and Measham and far beyond.

Wherever industries develop they have important human and social implications. Some attempt has therefore been made to examine the impact of industry upon local society and to analyse, where possible, the qualities of the leaders of industry in terms of entrepreneurial ability and their contribution to society. Primarily, however, this work is an attempt to reconstruct the evolution of local industries and to fill the gaps left by previous writers. Inevitably, lack of time has curtailed my research in certain directions and I readily acknowledge the fact that I have failed to answer certain questions and that there is scope for further work to be done. One final point that I would like to make for the benefit of the local reader concerns my original thesis ('The Development of Industry in Burton-on-Trent prior to 1900') which I submitted to the University of Sheffield in 1969. This contains much additional information, illustrations and appendices which, in the interests of economy, had to be omitted at the time of publication. Items such as lists of workers connected with the various Burton industires, particularly during the 17th and 18th centuries, may be of considerable interest to the local historian.

ACKNOWLEDGMENTS

The preparation of an industrial history depends to a considerable extent upon the volume and quality of original material that the writer is able to bring to light and upon the co-operation and assistance of many organisations and individuals. I feel that I have been extremely fortunate in both respects. The Allsopp Records and the Paget MSS, in particular, have provided such a wealth of information that it has been possible to reconstruct in great detail much of Burton's early industrial history.

I am especially indebted to Allied Breweries (U.K.) Ltd. for allowing me to examine at length both the Allsopp Records and many of their early property deeds and to publish the results of my research. I would like to thank Mr. R. L. Thompson, their Public Relations Officer, and also Messrs. R. Arnold and R. Carrington-Porter of their Property Department for their very kind co-operation.

Throughout the period of my research I was surprised by the interest taken in my work by many local firms. This was particularly noticeable during my visits to S. Briggs & Co., where Mr. R.S. Worth, the Company Chairman, and Mr. J. Staton, the former Sales Director, went to great lengths to provide me with the information that I required. I am very grateful to them. May I also thank Bass-Worthington Ltd. and Marston, Thompson and Evershed Ltd. for allowing me to extract information from their old property deeds and other records.

Historians inevitably spend many hours in reference libraries and record offices and therefore rely heavily upon the services of librarians, archivists and their assistants. With this in mind I would particularly like to thank Mr. F. B. Stitt, Staffordshire County Archivist, and his assistants, Mr. K. F. Stanesby, County Borough of Burton upon Trent Librarian, and his staff and the staff of Derby Reference Library.

Frequent visits to such establishments and occasional weeks spent at the Public Record Office and other centres of research in London and elsewhere were both time-consuming and expensive. I am indebted to the Burton upon Trent Education Committee for the generous financial assistance that they provided during the early years of my research.

The initial stages of research are often the most difficult in that one is dealing with so many unfamiliar and apparently unrelated names, places and activities. I would like to thank Charles Underhill of Burton for his valuable help in providing a base on which to build. At a later stage professional guidance in respect of sources of information and thesis preparation becomes important. I am greatly indebted to Professor S. Pollard of the Department of Economic History at the University of Sheffield for this guidance and for making my visits to Sheffield pleasurable as well as instructive.

I am also indebted to Humphrey Lloyd of Wotton under Edge for his stimulating correspondence over several years and for allowing me to use material from the Lloyd MSS. May I also thank Harry Curtis for his help with the illustrations for my book, Eric Brown for his photographic work, and Ray Brown, of S.E. Derbyshire College of Further Education, for the many hours spent in indexing the book. May I also thank my father, Mr. H. C. Owen, for his secretarial assistance and for the use of his extensive private library. Lastly, but by no means least, may I express my gratitude to my wife, Ann, for her encouragement, patience and help during eight years of writing and research.

I

PHYSICAL ENVIRONMENT

Burton upon Trent (population–50,000 in 1970) is situated in the Trent Valley, in the extreme eastern part of Staffordshire, eleven miles south-west of Derby and 28 miles north-east of Birmingham. Two miles to the south-east of the town, at Newhall and Stanton, lies the western margin of the South Derbyshire and Leicestershire Coalfield, one of the minor industrial zones of the Midlands, while to the west lies the entirely rural area of Needwood Forest. The Trent Valley, a corridor some two miles in width, separates these two economically contrasting districts and provides a major routeway between the north and south Midlands.

At Burton the valley floor lies entirely between the 140 ft. and 170 ft. contours and contains low but extensive gravel terraces and a broad flood plain. The latter forms a continuous line of meadows separating the main urban area from Winshill and Stapenhill to the east but the terraces have provided land ideal for settlement, in addition to copious supplies of easily-tapped hard brewing water. The town centre has developed on the first river terrace which lies roughly seven feet above the flood plain around a height of 152 ft O.D. Of the satellite settlements, Stretton and Branston are similarly sited, while Winshill, Stapenhill, Shobnall and Horninglow have been built mainly on and above the valley bluffs which rise 50–150 ft. above the first terrace. A distinct narrowing of the flood plain at Burton allowed the river to be bridged at an early date,[1] thus making the town a focus of north-south and east-west routes. The meandering Trent has played a significant part in the town's development, mainly by providing power for a variety of industries as well as a navigable outlet to the sea.

The Needwood Plateau to the west forms an undulating upland with an average summit level of 350–400 ft. and prominent scarps on its northern and eastern margins. It has undergone considerable dissection both by the main south-flowing streams, such as the Swarbourn and the Lin Brook and by short but vigorous east-flowing streams in the Shobnall and Tatenhill areas. As far as Burton is concerned, the Plateau's importance lies in the fact that it forms the main catchment area for the town's supplies of hard brewing water. It has, moreover, yielded quantities of alabaster, a soft white stone previously used for church monuments and ornaments, and large supplies of timber suitable for building and charcoal production.

The South Derbyshire Plateau to the east rises abruptly to a height of over 400 ft. at Waterloo Mount, only three-quarters of a mile from the river. Like the Needwood Plateau, it has a general summit level around 350–400 ft. and has been deeply dissected by short streams such as the Dale, Brizlincote and Repton brooks. Its Carboniferous rocks contain valuable coal seams which have been exploited since mediaeval times and have assisted Burton's industrial development.

Over most of the area the surface is formed by Triassic marls and sandstones with patches of alluvium and glacial drift. Generalised thicknesses of these Triassic beds and those of Carboniferous age that underlie them are as follows:[2]

			Feet
Triassic	Rhaetic Beds		30
	Keuper—	Tea-green Marl	50
		Keuper Marl	1,100
		Lower Keuper Sandstone	2-300
		Bunter Pebble Beds	330-470
Carboniferous	Productive Coal Measures		1,700
	Millstone Grit		80
	Limestone Series		1,300

On the Needwood Plateau Keuper Marl, in the form of red, chocolate and grey marls with thin bands of white siltstone or sandstone and occasional beds of salt and gypsum, covers well over half the surface. The main gypsum bed, or Tutbury Gypsum as it is often known, has an average thickness of nine feet and generally occurs 150 ft. below the top of the Keuper Marl. It may well extend under the whole of the plateau but it has been mined chiefly at Fauld and Castle Hay, near Tutbury, Row Bank, near Coton-in-the-Clay, and at Horninglow for use in the manufacture of plaster, ornaments and pottery moulds.[3] From an industrial point of view, however, its main contribution has been to impart to water percolating through it a very high calcium sulphate content, thereby providing Burton with a water supply ideal for the brewing of pale ale. The Keuper Marl itself has been excavated at Stapenhill, Winshill, Shobnall and Anslow for brick manufacture.

The Lower Keuper Sandstone outcrops in the north-south belt immediately to the east of the Trent Valley. It contains the Building Stones Group which was formerly quarried at Winshill, Newton Solney and Repton and used for local construction purposes.

Over wide areas the solid rocks are masked by superficial glacial and alluvial deposits. Boulder Clay, up to 60 ft. in depth, is widespread, particularly on the Needwood Plateau. Glacial sands and gravels form thin hilltop cappings on both sides of the valley, while fluvio-glacial gravels at Horninglow, Stretton and Clay Mills have been excavated for building purposes. Alluvium, peat beds and river terrace gravels cover the whole of the valley floor, the latter yielding copious supplies of shallow well water.

Beneath Burton the solid rocks have been considerably disturbed by faulting which makes it extremely difficult to predict the depth at which a particular bed may be encountered.[4] A large fault running along the eastern edge of the Trent Valley has a downthrow of 100 ft. to the north-west. A number of other faults radiate from this beneath the town, enclosing a horst bounded by downthrows of 300 ft. or more. As a result the supply of water likely to be obtained from wells sunk beneath the base of the valley gravels is highly unpredictable. Prior to 1860 all brewing water was obtained from shallow wells, less than 25 ft. in depth, sunk into the terrace gravels. Rapid expansion of the brewing industry and the resulting water shortage soon forced many firms to search for water at greater depth. Unsuccessful attempts by Bass & Co. and Allsopp's during the 1860's suggested that the marls below the gravel were not water-bearing strata but by the 1890's at least eight breweries were using water from wells sunk into the Keuper Marl.[5] Since then increasing quantities of water have been obtained from deep bores sunk through the Keuper Marl and the Lower Keuper Sandstone into the Bunter Pebble Beds to a depth of over 1,000 ft.

The suitability of Burton water for brewing lies in its extreme hardness and, in particular, its high content of magnesium and calcium sulphates.[6] Gypseous liquors assist coagulation during boiling and cooling, permit the use of a higher hop ratio without fear of harshness and promote yeast growth during fermentation, thereby producing a sparkling, light-coloured ale.[7] In contrast, hard liquors with a high sodium carbonate content, such as those used for brewing in the London area, tend to impede filtration as well as to adversely affect the hop flavour. Although varying remarkably in their degree of hardness and precise composition, Burton waters may be broadly classified into hard gypseous brewing waters from shallow wells sunk into gravel beds and bore tubes in the Keuper Marl and the Lower Keuper Sandstone, softer water, used for blending purposes, from South Staffordshire Waterworks reservoirs and from bore tubes in the Bunter Pebble Beds, and soft Trent water used for washing and cooling. During the 1890's, when the town's brewing industry reached its peak, it was estimated that its annual water requirements amounted to 1,800,000,000 gallons. Of the many factors that contributed towards Burton's development as a great brewing centre the possession of this unique water supply must rank of prime importance.

The Carboniferous rocks that outcrop within two miles of the eastern edge of Burton have also contributed towards the town's industrial growth. Records of coalmining in the Swadlincote and Swannington areas of South Derbyshire and Leicestershire go back as far as the 13th century.[8] The earliest known reference to mining in the extreme western section of the coalfield is contained in an indenture of 1608 in which Sir William Paget, Lord of the Manor of Burton, leased to Richard Almonde the coal mines in Winshill Heath and Winshill Wood for an annual rent of £80.[9] These early pits lay in the area around Brizlincote and Stanhope Bretby, a little over one mile to the east of the Trent Valley. It was not until the mid-nineteenth century, however, that the Anglesey, Stanhope, Eureka and Stockings seams in this area were exploited on a large scale. Until then Burton relied mainly upon coal brought by river from districts further north in Derbyshire and Nottinghamshire and by wagon from the pits in the Newhall-Swadlincote area.

The latter were considerably extended during the second half of the 18th century by the Bullivant and Nadin families. In 1777, for example, J. Bullivant advertised for 20 additional colliers at Swadlincote Colliery and announced that 'there are now four pits at full work and between four and five hundred stacks upon the Banks ... Exceeding fine Blacksmith's coal sold at 7s. per waggon load'.[10] In 1782 the Nadin's, who had recently moved from Yorkshire to Brizlincote Hall, purchased 'an undivided moity of all the coal mines, within the Liberties of Newhall, Stapenhill and Hartshorne and proceeded to develop the area extensively.' During the 1790–1810 period several unsuccessful schemes were proposed to link these and other pits by canal and railroad to Burton but it was not until the opening of the Ashby-Burton Railway in 1849 that the communications problem was solved. Nevertheless, the coalfield continued to expand and by 1810 there were 27 active pits in the Derbyshire section alone, many of which lay within five miles of Burton.

Undoubtedly, the presence of this nearby coalfield helped to stimulate industrial development in the town by supplying its manufacturers with essential supplies of cheap fuel and by providing a market for steam-engines and mining equipment.

Although the link between physical environment and industrial evolution in a deterministic sense is often questioned by modern geographers and economic historians it would, nevertheless, seem apparent that Burton's development has been guided by a special type of water supply and aided by the availability of coal and water power and by access to a formerly navigable river and to important Midland routes. As will be seen in the ensuing chapters, however, its industrial development has pursued a rather more devious course than its modern structure might suggest. Some attempt will also be made to explain why a town so richly endowed in terms of natural resources and accessibility has attained only a modest level of economic growth.

References

1. W. Molyneux, '*Burton-on-Trent: its History, its Waters and its Breweries*' (1869)—contains numerous references to the antiquity of Burton Bridge.

2. Geological Survey (1955), '*Geology of the Country between Burton upon Trent, Rugeley and Uttoxeter*'.

3. J. Farey, '*General View of the Agriculture and Minerals of Derbyshire*', (1811–17), Vol. 1, p. 151.

4. see Appendix.

5. F.E. Lott, '*Burton Waters—Drinking and Brewing*'; Transactions of the Burton-on-Trent Natural History and Archaeological Society, (1896). (T.B.N.H.A.S.).

6. see Appendix.

7. H. Lloyd Hind, '*Brewing Science and Practice*' (1938–40), Vol. 1, paras. 333–40.

8. A.D. Butterley, '*The Ashby Coalfield*' (Presidential Address to the Institute of Mining Engineers, October 1951).

9. *Paget Deeds*, (P.D.), 22 Oct. 1608.

10. *Derby Mercury*, (D.M.), 28 Feb. and 13 June 1777.

11. *D.M.*, 14 Nov. 1782.

II

HISTORICAL SUMMARY

During the five centuries following the establishment of Burton Abbey by Wulfric Spott, Earl of Mercia, in 1002 A.D. the affairs of the town and its surrounding villages and hamlets were largely controlled by the abbots and their officials. The history of the town during this period, so vividly portrayed by the charters and muniments of the abbey,[1] is relevant to the topic of industrial development in so far as it concerns the evolution of the town and its institutions, many of which survived until a much later date. The layout of the settlement, the system of administration, the siting of mills along the Trent and many of the town's other characteristics, some of which persisted until the mid-nineteenth century, had their roots in monastic Burton.

When Abbot Nicholas 'made the first borough of Burton' towards the end of the 12th century and Abbot Melbourne shortly afterwards established burgages along the street leading from 'the great bridge at Burton to the new bridge towards Horninglow' they formed the basic structure of a settlement that was to last for six centuries. The surrounding villages and hamlets of Winshill, Stapenhill, Horninglow, Wetmore, Shobnall, Stretton and Branston, which remained detached from the main urban area until the second half of the 19th century, also came within the jurisdiction of Burton Abbey. The reeve of Burton, who was responsible for the management of the abbot's demsnes, the summoning of his courts and the witnessing of his leases, continued to be the leading official of the manor (later known as the bailiff) long after the dissolution of the abbey, while the manor courts continued to be held until 1855. The mills at Winshill, Stapenhill and Clay Mills, later used for a variety of industrial purposes, were all under the control of Burton Abbey by the 13th century. When Burton and its adjoining manors passed from monastic to secular control in the mid-sixteenth century its basic structure and institutions were thus well-established.

On 4 November 1540 William Edys, the 35th Abbot, surrended the abbey for dissolution and shortly afterwards became the first dean of the newly-formed collegiate church. In 1546, following the latter's suppression, the lordship and manor of Burton, together with extensive lands and properties in Staffordshire, Derbyshire, Leicestershire and Warwickshire, were granted by Henry VIII to Sir William Paget, one of his chief secretaries. According to a survey of 1549 the total annual rental of the estates, including tithes, in Burton and its surrounding villages alone, amounted to almost £270.[2]

William Paget, son of one of the Sergeants of the Mace of the City of London, had entered the King's service between 1525 and 1530, following an education at Trinity College, Cambridge. His ability and integrity had earned him a knighthood in 1527 and appointment as Clerk to the Privy Council in 1540. Further honours bestowed upon him included appointments as Ambassador to France (1541), Secretary of State and Privy Councillor (1543), Comptroller of the King's Household (1547) and Chancellor of the Duchy of Lancaster (1547). Subsequent to his acquisition of the estates of the dissolved Burton Abbey he represented Staffordshire in Parliament (1547–9) and served as Lord Lieutenant of the county (1551). Burton thus passed under the control of a highly capable administrator, whose agents set about the task of enhancing the value of his newly-acquired estates.

At the time of the dissolution Burton contained only 51 free tenants and a population of little more than 1,000 (including the surrounding villages). Apart from agriculture, which, as elsewhere, formed the staple occupation, the only trades of any note in the town were the carving of alabaster tombs and ornaments and small cloth, malting and brewing industries. Like most settlements of comparable size it possessed its complement of mercers, cordwainers, tanners, butchers, chandlers, bakers and other tradesmen. Its most notable feature was the great bridge of 36 arches spanning the Trent, later described as 'The most notorious piece of work of a civil public building in this country'.[3]

To the Pagets and their agents the woollen cloth industry appeared to offer the best prospects for the town's commercial advancement and it was mainly by developing this that they were able to raise Burton's population to around 1,700 by 1580. Towards the end of Elizabeth's reign the family's Catholic sympathies resulted in the loss of lands and properties but these were later recovered by William, 4th Lord Paget. His son, William, 5th Lord Paget, was a strong supporter of the Royalist cause and during the Civil War Burton was occupied on several occasions by both sides, the church and other important buildings being severely damaged. Nevertheless, by 1660 the total annual value of the Burton estates had increased to almost £5,000 and the town's population to approximately 2,500.

The following 50 years witnessed a marked decline in the town's population and prosperity, the main reasons for which appear to have been the collapse of the cloth industry, the effects of the Civil War and the continued lack of adequate communications between Burton and other areas. By 1690 Burton's population had fallen to around 2,300, the bridge across the Trent, the corn mill at Winshill, and other important properties were in a ruinous condition, while trade and industry were thoroughly depressed.[4] This decline may have been partly due to mismanagement on the part of the Paget's agents, although it must be noted that a similar malaise affected a number of Midland towns during this period.

The passing of the Trent Navigation Act of 1699 heralded Burton's economic revival by placing the town at the head of one of the country's most extensive navigation systems. Provided with fresh commercial and industrial opportunities the town expanded steadily after 1720, although the town depicted by William Wyatt's map of 1760 still closely resembled the linear settlement of mediaeval times. High Street formed the core of the town, with its continuous lines of shops and tenements, backed by long, narrow burgage plots. Horninglow Street, Anderstaff Lane, Cat Street and New Street, with fewer buildings, projected from it towards the town fields and the neighbouring commons, while Bond End formed a small but compact hub of settlement at the southern end of the town. As the brewing, hardware, hat and worsted industries expanded the empty spaces were filled in with small manufactories and additional tenements and the population increased to over 3,000 by 1770 and 6,000 by the time of the first census in 1801. The growth rate was particularly high during the last 20 years of the century, when the new cotton spinning industry attracted many people to the town.

Throughout the 18th century the most important town official continued to be the High Bailiff of the Borough, who often combined the office with those of Steward of the Manor and Coroner. He was appointed by the lord of the manor and it was customary for him to reside at Sinai (or Seany) Park in the ancient moated house that passed to the Pagets at the time of the dissolution. The most outstanding holder of the office was William Wyatt (1739–73), a member of a large and highly talented Lichfield family, whose sound administration did much to further local industry and commerce. Management of the town's affairs was also vested in a committee of 10 or 12 burgesses known as the Feoffees, who were responsible for the town's lands granted in fee for charitable purposes and for the appointment of various officials. At their annual meeting on St. Thomas's Day they dispensed funds from the charities to the poor of the town and appointed two Town Masters for the coming year. The latter were generally tradesmen of high repute who had previously served as churchwardens, overseers and constables. Their duties included the collection of rents from the tenants of town lands and houses, payment of the constables' expenses, maintenance of the town's cross, pinfold and stocks, upkeep of the bridges in Horninglow Street and Cat Street and the apprenticing of poor children.[5] The two constables responsible for the preservation of law and order were appointed annually in October at the meetings of the Court Leet and the Court Baron. The churchwardens and overseers, appointed by the vestry in March or April, were concerned with such matters as vagrancy, upkeep of highways and repairs to the church.

The growing prosperity of the town after 1750 was accompanied by a general improvement in its amenities. A new Town Hall was constructed in 1772 to replace the old 15th century Guild Hall. An Act of 1779 authorised Town Commissioners to levy a rate of between twopence and sixpence in the pound for the re-paving of the streets, the installation of street lighting and culverting of sewers.[6] Turnpikes were instituted on all of the main roads leading out of the town and regular coach and wagon services increased. In 1770 the Burton section of the Trent and Mersey Canal was opened to supplement the somewhat inefficient Trent Navigation. Around 1785 Joseph Wilkes, a Measham industrialist, and Thomas and William Pyecroft of Overseal established the first commercial bank in the town. This was followed shortly afterwards by a second bank belonging to John Walker Wilson, a Burton brewer and merchant, and Daniel Dalrymple, a local attorney.[7] These country banks provided valuable services to industrialists by discounting bills of exchange and by granting short-term loans.

By the end of the 18th century Burton had thus become a bustling industrial and commercial centre of 6,000 inhabitants, with its facilities substantially improved and its appearance radically altered by the construction of industrial premises in the shape of breweries, malthouses and cotton mills. Outside the urban area, in Winshill, Stapenhill and the districts to the west, notable changes had also occurred as a result of widespread enclosures during the 1770's.[8] The strong personal influence of the Pagets (created Earls of Uxbridge in 1714 and subsequently Marquesses of Anglesey in 1815) in local affairs had gradually waned, although they still remained substantial property owners.

During the first 40 years of the 19th century the rate of growth and change slackened, with the result that the population of Burton and its surrounding villages was still under 7,000 in 1831. This can be attributed to the collapse of the Baltic system of trade, upon which Burton's brewing industry, in particular, had depended, as well as to the progressive decline of the town's textile, hardware and hat industries. Wood's map of the town in 1837 showed only modest expansion along Horninglow Street, Cat Street and New Street and it was not until after the opening of the Birmingham—Derby railway through Burton in 1839 that the picture began to change significantly.

The following 50 years witnessed an unprecedented industrial and urban growth which raised the town's population to 46,000 by 1891. This was almost entirely due to an extremely rapid expansion of the brewing industry. By the 1860's the old linear settlement had developed into a compact rectangular town largely contained within the river, the main railway, Horninglow Street and the Bond End Canal.[9] Much of the town centre had been filled-in with extensive brewery premises, while zones of terraced housing covered the former Goose and Horninglow Moors to the west. Contemporary writers described the developments thus—

> 'The recent great development of the Brewing Trade has caused such an influx of labourers that the present house accommodation has proved utterly inadequate, indeed, it is estimated that at this time not less than five hundred cottages are required for residents in the town, whilst there are numbers of labourers living five, six and even seven miles from Burton, who are compelled to walk to and from their daily work.'[10]

> 'During the last five years, the Marquess of Anglesey and the Feoffees of the Burton Town Lands have leased upwards of 200 acres of land for building and trade purposes, five miles of new streets have been laid out and completed or are in course of formation, and 1,100 houses erected.'[11]

Expansion continued unchecked for a further 20 years, particularly in the Victoria and Uxbridge areas, and by the end of the century Burton and Bond End had merged with Horninglow, Shobnall and Wetmore to form a single urban zone. Across the Trent Meadows

Winshill and Stapenhill had also grown considerably as a result of residential development.

An Act of 1853 completely re-organised the town's administrative system by creating the three wards of Burton upon Trent, Burton Extra and Horninglow, which were to elect 18, six and three commissioners respectively.[12] The commissioners were to be assisted by the High Bailiff of the Borough but the Feofees ceased to act as commissioners, thereby losing the responsibility of the County Police Force.

Continued expansion of the town led to its incorporation as a Municipal Borough in 1878, while in 1901 it attained the status of a County Borough with a population of 50,000. As will be seen later, the brewers played a leading part in this re-organisation and several of them became prominent in national politics as well as in local government.

In order to cater for the growing community there was a substantial increase in expenditure on public works such as sewage works and cemeteries. The many fine churches built between 1850–80 and the new bridge across the Trent, completed in 1864, were financed by private individuals and companies. Between 1855–60 three Burton weekly newspapers were initiated and a wide range of sports clubs and other social institutions emerged.[13] By 1890 Burton thus possessed all the outward signs of a progressive and successful town basking in the prosperity and prestige earned for it by its great breweries. It was unfortunate that the attainment of County Borough status was not the prelude to further growth and that the ensuing stagnation of the brewing industry was not compensated for by alternative commercial and industrial development.

References

1. '*Collections for a History of Staffordshire*', ed. by The William Salt Archaeological Society, (H.C.S.), vol. 5, Old Series, (1884) and special edition, 'Burton Abbey', (1937).

2. W. Molyneux, op. cit., pp. 50–51.

3. R. Plot, '*Natural History of Staffordshire*', (1686), p. 372.

4. Anglesey Papers; estate letters and accounts, c. 1690. Burton Parish Church Registers, 1680–1710.

5. Burton Parish Chest Documents: Town Masters' and Constables' Accounts. W. Molyneux, op. cit., pp. 78 and 104.

6. Burton upon Trent Town Act, 19 George III.

7. Universal British Directory, vol. 1, (1791), p. 415. W.R. Crick and J.E. Wadsworth, '*A Hundred Years of Joint Stock Banking*', pp. 244–51. L.S. Pressnell, '*Country Banking in the Industrial Revolution*', p. 111.

8. C.H. Underhill, '*History of Burton upon Trent,* (1942), pp. 147, 150 and 243.
9. T. Spooner, Maps of Burton upon Trent, 1857 and 1865.
10. Burton Weekly News, 10 Feb. 1865.
11. W. Molyneux, (1869), op. cit., pp. 122–3.
12. '*An Act for more effectually improving the Town of Burton upon Trent in the County of Stafford*', 16 & 17 Victoria.
13. W. Molyneux, op. cit., pp. 122–31 and 214–8.

III

THE DEVELOPMENT OF COMMUNICATIONS AND TRANSPORT

The gradual emergence of specialised areas of industrial and agricultural production during the 16th and 17th centuries stimulated a mounting volume of internal traffic with which the antiquated system of communications was unable to cope. In the pre-canal era merchants often had little choice but to utilise the slow and expensive road transport in the shape of packhorses and horse-drawn wagons. Despite the introduction of the turnpike system shortly after the Restoration and legislation designed to effect improvements, many highways remained seriously impeded by deep mud and ruts and decaying bridges. Road transport was generally at least five times as expensive as water transport and it was uneconomic to convey bulky commodities more than a few miles. It was not surprising, therefore, that merchants and manufacturers turned increasingly to the use of waterways, and that between 1650 and 1750 Parliament passed 53 River Acts and considered many other schemes.

Below Nottingham the Trent had been used for centuries as a navigable waterway and by 1650 both Gainsborough and Stockwith had become thriving ports with fleets of vessels engaged in river and coastal trade.[1] The river formed a vital artery between the port of Hull and its extensive hinterland, and the traffic in commodities such as coal, corn, iron, timber, hardware, cloth, cheese and malt was considerable. Several unsuccessful attempts were made during the 17th century to extend navigation along the River Soar as far as Leicester and along the River Derwent to Derby.[2] The failure of these and other similar schemes was largely due to the attitude of influential landowners who feared that corn prices would be adversely affected and their mills, weirs and fisheries damaged, and also to the strong opposition of Nottingham Corporation who had a vested interest in keeping Nottingham at the head of the navigation.

By the 1690's, however, the Trent Navigation had been extended above Nottingham as far as Wilden Ferry, mainly due to the efforts of the Fosbrooke family of Shardlow.[3] Despite vigorous, and sometimes violent, opposition from merchants at Nottingham and Derby the Fosbrookes developed a lucrative river traffic. The main item of trade at this time was cheese, which was taken to Wilden from many parts of the Midlands for despatch to London.[4] The success of the navigation did not pass unnoticed in Burton which lay 20 miles up the river from Wilden and the inhabitants there soon began to press Lord Paget for action—

> 'And because the Wealth and Honour of all cityes, townes, and societyes of men do very much depend upon and follow the publicke trades, manufactures and employment of the nation for want of which ye sayd towne [Burton] is very much ruined and decayed in its buildings and the inhabitants in generall much impoverished. And because the River Trent, which so conveniently waits upon the sayd Towne, by its being made a navigable river, may and without doubt will much advance and favour ye designe of Trade within ye Township, it is therefore recommended that ye navigation of ye sayd River by considered'.[5]

Lord Paget and his agents reacted favourably and were soon able to arouse considerable support for an extension of the navigation amongst landowners and merchants in neighbouring areas. This culminated in a 'Bill for making and keeping the River Trent in the Counties of Leicester, Derby and Stafford Navigable', which was presented to Parliament on 24 Aug. 1698 and became law on 4 May 1699.[6]

The Act authorised Lord Paget to construct 'such Locks, Wears, Turnpikes, Pens for Water, Cranes, Wharfs, Warehouses and other things proper and convenient' between Burton and Wilden. He was to provide £600 towards the cost, while the commissioners named in the Act were granted the right to raise a further £600 from the inhabitants of Burton. The task of completing the navigation proved far more difficult and expensive than anticipated and in 1705 Parliament considered 'A Petition of divers of the Inhabitants of the Town of Burton upon Trent' complaining that the financial provisions of the Act were inadequate.[7]

In 1711 Lord Paget was able to solve the financial problem by concluding an agreement with George Hayne, a Wirksworth merchant, whereby Hayne would complete the navigation providing he became its undertaker for a period of 31 years.[8] Hayne, in collaboration with Fosbrooke at Wilden, was particularly interested in the trade in cheese and salt along the Trent to London. In the previous year he had reached agreement with Fosbrooke over the 'Salt Rock workes belonging to William Lawton of Lawton in the County of Chester ... and all other Salt Rock or workes that the said George Hayne shall be concerned in', while Fosbrooke had signed a contract concerning the supply of Midland cheese to 58 London cheesemongers.[9] During 1712 Hayne successfully completed further improvements to the river between Burton and Wilden and opened the navigation to traffic.

The early years of the navigation were marred by bitter disputes between Hayne and Fosbrooke on the one hand and those wishing to use the river on the other.[10] A Petition to Parliament from the 'Merchants, traders and other inhabitants of Birmingham', submitted in opposition to a proposed Trent Navigation Bill in 1714, summarised the main reasons for the discontent—

> 'and one Haynes, having obtained an Assignment of the Lord of the Manor's Power, under the said Act, takes advantage thereof, and refuseth to join any such Appointment, insisting, That his is a private Wharf, as well as Fosbrooke's, at which no Goods can be landed, or received, without his, or Fosbrooke's Boats; by which illegal Practices they engross the whole Navigation to their Boats; to the Destruction of Trade.'[11]

Gradually, however, dissatisfaction with the navigation lessened as Hayne gained greater control and effected considerable improvements.[12] These included the construction of navigation locks at Burton and King's Mills and of wharves and warehouses at Burton and Willington at a total cost of around £8,000.

It is clear that by 1720 the Trent Navigation was to a large extent fulfilling the aims of its promoters. It was providing a vital link between a wide area of the Midlands and the port of Hull. The cheese trade continued to be of great importance, with large quantities arriving at the wharves at Wilden, Willington and Burton for despatch to London. Flints from eastern England were collected by land carriers at Willington and taken to pottery manufacturers in North Staffordshire, the same carriers returning with crates of pots, butter and cheese. Imported bar iron from Sweden and Russia passed upstream to Burton Wharf, where it was collected on behalf of Birmingham and South Staffordshire hardware manufacturers. Other important commodities taken downstream were hardware, coal, lead, millstones, scythestones, ale, coney skins, timber and salt, while on the return journey the boats carried hemp, flax, groceries, timber, potash, corn and linen, brought from London or from ports in northern Europe.[13] The navigation was not without its problems; freight charges were high (12s. to 15s. per ton between Burton and Gainsborough), and traffic was hindered by abnormally wet, dry or frosty weather, by the presence of numerous shallows in the river and by the need for flushes of water from the mills at Burton and King's Mills.

Apart from its regional significance, the extension of the Trent Navigation to Burton greatly stimulated the town's trade and industries. The isolation from which it had suffered for so long was finally broken and its position at the head of navigation made it a significant distributing centre. The Burton Boat Company, headed by George Hayne, and later by his brother Henry, operated a large fleet of sailing barges, with capacities of up to 40 tons, downstream as far as Gainsborough, the limit of sea-going ships. Access to the raw materials carried by these vessels and to distant markets enabled Burton to develop significant brewing, textile, hat and hardware industries. The town's brewers, in particular, were able to take advantage of markets in London and the Baltic countries and to profit from the import of a wide range of commodities. Men with commercial ability and capital, such as Sampson Lloyd of Birmingham, Joseph Wilkes of Overseal and Henry Evans of Derby, whose activities will be discussed in later chapters, were attracted to the town by the opportunities that the navigation offered.

Following the death of George Hayne in 1724, the navigation rights and properties passed to his brother Henry, who continued to operate the navigation until his death in 1757. During the early years of control he was hard-pressed to defend his rights against interlopers, who attempted to establish unauthorised wharves and warehouses along the river. By 1734 he had spent over £3,000 on legal proceedings against them, the disputes having been 'through most of the Courts in England'.[14] After 1739, however, conditions on the river became more settled and for a time the Nottingham Boat Company was allowed to take possession of a warehouse at Willington and to operate boats between there and Gainsborough. During the 1750's lock dues collected at King's Mills amounted to around £90 per annum, indicating the passage through the lock of approximately 300 vessels carrying 7,000 tons of freight. Almost half of the freight was handled by the Burton Boat Company and Henry Hayne's receipts from freight charges (as distinct from lock dues) averaged around £2,500 per annum between 1740 and 1757, giving him a clear profit of £1,000 per annum.[15]

Following the death of Henry Hayne in 1757 control of the navigation passed to his son John and to Abraham Hoskins, a Burton solicitor. They promptly spent nearly £1,300 on the repair and reconstruction of locks and weirs, including £850 on an excellent stone lock at King's Mills. In 1762, however, when several of the navigation and mill leases expired, the Earl of Uxbridge, on the advice of William Wyatt, his steward, demanded that the old navigation company should pay a fine of £3,900 in order to renew the leases.[16] When the latter refused Wyatt quickly came to terms with a syndicate comprising Sampson Lloyd (sen. and jun.), ironmasters of Birmingham and Isaac Hawkins, a Burton attorney, Joseph and John Wilkes, cheesefactors of Overseal, Robert Palmer, a Burton cheesefactor and William Wyatt himself; they were later joined by Nehemiah and Charles Lloyd of Birmingham and Abraham Hoskins and Henry Evans of Burton.[17] These 'Lessees of the Trent Navigation' became the proprietors of the new Burton Boat Company, and towards the end of 1763 Wyatt was able to report to the Earl of Uxbridge that—

> 'The new Company of Navigators are now in full possession of all the Wharfs, Warehouses, Fulling Mills, Boats, Barges etc. of the late Company, which possession cost £6,000, and about £800 they have laid out in a new Wharf and Warehouse, which with repairs now wanting and the fine to your Lordship will amount in the whole to near Ten Thousand pounds'.[18]

John Hayne ceased to take any part in navigation affairs, although he retained possession of the manor house and the nearby wharf and warehouse in Bond End until 1775, when he retired to London and Bath.

By this time the existence of the Trent Navigation was already being threatened by a proposed Grand Trunk Canal which would pass to the west of Burton and enter the Trent lower down the river at Wilden. As early as 1717 Thomas Congreve of Wolverhampton had proposed the construction of a navigable link between the Severn and the Trent,[19] but it was not until the 1750's that canal building became a reality. In 1758, following a preliminary survey on behalf of a group of Liverpool merchants, James Brindley, and John Smeaton began a series of detailed surveys for a Grand Trunk Canal that would link the rivers Weaver and Trent and, thereby, the ports of Hull and Liverpool.[20] In his report, presented in July 1761, Smeaton estimated the total cost of the canal from Wilden Ferry to Longbridge, near Burslem, including branches to Stoke, Lichfield and Tamworth, at just over £100,000. The section from Wilden to King's Bromley, a distance of 25 miles, was to cost £32,000, and the ascent of 110 ft. was to be accomplished with the aid of 19 locks. Despite the additional cost, the Burton to Wilden section of the Trent was to be avoided, for—

> 'There are upwards of twenty shallows between Burton and Wilden (along the Trent), which are not navigable, except when there are freshes in the river, but by means of flushes of water let off from the mills; and by withholding this water the lessees may interrupt, and frequently have interrupted, the navigation below Burton lock; so that the navigation of this part of the Trent depends entirely upon their pleasure.'[21]

So great was the support of merchants, manufacturers and landowners in the areas concerned, that by 1766 Parliament had passed an Act authorising a navigable link between the Trent and the Mersey.[22]

The lessees of the Trent Navigation were naturally fearful of the scheme to by-pass Burton, and they soon devised a solution involving the construction of a short canal from the Trent at Bond End to join the Trent and Mersey Canal at Shobnall. In this way they hoped that the vessels of the Burton Boat Company would be able to use both the river and the canal. In 1769, by which time the Canal Company had over 1,000 men working in the Burton area, the Earl of Uxbridge agreed to lease to the Burton Boat Company a strip of land between Bond End and Shobnall, at an annual rent of £20.[23] The Bond End Canal was duly completed in the following year but its effectiveness was largely destroyed by the refusal of the Canal Company to sanction a connecting lock at Shobnall and by the restriction of the width of the Trent and Mersey Canal south of Horninglow.

After a series of disputes between the Earl of Uxbridge and the Canal Company, concerning the price of land, the supply of water to the canal and the erection of a warehouse at Horninglow Wharf, the Wilden to Great Haywood section of the Trent and Mersey Canal was finally opened in September, 1770.[24] The Burton to Wilden stretch was 31 ft. wide at the top, 18 ft. wide at the bottom and 5½ ft. deep; it included six locks, each of which was 14 ft wide and could accommodate Trent boats of up to 40 tons. South of Horninglow the canal measured 29 ft. by 16 ft. by 4½ ft. and the locks were only 7 ft. wide. Horninglow Wharf, the limit of navigation for river barges, gradually developed as a small industrial centre, with limekilns, timber yards and a steam-operated corn mill.

By 1777, when the Trent and Mersey Canal was fully completed, Burton had become linked by navigable waterways to wide areas of the country, including the three major sea-ports of Hull, Liverpool and Bristol. The new system proved to be substantially cheaper and more efficient than its predecessors, freight charges between Burton and Gainsborough, for instance, being reduced on average by one-third. Traffic on the canal and on the Trent below Wilden increased rapidly. Apart from local traffic in corn, coal, timber, stone, bricks and gravel, large quantities of lead, ale, hosiery, woollen goods, tinplate, earthenware, wheat, nails, cheese, butter, millstones, plaster and potatoes moved downstream, and barley, groceries, glass, salt, iron, clay, flint, timber, flax, hemp, rye, peas and paving stones upstream.[25]

In order to cater for this increase in trade further surveys of the Trent between Wilden and Gainsborough were carried out by William Jessop. These culminated in an Act of 1783 which authorised the Proprietors of the Trent Navigation to scour the river so that it was 24 ins. deep at the fords and at least 27 ins. deep elsewhere and to construct a towpath in order that boats could be 'haled' with horses.[26] It was estimated by Jessop that in 1790, 89,000 tons of freight passed along the river, 55,500 tons going upstream and 34,500 tons downstream.

Meanwhile, nothing was done to improve the river between Wilden and Burton, although it remained open to traffic for many years. The Burton Boat Company continued to flourish, however, and in 1795 owned a fleet of ten river barges of 33 tons, most of which were manned by a master and five 'thoroughmen', and eight canal boats, each with a master and a man to drive the horse.[27] The latter operated between Shardlow and Manchester, Runcorn, Coventry, Dudley, Stourbridge, Wolverhampton, Birmingham, Stafford and Froghall, while of the former, seven worked between Burton and Gainsborough and three carried iron from Burton Forge to Shobnall Wharf via the Bond End Canal. The Company owned two wharves in Bond End, warehouses in Bond End and at the western end of Burton Bridge, and a number of similar facilities outside Burton, including a wharf at 'Love Lane, Gosty Green' in Birmingham.

It is likely that well over 200 boats and barges were operating through Burton by the 1790's. Of the 531 registered Staffordshire vessels, 147 passed regularly through the town, Henshall & Co. of Stone, who owned 75 vessels, being by far the largest company. In addition, vessels belonging to the Cavendish Boat Company of Shardlow, the Gainsborough Boat Company and other outside concerns also used the canal and the river.[28]

The success of the Trent and Mersey Canal aroused considerable interest in the surrounding districts, and between 1770 and 1810 a number of additional schemes for extending and improving local waterways were considered. The most significant of these was the proposal to construct a canal from Atherstone to the Trent at Burton, via Ashby and Swadlincote, with the intention of providing outlets for the collieries in South Derbyshire and Leicestershire. From 1786 onwards, several public meetings were held and various schemes proposed but it was not until 1793 that William Jessop and Robert Whitworth were commissioned as surveyors.[29] Despite many years of effort on the part of Joseph Wilkes of Measham, the terms of the Ashby Canal Act of 1794 were never completely carried out. Eventually in May 1805, after many financial and technical problems had been overcome, the main canal from Marston Bridge, near Atherstone, to Moira was opened, together with connecting tram roads to lime-works at Ticknall and Cloud Hill and to collieries at Moira, Lount, Park Wood, Swadlincote and Church Gresley. Additional schemes to make the Trent and Tame navigable between Burton and Tamworth and to build a 'commercial wide canal for river barges' from Ashby to Burslem via Burton were also considered but not effected.

The Burton Boat Company tried unsuccessfully on many occasions to persuade the Grand Trunk Company to build a connecting lock between their canal and the Bond End Canal at Shobnall. Traffic on the Trent between Burton and Wilden gradually dwindled until finally, in 1805, the Burton Boat Company reached an agreement with Henshall & Co., the leading canal carriers, which included the closure of the river navigation above Wilden.

As previously noted, the considerable time, effort and money devoted during the 18th century to developing navigation systems stemmed partly from the inadequacies of road transport. Abundant evidence is available of the appalling state of many Staffordshire roads during the 1650–1750 period.[30] Roads in the Burton area were certainly no exception, and the bridge across the Trent, one of the largest and most important in the Midlands, proved to be a serious drain upon the resources of Lord Paget.[31] However, although totally inadequate for the movement of heavy goods, the roads had to be used by passenger and postal services. With this in mind, the 18th century saw a progressive application of the turnpike system, first introduced in 1663. The Burton to Lichfield road was one of a number of highways included in a Bill sponsored by the inhabitants of Lichfield and Stone in 1728.[32] In 1753 both the Burton to Derby and the Ashby to Tutbury roads were turnpiked, Burton men playing a prominent part in both of these schemes.[33] Incorporated into the latter were toll gates at Smisby Lane, Ashby or (Geary) Lane, Bearwood Hill, Horninglow and Tutbury and a weighing machine at the eastern end of Burton Bridge. The Burton-Measham (1763), Ashbourne-Yoxall (1766), and Burton-Abbots Bromley (1793) were other local highways similarly improved.[34]

Technical and administrative improvements to the road system were accompanied by the introduction of regular, and increasingly efficient, wagon and coach services. The Derby to London wagon service began in 1734—

> 'The Derby wagon begins on Tuesday, the 14th May 1734. Sets out from the White Hart Inn at Derby, every Tuesday morning, and comes to the White Horse Inn in Friday Street, London on Saturday following. In the winter, sets out from Derby every Monday at ten o'clock, carries goods and passengers to Loughborough, Leicester, Market Harborough, and places adjacent . . . Thomas and Henry Partridge!'[35]

By 1750 similar services were being operated to Manchester, Nottingham, Birmingham and other towns throughout the region. Stage-coach services were introduced between Derby and London in April 1735 and between Derby and Nottingham in July, 1737, single journies taking three days and one day respectively. The Derby to Birmingham service began in June 1764; coaches set out from Derby on Tuesdays and Fridays at 5.0 a.m. reaching Birmingham the same night; meals were taken at Burton and Lichfield, and the single fare charged was 10s. inside the coach and 5s. outside. The introduction of 'flying machines' with steel springs during the 1760's speeded-up services considerably, the Derby to London journey being reduced to one day.

It is thus evident that by 1780 Burton was linked to wide areas of the country by a vastly improved and enlarged network of roads and waterways. The contribution made by this network to industrial growth during the 18th century cannot be over-stressed. The opening of the Trent Navigation in 1712 set in motion a train of events that changed Burton from an isolated and impoverished market town into a prosperous industrial centre. Transport improvements and industrial expansion proceeded simultaneously, each helping to finance the other. Manufacturers invested profits in boat companies, canal companies and turnpike trusts, which in turn yielded them dividends and assisted their commercial activities. The Wilkes family of Overseal invested part of their proceeds from farming and cheese-trading in the Trent Navigation, while navigation revenues later helped them to purchase estates, coal mines, brickworks and cotton mills. Henry Evans of Burton was at the same time a lessee of the Trent Navigation, a boat owner, an iron merchant and a brewer. As the development of each major industry is traced the overwhelming significance of communications becomes apparent. In the case of the brewing industry, for instance, the purchase of prime barley from eastern England and of hops from Kent and Worcestershire, and the export of ale to Continental markets would all have been uneconomic without the transport improvements described.

Early 19th century directories indicate a steady increase in road and canal services, without any fundamental change in the system that had evolved 50 years before. Already, however, the first steps had been taken towards the introduction of a cheaper, faster and more efficient mode of transport. Short iron railroads, for carrying coal and stone in horse-drawn wagons to nearby canals, had been constructed in a number of the mining and quarrying districts of Derbyshire and Staffordshire since the 1770's. In 1792 links of this type between the collieries at Newhall and Swadlincote and the Trent near Burton had been suggested, while a proposal to revive the scheme in 1809 stated that—

> 'It is the general wish of the Inhabitants of Burton upon Trent and its neighbourhood to have a Rail Road made from the Collieries of Newhall and Swadlincote to Burton. It would very considerably reduce the price of coal and would be a great convenience in supplying the neighbourhood with lime up the River Trent, for slack could be brought down from the Collieries to burn it with, at a very trifling expence'.[36]

Although this railroad was never built, several others, linking collieries and limeworks to the Ashby Canal further east, were, and these undoubtedly fulfilled a need.

The technical failure of the Loughborough to Swannington Canal in 1799 and the limited success of the Ashby Canal induced Leicestershire colliery owners to turn to railways at an early date. In October 1828 William Stenson, one of the partners in Whitwick

Colliery, began to negotiate with George and Robert Stephenson for the construction of a railway for locomotives from Swannington to Leicester, where he hoped to secure many customers.[37] Work on the line began in October 1830, with Robert Stephenson as engineer, and was completed in July 1832, but it was not until August 1849 that the railway was extended westwards as far as Burton.

In 1836 the Birmingham and Derby Junction Railway Co. began work on a line from Derby through Burton to Hampton Junction, where it linked up with a line to London. The opening of the railway in August 1839 proved to be a great stimulus to industrial growth, just as the completion of the Trent Navigation had been over a century before. By 1839 several of Burton's staple industries, such as cotton spinning and weaving and hat and hardware manufacture were declining rapidly, while the expansion of the brewing industry was being held in check by high freight charges on the canals. Railways provided a transport system substantially faster and cheaper than any previously used; freight charges between Burton and London, for example, fell from £3 to 15s. per ton and the time taken from a week to 12 hours. Immediately, domestic markets became more important to the brewers than those overseas. Burton rapidly developed into a specialist brewing centre, with ale output increasing more than threefold each decade and the town's population expanding almost as rapidly.

The Midland Railway Company formed in 1844, found it increasingly difficult to cope adequately with the mounting volume of traffic. They laid out extensive sidings along the main railway, particularly at the north end of the town, and in 1859 obtained permission to open a branch line to serve brewery premises in High Street and Anderstaff Lane, which involved the reconstruction of Burton Bridge.[38] In 1865 Bass & Co., alone, despatched 100,000 tons of freight and received 72,000 tons by rail. During the following year M.T. Bass commented, 'We have paid the Midland Company nearly £17,000 for a single month's traffic ... Last year, I think we paid the Midland Company £100,000 beside what we paid the other companies. The traffic of Burton is very nearly £400,000 a year.'[39] Shortage of rolling stock caused the Midland Company much embarrassment and in 1869 it was requested to provide 'a more consistent class of station accomodation' and 'to pay some little complimentary attention to the requirements of a town to which it is so largely indebted'.[40] By 1880, however, the construction of branch lines, sidings and a new station, together with a slackening in the rate of industrial growth, had helped to relieve the congestion.

The construction of the main railway during the 1830's three-quarters of a mile to the west of the existing town centre and the main breweries produced an acute internal communications problem. For the next 20 years the town's streets were choked with 'floaters' moving between the breweries in High Street and the railway station, much to the annoyance of other road users. The eventual solution was the building of a network of private railways, which, at the time, was strongly opposed by a section of the community, who complained that 'our two main streets and thoroughfares are to be crossed in three different places, and a cost of perhaps £150,000 incurred, for no other purpose than to give Messrs. Allsopp & Sons an advantage over their neighbours'.[41] Between 1860–80, however, Parliament passed a series of Acts authorising the railway companies and the leading breweries to construct this network, with the result that by the end of the century 40 miles of private railway had been laid, of which Bass & Co. owned 26 miles and Allsopp & Sons ten.[42]

The great success of railways in respect of both passenger and freight services naturally led to a rapid decline in alternative forms of transport. By 1851 the Trent and Mersey Canal Company had re-organised itself to become the North Staffordshire Railway Company, with an integrated system of canal and rail services. It maintained the wharves, warehouses and granaries at Horninglow and existing carriers, such as J. & W. Soresby and Joseph Smith & Sons, continued to operate services between Hull and the Potteries.[43] Much of the traffic in general merchandise was lost to the railways but bulk cargoes, in the form of coal, stone, gravel, bricks, iron and timber, remained important. Tolls on the Trent Navigation below Shardlow fell from an average of £6,000 per annum during the 1830's to £3,000 during the 1880's.[44] Several unsuccessful attempts were made to revive traffic on the river, including a proposal by 'The Upper Trent Navigation Company' in 1886 to re-open the section from Burton to Wilden. All other local waterways fell into disuse shortly after the introduction of railways. The Ashby Canal passed into the hands of the Midland Railway Company in 1846, while the Bond End Canal was filled-in in 1874 and used as a route for a branch railway.

During the same period many of the road wagon and coach services through Burton were discontinued in the face of railway competition. The 40 mile journey from Derby to Birmingham, for example, that during the late 18th century had cost coach passengers 10s. and taken eight hours, could, by the 1840's, be accomplished by rail in two hours at a cost of 5s.6d. Road transport thus maintained its importance only at local level and it was not until the widespread introduction of motor vehicles during the following century that long distance services were revived.

In tracing the evolution of communications and transport their outstanding influence upon the extent and pattern of industrial growth can be immediately recognised. As will be seen in the ensuing chapters, the years 1712, 1770 and 1839 stand out as landmarks in Burton's economic development. Each year heralded the dawn of a new transport era in which the town's merchants and industrialists were provided with greater opportunities. It is not surprising, therefore, that these men were foremost in initiating and financing the successive transport improvements.

References

1. I.S. Beckwith, 'Transport in the Lower Trent Valley in the Eighteenth and Nineteenth Centuries'; *The East Midland Geographer*, vol. 4, part 2, no. 26, (Dec. 1966), pp. 99–106.

2. A.C. Wood, '*The History of Trade and Transport on the River Trent*' (1950), p. 13. T.S. Willan, '*River Navigation in England*, 1600–1750,' (1964), pp. 42–43.

3. C.C. Owen, '*The Early History of the Upper Trent Navigation*', Transport History, vol. 1, no. 3, (1968).

4. *Coke MSS*; correspondence of Leonard Fosbrooke (sen. & jun.) and Thomas Coke of Melbourne Hall, 1698–1700.

5. *Anglesey MSS*; proposal signed by Peter Walter, agent to Lord Paget, Aug. 1694.

6. *Trent Navigation Act*, 10 Will. III, c. 26.

7. Journal of the House of Commons, (J.H.C.) vol. 15, p. 59, 10 Dec. 1705.

8. *Coke MSS*; 'Mr. Geo. Hayne's Agreement with Wm. Lord Paget for the Burton Navigation', 16 Nov. 1711.

9. Ibid., 'Mr. George Hayne's Bond for Burton Navigation and Salt Rock', 1 Feb. 1710; 'Agreement between Mr. L. Fosbrooke and the London Cheesemongers', 20 June 1710.

10. *Paget MSS* (S.C.R.O., D.603 unlisted); inhabitants of Burton to George Hayne, 1713. *J.H.C.*, 17, p. 607.

11. *J.H.C.*, 17, p. 586.

12. *Coke MSS*; 'New Articles between George Hayne and Leonard Fosbrooke', 1714; 'Agreement between George Hayne and Leonard Fosbrooke', 25 June 1720.

13. A.C. Wood, op. cit., pp. 9 & 15; D. Defoe, '*A Tour Thro' The Whole Island of Great Britain*', (6th Ed. 1762) vol. 3, pp. 58 & 62.

14. *Paget MSS* (S.C.R.O; D.603, unlisted); Henry Hayne to Peter Walter, 30 Nov. 1734.

15. Ibid; letters from William Wyatt to the Earl of Uxbridge, July, 1762.

16. Ibid; correspondence of William Wyatt, July to Sept. 1762.

17. P.D., 29 May 1762 & 10 Feb. 1763.

18. *Paget MSS.*, William Wyatt to the Earl of Uxbridge, 7 Nov. 1763.

19. Dr. Thomas Congreve, '*A Scheme or Proposal for making a Navigable Communication between the Rivers Trent and Severn, in the County of Stafford*', (1716–17).

20. A.L. Thomas, 'Geographical Aspects of the Development of Transport and Communications affecting the Pottery Industry of North Staffordshire during the 18th century'; *H.C.S.*, (1934), p. 104.

21. J. Phillips, '*A General History of Inland Navigation, foreign and domestic*', (1795), p. 186. *Wyatt MSS*, 'Report of John Smeaton, Engineer, concerning the practicability of a navigable canal from Wilden in Derbyshire to King's Bromley Common and then by several branches to Longbridge near Burslem', 11 July 1761.

22. *Trent & Mersey Canal Act*, 6 George III, c. 96.

23. *Paget MSS*; Proprietors of the Burton Boat Co. to the Earl of Uxbridge 4 Jan. 1766, 19 June, 12 July, 11 Oct. 1769.

24. *D.M.*, 7 Sept. 1770.

25. Ibid; i773; arrivals and departures of vessels at Gainsborough.

26. *Trent Navigation Act*, 23 George III, c. 41. British Transport Commission Archives; 'A State of the depths of water upon the shallows in the River Trent between Cavendish Bridge and Gainsborough'—W. Jessop, Engineer, Aug. & Sept. 1782.

27. *S.C.R.O.*, Register of Staffordshire boats and barges, 1795.

28. *D.M.*, 21 Apr. 1780, 27 Apr. 1781, 1 Aug. 1793.

29. Ibid., 5 Sept. 1782, 8 Sept. 1791. C.E. Stretton, 'The History of the Midland Railway', (1901), p. 98. C.R. Clinker and C. Hadfield, 'The Ashby-de-la-Zouch Canal and its Railways'; *Transactions of the Leicestershire Archaeological and Historical Society*, vol. 34, (1958).

30. A.L. Thomas, op. cit., p. 25. Joan Parkes, '*Travelling in the 17th Century*', p. 221.

31. *Paget MSS*; estate papers, including the accounts of John Barker, Bailiff of Burton, 1689–90.

32. *Turnpike Act*, 2 George II, c. 5.

33. *D.M.*, 29 Sept. 1752, 8 June 1753.

34. Ibid; 23 May 1766, 8 Dec. 1775, 26 Aug. 1793.

35. Ibid; 9 May, 1734.

36. *Paget MSS*; Oswald Mosley to the Earl of Uxbridge, Aug. 1809.

37. C.E. Stretton, op. cit., p. 4 & pp. 99–100.

38. '*Burton-on-Trent Railway and Bridges Act*, 22 and 23 Vict., c. 136, (1859). W. Molyneux, op. cit., p. 119.

39. F.S. Williams, '*The Midland Railway: its rise and progress*' (1878), pp. 546–7.

40. W. Molyneux, op. cit; p. 251.

41. *Burton Weekly News*, 16 Mar. 1860.

42. *Burton-on-Trent Railway Acts*—

23 & 24 Victoria, c. 65 (1860).
30 & 31 Victoria, c. 71 (1867).
41 & 42 Victoria, c. 67 (1878).
44 & 45 Victoria, c. 59 (1881).

Burton-on-Trent, London and N.W. Railways Act—

24 & 25 Victoria, c. 208 (1861).

Burton-on-Trent, Great Northern Railway Act—

37 & 38 Victoria, c. 157 (1874).

Burton-on-Trent, N. Staffs. Railway Act—

26 & 27 Victoria, c. 132 (1863).

G.A. Wade, A Town of Railways and Beer; *Railway Magazine*, vol. 9, Aug. 1901.

43. W. White, *History, Gazetteer and Directory of Staffordshire*, (1851).
44. *B.T.C.A.*, Statements of Accounts, Trent Navigation Co. 1830–90.

IV

THE BREWING INDUSTRY PRIOR TO 1807

Brewing is a comparatively simple manufacturing process which relies mainly upon the use of four raw materials, namely barley in the form of malt, water, hops and yeast. The conversion of barley into malt is accomplished in a malthouse by screening, steeping, germination and drying processes carried out under carefully regulated temperature conditions. Ground malt is then mashed with warm water to enable the enzymes in the malt to convert the soluble starch into fermentable sugars. The resulting wort is then boiled with hops, sterilised, cooled and run into fermenting vessels, where the fermentable part of the wort is changed into alcohol and carbon dioxide by the addition of yeast. Finally, the beer is racked into casks where secondary fermentation occurs and further hops and sugar may be added.

Although modern chemistry and technology have helped brewers to carry out their work more swiftly and accurately and greatly reduced the element of personal skill and experience required, the basic processes of manufacture have changed surprisingly little over a long period of time. Until the 15th century English ale consisted of a sweet malt liquor brewed without hops but the use of imported and locally-grown hops by Flemish immigrants in London and Kent after 1420 gradually brought about a change in brewing methods, much to the dislike of native brewers.[1] By the second half of the 16th century it was widely recognised that hops not only imparted a flavour to beer but also assisted in its preservation. It was probably not until the middle of the 18th century that the use of isinglass for the fining of beer replaced the old method of using flannel filters. The addition of sugar to wort did not become legal until 1847. The raw materials used by the 19th century brewer were thus fundamentally the same as those used by his mediaeval counterpart.

In another respect, however, the two differed considerably, in that the latter was entirely ignorant of the chemical processes involved in brewing. Even the leading brewers and scientists of the 18th century were unaware of the reasons why certain types of barley and water and certain methods of malting and fermentation produced high quality beer. Their uncertainty was conveyed in the words of Erasmus Darwin, writing around 1770—

> 'I suppose from the affinity between calcareous earth and saccharine acid may be explained a circumstance, the theory of which has never been understood, and therefore the fact has generally been doubted; and that is, that hard waters make stronger beer than soft ones. I appeal to the Brewers of Burton for the fact, who have the soft water of the Trent running on one side of their brewhouses and yet prefer universally the hard calcareous water supplied by their pumps. I suppose there may be some saccharine acid in the malt (which is not all of it equally perfectly made into sugar by the vegetable digestive power of the germinating barley) which, by its attracting the calcareous earth of hard waters may produce a kind of mineral sugar; which, like the true sugar, may be convertible into spirit.'[2]

Lavoisier (1743–94) and Gay-Lussac (1770–1850) both worked on the fermentation process and were able to describe the break-down of sugar into alcohol and carbon dioxide, but it was left to later researchers, such as Pasteur (1822–95) to explain the process in precise chemical terms. Prior to 1860 brewing was thus a very inexact art that relied heavily upon trial and error and experience.

The brewers' ignorance of chemistry was matched by their lack of technical progress. Even by the end of the 18th century most breweries were powered by men and horses and, apart from the thermometer and the saccharometer, were devoid of scientific instruments.[3] Steam power was first applied to the processes of pumping and malt-milling in a brewery in 1784, when Boulton and Watt supplied engines to H. Goodwyn and S. Whitbread of London but it was not widely used until after 1820.

Whatever the technical shortcomings of the industry may have been, however, it was nevertheless of great national importance. It was estimated by Gregory King in 1689 that 21s. out of every 76s. spent on food and drink each year by an average member of the community went towards the purchase of beer and that the taxes on beer yielded a gross annual revenue of £700,000. It is not surprising, therefore, that brewing was one of the most widely distributed industries and that it was customary for almost all inns and large houses to possess a brewhouse. In Coventry in 1520 the 6,600 inhabitants were served by 60 brewers; in Burton-on-Trent in 1604 there were 46 licensed victuallers to supply a community of around 1,500, while in Derby in 1693 there were 120 alehouse-keepers out of a total population of just over 4,000.[4] In 1700 the 39,469 brewing victuallers in the United Kingdom produced almost the same amount of beer as the 746 common brewers, of whom 200 were established in London.[5] Apart from the universal demand for beer, the division of the industry into a large number of small units can be mainly attributed to the small size of urban centres and to the lack of adequate inland communications. It was only in London that the market was of sufficient size to enable large breweries to develop. These expanded considerably during the early 18th century when they began to brew porter, a thick, dark, bitter beer, that could be produced cheaply and possessed superior keeping qualities. Outside London the scale of production remained small as it was unusual for beer to be transported more than 10 miles from its place of manufacture. Burton-on-Trent was one of the few provincial towns that was able to emerge during this period as a significant brewing centre by serving distant markets.

The first records of brewing in Burton are connected with the Benedictine Abbey, which, like similar establishments, possessed its own brewhouse. The Abbey muniments contain a number of references to brewing dating back to 1295 but they provide no indication of total output or employment. Two early workers engaged in the industry were Hugh Crispe, a 'couper', who was granted a burgage in 'Catte Streete' in 1368, and John Wolston, a brewer, who was involved in an affray in 1453.[6] At the time of the dissolution in 1540 the Abbey brewhouse contained—

Item	xiii wort leddes in iii frames	xxii s.
Itm	one grett malt Fate	V s.
Itm	one yelyng Fate	V s.
Itm	a cest're of ledd	xxvi s. viii d.[7]

according to an inventory taken, while there were, in addition, large malthouses in the Market Place and a number of smaller ones in other parts of the town.

After the dissolution the brewhouse and malthouses passed with other Abbey properties to Sir William Paget. In April 1585 Sir Amyas Paulet, the keeper of Mary Queen of Scots during her imprisonment at Tutbury Castle, wrote to Lord Burghley—

> 'The brewer that serveth this house with beer breweth his beer in the Lord Paget's house at Burton, where he is lodged with his wife and family.'[8]

It is clear, however, from the number of licences granted to Burton victuallers and coopers that by the end of the 16th century the town's brewing industry was growing steadily in importance and becoming increasingly concentrated at the inns. The existence of 46 licensed victuallers in Burton in 1604 suggests that some beer was already being sent out of the town, probably as far afield as London.[9] It is known that by the early 1620's Burton ale (sometimes under the name of 'Darbie Ale') was being sold at 'The Dagger' in Holborn and at the 'Peacock' in Gray's Inn Lane, where it was held in high esteem.[10] The significance of this lies in the fact that even at this early date the superior quality of Burton ale and its ability to withstand long and arduous journeys without deteriorating was enabling it to command a higher price than beer brewed elsewhere.

Throughout the first half of the 17th century brewing undoubtedly remained subordinate to the cloth-working industry, while the damage done to properties in the town during the Civil War seriously affected all commercial activities. Of the 57 tradesmen mentioned in the Caldwall Charity Deeds of 1662 only three belonged to the brewing industry: Edward Lambe, William Melburne and Thomas Browne, all of whom were maltsters.[11] From the information available it appears that Peter Bunne was the most important property owner connected with the industry during this period. In 1656 he held the leases of the lower corn mill at Winshill and the malt mill in Burton Market Place, while shortly afterwards he gained possession of the Manor House with its old brewhouse and a group of premises on the east side of High Street which included tenements, outhouses, malting rooms, barns and stables.[12] After his death around 1665 most of these properties passed to Daniel Watson, a local barrister, who in 1669 paid tax on nine hearths in Burton Extra, including those in his 'brore house' (brewhouse), and a further eight in Burton.[13]

It is clear that by the end of the 17th century Burton possessed a thriving, if small, brewing industry that had already gained a national reputation for the high quality of its products. It was organised entirely in small units comprising inn brewhouses along High Street and Horninglow Street and the larger brewhouse in Burton Extra. Occupiers of leashold properties used as inns or alehouses were obliged to send their barley to the malt mill or, if they possessed their own facilities, to pay a toll amounting to one-sixteenth of the malt used. Between 1704 and 1709 Lord Paget's receipts from the mill averaged £130 per annum; he paid William Bowers, the miller £13 and Joseph Knapper, the loader £6 for their work during the year.[14] In Derby, where at this time brewing and malting were considerably more important, the industry was organised in a similar manner, with 120 alehouses and 76 malthouses but again no brewery. Derby regularly sent large quantities of fine quality malt to Lancashire and Cheshire but there is no indication that Burton participated in this trade. When Dr. Plot visited the town around 1680 he commented on the thrashing of corn 'as I saw them upon the pavement in the open streets' and he no doubt had Burton in mind when he referred to Staffordshire beer 'the management of which they have a knack of fineing it in three days, to that degree that it shall not only be potable but as clear and palatable as one would desire any drinke of this kind to be.'[15] Both Plot and Celia Fiennes, who passed through Burton a few years later, seemed, however, to find the bridge across the Trent far more impressive than the brewing industry.[16]

Even by the 1750's, by which time Burton's brewing industry had expanded considerably, the amount of strong beer taxed in the Lichfield Excise District, which included Burton and other Staffordshire towns, was not above average.[17] Output was inevitably restricted by limited markets and inadequate communications. The leading London breweries each produced more than all the Burton brewhouses together. Nevertheless the sweet, nut-brown Burton ale was still demanded by those Londoners who could afford to pay the high price. London newspapers of the period advertised 'genuine Burton ale brew'd to the greatest perfection for keeping by sea or land . . . procurable in Essex Street in the Strand' at 7s.6d. per dozen bottles.[18]

The turning point in the history of Burton's brewing industry was unquestionably the opening of the Trent Navigation in 1712 which immediately placed the town in direct contact with the ports of Gainsborough and Hull from which vessels sailed regularly for London and other English and foreign ports. It is possible that small quantities of Burton ale were already being sent to London via the Trent route. As early as 1680 ale was passing regularly through Hull in Stockwith and Gainsborough boats bound for London and in 1712 this amounted to 638 barrels per annum.[19] If any ale was exported direct to the Baltic ports from Hull at this time it was certainly not recorded by the customs officials. The long-held belief that 'both Peter the Great and the Empress Catherine' were 'immoderately fond of Burton ale'[20] suggests that either the ale was exported unofficially or was sent to St. Petersburg via London. The latter procedure is supported by the fact that after 1740, when exports of ale from Hull to the Baltic were increasing, the coastal trade to London was declining. Although the use of the Trent by Burton brewers prior to 1712 is largely a matter of speculation, an agreement between George Hayne and Leonard Fosbrooke proves that the ale trade was in existence by that year. One clause in the agreement specifically stated that Hayne had no rights below Wilden except that he

> shall from time to time navigate and carry from Gainsborough to Wilden Ferry aforesaid all empty ale casks or vessels (of William Dilke, Henry Shorthouse, Gervas Littlefere, Joseph Smith, John Wilders, William Wilders, Richard Tyler, Anne Walker and Thomas Wilmore) which he the said Leonard Fosbrooke had first navigated and carried down with Ale in them from Wilden Ferry.[21]

All of the persons named in the list who can be traced were Burton innkeepers; Gervas Littlefere was the proprietor of the 'Vine', William Wilders of the 'Three Queens' and John Wilders of the 'Lamb', all of which were situated in Horninglow Street, while Joseph Smith owned an inn and brewhouse in High Street.

The one surprising omission from the list is Benjamin Printon who established a small brewery in Horninglow Street around the time of his marriage to Maria Bannister of Burton in 1708. Later in the century Stebbing Shaw commented—

> 'The first origin of this business here was about ninety years ago and simply commenced with a few public houses; and one Benjamin Printon was the first who began in a small way (by employing three men) anything like the business of a Common Brewer.'[22]

There is some reason for believing that Printon moved to Burton from the Wapping district of London, no doubt attracted by the excellent reputation that Burton ale had gained there. His brewery stood close to the Trent on the north side of Horninglow Street and was later referred to as—

> 'all that messuage dwelling house tenement with the malthouse malting rooms Brewhouse ... situate standing and being in Burton upon Trent aforesaid in a certain street there commonly called or known by the name of the Horninglow Street at or near

> the Bridge foot sometime ago the estate and inheritance of Benjamin Printon and now in the possession of the said John Musgrove.'[23]

Printon became an influential man in the town and between 1719 and 1724 served as overseer of the poor, churchwarden and townmaster.[24] He died in 1729, leaving all his properties and possessions to his second wife, Elizabeth.[25]

Another notable Burton brewer of the early 18th century was Joseph Smith whose inn and brewhouse on the east side of High Street were later purchased and enlarged by William Worthington.[26] Like Printon he also held various public offices, including that of townmaster in 1721. He died in 1727, leaving properties and lands in Burton and Rolleston to his wife Ann and his son Joseph and £400 to his daughter Ann.[27]

It is evident from the numerous local deeds and other documents that have survived from the early 18th century that the numbers of brewing victuallers, maltsters and coopers in the town were steadily increasing. Moreover, many of the brewing premises, which later formed the nuclei of the larger breweries, were established during this period. William Newton, the landlord of the 'Three Queens' during the 1720's purchased a house on the south side of Horninglow Street to which he later added a brewhouse and a malthouse, this later became Charles Lesson's brewery. A short distance away John Wilders extended the premises at the 'Lamb Inn' which later formed Joseph Clay's brewery. In High Street the 'Blue Stoops' belonging to John Walker and the premises of Thomas Pearsall, a cooper, were improved; these later helped to form the breweries of Benjamin Wilson and Henry Evans.[28] The first 40 years of the century thus produced a modest but significant growth of the brewing industry, particularly at the northern end of the town. Although output remained small and much of the ale was still sold locally, there is evidence to suggest an increasing concentration on quality brewing with London and Baltic markets in mind. With the assistance of the Trent navigators a co-ordinated and efficient system of trade was steadily developing. Exports of ale overseas from Hull remained small but the coastal trade with London increased, reaching almost 1,000 barrels by 1722.[29]

Around 1740 Burton's brewing industry entered a new and important phase in its development which was symbolised by the conversion of many of the small inn brewhouses into larger and better equipped premises. The following advertisement is typical of a number that appeared in the 'Derby Mercury' at this time—

> 'To be let and entered upon immediately at Burton upon Trent in the County of Stafford. A New compleat Brewhouse fit for a Common Brewer, ready furnished with all sorts of new materials for brewing, as Coppers, Coolers etc. which will be sold to the person who takes the Brewhouse at reasonable rates, or in case the said Brewhouse should not be let, the same materials will be sold in any manner, together with all sorts of empty casks iron bound—Enquire of Mr. James Butterfield, Woollen-Draper in Derby, or Mr. William Bowers, Cooper in Burton'.[30]

These premises which which were situated on the north side of Horninglow Street, were acquired by Samuel Sketchley of Nottingham who became a notable brewer and Trent merchant.

At the same time this expansion was heralded by the migration into the town of men with capital, ability and progressive ideas. These included Joseph Clay and Henry Evans of Derby, Benjamin Wilson, also probably from the Derby Area, William and John Davies Greaves of Ingleby, Samuel Sketchley of Nottingham, William Bass, probably from London, and William Worthington, who is said to have originated from Orton-on-the-Hill, Leicestershire. The drift of men from Derby to Burton is of particular interest, for there is little doubt that at the end of the previous century Derby had been a considerably more important centre for brewing and malting than Burton. By the 1730's these industries were declining rapidly in Derby, judging by the number of brewhouses and malthouses unsuccessfully offered for sale. There may have been a number of reasons for this trend. Firstly, the Trent Navigation, which was so vital to the success of the ale trade, was very carefully controlled by the Hayne family at Burton Wharf and, in consequence, Burton was rapidly developing as a distributing centre for commodities flowing between Hull and the Birmingham area. Secondly, the Burton water supply may well have proved superior for the brewing of strong ale capable of withstanding the long voyage to the Baltic ports. Thirdly, the fact that Derby capital and commercial expertise were being increasingly devoted to the expansion of the silk and hosiery industries may have led to a neglect of less important occupations such as brewing.

Whatever the precise reasons may have been, the fact remains that considerable impetus was given to the brewing industry in Burton which was reflected in national trade statistics. English ale exports to

Russia and the East Country increased rapidly from a mere 740 barrels in 1750 to 11,025 barrels in 1775.[31] Entries in the 'Hull Port Books' show that Hull completely monopolised this trade; indeed, its exports to Russia and the East Country (mainly to St. Petersburg, Danzig, Riga and Konigsburg) in 1750 were unaccountably in excess of the figure shown in the national statistics.[32] In the absence of detailed local records it is impossible to say what proportion of the exports can be attributed to Burton brewers. Occasionally the 'Hull Port Books' specifically recorded Burton ale; on 19 January 1751, for example, the 'Alice and Elizabeth', bound for Danzig, carried 1,364 gallons of 'Burton Ale' together with lead, ironmongery and woollen drapery. In the spring of 1756 the 'Mary Ann' carried 10 tons and 51 gallons of 'Burton Ale' to Danzig and the 'Baltimore' 15 tons to Narva.[33] Unfortunately, the sporadic nature of such references make it impossible to arrive at an accurate assessment of the Burton contribution. Nevertheless, as will be seen later, the remarkably close correlation between the increase in Hull's exports and the expansion of Burton's breweries suggests that this contribution was well in excess of 50 per cent.

The period from 1740 until 1807 formed a highly distinctive phase in Burton's economic development in that so many facets of its commerce and industry were linked to the Baltic system of trade. It is, therefore, extremely fortunate that the business records of Benjamin Wilson (jun.), who was the leading brewer in Burton between 1773 and 1807, have survived. This fascinating collection has yielded a detailed insight into such aspects as transport arrangements, Baltic customers and ports, financial arrangements, brewing techniques and business organisation. Certain points revealed by the records, such as the partial use of a system of barter, the stimulus given to exports by low outward freight charges and the diversity of commercial interests shared by many of the leading brewers of the period, are of particular significance.

Benjamin Wilson (sen.) was born in 1712 or 1713 (possibly in the Derby area) and all that is known about his early life is that he began his career as a rope-maker. It was probably in 1736 that he married Hannah Walker, the daughter of Mary Walker and the late John Walker, the former landlord of the 'Blue Stoops', an inn on the east side of High Street in Burton. It was here that Benjamin went to live with his wife and mother-in-law and where he first learnt the art of brewing. In January 1742, following Mary Walker's death, he purchased the 'Blue Stoops', 'together with outhouses brewhouses barnes and stables' from his brother-in-law for £164.[34] It is likely that his experience in the rope business, which relied mainly on imported Russian hemp, had already given him an insight into the workings of the Trent Navigation and, possibly, contact with Hull merchants, such as William Wilberforce, Henry Etherington and Samuel Watson. By 1750 he had substantially improved and extended his business premises, increased the output of his brewery to around 1,000 barrels per annum, by brewing mainly for export, and had 30 men in his employ. So successful was his business that during the next decade he was able to pay off the mortgage on his premises and also acquire additional lands and properties in High Street, Horninglow Street and at Winshill.[35]

Some indication of the growth of Wilson's business is given by the following ledger extracts—

> 'in 1765 the account of Messrs. Blayden of Hull, from October to March, was £373 9s. 10d.; and that of Messrs. John and William Mornby [probably a mistake for Horner] of Gainsborough, for the same period, was £288 5s. 10½d. In 1766 the account of Messrs. Samuel Watson & Sons of Hull was settled by £655 0s. 4d. Messrs. George Storey & Co. £359 13s. 3d.; and Mr. Robert Wilberforce, £428 13s. 2d.; which he paid in flax'.[36]

Moreover, they show that Wilson dealt mainly or entirely with intermediaries at Hull and Gainsborough rather than with merchants in the Baltic ports and that the barter system was already in operation. Unfortunately, there is no way of knowing whether the extracts were random selections or complete accounts for particular years. It might be useful to record, however, that the three accounts for 1766 represent in total the sale of 550 barrels of ale.

In 1773 Benjamin Wilson (sen.) handed over the running of the business to his three sons, John Walker, William and Benjamin, all of whom were common brewers.[37] Contrary to his father's wishes John Walker Wilson established a separate business as a brewer and timber merchant and in 1774 sold his share of the family business to his younger brothers for £1,300. Benjamin proved to be the most able and single-minded of the three. He remained a bachelor all his life, kept aloof from public affairs and apparently had few interests outside the brewery. His letters and other business records show him to have been efficient, meticulous, persevering, cautious and honest in everything that he did. By 1778 he had paid off a mortgage of £1,000 on the brewery and also secured William's share of the business for £650.[38] When he retired from business thirty years later he was a wealthy man with extensive lands and properties and a brewery valued at nearly £10,000.

The story of his success is one of steady and cautious development rather than of meteoric growth. Until 1790 his brewing activities were based entirely at the family premises in High Street, where he opened a third brewhouse in 1774—

> 'We have already two large Brewhouses employ'd and about to use a third, the whole of which will take all the money I can raise with convenience to myself, beyond which I do not choose to go.'[39]

According to Wilson it took him 'more than two months in the full spirit of my business to brew 1,000 barrels of ale', which gave the brewery an annual capacity of around 3,000 barrels, bearing in mind that brewing was a seasonal occupation largely confined to the October to April period. In times of favourable trade his limited output was a constant source of embarrassment—

> 'With respect to the Quantity of Ale likely to go to St. Petersburg it would be very considerable could the orders be compleated, but from various causes that is impossible. The other ports have made great demands upon us this year, so that, though a great deal of Ale will be brewed from this time to the 5th April, yet we hope and believe Petersburg cannot be overcharged. Our orders for that place exceed 600 Hogsheads'.

Wilson's reluctance to expand the capacity of his brewery was due not to lack of capital but to the risky nature of the Baltic trade. Its serious decline after 1792 and complete collapse in 1807 certainly proved the wisdom of his cautious policy.

While trade continued to expand Wilson solved the problem of excess orders by modest brewery extensions, by hiring additional malthouses on short-term leases and by purchasing ale from other Burton brewers. In January 1790 he purchased Samuel Sketchley's brewery on the north side of Horninglow Street, comprising—

> 'a handsome sashed and modern, well-built and finished dwelling-house of brick and stone, covered with slate; with a brewhouse, store-rooms, three malt offices that will steep 40 quarters every four days, coopers' shops, stables and other conveniences'.[40]

The only other significant addition to his brewing premises was the purchase of two large malthouses on the west side of Anderstaff Lane from the executors of Charles Leeson in 1800. Between 1785 and 1787, when exports were rising, Wilson leased malthouses from Messrs. Yeomans, Sketchley, Wayte, Standley, Whitehurst, Sergeant, Reynolds, Morecroft, Greaves and Wilders, an expedient to which he resorted on numerous occasions.[41] In 1785 Hill and Sherratt's of Burton supplied him with 200 barrels of ale, while in 1791 Charles Leeson provided him with 300 barrels so that he could satisfy his Baltic customers.[42] As Wilson explained to J.J. Roskampff of Elbing, one of his leading customers, in 1791, his ability to supply the requisite amount of ale depended very much upon weather conditions, particularly in spring and autumn, and upon the activities of the captains of the Baltic ships—

> 'From the unusual impatience of the Ship owners and masters to depart so early in the spring, I ought to begin to brew before the winter sets in, but let me tell them and all whom it may concern, that it would be very dangerous to the preservation of the ale, which is a material object both for me and my friends to consider. I commonly begin to brew in the beginning of November, and am not willing, not withstanding the importunity of the Ship owners, to open my winter business sooner'.[43]

As previously mentioned, the 18th century brewers' knowledge of brewing science was very limited and he experienced considerable difficulty in manufacturing a consistent product. Wilson repeatedly stressed the importance of temperature control in the malting and fermentation processes and the dangers of working out of season. He never began to brew before mid-October and even in winter mild spells of weather sometimes forced him to suspend activities. Although highly experienced and in possession of the best materials, methods and equipment available he was unable to produce ale of uniform colour and strength from one season to the next. Complaints from several of his best customers in 1791 forced him to admit—

> 'I have committed one fault in the Brewing of my Ale last winter, and that is, in making it too strong ... If I had made it weaker it certainly would have been lighter colour'd and would have pleased better at first sight, but it is certainly better for the Interest of the Adventure to possess strength sufficient for its

> certain conservation, than to be otherwise and in danger of turning sour'.[44]

Experiences such as this induced him to search for better methods, particularly from the large brewers. The following extract from a letter to Joseph Brooks of London was typical of his attitude towards improvements—

> 'every part of the business is done with hand pail, from drawing off the mash to filling the casks for exportation. It occurs to me that this quantity of business could be done with the aid of machinery to save great expense and with equal certainty of purpose'.[45]

Throughout his working life Wilson was without doubt the leading brewer in the town. His acquisition of Sketchley's brewery in 1790 raised the total capacity of his business to at least 4,500 barrels per annum. During the 1791–2 season, when export orders reached a peak, he used over 17,000 strikes of malt to attain an output of 4,500 barrels of ale. Exports travelled in whole (hogsheads), half or quarter casks containing 80, 40, and 20 gallons respectively. Ale for the home market was also despatched mainly in casks, although by 1796 he was bottling small quantities for London customers. The price of ale varied from year to year in accordance with the cost of raw materials and the size of his malt stocks. Between 1784 and 1792 the price varied between 18d. and 21d. per gallon; even in 1791 and 1792, when harvests were poor and barley expensive, he was able to assure his Baltic customers that the price would not exceed 20d. per gallon because he was 'in the possession of the largest stock of the best old malt I ever saw'.[46] After 1793 the rapid rise in barley prices, coupled with the need to pay convoy dues and increased freight and insurance charges, inevitably drove-up ale prices well above the previous level.

As far as Wilson and the other Burton brewers were concerned the key to successful brewing with the use of top quality barley and malt. The best malting barley was the short, plump, thin-skinned, 'mealy' type, with its high starch and low nitrogen content, grown on light sandy, chalky or loamy soils. In consequence, practically all the supplies were purchased from farms to the east of the town and from farmers and merchants in certain parts of Nottinghamshire, Lincolnshire and East Anglia. The following extract from a letter to Samuel Sanders of Newark was typical of his instructions to his agents—

> 'When you have completed one cargo proceed on another and buy me 50 or 60 qrs. weekly till you hear to the contrary, but I beseach you to buy me none if you can't buy it sound and dry. The price I submit to your candour and regard to my interest. If I can meet with barley that is sound and useful I may want much, if it is otherwise I shall want little or none'.[47]

Throughout the second half of the 18th century barley prices showed a general upward trend accompanied by sharp annual fluctuations in accordance with the quality of harvests. During the early 1770's Wilson paid around 25s. per quarter but by 1800 the price had risen to an average of 40s. He did his utmost to offset this by storing large quantities of malt and by purchasing barley when it was unusually cheap. In December 1791, for example, when the Trent Navigation was closed by a severe frost, the local farmers were unable to obtain supplies of barley from Newark and were forced—

> 'to thrash for the support of their cattle, and thereby produced such a supply as I never saw exceeded. The consequence of which is that much good barley has been bought for the last two market days at 34s. and 35s per quarter'.[48]

Wilson took advantage of these unusual circumstances to build up a large stock of malt for the following season. During the 1785–6 season when barley prices were high he purchased only 717 quarters, whereas in the following year, when plenty of good barley was available at 25s., he malted 1,307 quarters.

Unlike most of the large London porter brewers Wilson very rarely purchased malt, for in his opinion the final quality of the ale was largely determined by the quality of the malt used. Highly skilled local maltsters were engaged to operate his malthouses and paid by results. In 1771, for example, John Hopkin was commissioned to work three malthouses at one penny per strike and Wilson promised—

> 'to furnish him with barley or pay him for the vacant time, and he engages to steep no more than once in five days and to turn off a pale well-worked and thoroughly dried malt'.[49]

Wilson carefully supervised work in the malthouses and also visited farmers and agents over a wide area in order to inspect barley. Local supplies came particularly from the Ibstock, Ticknall and Smisby areas, where the relatively light soils yielded excellent grain. His main supplies of 'water barley', so called because it was transported by river and canal, were obtained from Messrs. J. Parnell, S. Sanders, J. Jackson, G. Ashforth and Winrow of Newark, Messrs. Pheasant and Manton of Grantham and P. & J. Denton of King's Lynn, each of whom was normally paid a commission of 1s. per quarter. During the 1780's Wilson relied mainly on local growers but as time went by he purchased increasing quantities from eastern counties, only 40 per cent coming from local sources during the 1801–2 season.

The overwhelming importance of malt as a brewing material implied that fluctuations in barley prices significantly affected brewers' profits. In the interests of trade Wilson endeavoured to keep ale prices reasonably stable; thus, if the price of barley rose from 25s. to 35s. per quarter he might increase the price of ale from 18d. to 19d. or at the most, 20d. per gallon but he could not absorb the whole of the extra cost in this way. Moreover, the better the quality of the barley, the greater the amount of wort that could be extracted from the malt. The price and quality of malt was thus the key to profits and it is scarcely surprising that Wilson devoted so much of his time to that side of the business. To some extent the price of barley was more important than the demand for his ale and it is no wonder that he frequently complained about 'the oppressive tax on malt' which rose from 1s. 4½d. per bushel in 1780 to 2s. 5d. in 1802 and 4s. 5¾d. in 1803.[50]

Also liable to marked seasonal fluctuations was the price of hops. In 1800, for example, hops were scarce owing to abundant rain and strong winds during the ripening and picking season, with the result that prices rose to nearly three times the normal average. As with barley, therefore, it paid the brewer to exercise a careful control over hop-buying in order to secure the best materials at a fair price. Wilson purchased most of his Kent hops from merchants in Southwark, the three main suppliers being Sir William Stephenson, Yeats and Brown and Sir James Sanderson, Roxby & Co. From time to time he also dealt with various other London and Worcester merchants and with Flower, Ellis & Co. of Ollerton who marketed the North Clay hops grown on the heavy clay lands around Southwell, Tuxford, Ollerton and Retford in Nottinghamshire.[51] Hops were bought in bags weighing roughly 2¾ cwts. or, in the case of the finest hops, in pockets of 1½ cwts. For a season's brewing of 2,000 barrels of ale Wilson required 100 cwts. of hops, the price of which might vary between £6 10s. and £4 5s. per cwt. Occasionally, he purchased hops far in excess of his own requirements, with the intention of selling the surplus to other Burton brewers or of storing them in London until he could take advantage of the market. With such speculations he was generally successful. In May and June, 1798, for example, Wilson bought several large consignments of hops, including 70 bags and 71 pockets from Bolland and Prestwidge of London for £1,727 which he sold five weeks later for £2,082.[52]

Apart from barley and hops, Wilson was constantly engaged in the purchase of timber, iron hoops, coal and coke. Unlike their London counterparts, the Burton brewers employed a considerable number of coopers for cask manufacture. Russian and Polish timber was obtained either direct from Baltic ports or from merchants in Hull and London, with quality very much in mind—

> 'the staves that suit me are those wherein the quality is as large as may be and the grain of the wood be fine, straight and close ... the best ale that man can brew will degenerate or become indifferent if it is put in a cask of indifferent or coarse-grained timber ... I should buy more Danzig staves than I do, but the wood is so coarse-grained. Stettin wood is much finer in grain, which is the reason I prefer it.[53]

Wilson kept large stocks of staves at the brewery and also various types of timber at Gainsborough in order to guard against price fluctuations, particularly after 1793 when shipping conditions in the Baltic became hazardous. Casks were expensive items equal to almost a quarter of the value of the ale they contained and Wilson was obliged to charge his Baltic customers 14s. 6d. for each half-cask and 9s. for every quarter-cask sent to them.

Iron hoops for the casks were purchased from Thomas Thornewill and Lloyd & Co. of Burton and from manufacturers in Derby, Birmingham, Coventry, Market Bosworth and Stratford-on-Avon. These were generally bought in lots costing £10 10s. but occasionally large consignments in excess of £100 were obtained.[54] They were often accepted by Wilson in part-exchange for imported Russian bar iron.

Wilson's annual expenditure on coal and coke usually amounted to approximately £100; during the 1798–9 brewing season, for example, he purchased 150 tons of coal and 570 quarters of coke at a total cost of £112 8s.[55] Coal was required for heating liquor and for various other purposes in the brewery and in the cooperage, while coke was needed for drying malt. The use of coke in malthouses was practised in Derby during the 17th century and was almost certainly used in Burton during the same period. Coal supplies were purchased mainly from Bullivant & Co. of Swadlincote, William Nadin of Stanton, William Brearley of Newhall and Fletcher & Co. of Ripley, while coke was obtained from various merchants in the Chesterfield and Staveley areas of north Derbyshire. Unlike barley, hops and staves, which at times were scarce and expensive, supplies of coal, coke and hoops were generally easily obtainable and constant in price.

Undoubtedly, the most unusual characteristic of Wilson's business and, indeed, of many of the other Burton breweries during the second half of the 18th century was the high degree of dependence upon distant overseas markets. This necessitated elaborate transport and financial arrangements. Most of the ale was despatched by canal and river, during the first four months of the year, via Gainsborough to Hull, where Wilson maintained a close liaison with merchants and ships' captains. Theoretically Wilson's customers were responsible for the ale after it left Burton but in practice Wilson himself usually made the necessary shipping and financial arrangements and accepted some responsibility for loss of ale in transit. Between 1780 and 1805 he mainly used the services of John Smith of Gainsborough and Henshall & Co., sending to them full details of each consignment, including cask numbers, marks and sizes and the names of the Hull ships onto which they were to be loaded. The chief problem encountered during the 150 mile journey from Burton to Hull was the delay of vessels by severe frosts or floods which sometimes resulted in the ale missing the appropriate ship at Hull. Pilfering of cargoes by 'river pirates' also occurred, although this could usually be prevented by sending an experienced waterman with the boat.

Wilson's main shipping agents in Hull were Carlill, Gilder, Kirkbride & Co. and Terry & Wright but he also engaged the services of Thomas Barmby, Christopher Thorley, Charles and Isaac Broadley, George Etherington, James Thompson, Benjamin Metcalf and a number of others.[56] The first two were important companies engaged in trade from the Baltic to the Mediterranean and also in marine insurance. They owned offices and warehouses in High Street in Hull, behind which were staithes at which their ships could take-up and discharge cargoes.[57] The main ships that carried Wilson's ale to the Baltic ports were 'Humber' (Capt. J. Wright) and 'Porter' (Capt. Mentrup), in which Wilson himself owned one-third shares, and also 'Phoenix' (Capt. Leonard), 'Sally' (Capt. Metcalf), 'Amity' (Capt. Mallison), 'Traveller' (Capt. Horwood), 'Olive Tree' (Capt. Thompson), 'Deuro', 'Argo' and 'Charming Harriott'.

Much to Wilson's annoyance they sailed for the Baltic as soon as the weather permitted, rather than at stated times. In 1791, for example, several ships took advantage of 'the finest westerly wind that almost ever blew' and 'went out in Ballast'.[58] Early departure could, however, entail great hazards; in 1792 several vessels 'met with strong winds and were driven against the ice', arriving at Pillau six weeks late.[59] The eagerness of the ships' owners and captains to take such risks and to leave in ballast, rather than to wait for a cargo, clearly demonstrates the overwhelming importance of commodities imported into England in relation to exports. Throughout the 18th century England imported substantial quantities of timber, iron, flax, hemp, grain, tallow and other goods from the Baltic states which greatly exceeded in value the commodities sent to them.[60] In 1749, for example, British exports to St. Petersburg totalled one million roubles, while imports from there amounted to 2·25 million roubles.[61] As time went by this adverse trade balance became increasingly pronounced in respect of all Baltic countries, so that by 1783 English exports to and imports from the whole of Russia totalled £216,138 and £1,288,314 respectively.[62] In terms of shipping space the discrepancy was even greater, for many of the imported commodities, such as timber and iron, were of considerable weight and bulk. Burton brewers benefitted enormously from this situation in that inward cargoes bore the brunt of the shipping charges in both directions, while exports, such as ale, tended to be treated almost as ballast and to be carried at highly favourable rates. Thus, despite high freight rates between Burton and Hull and, after 1793, convoy dues and high insurance charges, the Baltic ale trade proved to be a lucrative business.

Prior to 1775 Wilson sent the bulk of his exports to St. Petersburg via intermediaries in Hull; during the 1770–1 season, for example, 85 per cent of his exports were sold to Hull merchants. Direct contact with Danzig customers began during the 1775–6 season when he sent 72 barrels of ale to Frederick William von Ankum, who remained his client and friend for over 20 years. Gradually, such contacts were increased with merchants in Danzig and Elbing taking a larger and larger proportion. This transition was largely the result of a steady deterioration in Anglo-Russian relations arising from Russian aggression in the Crimea and Poland. During the American War of Independence she played an active part in the armed neutrality directed against England's command of the seas. Political enmity was also manifested in a general decline in Anglo-Russian trade and in a series of repressive measures directed against English merchants. In 1783 tariffs on British goods imported through St. Petersburg were increased by as much as 300 per cent, while a duty of 20 roubles per hogshead, later increased to 40 roubles, was imposed on imported ale.

By 1787 practically all of Wilson's old St. Petersburg customers, such as Shairps, Maude & Co. and Messrs. William Glen & Co. had ceased to place orders for ale owing to the difficulties. In 1791 Wilson was forced to revoke orders for various commodities placed with Ivan Kusoff of St. Petersburg 'on account of the threatening appearance of war' and had to send ale to him in an American vessel at the rate of five roubles per hogshead.[63] All trade between the two countries finally came to an end in 1800 when Russia placed an embargo on all British ships and merchandise.

These unfortunate developments forced Wilson to rely increasingly upon markets in Prussia and Poland where conditions up to 1792 were relatively more stable. During the 1782–3 season 44 per cent of his ale shipments went to Danzig and 2 per cent to Elbing, while by 1791–2 the proportions were 49 per cent and 38 per cent respectively. Moreover, his total exports showed a marked increase from 1,300 barrels in 1786–7 to at least 3,500 barrels in 1791–2.[64] Unfortunately, just as Wilson's export business reached its peak, trade was totally disrupted by the invasion of Poland by Russia in 1792 and the second partition of the country during the following year. Wilson commented on the events thus—

> 'In the previous year [1791–2] the market was greatly overdone for I sent myself that year between 4 and 5,000 casks to Elbing and Dantzig ... In the Spring of 93 I did not send so much by 1,000 casks as in the preceeding year—the events of that year notwithstanding, this great difference proved more injurious than the former one, for some persons lost nearly their whole capital—this circumstance arose from the bankruptcies then prevailing and partly from the stagnation of business and of public credit, but principally from the violent usurpation of the Country. This Spring [1794] I have not sent more than 1,450 casks to both places or ports—it may possibly happen from the commotions existing in Poland that this reduced quantity may either find a good market or one worse than all'.[65]

Like many other English merchants and manufacturers, Wilson suffered heavy losses through bad debts. Carl Zimmerman of Danzig, for example, one of his best and most reliable customers of 14 years standing, was unable to settle his account for almost £600.

Although Wilson managed to obtain a number of small compensatory orders in London, Liverpool and other English towns, he was forced to operate his brewery well below capacity—

> 'The stagnation of this trade is really hurtfull to me, not only on account of a large stock of casks which I have on hand and which are fit for no other purpose, but also I have locked up a great capital in other materials and which, unimployed, occasion a great loss to me'.[66]

The net profits of the brewery for the year ending 30 April 1795 amounted to a mere £411, so that Wilson began to supplement his income by speculating in various commodities such as wheat, timber and calico.

Towards the end of 1795 trade began to revive and shipments to Danzig and Elbing during the 1795–6 season totalled almost 2,000 barrels. From then until 1800 they averaged around 1,900 barrels per annum but after 1800 exports increased substantially, attaining a new peak of just over 3,000 barrels in 1802–3, of which 80 per cent went to Danzig.[67]

During most of the 1793–1806 period trade between England and the Baltic States was also threatened by the war with France so that it was necessary for ships to travel in convoy. Apart from convoy dues, Wilson was forced to pay rising freight and insurance charges. During the 1794–5 season insurance rates on his ale varied between 10 and 11 per cent; in April 1795, for example, he paid J.W. Anderson & Co. £139 on a Danzig consignment worth £1,280. The French invasion of Holland in 1793 also forced Wilson to transfer his financial arrangements from companies in Amsterdam to others in Hamburg. The Berlin and Milan Decrees of 1806 and 1807 and the retaliatory Orders in Council abruptly brought to a standstill the Baltic ale trade and effectively severed the links between the Burton brewers and the merchants in Danzig and Elbing. During the 1806–7 season Wilson sent no more than 200 barrels of ale along the Trent to Hull and most of this was destined for London, thus bringing to a close a highly significant phase in Burton's brewing history.

The overwhelming importance of foreign markets prior to 1806 made it essential for Wilson and other Burton brewers to employ a precise trading system designed to eliminate as many risks as possible.[68] Freight, cask and insurance charges were added to the price of the ale invoiced to Baltic merchants or intermediaries in Hull or London. Financial arrangements concerning payment and insurance were made with 'some indubitable House' in Amsterdam or London and all new customers were strictly required to prove their credit-worthiness. Once Wilson had been advised that his customer was sound and had lodged sufficient credit he despatched the ale and forwarded a bill of lading together with a bill of exchange, usually drawn at three months, to the intermediary.[69] He normally discounted the bills almost immediately in exchange for £50 bank notes or used them to offset existing debts. The main finance houses that he used were B.D. Weyland, J. & W. Anderson, Isaac Solly, W. & T. Raikes, C.A. Petersson, Henry Law & Co. and Smith, Wienholt & Co. of London, Muilman & Sons, J.W. & M. van der Schaaf, Messrs. Pye, Rich & Co., Melvill & Wolff, Dupper & Co. and W. van Bruiven & Sons of Amsterdam and M.H. Opman & Co. of Hamburg.[70]

Generally the system worked smoothly enough but occasionally customers defaulted or attempted to extend the term of credit—

> 'Mr. Lewis Paleske on whom one of my drafts were made has wrote to me that my letter of advice states that the account was made out at 2 months and that the draft itself was filled up at 1 month, for which reason he cannot accept but at the term of 2 months. Foreigners are fond of chicanery—I have wrote to him by this day on the subject and I have no doubt but all will be right'.[71]

In 1791 Rosler and Hurtig of Warsaw refused to accept 150 barrels of Wilson's ale and he was obliged to ask Barstow and Elliot of Danzig to dispose of the consignment as best they could. Surprisingly, participation in the Baltic ale trade often proved less hazardous and frustrating than that in internal trade. There is little doubt that the principal reason for this was the mutual interest that Burton brewers and Baltic merchants possessed in it. The latter found Burton ale an acceptable commodity but they were far more interested in selling timber, iron, hemp, flax and other commodities to English merchants. The Burton brewers for their part were often willing to accept these commodities in part-payment for the ale, in the knowledge that they could usually be disposed of at a profit. Goods were frequently entered on both sides of an account in Wilson's ledgers and there is good reason for supposing that up to a quarter of Baltic ale sales were covered by this system of 'bookkeeping barter'. Moreover, commodities such as iron and timber might be involved in triangular transactions in which they were used to satisfy creditors. Thus, Wilson accepted bar iron from Sutherland & Co. of St. Petersburg in settlement of an ale account and arranged for the iron to be sent direct to Thomas Thornewill at Clay Mills Iron Works to offset the cost of iron hoops supplied by Thornewill to the brewery. Similarly, Wilson used timber from M. & W. Fischer of Riga and Barstow &

1. 'The East prospect of Burton upon Trent in the County of Stafford' by S. and N. Buck, 1732 (by permission of County Record Office, Stafford)

2. View of Burton upon Trent from the east by White, 1753 (from W. Molyneux, 1869)

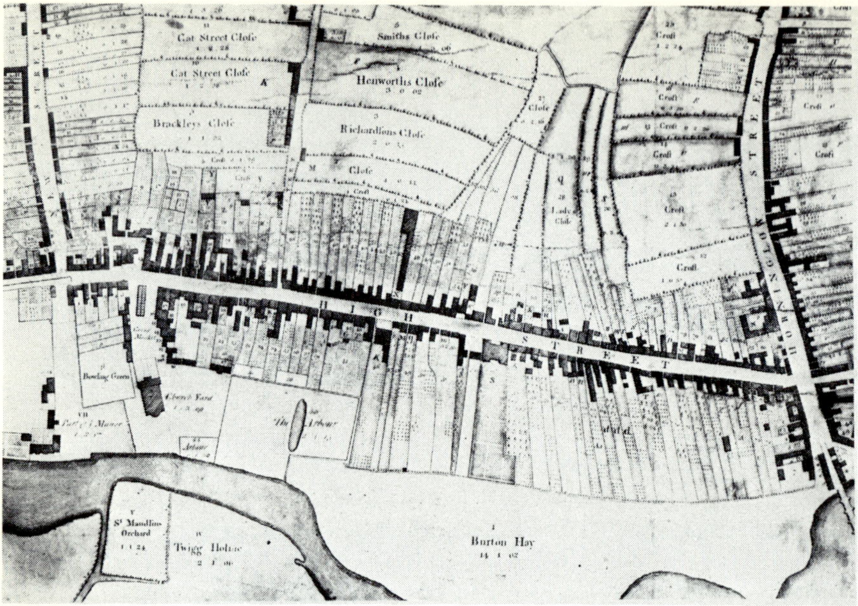

3. Plan of Burton upon Trent by William Wyatt, 1757-60 (by permission of County Record Office, Stafford)

4. View of Burton upon Trent from the north by Wilson, 1779 (by permission of County Record Office, Stafford)

5. View of Burton upon Trent from the east by K. Thomas, *c.* 1840 (by permission of County Record Office, Stafford)

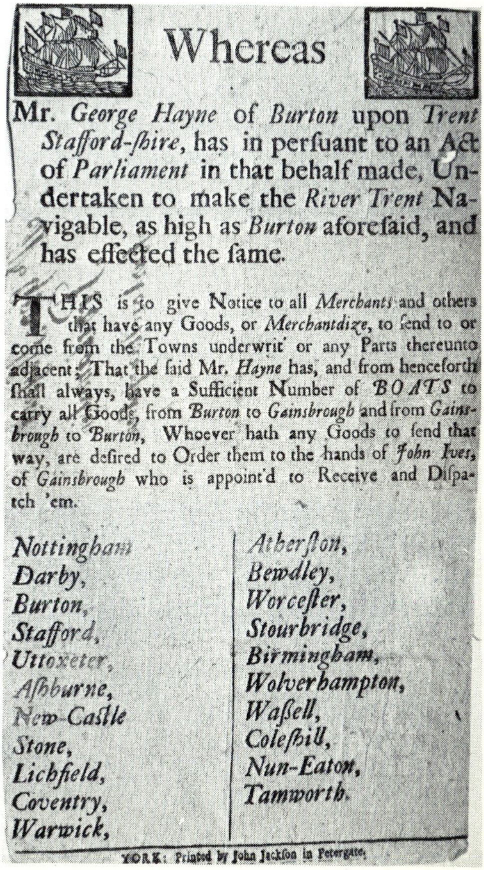

Whereas

Mr. *George Hayne* of *Burton* upon *Trent Stafford-ſhire*, has in perſuant to an Act of *Parliament* in that behalf made, Undertaken to make the *River Trent* Navigable, as high as *Burton* aforeſaid, and has effected the ſame.

THIS is to give Notice to all *Merchants* and others that have any Goods, or *Merchantdize*, to ſend to or come from the Towns underwrit' or any Parts thereunto adjacent; That the ſaid Mr. *Hayne* has, and from henceforth ſhall always, have a Sufficient Number of *BOATS* to carry all Goods, from *Burton* to *Gainsbrough* and from *Gainsbrough* to *Burton*, Whoever hath any Goods to ſend that way, are deſired to Order them to the hands of *John Iver*, of *Gainsbrough* who is appoint'd to Receive and Diſpatch 'em.

Nottingham	*Atherſton,*
Darby,	*Bewdley,*
Burton,	*Worceſter,*
Stafford,	*Stourbridge,*
Uttoxeter,	*Birmingham,*
Aſhburne,	*Wolverhampton,*
New-Caſtle	*Waſell,*
Stone,	*Coleſhill,*
Lichfield,	*Nun-Eaton,*
Coventry,	*Tamworth.*
Warwick,	

YORK: Printed by John Jackſon in Petergate.

6. Advertisement for the Opening of the Trent Navigation, 1712 (private collection)

7. Warehouses in Bond End, Burton upon Trent, *c.* 1850

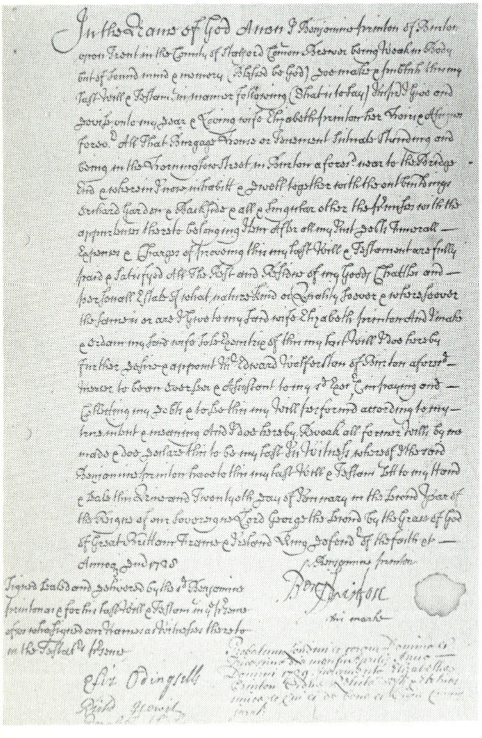

8. Will of Benjamin Printon, 1728 (National Probate Registry, Somerset House)

9. Portrait of Henry Evans (1731-1805) (from A. Barnard, 1889)

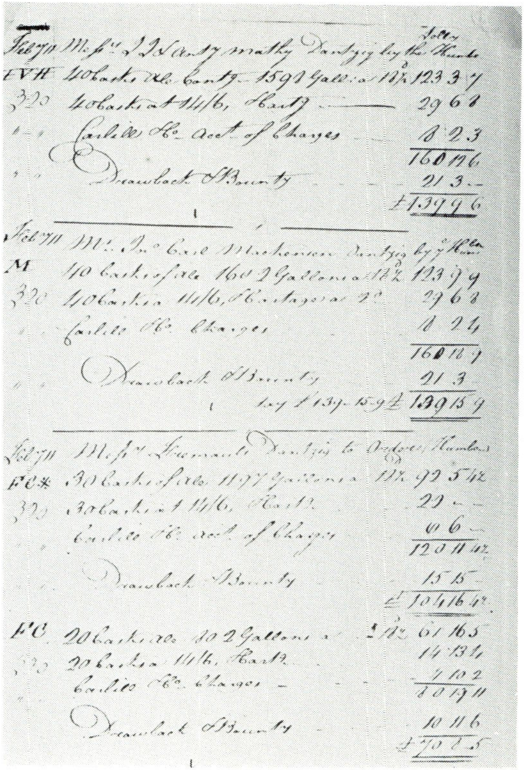

10. Extract from Benjamin Wilson's Day Book, 1791 (Allsopp Records)

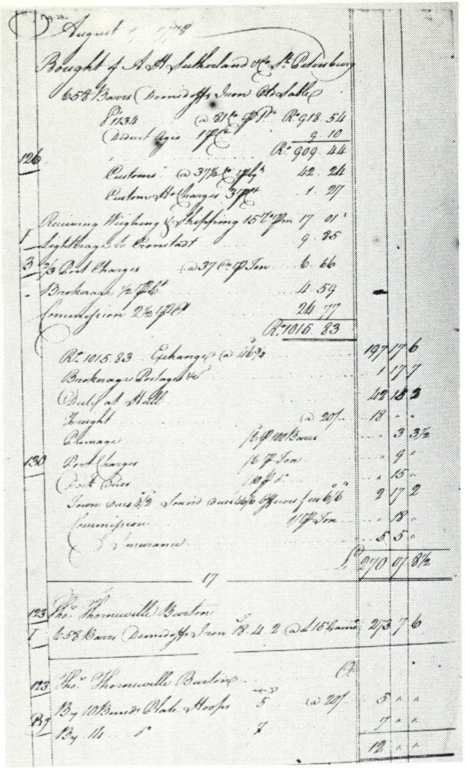

August 1778

Bought of A.H. Sutherland & Co. St. Petersburg

658 Barrs Demidoffs Iron

Customs @ 37½ ... 42. 24

Lighterage to Cronstadt ... 9. 35

Brokerage ½ p Ct ... 4. 59

Commission 2½ p Ct ... 24. 77

R. 1016. 83

R. 1015. 83 Exchange

Brokerage Postage &c ... 1 17 7

Duty at Hull

Freight @ 20/- ... 18

Primage

Port Charges

Dock Dues

Commission

Insurance ... 5 5

£ 270 07 8½

Thos. Thornewill Burton

658 Barrs Demidoffs Iron ... 273 7 6

Thos. Thornewill Burton

By 10 Bundles Hale Hoops 5 @ 20/- ... 5

By 11 ... 7 ... 7

12

11. (*left*) Extract from John Walker Wilson's Day Book, 1778 (Allsopp Records)

12. (*right*) Portrait of Michael Bass (1759-1827)

13. Robert Peel's first Cotton Mill (1780) and Burton Corn Mill (reproduced from 19th century painting, by permission of G. H. Gopsill Esq., of Burton upon Trent)

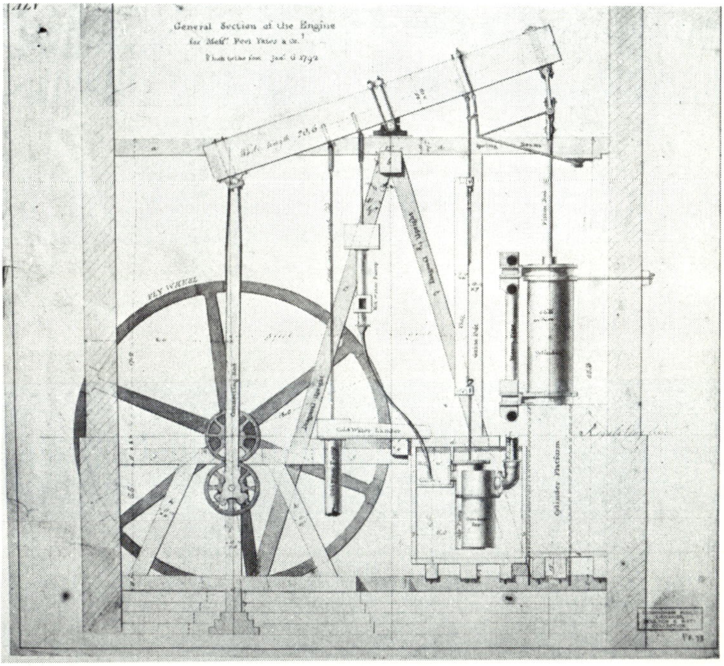

14. Design of Steam Engine installed in Peel & Co's Cotton Mill, Bond End, Burton in 1792 (Boulton & Watt collection)

15. Burton Forge Mills *c.* 1900

16. A Feltmaker at work (from J. H. Hawkins, 1917)

Elliot of Danzig to balance their ale accounts and also to settle his own barley account with Samuel Sketchley of Newark. 'Bookkeeping barter' remained a feature of the Baltic trade until its disruption in 1806 but it is noticeable in Wilson's accounts that it was used more extensively prior to 1785 than later. This might, perhaps, indicate that it was a survival of an earlier and more primitive system of trade in which bills of exchange were used less frequently. Mutual interest was occasionally strengthened by personal visits that Wilson made to all the main Baltic ports and, in particular, to Danzig where he enjoyed the hospitality of his lifelong friend and customer, Frederick von Ankum.

Outside the Baltic trade Wilson's sales were relatively insignificant. He sent small consignments of ale to Italy, Portugal and Ireland and, occasionally, larger ones to merchants in London and Liverpool who probably exported it to Southern Europe and the West Indies. In addition, he supplied innkeepers over a wide area; during the 1794–5 season, for example, he served customers in Burton, Derby, Oakthorpe, Overseal, Hilton, Rolleston, Stanton, Newhall, Hartshorne, Measham, Yoxall, Ashby, Melbourne, Castle Donington and Nuneaton as well as more distant clients in Norwich, Bristol, Oxford, Edinburgh, Wakefield, Bawtry, King's Lynn, and Manchester. Wilson never developed any great interest in the home trade, however, for he found it far more profitable and less tedious to despatch 50 large consignments to the Baltic than to send hundreds of small lots to various parts of the British Isles.

Wilson, like many of his contemporaries, could be described as a merchant brewer. His breweries formed the heart of his business and kept him fully occupied during the October to April period but for the remainder of the year he turned to dealing and speculating in a wide range of commodities. With his substantial capital and commercial knowledge he was well equipped to do this. His annual expenditure on timber did not normally exceed £3,000 but occasionally his purchases were considerable; between December 1789 and September 1790, for example, he bought staves to the value of £16,500 from Danzig merchants.[72] His main Baltic suppliers were Ivan Kusoff and W. Glen & Co. of St. Petersburg, Herman Ramm and Matthew Fischer of Riga and John Paleske, Barstow & Elliot and Guillaume du Bois of Danzig. The types of timber bought were mainly Stettin staves, excellent for cask-making, Danzig crownpipe and brack staves, generally of lower quality and St. Petersburg red deals. Wilson selected the best staves for his own use and sold the remainder to merchants, brewers, builders and other tradesmen in

Burton, Tamworth, Wolverhampton, Birmingham, Nuneaton and elsewhere. Some large consignments stored at Hull and Gainsborough were used periodically for settling accounts with merchants in those areas.

Russian tallow was another commodity that Wilson considered worthy of speculation. A 'Tallow Advanture' in 1785, involving 27 casks of tallow purchased from Shairps, Maude & Co. of St. Petersburg for £350 13s., resulted in a profit of £64, while several purchases in 1799, amounting to over £3,900, were considerably more lucrative.[73] Wilson was also generally successful in his speculations in foreign wheat. In May 1800, for example, he made a net profit of £106 on a cargo of wheat purchased for £5,054 from Jacob Kabrun and shipped from Danzig to Liverpool. Later in the year he bought several similar consignments from the same source amounting to £8,150. During the year ending 30 April 1801 Wilson made a net profit of £1,310 on his wheat speculations. On other occasions his opportunism proved less successful—

> 'I happened to be on the Corn Exchange and was tempted to purchase of Mr. Prest a small cargo of very fine Dantzig wheat at 104s. which comparatively was very cheap. I thought it could do no harm and that as wheat was so fluctuating an article I probably might sell it again to pay my expenses of my journey to and from London. It is curious to tell you that in 10 days after I bought it, it was not worth more than 70s. and perhaps less'.[74]

Hemp and flax were acquired from Hull and Baltic merchants both as payment for ale and as occasional purchases. They were normally disposed of to rope makers and flax dressers in Burton, Tutbury and other local centres. One unusual but lucrative speculation recorded in Wilson's accounts for 1799 was the purchase of 74 bags of 'Red Clover Seed' from Richard Harris of London for £589 and the subsequent sale of 53 bags for £789. Prior to 1790 it was customary for Wilson to buy at least one large consignment of iron each year from St. Petersburg. In 1785, for example, he imported 1,189 iron bars from Shairps, Maude & Co. at a cost of £350 and sold them over a period of two years to Thomas Thornewill of Clay Mills, Carson & Co. and Staniforth & Co. for £483.[75]

Wilson's association with Thomas and Francis Dicken of Alrewas Cotton Mill provides a further instance of his diversity of interests, for betweeen 1800 and 1809 he was not only a partner in the Company but also their chief buyer of raw cotton. His purchases from C.D.

Peters and De Visme & Co. of Lisbon and from various merchants in Charleston, Philadelphia and New York were considerable, amounting to £11,000 during the last three months of 1801. His share of the profits of Alrewas Mill during the year ending 30 June 1801 amounted to £2,451, which was only slightly less than his brewing profits. Wilson also occasionally exported cotton products. In 1793 and 1794, for example, he joined with Richard Hoskins, a partner in the firm of Hoskins and Hand of Manchester, in the sale of calico and between 1803 and 1806 he sent several large consignments of cotton yarn and twist from Alrewas Mills to customers in Danzig, Konigsburg and Hamburg.[76] The marked deterioration in trade relations with Russia after 1785 caused Wilson to turn his attentions from iron, flax, hemp and tallow to raw cotton, cotton products and wheat.

As previously mentioned, Wilson's involvement in the Baltic trade induced him to become part-owner of a number of Hull ships. By 1789 he held one-third shares in the 'Humber' and 'Porter'. During the year ending 30 April 1790 the two vessels each made eight voyages to Baltic ports, thereby providing Wilson with a total profit of £358. He also invested in a one-sixteenth share in a 'Greenlandmen' ship (presumably a whaler), whose two voyages in 1790 yielded him £18 15s.

Wilson also indulged in long-term loans to local property owners and manufacturers and in short-term share transactions. In 1790 he provided William Nadin of 'Brizencote', a local colliery proprietor, with £3,200, secured on lands and coal mines at Newhall, Stapenhill, and Hartshorne; this was increased to £4,444 in 1792.[77] In 1793, however, with brewing profits falling drastically and barley prices rising, he began to press for repayment and in the following year, after much persuasion, was eventually successful. After 1795 Wilson frequently became involved in short-term share transactions through his bankers, Robarts & Co. of London. Both of these types of speculation were appropriate to his business; the former suited his well-justified policy of not over-investing in brewery premises, while the latter accorded well with the spasmodic nature of his business. As previously noted, if barley prices were excessive in a particular year Wilson might be able to rely entirely upon stocks of malt accumulated in previous years. This would have inevitably provided him with a short-term capital surplus which he would obviously have tried to use profitably in some type of commodity or share speculation.

The absence of final accounts from many of Wilson's records makes it impossible to state precisely what his overall profits and losses were throughout the 1770–1807 period. The years 1789–92, when barley prices were moderate and exports above average, were unquestionably the most prosperous and it is likely that his profits exceeded £4,000 per annum. In 1793–4 Wilson's business, like so many others, was enveloped by 'the gloomy apprehensions of the sinking state of the country, its commerce and manufactures'[78] and it is likely that his losses were considerable. In the following year his profits were again well below average but from 1796 to 1806 brewing profits were generally in excess of £2,000 per annum; 1800–01 was a particularly successful year in which net profits amounted to just over £7,600.[79] It is interesting to note that in this particular year brewing profits, although high, amounted to only 40% of the total profits, speculations in cotton and wheat being particularly rewarding. One of the two surviving balance sheets shows that in April 1806 the brewing premises were valued at £7,000 and stock at a little over £10,000. Bank deposits stood at just over £6,000, sundry debtors at £6,000 and creditors at £800, not including £3,400 owing to the excise account. Wilson's share of the business totalled nearly £21,000 and Samuel Allsopp's £5,153.[80] A profit and loss account for the year ending 30 April 1802 again illustrates the versatility of the 18th century brewer, with substantial profits coming from dealings in cotton twist, wheat and cheese. Its inclusion of housekeeping expenses shows also the inseparable nature of business and household affairs, with the brewery being merely an extension of the brewer's living accommodation. It was not until well into the 19th century that the Burton brewers became specialist manufacturers and the semi-domestic nature of their business disappeared.

After 1800 Wilson's nephew, Samuel Allsopp, played an increasingly active part in the running of the business. He was the eldest son of Wilson's sister, Ann, who had married James Allsopp, a gentleman of Derby in 1778. In 1807, following the collapse of the Baltic trade Wilson, a wealthy bachelor of 56, sold his breweries in High Street and Horninglow Street to Samuel Allsopp for £7,000.[81] He withdrew £2,750 but agreed to leave the remainder in the business and to receive interest on it at the rate of 5% per annum. When he died in March 1812 the business passed entirely into the hands of the Allsopp family, while the main beneficiaries under his will were Ann Noble, his niece, who received the interest on £5,000, Edward Moore Noble, her husband, James Nettlethorpe Fowler, Thomas Allsopp and Thomas, Benjamin and Jane Wilson, the children of Benjamin's late brother, John Walker Wilson.[82]

Although the Wilson brewery was undoubtedly the leading concern in Burton during the 1740–1807 period, many of the other breweries are well worthy of consideration. Unfortunately, with one exception, no other business records have survived and it is matter of piecing together scraps of information from a wide range of sources. The one exception concerns a group of accounts books within the Allsopp Collection which refers to the business of John Walker Wilson, who worked independently in Burton as a brewer and raff merchant between 1773 and 1797. As previously mentioned, J.W.W., having spent his early working life in his father's brewery, decided to establish his own business at the time of the latter's retirement in 1773. In June 1774 he succeeded in purchasing, for £1,040, 'new-erected dwellings, brewhouse, malthouse and malting offices' on the west side of High Street opposite to the family business.[83] By 1781 he had built 'a tunhouse and coolhouse' on adjoining land, opened a timber yard in Bond End and acquired the 'Hopyard' in Cat Street, Guildables Close and various pieces of meadow. His properties in Burton and elsewhere were valued at £7,375, including an estate at Maldon, Essex worth £3,500 and another in Bedfordshire valued at £600.[84]

J.W.W. was even less specialised than his brother, Benjamin, and could almost be described as a general merchant, for he was just as much interested in timber, iron, hemp, flax and canal shares as he was in brewing. As a brewer he appears to have been less successful than his brother and rather more concerned with the home market. Otherwise, the incomplete set of accounts indicates a close similarity between the two breweries. He purchased hops from Weston & Fife and J. Sanderson of London, Dowding and Smith & Mousley of Worcester, R.J. Sanders of Birmingham, Buxton & Dale of Nottingham and Flower, Ellis & Co. of Ollerton. Both local and 'water' barley were used, regular suppliers being Thomas Paget and Thomas Catway of Ibstock, Robert Creswell of Ravenstone, William Worthington of Tamworth and John Peart and Mr. Tomlinson of Newark. Baltic staves, coke from North Derbyshire and coal from Newhall Colliery were also regularly used in the brewery. A valuation of stock and premises, taken in June 1782, revealed a brewing stock of £4,635 and brewing premises worth £2,400. These and other records indicate an annual brewing capacity of around 1,500 barrels per annum.

J.W.W. normally sold at least half of his ale to the home market, consignments going regularly to many inns within 15 miles of Burton and occasionally to more distant centres such as Shrewsbury, Worcester, Hull, Sandbach, London, Edinburgh and Belfast. He also regularly exported ale to the Baltic. In March and April 1775 his exports were well above average, amounting to 995 barrels, 352 of which were sent direct to customers in Riga and Hanover but the remaining 600 barrels travelled via Hull merchants.[85] Between 1779 and 1785 shipments to the Baltic averaged around 500 barrels per annum. Wasily Kusoff of St. Petersburg, Christian Hubbernett, J. Holst, M.W. Fischer, Lorentz Helmsing and Herman Ramm of Riga and W.M. Kenworthy of Danzig were regular recipients of his ale and suppliers of timber, iron, flax and hemp. 'Bookkeeping barter' was again a prominent feature of the transactions.

In 1790, at the age of 52 J.W.W. decided to sell his brewery—

> 'To be sold by aution on 27th May at the Old Crown Inn, Burton—A capital Freehold Messuage and dwelling-house, sashed, fit for the residence of a large family, situate in the High Street in Burton-on-Trent, together with the Brewing Office, store-rooms, four malt-houses, spacious yards, coopery, beast sheds for feeding cattle, and a large kitchen garden adjoining; the whole containing together near one acre, with two whole seats or pews in the Parish Church of Burton; now in the occupation of Mr. John Walker Wilson, carrying on the Brewing Business there under the firm of John Walker Wilson & Co.'[86]

The property was purchased by Henry Evans, another Burton brewer, for £2,500 and shortly afterwards passed by marriage into the possession of the Worthington family.

Between 1770 and 1790 J.W.W. was the most important timber merchant in Burton and held considerable stocks of 'wainscott logs and Dantzig, Stettin and Hambro Crown Pipe Staves' in his yard in Bond End. He normally spent between £1,000 and £1,500 each year on timber from St. Petersburg, Riga and Danzig and imported it through Hull, where he held an interest in the firm of Carlill, Gilder, Kirkbride & Co. During the year ending 31 Aug. 1779, for example, he purchased timber to the value of £1,113, while his stock in June of the same year amounted to £1,016.[87] At the head of the Trent Navigation, Burton was an ideal centre for timber distribution and J.W.W. despatched consignments to most parts of the Midlands. William Owen and John Chamberlain of Birmingham, James Winn, John and Randle Walker and James Henderson of Wolverhampton, Thomas Nock of Walsall and Benjamin Woodcock of Tamworth were particularly important customers. Most of the Burton brewers regularly bought barrel staves from him, while in 1782, when Robert

Peel was building a large cotton mill in Bond End, J.W.W. supplied him with over £100 worth of timber.

Between 1778 and 1784 J.W.W. also purchased several large consignments of Russian bar iron each year, disposing of it to forge owners or iron merchants in the Burton area and South Staffordshire. Thomas Thornewill of Clay Mills was a particularly good customer and also supplied J.W.W. with large quantities of barrel hoops. J.W.W. also regularly imported Russian hemp and flax and, occasionally, Baltic wheat, barley and rye. In 1782 he added to his commercial activities by selling his Maldon estate and investing most of the proceeds in Alrewas Mill. By 1791 he had relinquished this interest, disposed of his brewery and timber business and rather unwisely turned to two quite different ventures. In association with Danial Dalrymple, a local solicitor, he founded the Burton Bank, while in collaboration with Joseph Bewick of Worcester, he began to speculate freely in canal shares. It is likely that during the crisis of 1793, when many banks failed and share values plunged, J.W.W. lost heavily. In 1794 he held shares in 11 canal companies, while in the following year he was paying calls on £19,000 in canal stock and had at least a further £7,000 in Consols. His final years were fraught with disappointment and he died intestate in February 1797.

Far less information is available about the third Wilson brother, William, who also worked in his father's brewery, until 1773. He remained in partnership with Benjamin until 1778, when the latter paid him £650 in order to become sole owner of the brewery. William apparently retained an active interest in the business for he became manager and part-owner of Sketchley's brewery in Horninglow Street when his brother purchased it in 1790. He was listed as a common brewer in the 'British Directory' of 1791 but he was also in business as a dealer in hemp and flax and was a partner in the firm of Anthony Bradley & Co. of New Mills Cotton Mills near Ashbourne. When he died in 1805 his business interests and properties in Horninglow Street and Anderstaff Lane passed to Benjamin.[88]

Apart from the Wilson family, which undoubtedly contributed more than any other to the development of the brewing industry in Burton during the second half of the 18th century, there were several others, some of whom eventually became world famous. One of these was the Worthington family, headed by William Worthington I, who is said to have been born at Orton-on-the-Hill, Leicestershire, and to have moved to Burton in 1744.[89] Until 1760 he worked as a cooper, probably at Joseph Smith's brewery on the east side of High Street. In October 1760, with the assistance of Ann Tarratt who later became his wife, Worthington purchased the premises from Richard Commings of Repton for £320.[90] In 1761, following extensions and improvements, they were described as—

> 'all that brewhouse tunhouse and other buildings now erecting or to be erected upon the premises situate standing and being on the east side of High Street in Burton upon Trent aforesaid heretofore the estate and inheritance of Joseph Smith and lately purchased by the said William Worthington of and from Richard Commings and now in the possession of the said William Worthington and his tenant Adam Bell'.[91]

Assuming Barnard's comments to have been correct it appears that Worthington conducted his business in a similar manner to that of Benjamin and J.W. Wilson and that by the 1780's his brewery had a capacity of around 1,500 barrels per annum.[92] As previously noted, when his two sons, William and Thomas, married Martha and Sarah Evans, the daughters of Henry Evans, in 1791, the former J.W. Wilson brewery also passed into Worthington hands. When William Worthington I died in 1800 he was able to leave to his sons and widow the two breweries, several adjoining premises, farms at Hartshorne and Gresley and various minor properties and other assets.[93]

Meanwhile, a short distance away, the Bass family had also succeeded in establishing a highly successful brewery. William and Mary Bass had moved to Burton, probably from London during the late 1750's in order to operate a carrying business. Bass ran a weekly freight service between London and Manchester via Burton which carried, particularly, London groceries and raw cotton northwards and ale, cheese, hardware and hats on the return journeys.[94] This highly lucrative business was rapidly expanded to include many local services, the profits being invested in a number of large properties in Burton. One of these, purchased from the Rev. John Hepworth and Nathaniel Dawson for £1,050 in 1777, included—

> 'A large capital, well-built and commodious Freehold Dwelling House on the E. side of High Street—containing spacious hall, five large parlours, bed chamber, butler's pantry etc. on lower floor; Bed chambers on 2nd floor; attic storey. Stable for 8 horses, malt-house, brew-house, pigeon-house, coach-house etc. walled garden with fishponds.'[95]

Shortly afterwards he secured by purchase and lease the two adjoining properties, both of which included extensive brewing premises. These formed the nucleus of what was to become the largest brewery in the United Kingdom. Under the guidance of William Yeomans, the Officer of Excise, who lived in one of the properties, Bass and his two sons, Michael and William, rapidly learnt the arts of malting, brewing and brewery management, sufficient to earn for himself a reputation as 'a considerable brewer' by 1786.[96]

Following his death in 1787, Michael and William inherited the business and considerable estates in Burton and Ashbourne.[97] By 1795 Michael had gained complete control of the brewery and William had moved to Ashbourne where he was in business as a carrier. In the following year Michael Bass and John Ratcliffe, a 'writer' at the brewery, became 'co-partners as brewers, maltsters and farmers', an association that was to last for many years.[98] They proceeded to build-up a thriving brewery which by the end of the century had a capacity of around 2,000 barrels. Approximately half the output was sold locally and the remainder was sent to Manchester, Liverpool, Birmingham and the Baltic Ports.

Opposite to the Worthington and Bass breweries in High Street lay another belonging to the Evans family. Henry Evans, son of Thomas Evans a Derby merchant, moved to Burton in 1754 when his father paid £250 for a freehold property on the west side of High Street, previously used as a cooperage by Thomas Pearsall, Thomas Taylor and William Jordan.[99] Three years later it comprised a house fronting the street and 'all those two malting houses and brewhouse lately erected and built upon part of the said premises'. During the next 40 years Henry Evans became involved in practically every major commercial activity in the town with the result that he was variously described in legal documents as a common brewer, merchant, ironmonger and gentleman. Between 1762 and 1766 he joined with the Lloyds and others in acquiring the leases of the Trent Navigation and the mills along the river. He proceeded to play a very active part in the affairs of Burton Boat Company and in the running of Burton Corn Mill. He owned a barge of 40 tons which he used for carrying ale, iron and timber along the river between Burton and Gainsborough.

His diverse activities enabled him to become one of the wealthiest men in the town with valuable freehold premises in High Street, leasehold property with an annual rental of £180 and extensive lands in Burton Lower Meadow and Burton Extra.[100] Indicative of his wealth was his purchase of J.W. Wilson's brewery for £2,500 in 1791 for the benefit of his two daughters, Martha and Sarah, and of Caldwell Hall, with its 3,000 acres of land. Henry Evans retired to Caldwell in 1795 at the age of 64, leaving his son John in charge of the brewery. He died in 1805, the brewery passing to John and Caldwell Hall to his wife Martha and his daughter Rebecca.

By 1780 there were thus five notable breweries in close proximity to one another along High Street between Cat Street and Horninglow Street. Between them they produced around 10,000 barrels of ale per annum, of which at least half was sent down the Trent to Hull for export to the Baltic. They had evolved by the systematic improvement and extension of freehold premises over a period of 40 years or so. All possessed living accommodation for the owner and his family and some still retained an alehouse for which the brewing had originally been carried out. A second group of similar breweries lay a few hundred yards away in Horninglow Street, the oldest of which was the one opened by Benjamin Printon early in the century and later acquired by the Musgrave family.

The Musgraves (or Musgroves or Musgreaves) were an old Burton family whose connection with the brewing industry may have begun during the 17th century. Following Printon's death in 1729 his brewery was acquired by John Musgrave, who, in turn bequeathed it to his son William. The latter expanded the business considerably between 1748 and 1760 and was able to open a second brewery in Horninglow Street, which he sold to Samuel Sketchley in 1761.[101] An advertisement relating to his main brewery, which appeared in the 'Derby Mercury' shortly after his death in 1784, gives some idea of the nature and extent of the business—

> 'Burton Brewery, Staffordshire.
> To be sold or let, and entered upon immediately, A Freehold Estate, consisting of a Brewery with four Malt Offices, Cooper's Shops, Stables, Dwelling-house, and a variety of other buildings, all on the same premises, the Brewhouse and Offices belonging to it are calculated for an extensive business, the malt offices will produce about 80 quarters weekly, the dwelling-house is handsomely furnished and fit for a genteel family ... The coppers and other brewing utensils, with a quantity of casks proper for exportation, will be sold at a fair valuation. There is a person on the premises, who for a consideration, would assist the purchaser in the Brewery, and give him an insight into the Russia Trade, which is partly connected with the Brewery; and the centrical situation of the town of Burton, having a

> communication with every capital Sea Port in the Kingdom, makes it a most eligible situation for the disposal of all importable goods.'

Apart from these premises, which stood close to the river, Musgrave also owned three malthouses in Anderstaff Lane at which William Simnett, John Whitehead and William Holloway were employed. The Musgrave brewery was clearly an important concern, probably capable of producing around 2,000 barrels of ale per annum. Musgrave was also a general merchant and a considerable importer of Baltic timber, iron, flax and hemp. His persistent use of an unauthorised landing place on Umpler Green, near to the west end of Burton Bridge, involved him in a lengthy dispute with the Burton Boat Company.

Following William's retirement in 1779 and his elder son Henry's premature death in 1781, the business passed to his younger son, James Wood Musgrave who, with some reluctance, continued to operate the brewery in association with the Bass family. After the death of J.W. Musgrave in 1803 the brewery was purchased by John Greaves, the son of J.D. Greaves, a former Burton brewer. A few years later the business failed owing to the disruption of the Baltic trade and most of the brewing premises eventually passed into the hands of Bass & Co.[102]

A short distance away, on the south side of Horninglow Street, lay the breweries of Charles Leeson and Joseph Clay. Charles Leeson, the son of a Burton chandler, used his small inheritance to purchase one of these properties for £250 in 1753. It included a brewhouse and a malthouse, that had been added to it by William Newton, the former landlord of the 'Three Queens', earlier in the century. Leeson improved the property and also later acquired further malting and brewing premises on the west side of Anderstaff Lane and the east side of High Street. His business remained a relatively modest concern that, unlike most of the other Burton breweries of the period, catered primarily for home markets. Leeson developed few business interests outside the brewery and generally purchased his supplies of raw materials from other brewers. Nevertheless, his efforts apparently met with success, for when he died in 1794 he was able to leave to his wife the freehold 'dwelling-house, garden, brewhouse, tunhouse, malt-houses and other buildings adjoining' and various other properties together with £4,800 to his six surviving children.[103] His brewery eventually passed into the possession of

Joseph Clay, while his malthouses in Anderstaff Lane were acquired by Benjamin Wilson.

Joseph Clay, a Derby maltster, moved to Burton in 1751 when he purchased the 'Lamb Inn' on the south side of Horninglow Street, described as a freehold house of—

> 'six rooms, a malthouse to steep 10 quarters, brewhouse, tun house etc., lately used as an inn—the Lamb Inn—now compleated for a common brewer'.[104]

Clay's brewery was probably similar in capacity to that of Leeson but it was certainly more concerned with brewing for export. By 1790 he was the proprietor of two houses and a brewery on both sides of Horninglow Street and a cooperage on the west side of High Street. When he died in 1800 he was one of the wealthiest men in the town. His elder son, Joseph, inherited the business and in the following year purchased the nearby Leeson brewery for £700. Shortly afterwards Joseph and his son, Henry, became partners in a commercial bank, using the front of their old brewery as offices. As the banking business increased they left the management of the breweries to Thomas Salt, who had been employed by the Clays as a maltster since 1774 and who had established his own brewery on the east side of High Street in 1800. Eventually the Clays withdrew from brewing entirely and most of their premises were acquired by Salt & Co.

Horninglow Street possessed at least three additional breweries during the second half of the 18th century. The first of these stood on the north side of the street opposite to Clay's first brewery and was owned by John Davies Greaves, the son of William Greaves, a wealthy farmer of Ingleby. The latter purchased the premises in 1774 from Thomas and Mary Hacket for £1,000 and at the same time provided his son with a warehouse at Willington Wharf together with several boats for use on the Trent. By 1781 J.D. Greaves had established himself as a brewer and cheese merchant, thanks to a loan of almost £5,000 from his father.[105] He extended the premises in Horninglow Street and acquired additional malthouses in Anderstaff Lane in order to increase the production of ale for export. Like so many of the other brewers, his business activities were wide-ranging, as the following advertisement indicates—

> 'Flax. To be sold, a considerable quantity of the best Oberland Flax, now lying in the warehouse of Messrs. Smith & Mosley in Gainsborough—Samples may be seen and the price known, by

> applying to John Davies Greaves, Common Brewer in Burton-on-Trent.[106]

Unfortunately, Greaves proved to be a poor businessman with the result that after his death in 1784 his younger brother, Robert Charles Greaves, tried unsuccessfully to dispose of the brewery on several occasions. J.D. Greaves' widow, Elizabeth, continued to live there and eventually with the aid of her second son, John, and Thomas Salt, revived the business for a short time.

The other two breweries in Horninglow Street were developed by the Sketchley's, who were undoubtedly one of the most active and capable families to be connected with the industry during the 1740–90 period. From humble origins they built up a thriving business as brewers and Trent merchants out of which they derived considerable wealth and influence. Samuel and Elizabeth Sketchley began their married lives in 1734 in Nottingham, where Samuel practised as a barber and also ran a small public brewhouse at the rear of the 'Crown and Cushion' in Pilcher Gate.[107] In 1741 they moved to Burton to take possession of a small brewery that had recently been built on the north side of Horninglow Street.[108] By 1758 Sketchley had developed a highly successful business as a common brewer and merchant. He had established direct contact with a number of Baltic merchants and was regularly importing and exporting a wide range of commodities. In 1758 he exported lead and ale to Danzig and imported large quantities of timber from Riga and one consignment of flax from Konigsburg. In 1763 he imported timber, flax, linen yarns, hogs' bristles, hemp and iron from St. Petersburg, Konigsburg and Riga. His ale exports were considerable: in 1758 he exported 20 tons (160 barrels approximately) to Danzig; in 1760, 200 tons (1,600 barrels) to Elsinore; in 1765, 123 tons (984 barrels) to Konigsburg, St. Petersburg and Bremen; and in 1771, 200 tons to St. Petersburg and Rotterdam.[109] His ale exports in 1760 amounted to almost one quarter of the entire ale exports from Hull, which demonstrates conclusively the overwhelming importance of Burton in this aspect of trade and also suggests that Sketchley exported not only his own ale but that of a number of other Burton brewers.

The great success of Sketchley's efforts can be seen in the rapidity with which he built and purchased additional premises. In 1758 he built a new warehouse, 60 ft. long, on the east side of High Street near to the Bargates. In 1761 he bought a 'new built messauge, malthouse, brewhouse, tunhouse, outbuildings and yard', near to his own brewery, from William Musgrave and in the following year acquired a nearby leasehold property from the Earl of Uxbridge.[110]. During the same period he also built a fine house near to the river on the south side of Horninglow Street. It is likely that his brewery was the second largest in the town at this time, with an annual output of around 1,500 barrels.

When Samuel Sketchley died in 1775 his sons, Samuel and William, inherited most of his properties and immediately entered into partnership as brewers and merchants. Having disposed of two houses in Horninglow Street, the former moved to Newark to organise the buying and transportation of iron, timber, barley and other commodities, while William stayed in Burton to manage the brewery and warehouse. The following advertisements give some indication of the variety of their business—

> 'Russia and Swedes Iron, of all sorts, in Bars, neatly drawn and of good Quality, sold on the most reasonable terms, wholesale and retail, at Gainsborough and Burton by Samuel and William Sketchley & Co. Burton, Aug. 2, 1776.'

> 'To be sold at Messrs. Sketchley's Warehouse at Burton-on-Trent—Forty barrels of exceeding fine Porter at 39/- money—also considerable quantity of well-cured Irish Hams at 5½d. per lb., warranted as good as any imported.'[111]

So successful were the Sketchley's that they were able to widen their business interests still further and to become highly influential both in Newark and Burton. Samuel played a leading part in the affairs of the Trent Navigation Company; at a meeting held at Nottingham in June, 1783 both he and Henry Evans of Burton were elected to the Committee, while at subsequent meetings Samuel often served as Chairman. In conjunction with William Handley, a Newark mason and Trent merchant, he established a successful brewery at Newark and later opened a large cotton mill there. He was elected Mayor of Newark in 1778, 1791, and 1804.[112] William became a considerable property owner in Burton; he played a leading role in local affairs, serving as Townmaster in 1782. In 1787, however, he too moved to Newark and by 1790 the Sketchley's had sold most of their Burton properties, including their brewery in Horninglow Street. Henceforth, their interest in Burton waned but there is no doubt that they and their father had contributed in no small way to the development of the Baltic ale trade as well as to the general economic progress of Burton. It was to the vision and expertise of men such as the

Sketchley's that Burton owed its ever-expanding reputation as a brewing centre.

Although most of Burton's 18th century breweries developed in Horninglow Street and High Street, a small number also thrived at the southern end of the town. The most important of these, operated by Hill and Sherratt, was in existence in Abbey Street as early as 1740 and may well have evolved from the large brewhouse owned by Daniel Watson during the previous century.[113] Unlike most of the other breweries their premises were leasehold and were almost entirely concerned with producing for local demand. Moreover, they appear to have relied upon other brewers, such as Benjamin Wilson, for supplies of staves, hoops and other materials. Nevertheless, it is evident from the extent of the properties owned in Bond End during the 1780's by John and William Sherratt and the wealth amassed by the latter by the time of his death in 1814, that their business was highly profitable.[114] Nearby, two other small breweries of relatively short duration also developed. Thomas Morecroft, a carpenter and builder by trade, ran a small brewery on the west side of Lichfield Street between 1775 and 1795.[115] Thomas Dicken, a wealthy mercer and textile manufacturer, leased the Angel Inn on the west side of High Street and a nearby house and malthouse from the Earl of Uxbridge in 1775 in order to start a brewing business. He brewed ale for St. Petersburg and also for clients in London, Bristol and Bath.[116]

The great success of the industry between 1750–90 attracted to it many men additional to the main brewers so far discussed. Other common brewers were John Gretton and John Ratcliff, who became associated with the Bass brewery, Thomas Robinson, who was an employee of William Worthington and Thomas Hackett, who ran a small brewery on the north side of Horninglow Street that was later acquired by Samuel Sketchley. William Kinder, a timber merchant who owned a raff-yard in Burton at which he sold 'Datzick Crown Pipe staves, Stretteen Pipe, Hogshead and Barrel Staves and Wainscot', also became involved in brewing following his marriage to Mary Sketchley in 1772.[117] William Morris, a 'stage-waggoner' and carrier, also became concerned in brewing and malting for the Sketchley's after 1785. Moreover, it must also be remembered that many of the inns in the town, such as the 'White Hart' and the 'George' in High Street and the 'Vine' and the 'Bear' in Horninglow Street brewed ale for local consumption. Some had malthouses attached to them; the 'Blue Posts' in High Street, for example, possessed a ten-quarter malthouse belonging to the Yeomans family.

The 1740–90 period was thus one of great significance in the development of Burton's brewing industry in that production was substantially increased and the small inn brewhouses that had previously dominated the industry were largely replaced by non-retail breweries. Prior to 1740 only the Printon-Musgrave brewery and possibly those of Joseph Smith and Hill & Sherratt belonged to the second category. The establishment of Sketchley's brewery in 1741 and that of Benjamin Wilson (sen.) in 1742 proved decisive, for both were able to successfully exploit the unique qualities of Burton ale and the great opportunities offered by the Baltic trading system. During the 1750's Joseph Clay, Charles Leeson, Henry Evans and William Worthington I swelled the ranks of the brewers, while by 1780 the number of breweries had increased to thirteen—

William Bass	High Street E.
Joseph Clay	Horninglow Street S.
Thomas Dicken	High Street W.
Henry Evans	High Street W.
John Davies Greaves	Horninglow Street N.
Hill & Sherratt	Abbey Street W.
Charles Leeson	Horninglow Street S.
William Musgrave	Horninglow Street N.
Thomas Morecroft	Lichfield Street W.
Samuel & William Sketchley	Horninglow Street N.
Benjamin Wilson (jun.)	High Street E.
John Walker Wilson	High Street W.
William Worthington	High Street E.

In comparison with the leading London breweries of the time, six of which brewed over 60,000 barrels per annum, the Burton breweries were small concerns, only one producing an annual output in excess of 2,000 barrels. Nevertheless, the gradual displacement of inn brewhouses by public breweries had resulted in a substantial increase in the size of the unit of production. This was further increased after 1790 by a series of amalgamations which reduced the number of firms to only seven by 1806; particularly significant were the absorbtion of the Sketchley and J.W. Wilson breweries by B. Wilson and Worthington respectively. The deterioration of the political situation in the Baltic, increases in the prices of raw materials, such as barley, and the rising costs of insurance, shipping and brewing equipment tended to drive out the small breweries and to stimulate large-scale production.

By using the production and export figures of the two Wilson breweries as a guide it seems likely that in 1780 the 13 Burton firms produced around 20,000 barrels of ale of which 40 per cent was exported. B. and J.W. Wilson, Sketchley, Evans, Worthington, Bass and Musgrave were especially concerned with the brewing of strong export ale. In particularly favourable years, such as 1790–1 and 1791–2, Burton exports were almost certainly in excess of 10,000 barrels. The statistics for ale exports provided by the Hull Port Books indicate that Burton contributed a substantial proportion, particularly during the 1740–1770 period. The 2,000 barrels exported from Hull in 1756 were probably provided mainly by Wilson, Sketchley, Musgrave and Evans. By 1765, when exports had risen to almost 6,000 barrels, the amount of Burton ale sent down the Trent was sufficiently large to attract the attention of the promoters of the Grand Trunk Canal—

> 'The fine ale made at Burton upon Trent which is now exported to Germany, Denmark, Sweden, Russia and the West Indies may, by means of the intended canal, be exported from Liverpool as well as from Hull, to those places where it has become a very considerable article of commerce'.[118]

After 1770, however, Burton contributed a decreasing proportion of Hull's exports as other towns along the Trent, such as Newark, began to develop large breweries. It is probable that by 1790 the proportion had fallen to less than half.

Although the Baltic trade and the Trent Navigation were of prime importance in the expansion of the breweries, the long-established London market continued to be supplied to some extent by the relatively difficult and expensive overland service costing £6 per ton. During the 1762–3 season, for example, William Bass's wagons carried over 100 barrels of Burton ale to London on behalf of Messrs. Evans, Leeson, Clay, B. Wilson, Musgrave, Lovatt, Dicken, Littlefear and Sketchley and later brought back the empty casks.[119] Other carriers were no doubt similarly engaged.

For the first time in its history the growth of the brewing industry had a marked effect upon the town's population, which increased from under 2,000 in 1700 to almost 5,500 in 1800 (excluding Branston and Stretton). The breweries developed particularly at the northern end of the town in Horninglow Street and High Street rather than around the wharf in Bond End. This enabled the brewers to take advantage of available freehold land and premises there and to escape the local toll on malt that leaseholders were obliged to pay.

Commenting on this point in 1762, William Wyatt, Lord Paget's steward, remarked—'tis no wonder as every 16th strike of malt goes for toll which to those that Brew least would come to £20 per annum and to one Brewer who Brews the most would come to above £100 a year'.[120] Wyatt, rather belatedly, attempted to reverse this trend by demolishing the old malt mill in the Market Place and by exempting exporting brewers from payment of the malt toll. It is possible, however, that supplies of shallow well water for brewing may have been more readily available at the north end of the town for physical reasons.

As the 18th century progressed the leading brewers emerged as a new dimension within local society. Most of them began their careers as humble tradesmen; Benjamin Wilson I as ropemaker, William Worthington I as a cooper, William Bass as a carrier, Charles Leeson as a chandler and Samuel Sketchley I as a barber. Only Henry Evans, the son of a wealthy merchant who also owned mines and ironworks, and John Davies Greaves, the son of a wealthy farmer, entered the industry with capital. Nevertheless, within a few years, they all became important property owners and influential men in the town, often serving as churchwardens, constables, town masters and feofees. In 1790 three of the nine feofees were brewers (Henry Evans, Thomas Dicken and Charles Leeson), while between 1780 and 1800 William Sketchley (1782), Joseph Clay (1788), James Wood Musgrave (1793) and Michael Bass (1794) served as townmasters. They greatly enhanced the values of properties within the town, increased local employment and invested liberally in a wide range of other local commercial and industrial enterprises. Benjamin Wilson II, for example, helped William Nadin to develop the collieries in the Newhall-Stanton area and also greatly assisted Thomas and Francis Dicken in the affairs of Alrewas Cotton Mill. The Sketchleys and Henry Evans helped considerably to make the Trent Navigation efficient and profitable, while J.W. Wilson and Joseph Clay were largely responsible for the establishment of the first commercial banks in the town. It is probably true to say that by 1780 they had become the most influential and dynamic group within the community.

The most distinctive characteristic of the 18th century Burton brewer was undoubtedly the diversity of his business interests. Apart from Charles Leeson and Hill & Sherratt, who catered mainly for local demand, all of the 13 brewers operating in 1780 traded in timber, iron, hemp, flax and other Baltic commodities. In certain years Benjamin Wilson II derived a greater profit from commodity dealings that he did from brewing. Henry Evans derived considerable benefit from his share of navigation profits and from the import and sale of bar iron as well as from his brewery. J.W. Wilson was as much concerned with timber dealing as with brewing, while the Sketchleys could appropriately be described as import/export merchants who owned several breweries. In its infancy the brewing industry of Burton was still incapable of supporting large-scale specialist brewers, while the great demand for Baltic commodities in England presented the brewers with opportunities too good to miss. The Trent provided the main avenue along which these commodities flowed between Hull and the rising industrial areas of the Midlands, thus making Burton an ideal distributing centre. By accepting timber and iron in exchange for ale the brewers discovered that they could sell more ale and also make a handsome profit from the goods received. A mixed trading system thus evolved in which both financial settlement and barter existed to the mutual advantage of all parties.

To the great regret of all concerned this unique phase in the development of Burton's brewing industry ended abruptly in 1807, when the Napoleonic blockade seriously curtailed Baltic trade. During the ensuing years all the Hull merchants lost heavily; writing to his London partners in October 1810, Thomas Thompson, a Hull banker, commented—'We go on here as usual, a minor man or two in the Russia trade failing every week'.[121] There was no radical improvement in the situation until after the war with France ended in 1815 and even then the Baltic ale trade failed to regain its former importance. The Burton merchant brewer disappeared from the scene and the ensuing years saw the gradual emergence of specialist brewers whose activities lacked the diversity and interest of those of their predecessors. The leading breweries in the town weathered the storm but many of the smaller concerns either collapsed or were absorbed by their competitors.

References

1. P. Mathias, '*The Brewing Industry in England, 1700–1830*', p. 3. H.A. Monckton, *A History of English Ale and Beer*, (1966), p. 70.

2. W. Molyneux, op. cit. p. 248 (extract from J. Pilkington, '*The Present State of Derbyshire*' (1789).

3. J. Richardson, '*Philosophical Principles of the Science of Brewing*', (1784).

4. S. Strong, '*The Romance of Brewing*', (1951), p. 20. C.H. Underhill, '*History of Burton upon Trent*', (1841), p. 116. J. Houghton, '*A Collection for the Improvement of Husbandry and Trade*', (1692–4).

5. P. Mathias, op. cit., p. 542.

6. *Burton Abbey MSS*; unpublished transcriptions No's. 1335 and 1492 by I.H. Jeayes.

7. F.A. Hibbert, '*The Dissolution of the Monasteries*; pp. 262–3.

8. C.H. Underhill, op. cit., p. 104.

9. *H.C.S.*, vols. 1929–48; transcriptions of Staffs. Quarter Sessions Rolls, 1586–1608.

10. J.S. Bushnan, '*Burton and its Bitter Beer*', (1853), p. 80

11. *Richard Caldwall's Charity Deeds*, 1662 (S.C.R.O.).

12. W. Molyneux, op. cit. p. 51. *Every Deeds*, Dec. 1663 and Oct. 1676 (D.R.L.).

13. H.C.S., 1923, '*The Staffordshire Hearth Tax*, 1669–70', see also vols. for 1920 and 1922.

14. Pagett MSS., 'Accounts for Burton Mills, 1704–9'.

15. R. Plot, op. cit., p. 338.

16. '*The Journies of Celia Fiennes*', (ed. C. Morris, 1947), p. 173.

17. P. Mathias, op. cit., p. 540.

18. '*The Spectator*', 26 May 1712. '*Burton Observer*', 12 Oct. 1899.

19. Hull Port Books; P.R.O., E. 190.

20. W. Molyneux, op. cit., p. 223.

21. *Coke MSS.*, 'Agreement between George Hayne and Leonard Fosbrooke, 8 May 1712.'

22. S. Shaw, '*History of Staffordshire*', (1798), vol. 1, p. 13. Burton Parish Church Register of Marriages, 2 Nov. 1708.

23. *Burton Deeds* (W.S.L.), 16 Aug. 1748.

24. *Burton Parish Church Vestry Book*, 31 Mar. 1719. B.P.C.D., Townmasters' Accounts, 1720 and 1724.

25. National Probate Registry; Will of Benjamin Printon, 21 Jan. 1728. B.P.C.R., 11 Sept. 1724 and 15 Feb. 1729.

26. Infra, c. 4 p.

27. *Lichfield Probate Registry*; Will of Joseph Smith of Burton, 'brewer', 10 Oct. 1727. B.P.C.D., Townmasters' Accounts, 1720. P.D., 24 June, 1717.

28. Burton Deeds (W.S.L.) 26 Mar. 1720. Bass-Worthington Deeds, 1720–50. L.P.R., Will of John Walker of Burton, 16 Mar. 1719.

29. See Appendix.

30. D.M., 26 Feb. 1741.

31. P. Mathias, op. cit., p. 176.

32. See Appendix.

33. Hull Port Books, P.R.O., E. 190, 367/6 and 370/2.

34. Allsopp Deeds; 12 Jan. 1742.

35. Ibid, 21 Dec. 1756. '*Plan of Burton-on-Trent and surrounding districts*' by William Wyatt, 1757–60.

36. A. Barnard, '*Noted Breweries of Great Britain and Ireland*' (1889), Vol. 1, p. 123. (Barnard's extracts are identical to those of Bushnan and, as far as is known, the ledger from which they were taken is no longer in existence.)

37. Allsopp Deeds, 12 & 13 Feb. 1773.

38. Ibid; 23 & 24 June, 1774, 9 Oct. 1775, and 1 & 2 April 1778.

39. A. Barnard, op. cit., Vol. 1, pp. 123–4; extract from letter of 12 Jan. 1774.

40. D.M., 24 Dec. 1789.

41. A.R., Benjamin Wilson's Malt Book, 1785–7.

42. Ibid. W.B.D.B., 1785–1791.
43. Ibid. B.W.L.B., 11 Mar. 1791.
44. Ibid. 11 June 1791.
45. Ibid. 31 Aug. 1791.
46. Ibid. 26 Sept. 1792.
47. Ibid. 3 Oct. 1792.
48. Ibid. 26 Dec. 1791.
49. Ibid. B.W.J. 2 May & 1 Dec. 1771.
50. P. Mathias, op. cit., p. 400.
51. Ibid. p. 485. A.R., B.W.D.B., 1782–95. R. Lowe, '*General View of the Agriculture of the County of Nottingham*', (1798) pp. 27 & 38.
52. A.R., B.W.J. 13 May and 21 June, 1798.
53. Ibid. B.W.L.B. Benjamin Wilson to Messrs. J. Gorr & Co. of Danzig 28 June 1791 and to John Paleske & Sons of Danzig, 14 Jan. 1792.
54. Ibid. Apr. & May 1805.
55. Ibid. B.W.D.B. 1798–9.
56. Bailey's '*British Directory*' (1784), vol. 2, pp. 489–90.
57. J.A.S.L. Leighton-Boyce, '*Smith the Bankers, 1658–1958*', pp. 186–237.
58. A.R., B.W.L.B., B.W. to J.D. Abegg of Elbing, 26 Mar. 1791.
59. Ibid. B.W. to Messrs. Melville & Wolff of Amsterdam, 6 Mar. 1793.
60. J.M. Price, 'Multilateralism and/or Bilateralism: the Settlement of British Trade Balances with 'The North', c. 1700'; *Economic History Review*, vol. 14 (2nd series), (1961–2), pp. 254–74.
61. D. MacPherson, '*Annals of Commerce*', (1805), vol. 3, p. 275.
62. Ibid. vol. 4, pp. 38 & 99.
63. A.R., B.W.L.B., B.W. to Ivan Kusoff of St. Petersburg, 26 Mar. 1791 and to Godfrey Thornton & Son of Hull, 20 Apr. 1791.
64. Ibid. B.W.D.B., 1782–92.
65. Ibid. B.W.L.B., B.W. to Barstow & Elliot of Danzig, 27 Apr. 1794.
66. Ibid. B.W. to Jacob Kabrun of Danzig, 22 Nov. 1794.
67. Ibid., B.W.D.B., 1795–1806.
68. See Appendix.
69. See Appendix.
70. See J. Sperling, 'The International Payments Mechanism in the Seventeenth and Eighteenth Centuries': *Econ. His. Review*, vol. 14, (1961–2), p. 452.
71. A.R., B.W.L.B., B.W. to Wm. Stephenson & Co., London, 25 Feb. 1791.
72. Ibid., B.W.D.B., 1789–90.
73. Ibid. 1785–1800.
74. A.R., B.W.L.B., B.W. to Jacob Kabrun of Danzig, 3 Sept. 1801.
75. Ibid. B.W.D.B., 19 Oct., 21 Nov., 3 & 10 Dec. 1785.
76. Ibid. 1793–1806.
77. Talbot Deposit (S.C.R.O.), 1 & 2 Jan. 1790. A.R., B.W.L.B., B.W. to William Nadin, 26 Dec. 1793.
78. D. Macpherson, op. cit., vol. 4, p. 266.
79. See Appendix.
80. See Appendix.
81. A.D., 25 & 26 Sept. 1807.
82. Ibid. Will of Benjamin Wilson, July 1811.

83. B.W.D., June, 1774. D.M., 19 Oct. 1770 and 10 Dec. 1773.
84. A.R., Journal of J.W.W., 1778–96. B.L.T.R., 1781. P.D., 2 Sept. 1775 and 6 Apr. 1789.
85. A.R., Ledger of J.W.W., 1775.
86. D.M., 29 Apr. 1790.
87. A.R. Day Book of J.W.W., 1778–90.
88. A.D., Will of William Wilson, 18 Dec. 1799.
89. A. Barnard, op. cit., vol. 1. p. 410.
90. B.W.D., 10 Oct. 1760.
91. Ibid. 23 Aug. 1761.
92. A. Barnard, op. cit., vol. 1, p. 410. Wray & Hollingsworth, Letter Books, Letters no's. 300, 380 & 393. *Burton Land Tax Returns,* 1781–90.
93. B.W.D., 5 Apr. 1799. D.M., 12 Mar. 1800. N.P.R., Will of William Worthington, 19 Apr. 1800.
94. B.W.R., William Bass Book, 1762–4. H.S. Twells, '*Mr* Drewry & the Derby Wagons'; Transactions of the Derby Archaeological Society, vol. 63 (1942). D.M., 21 Nov. 1766.
95. D.M., 7 July 1775. B.W.D., 4 Apr. 1777.
96. D.M., Mar. 1786.
97. B.W.D., Will of William Bass, 28 July 1787.
98. Ibid. 23 July 1792, 3 June 1795 & 18 Nov. 1830.
99. Ibid. 19 Dec. 1754 & 20 Aug. 1757.
100. P.D., 6 Apr. 1789. B.L.T.R., 1790.
101. Paget MSS., lease of 31 Aug. 1709. Anglesey MSS., 16 Aug. 1748, 10 Feb. 1753 & 9 May 1761. P.D., 23 Sept. 1762.
102. D.M., 9 Apr. 1779 & 13 Aug. 1779. B.L.T.R. 1790. J.S. Bushman, op. cit; pp. 79 & 90. B.W.D. 22 July 1803.
103. B.W.D., Will of Charles Leeson, 24 Oct. 1785 & 26 Sept. 1800.
104. D.M., 26 July 1751.
105. M.T.E.D., 4 & 5 Apr. 1774. D.R.L. Deeds, Will of William Greaves of Ingleby, 2 Aug. 1781.
106. D.M., 21 June 1781.
107. W. Stretton, '*The Stretton MSS*' (1910), pp. 161 & 220–1.
108. Supra, c. 4, p.
109. *Hull Port Books,* P.R.O., E. 190; 371/1, 371/2, 374/6 and 378/2. See also Appendix.
110. *Paget MSS,* 6 Aug. 1761. *Anglesey MSS*; 9 May 1761. P.D. 23 Sept. 1762. M.T.E.D., 24 Nov. 1845.
111. D.M., 2 Aug 1776 & 24 June 1784.
112. W. Stretton, op. cit., pp. 220–1. S.D. Chapman, '*The Early Factory Masters*', (1967), p. 86. W. Dickinson, '*The History and Antiquities of the Town of Newark*', (1819), p. 155, B.T.C.A., Trent Navigation Company Minute Books.
113. Supra, c. 4. p L.P.R., Will of William Hill of Burton, ('Maltster and Brewer'), 10 Apr. 1741.
114. Burton Extra L.T.R., 1781–90. P.D. 4 May 1789 & 5 May 1795.
115. P.D., 5 Apr. 1778 & 6 Apr. 1789. B.L.T.R. 1790.
116. P.D., 31 Aug. & 23 Sept. 1775. B.L.T.R. 1781–90. John Hayne's Letter Book, 1779–82.
117. D.M., 10 Dec. 1779 & 26 May 1780.

118. J. Phillips, '*A General History of Inland Navigation, foreign and domestic*', (1795), p. 168.
119. William Bass Book, op. cit., 1762–4.
120. *Paget MSS*, 20 Feb. 1762.
121. J.A.S.L. Leighton-Boyce, op. cit., pp. 236–7.

V

THE BREWING INDUSTRY DURING THE NINETEENTH CENTURY

For ambitious young brewers, such as Samuel Allsopp, Michael Bass and Thomas Salt, eager to develop their recently-acquired businesses, the outlook in 1807 was distinctly bleak. The long-established connections with Hull and the Baltic ports, that had taken over half a century to perfect and had enabled the Burton breweries to become larger than most provincial breweries, were rendered useless by the Napoleonic blockade. During the year ending April 1807 the Wilson-Allsopp brewery sold less than 600 barrels of ale and most of its working capital lay idle in the form of malt and cask stocks. Every effort was made to retain key workers but many others were forced to seek employment elsewhere. Believing that the blockade would soon end, Allsopp continued to export a few consignments, despite the risks involved and the high shipping and insurance charges. In June 1807 he sent 100 barrels of ale to Messrs. Kish & Co. of Konigsberg but the cargo was seized and in April 1808 he was still negotiating with the underwriters for compensation.[1] A few exports reached their destination but generally Allsopp and the other Burton brewers were forced to seek fresh markets at home. The most likely areas were clearly London, where Burton ale had been held in high esteem for at least two centuries, South Lancashire, where a large and expanding industrial community was linked to Burton by canal, and the Birmingham area, which offered similar opportunities.

Despite existing connections with merchants in London, Liverpool and Manchester the problems involved in this almost total reorganisation of business were immense. The main difficulty to be overcome was that of selling Burton ale at a price inevitably higher than that of the local beer; hence Allsopp's comment—

> 'If we lived only a few miles nearer we could sell our Malt liquor upon the same terms as the Liverpool Brewers do and would soon acquire a fortune'.[2]

Unlike their London counterparts, the Burton breweries possessed few, if any, tied houses, at this time and were thus obliged to sell to merchants and publicans over whom they had no control. The latter frequently tried to persuade Allsopp to lower his prices or to bear the cost of freight. He consistently refused their demands, however, and wisely co-operated with other brewers in the town in fixing prices—

> 'In consequence of the great advance in the price of barley and malt all the Brewers in this town have come to a determination to raise the price of their ales two pence per gallon . . . the lowest price at Burton to be 22d. per gallon'.[3]

In respect of the types of beer brewed Allsopp adopted a more flexible policy by modifying the flavour and colour to suit local tastes and by producing porter for the first time. He paid frequent visits to Manchester, London, Liverpool, Hull and West Bromwich, where he employed agents to promote sales. In Liverpool and Manchester Allsopp met with immediate, if modest, success, nearly 600 barrels of ale being sent there between October 1807 and April 1808. A. Heywood of Liverpool and W. Lawton of Manchester purchased several consignments exceeding 40 barrels, some of which may have been for export to Ireland or the West Indies. In London Allsopp rented a warehouse in Love Lane, Eastcheap and appointed Robert Oates and Thomas Shorthose as managers, initially for a salary of £80 per annum and, later, for a commission of five per cent. In letters to London merchants and innkeepers Allsopp explained that—

> 'Our time has been until lately occupied in supplying the Russian and Prussian demand. The sort of ale mostly used in London is that at 2/6d. per gallon; this price is 2d. per gallon higher than last year on account of the great advance in Barley, to that is to be added about 2d. per gallon expenses so that you get it delivered to you for 2/8d. payment in three months with a Bill at 2 or 3 per cent for ready money discount'.[4]

His efforts in the Birmingham area met with little success and poor sales and pilering on the canals persuaded him to abandon the West Bromwich agency before the end of 1808.

During the first season of reorganised trade the Wilson-Allsopp Brewery sold a modest 1,300 barrels of ale, including 400 barrels to customers within ten miles of Burton. The 2,500 barrels exported to the Baltic during the Spring of 1806 had thus been replaced by an additional 600 barrels sent to London, Liverpool and Manchester—a poor reward for Allsopp's determined efforts. Furthermore, his thirty foreign customers had been replaced by at least ninety English clients outside the Burton area. This radical change in marketing greatly increased the work of his clerks and managers without offering additional profits, although Allsopp did his best to mitigate this by concentrating on sales in specific areas and by consolidating ale despatches. The risk of incurring delayed payments and bad debts was magnified by the increased number of customers as well as by the lack of a mutual trading interest which had always been a feature of Baltic commerce. Unscrupulous English publicans were able to refuse payment on the grounds that the ale was bad or that the barrels were half empty on arrival, knowing that they need not deal with Allsopp again and that he was unlikely to take legal action against them for trifling amounts. Pilfering of cargoes on the canals was another nagging problem which eventually induced Allsopp to employ a Mr. Cartmeal to guard his large Lancashire consignments. Whereas Wilson's Baltic customers had normally ordered their requirements several months in advance, many of Allsopp's clients gave little notice of their needs and thus made forward planning very difficult. Moreover, Allsopp's business was frequently threatened by the increasing cost and scarcity of barley, staves and other raw materials. Whereas, in the 1790's, Wilson had complained bitterly at having to pay 38s. per quarter for barley and, in fact, often paid only 25–30s., Allsopp was forced to pay 53–60s. during the 1808–9 season and 65–70s. by 1813. When the 'Zulun' and the 'Juliana Catherina' arrived at Hull in July 1809 with a large cargo of staves from J.G. Walter of Stettin, Allsopp pleaded with Thomas Barmby to send him as many staves as possible because of their great scarcity.[5]

During the 1807–11 period the total sales of ale, stout and porter by the Wilson-Allsopp Brewery did not exceed 2,000 barrels in any one year. Sales in Liverpool continued to rise, reaching over 600 barrels in 1810–11, but these were offset by a decline in business in Manchester and London after 1809. So limited were the opportunities of increasing home sales that Allsopp continued to look towards the Baltic in the hope that the situation there might improve. Throughout the 1807–15 period, trade between Britain and the Baltic ports, although risky and spasmodic, by no means came to an end; indeed, between 1808 and 1810 it reached considerable proportions. As far as the Burton brewers were concerned, however, ale exports became unprofitable as soon as freight, insurance and convoy charges and foreign import duties became excessive. In February 1811 Allsopp successfully shipped 30 barrels of ale and 30 barrels of porter to Danzig and Konigsberg, while in the Spring of 1813 he sent a further 107 barrels of ale.[6] Profits were negligible but at least it helped to keep the brewery employed and to maintain connections in Hull and overseas. By 1814 the prospects for a resumption of the Baltic trade had brightened considerably and Thomas Allsopp, Samuel's brother, travelled to Danzig to visit Jacob Kabrun and a number of other former customers. He succeeded in obtaining orders in Danzig and Elbing for 300 barrels of ale. After the end of the war and the blockade in 1815 there was a marked revival in the Baltic ale trade, including a brief resumption of trade with Russia between 1820 and 1822, when the high tariff on English ale was lifted. Unfortunately, the absence of business records for this period prevents an accurate assessment of this revival from being made. It is highly improbable that ale exports, approached their pre-war level; they declined rapidly after 1822 and finally came to an end in 1825. This can be attributed to a combination of factors, the most significant of which were the establishment of breweries within the Baltic countries, their imposition of harsh tariffs on English imports and a sharp decline in demand in England for bar iron and certain other traditional Baltic commodities.

Meanwhile, the Burton brewers gradually increased their home sales. Between 1822–26 Allsopp sent ale to 346 customers in London, 234 in Liverpool and 128 in Manchester. In 1824 two-thirds of his output of 3,000 barrels went to London and Liverpool.[7] This was achieved by visits to likely areas and by advertising in the form of circulars, such as the following sent to potential customers in 1822—

> 'In consequence of the sudden prohibitory measures adopted by the Russian Government, affecting various exports from Great Britain, Wilson and Allsopp of Burton-upon-Trent will directly offer to the public a quantity of rich pale and fine-flavoured Ale, of uncommon strength, brewed expressly for that market, at the reduced price of 2/6d. per gallon, at Burton (from whence there is a water conveyance to every part of the Kingdom) in casks of about forty gallons each . . . It is too well known to comment that the ale from this Brewery has stood pre-eminent and unrivalled in the Baltic market for the last forty years'.[8]

In the same year the firm began to brew a new type of pale ale for export to India, which eventually proved to be an event of great significance.

English ale had been sent to India since the early years of colonisation but by 1775 exports still amounted to only 1,680 barrels per annum. After 1790 they increased rapidly, reaching just over 9,000 barrels in 1800 and 41,000 barrels in 1817.[9] Prior to 1830 the main exporter was Mark Hodgson, a London brewer who discovered that outward freight charges were extremely low owing to the dominance of homeward-bound cargoes in Anglo-Indian trade. He produced a bitter, sparkling ale that was much paler in colour than the traditional nut-brown Burton ale. This became known as 'India Pale Ale' and proved to be very popular, initially, amongst overseas consumers. Both Wilson and Allsopp had tried unsuccessfully to brew a similar ale on several occasions but it was not until 1822 that a determined effort was made. At the suggestion of two senior employees of the East India Company several bottles of Hodgson's ale were brought to Burton for examination and it is reputed that Job Goodhead, Allsopp's head brewer, succeeded in producing the first Burton pale ale in a teapot.[10] Later in the year a consignment of 45 barrels was sent to Calcutta via London. According to Messrs. Bailton and Hodson, merchants in Calcutta, this was very well received and sold at 90 rupees per hogshead—15 rupees higher than Hodgson's ale. Production began in earnest during the following year and in 1824 Allsopp sent almost 2,000 barrels of ale to ships' captains and merchants in London and Liverpool, most of which was destined for export to India and West Indies.

Encouraged by Allsopp's success other Burton brewers were quick to follow suit, both Michael Bass and Thomas Salt starting to brew pale ale in 1823. By 1832 Bass and Allsopp were contributing over half the ale exported to Calcutta and almost twice as much as Hodgson.[11] The pale ale trade with India had rapidly assumed an importance almost as great as that of the Baltic trade during the previous century. Throughout the 1830's Bass and Allsopp continued to send approximately 6,000 barrels to Calcutta each year, while additional consignments may well have gone to other Indian ports. Bass's contribution was consistently in excess of Allsopp's and this may indicate that he exported not only his own beer but that produced by Worthington, Salt and other Burton brewers. As in previous centuries, the strength, flavour and superb keeping qualities of Burton ale made it an instant success in the Indian market. Pale ale enabled the excellent qualities of the local water supply to be fully realised with the result that during the next few decades Burton became the world's leading centre for its production. The year 1822 thus marked a turning point in the development of the town's major industry and the end of 15 years of frustration during which brewery plant and capital had stood idle.

The popularity of Burton pale ale overseas very quickly spread to the home market. It is believed that this began in 1827 when a vessel carrying 300 hogsheads of ale was wrecked in the Irish Sea and several salvaged casks were sold by the underwriters in Liverpool.[12] Sales of pale ale to the Liverpool, Manchester and London areas in particular increased rapidly after this date but the lack of business records for any of the Burton breweries during this period makes it impossible to give a detailed and accurate account of the rate of growth. All that can be said is that it was steady rather then meteoric, for, until the Birmingham to Derby Railway was opened in 1839, Burton brewers remained entirely dependent upon relatively slow, inefficient and expensive canal and river transport.

The period from 1806 to 1830 was thus one of fluctuating fortunes in which the resources of the Burton brewers were severely tested by rising costs and uncertain markets. By 1822 only five breweries remained in the town—those of Samuel Allsopp & Co., Bass & Ratcliff, Thomas Salt & Co., William Worthington and John Sherratt.[13] John Greaves of Horninglow Street had been declared bankrupt in 1815 and his premises offered for sale on several occasions without success.[14] They were eventually sold to Jonathan Mason by R.C. Greaves of Ingleby in 1834. The Evans brewery in High Street had been purchased by William Worthington in 1819 for £8,950 and it was about this time that Joseph and Henry Clay had withdrawn from the industry and leased a number of their premises to Thomas Salt. Of the five remaining breweries those of Michael Bass and Samuel Allsopp were undoubtedly the most important. The former had apparently been more successful in securing home markets and had been able to extend his brewing premises, particularly after the acquisition of an additional area of land in High Street in 1812.[15] When Michael Bass died in 1830, the firm's output had reached 10,000 barrels per annum, over half of which was sent to London and Liverpool for export. The business then passed under the control of five partners—Michael Thomas Bass, his son, Samuel Ratcliff, John Gretton, Charles Walter Lyon and Joseph Spender Clay.[16] The Allsopp breweries in High Street and Horninglow Street remained under the management of Samuel Allsopp until 1838, when they passed to his son Henry, by which time the firm's output had fallen below that of Bass & Co. Thomas Salt gradually extended his premises in High Street in addition to acquiring a number of properties in Horninglow Street that had been used previously by the

Clay, Leeson, Greaves and Musgrave breweries.[17] A small additional brewery had been opened around 1800 by Coats & Co. at Horninglow, a mile to the west of the town. In 1806 this had passed into the hands of the Marston family, who, later in the century, helped to develop one of the leading businesses in the town.[18]

The progressive reduction in the number of breweries in Burton between 1780 and 1822 reflected fundamental changes that were taking place in the structure and character of the industry during this period. While it is true that declining trade forced some of the smaller firms out of business and caused the larger ones to operate well below capacity, it is equally true that the latter emerged from the crisis as larger units. It was a process not of industrial decline but of reorganisation in which the need for more elaborate and expensive equipment and premises and the rising costs of materials and marketing were gradually forcing the brewers to operate on a larger scale. The merchant brewers of the previous century, who had been able to add to their profits by a variety of commercial activities, were gradually replaced by a group of specialists who were denied the opportunities of their predecessors and who were obliged to devote a much greater proportion of their time and capital to brewing. This move towards specialisation was undoubtedly hastened by the collapse of the Baltic system but it was not until after the development of a railway network that the Burton brewers were able to benefit fully from the economies of large-scale production.

The growing popularity of Burton pale ale both at home and overseas after 1830 enabled the established breweries to expand and a number of new businesses to develop. By 1834 the number of firms had increased to nine; the additional four were those of Charles Hill of Lichfield Street, Jonathan Mason of Horninglow Street and Jonathan Meakin and John Yeomans of High Street.[19] Charles Hill, whose father had been in partnership with the Sherratts for many years, built his new brewery on the north bank of the Bond End Canal around 1830. The partnership had been dissolved in 1820, with John Sherratt continuing to operate the old brewery in Abbey Street until 1823, when it had passed under the control of Lewis Meakin, a former employee.[20] Jonathan Mason, who had owned a group of malthouses in Anderstaff Lane since 1820, purchased the former Greaves brewery in 1834 for £1,500 and went into partnership with his son-in-law Robert Gilbertson, who was also a brewer.[21] They opened an agency at the 'Town Hall Cellars' at Derby, at which they kept a large stock of ale and porter. The firm was of short duration, for four years after Masons's death in 1845 it was acquired for

£2,000, by John Thompson, the proprietor of the neighbouring 'Bear Inn'. The breweries of Jonathan Meakin and John Yeomans were small concerns on the west side of High Street, the latter's being attached to the 'Blue Posts' public house. By 1840 these modest additions had helped to make Burton one of the foremost brewing centres in the country, with an annual output of around 60–70,000 barrels and approximately 350 workers engaged in the industry. Although still very much smaller than the leading London breweries, Bass and Allsopp were by this stage each producing 15–20,000 barrels of ale per annum.

The opening of the Birmingham to Derby Railway through Burton in August 1839 set in motion a chain of events that in the space of 30 years completely transformed both the brewing industry and the town. For the first time in its history Burton was linked to all parts of the country by a communications system that allowed large quantities of freight to be transported swiftly, cheaply and safely. At last the Burton brewers were able to reap the benefits of large-scale production, which their London counterparts had enjoyed for over a century. During the 1840's the output of Burton's breweries increased from 70,000 to 300,000 barrels per annum and their employees from 350 to almost 1,000. This was achieved particularly by a considerable expansion of the two leading firms of Bass, Ratcliff & Gretton and Allsopp & Sons. By ploughing-back profits they were able to greatly extend and improve their premises, to make more effective use of steam-powered equipment and to reduce wastage by using more scientific methods, thereby increasing efficiency and the output/labour ratio. Whereas Benjamin Wilson had required 25 men to produce 3,000 barrels per annum during the 1790's, the larger and better equipped Burton breweries of 1850 were able to produce 300,000 barrels with the aid of less than 1,000 workers. At the same time, many of the significant features of the modern brewing industry, such as the employment of brewery managers, engineers and chemists, the establishment of agencies in important centres throughout the country and the predominance of beer sales to the home market, began to emerge.

By 1851 the number of breweries in the town had increased to fifteen. Four of these were small inn breweries belonging to Messrs. Hicklin and Gretton and to Mrs. Yeomans and Measom. They were of little importance in terms of output and employment and were somewhat reminiscent of the businesses of the early 18th century. Hicklin's brewery, for example, established at the Crown Inn in High Street during the mid-1840's, had a capacity of only 300 barrels per week.[22] Far more significant was the Burton Brewery Company founded in 1842 by Henry and Thomas Wilders. Its premises stood on the site of an old tanyard in High Street next to Salt & Co.'s brewery.[23] After its incorporation in 1858 the firm expanded rapidly with the result that by 1861 it had become the third largest brewery in the town, with extensive premises in High Street, Station Street and Anderstaff Lane and 300 workers in its employ. Considerably less important was a brewery established on the south side of Horninglow Street, close to the Midland Railway, by John Perks, a local attorney, in 1846. It was never particularly successful and by 1879, when it was no longer in use, it had passed through the hands of three other companies. One of these was the firm of John Thompson, whose predecessors had worked as victuallers at the 'Bear Inn' in Horninglow Street since 1765. By the 1860's Thompson owned three small breweries in Horninglow Street and malthouses in Bond Street and Brook Street.[24] The rapid expansion and growing reputation of the industry during the 1840's attracted to the town many outsiders, some of whom came with the intention of establishing businesses. These included William Middleton from London, who opened a small brewery in High Street in 1846 and Joseph Nunneley, who commenced business in Bridge Street in 1845. Their premises were later acquired by Ind Coope & Co. and J. Marston & Son Ltd. respectively. An additional brewery that also operated during this period was that of William Saunders, who opened premises on the north side of Horninglow Street around 1835; these were probably absorbed into Allsopp's brewery in 1865.[25] Despite the appearance of these new firms in the town, however, Bass & Co. and Allsopp's continued to dominate the industry by producing 70 per cent of the output and employing a corresponding number of workers.

The events of the 1840's formed a prelude to the staggering developments that during the following 30 years made Burton the world's premier brewing centre. Between 1850–80 the town's brewing industry trebled in size every ten years in terms of output and employment. During the first decade, for example, the number of brewery workers rose from 956 to 3,086 and the output of beer from approximately 300,000 barrels to 971,000 barrels. Between 1851–65 Bass, Ratcliff & Gretton built two new breweries in addition to other large premises, raised their annual output from 100,000 to 600,000 barrels and increased their labour force from 367 to 1,555. According to the 'Burton-on-Trent Times' in May 1858—

> 'the quantity of ale sent out of Burton during the present season far exceeds anything previously done. In fact the streets have been literally crowded with floaters from morning till night, wending their way to the Railway Station and back again. Nearly one thousand tons of ale were carted to the station and to the canals on Tuesday last ... this represents no less than 186,900 gallons'.

So rapid was the expansion that the communications system and social services of the town were frequently overwhelmed and there was a continual shortage of water and accommodation. By 1869 the various brewery premises, comprising 26 active breweries, 104 malthouses, 76 ale stores and 20 cooperages, covered an area of 174 acres. The brewers were consuming 439,000 quarters of malt per annum, 63,000 cwts. of hops, over 70,000 tons of coal, 8½ million cubic feet of barrel staves and nearly 12,000 tons of hoop iron in order to produce 1¾ million barrels of ale and porter. They were employing 4,701 men and boys as brewery workers, 373 clerks and executives and were using 189 horses, 282 floaters, 8 private locomotives, 18½ miles of private railway and 67 steam engines.[26]

Around 1880 the rate of growth began to slacken and when Alfred Barnard carried out his intensive survey of the leading breweries in 1887 and 1888 most of the premises that were to serve them for the next 50 years had been erected. There were then 31 active breweries in the town which between them produced three million barrels of ale and employed 8,000 workers. Bass, Ratcliff & Gretton Ltd. had become the largest brewing company in the world, while S. Allsopp & Sons Ltd., Ind, Coope & Co., T.F. Salt & Co. and Worthington & Co. were amongst the largest producers in Britain. Barnard aptly described the bustling atmosphere of the town in the following words—

> 'We passed no less than four large breweries, all within a quarter-of-a-mile of our hotel, whose lofty buildings, water towers and tall chimneys seemed to hem us in on every side. As we proceeded a smell of beer, and the odour of hops pervaded the air, whilst burly brewers met us at every turn. Here and there engines glided noiselessly about, dragging trucks heavily ladened with casks, and the clean streets were full of animation and life'.[27]

Although Bass, Ratcliff & Gretton Ltd. and S. Allsopp & Sons Ltd. continued to dominate the industry, the opening of breweries by large London firms was also significant. They were attracted to Burton by the suitability of its water supply for pale ale brewing. The London water, in contrast, with its higher carbonate and lower sulphate content, tended to impede filtration, thereby producing a duller wort, and to increase and adversely affect hop flavour.[28] Charrington & Co. purchased and rebuilt Meakin's London and Burton Brewery in Abbey Street in 1872, Truman, Hanbury & Buxton acquired the newly-built premises of Phillips Bros. in Derby Street in 1873, while Mann, Crossman & Paulin erected the Albion Brewery in Shobnall Road in 1874. Newcomers from other areas were A.B. Walker of Warrington, who also built a brewery in Shobnall Road in 1877, Peter Walker of Warrington, who opened the Clarence Street Brewery in 1880, and Everard & Co. of Leicester, who acquired Henry Boddington's Trent Bridge Brewery around 1885. Some of the breweries changed hands with bewildering rapidity. Moor Street brewery, for example, built in 1863, was owned by John Dickenson of Wolverhampton, William Nicholls, a Burton brewer, and Samuel Stone of Knighton, Leicestershire, until 1872, when it was purchased by Edwin Dawson of Leeds. In 1890 Dawson sold it to the Burton & Lincoln Brewery Co., which came partly under the control of the Albion Brewery Ltd. in 1896. In October 1899 the former went into voluntary liquidation and the premises were acquired during the following year by S. Briggs & Co. the brewery engineers.[29]

Not only did the number of brewing firms increase during this period but so also did the size of the unit of production. In 1851 the average production of London breweries, which benefitted considerably from the size of the potential local market, was seventeen times the provincial average but only four times the Staffordshire average and less than three times the Burton average. So rapidly did the Burton breweries expand, that by 1888 their average production was more than double that of the London firms. Large-scale production was stimulated by the increasing need for brewers to possess large funds of capital, required for the building and equipping of laboratories, the employment of qualified chemists and engineers and the purchase of elaborate equipment such as bottling machines. Moreover, the severe restriction of licences after 1869, during a period of rising beer consumption, resulted in a scramble for licensed properties, which stretched brewers' capital reserves to the limit, while the need for additional sites for brewery premises and workers' houses helped to inflate the price of land. The inability of small firms to raise the necessary capital generally resulted in take-over or amalgamation, with the result that the number of breweries in Burton declined from 31 in 1888 to 21 in 1900. The most outstanding example of amalgamation during this period was the formation of Marston, Thompson & Evershed Ltd. John Marston of Horninglow Brewery and Joseph Nunneley of Bridge Street combined in 1888 and ten years later were joined by J. & F. Thompson of Horninglow Street to form J. Marston, Thompson & Son Ltd. In 1902 they moved to the Albion Brewery in Shobnall Road, previously vacated by Mann, Crossman & Paulin. Finally, in 1905, after absorbing a number of small Midland breweries, including Pettifor's of Anstey and Wright's Crown Brewery Co. Ltd. of Market Drayton, the firm was joined by S. Evershed of Bank Square, Burton, to form Marston, Thompson & Evershed Ltd.[30]

Although there were generally between 20 and 30 brewing firms in the town during the 1850–1900 period, the progress of the industry was determined mainly by Bass & Co. and Allsopp's, who between them produced well over half the total output of beer. Both were quick to exploit the Indian market after 1823 and by 1840 had secured almost complete control over it. Bass & Co. proceeded to forge ahead of its old rival, increasing its output from 60,000 barrels in 1847 to 130,000 in 1853 and 400,000 in 1863. By 1876, with an output of 900,000 barrels, it had become the largest brewing company in the world and it continued to increase production until 1900, by which time its output had reached 1½ million barrels. The firm's employees increased correspondingly from 367 in 1851 to 1,167 in 1861. When Barnard visited the brewery in 1887 they totalled 2,760, including 2 head brewers, 10 assistant brewers, nearly 200 clerks, 10 maltsters, over 400 malting workers, 546 in the engineer's department and 400 in the cooperages.[31] In addition, the firm employed over 400 at its agencies in the United Kingdom and France and a further 150 at its St. Pancras stores in London. By the end of the century its 3,500 Burton employees formed 40 per cent of the brewery workers in the town. Highly qualified and skilled workers were recruited nationally and often housed in cheap accommodation owned by the firm.

Until 1840 Bass & Co. coped with its growth in business by gradual additions to its premises on the east side of High Street but afterwards this was no longer feasible. In 1842 they acquired a number of properties on the west side of High Street from Worthington & Co. which later formed part of their Middle Yard, while in 1845 they bought a large block of malthouses in Anderstaff Lane from John

Mason.[32] Frequent additions were made to the Old Brewery, including the erection of a large water tower in 1856. So rapidly did their business expand, however, that they were obliged to open the Middle Brewery on the north side of Station Street in 1853, together with malthouses, a cooperage and a large hop store, and the New Brewery on the south side of Station Street in 1864. In 1873 and 1874 they built a block of 6 large malthouses, later increased to 8, with attached workers' cottages and railway sidings on the south side of Shobnall Road at a cost of nearly £100,000. By 1887 the Company's premises in Burton covered an area of 145 acres, while, in addition, the firm owned properties in many other towns, including 10 malthouses at Lincoln.

Supplies of raw materials continued to be obtained from traditional areas but increasing quantities were also imported. Prime barley was purchased from agents in Eastern England, the Bury St. Edmunds area of Suffolk being particularly important, and also from merchants in Germany, Austria, Holland and France. The firm's consumption of malt rose rapidly from 133,000 quarters in 1863 to 190,000 quarters in 1866. By 1895 it was operating 22 malthouses in Burton, 12 at Lincoln and Grantham and 8 at Sleaford but was obliged to purchase a further 100,000 quarters of malt from other suppliers. Increasing quantities of hops were obtained from Bavaria and the U.S.A. and by 1887 the company's average weekly hop consumption amounted to 60 tons. During the same period it used approximately 40,000 tons of coal and 2,000 tons of coke per annum, most of which was purchased from collieries in Derbyshire and Leicestershire. The firm's cooperages in the Middle Yard and Station Street employed 400 workers and consumed huge quantities of staves and 700 tons of hoop iron per annum. Supplies of brewing water were obtained from 17 wells at the three breweries, Shobnall and the Upper Mills, while water for washing and cooling came from the Trent and from Lichfield.[33]

The move towards large-scale production demanded the use of more elaborate and efficient brewing equipment. Unlike the large London breweries, which used steam power for various purposes before the end of the 18th century, the Burton firms relied entirely upon men and horses until at least the 1820's. By 1846 Allsopp's were using a beam engine of 20 h.p. for maltcrushing, winnowing, mashing, hoisting and ventilation in their High Street brewery. In 1869 all the Burton breweries together contained 67 fixed engines totalling 1,059 h.p., while by 1887 Bass & Co. alone owned 35 fixed engines and their Engineer's Department, with 546 employees, had become one of the largest sections of the firm.[34] At the same time the system of transportation was substantially improved, particularly after 1860 by the construction of an intricate network of private railways linking the leading breweries to the main railway. In 1866 Bass & Co. despatched over 100,000 tons of ale in over 36,000 wagons and in one particularly busy month paid the Midland Railway Co. £17,000 in freight charges. By 1880 the firm had bought 11 locomotives from Thornewill & Warham of Burton and had laid 17 miles of full-gauge track. The system proved so effective that it was still in partial use a century after its creation.

The enormous increase in the size and extent of the market after 1840 also called for a far more elaborate system of distribution. This was largely achieved by the opening of agencies in many large towns and the employment of managers, travellers and agents. By 1887 Bass & Co. had agencies in 22 centres extending from London to Glasgow and Bristol to Aberdeen, as well as in Dublin, Cork, Belfast and Paris. Overseas sales, although increased, were relatively unimportant after 1850 and in 1887 amounted to only 25,000 barrels out of a total production of nearly one million barrels. After the restriction of licences in 1869 home sales were secured by the acquisition of hundreds of tied houses, particularly in South Lancashire and North Staffordshire. The marketing of grains and other brewery bi-products throughout the Midlands also formed an increasingly important aspect of the firm's business.

S. Allsopp & Sons, the second largest brewery in the town after 1820, expanded its business at a similar pace, raising its output from 80,000 barrels in 1851 to 270,000 barrels in 1861. At the end of 1865 the firm's Executive Committee approved extensions to the brewery sufficient to enable it to use 150,000 quarters of malt per annum and to brew over half a million barrels. By 1875 ale output had risen to around 90,000 barrels per month during the winter season and approximately 700,000 barrels per annum.[35] From then until the end of the century, however, the brewery rarely operated at full capacity and despite the introduction of summer brewing during the early 1880's annual output was generally under 500,000 barrels. This was primarily due to ineffective marketing techniques and failure to secure sufficient retail outlets in the form of tied houses.

The extremely rapid growth of the firm after 1840 necessitated periodic reorganisation of its administrative machinery. In 1851 its Directors were Henry Allsopp, Henry Townshend, Henry Blundell Leigh, James Finlay and Thomas Poyser. Henry Allsopp continued to chair the monthly meetings of the Executive Committee until the

1870's but the family influence, so dominant in earlier days, gradually waned. Reorganisation culminated in the incorporation of Samuel Allsopp & Sons Ltd. on 8 Feb. 1887 and the approved prospectus invited the public to subscribe to a share capital of £2,200,000 and a 4½ per cent debenture stock of £1,100,000.[36]

Until 1860 Allsopp's relied mainly upon their old brewery in High Street and upon malthouses, cooperages and stores in Horninglow Street. Between 1857–60, however, they found it necessary to purchase an extensive area of land at Moor Mill Dam, near to the railway station, and to construct a new brewery there at a cost of £27,000. From then until 1880 expenditure on new plant and equipment was considerable. In April 1866, for example, the Executive Committee approved estimates totalling £12,266, which included extensions to the cooperage, alterations to the model brewery, machine shops and stores, the construction of a railway line to the Old Brewery and the purchase of boilers, coppers and hydraulic engines for the New Brewery. Improvements at the Old Brewery in 1872 and 1876 amounted to over £35,000 while new malt and barley stores at the New Brewery cost £17,600 in 1878.[37] By 1887 the New Brewery contained the largest ale stores in the town, a hop store with a capacity of 20,000 pockets, a cooperage employing 200 men and many other extensive departments. The firm had 30 malting floors at Shobnall and the New Brewery capable of handling 18,000 quarters of barley every four days, while its premises at Grantham and Beccles were able to produce 40,000 quarters of malt per annum.[38] The firm's brewery workers showed a corresponding increase from 304 in 1851 to 889 in 1861 and 1,600 in 1888, by which time it also employed 150 clerks and managers.

As with Bass & Co., supplies of prime barley were purchased from merchants and growers in Lincolnshire, East Anglia and various European countries, while hops were obtained from Kent, Worcestershire, Bavaria and California. Supplies of coal and coke arrived from Staveley, Chesterfield and other Derbyshire mining centres. The cooperages used mainly Memel oak and in 1881 the firm had £30,000 worth stacked at Church Croft timber yard. In the same year the firm owned 11 wells, ranging in depth from 20 to 120 feet, which yielded 100,000 gallons of water per hour. In order to facilitate the movement of materials between their scattered premises the firm emulated Bass & Co. by constructing a network of private railways during the 1860's. They purchased their first Thornewill & Warham locomotive in 1863 and by 1887 had acquired a further five.

Allsopp & Co. were probably the first Burton firm to establish outside agencies for promoting sales, the earliest being opened in London, Liverpool, Manchester and West Bromwich in 1808. By 1880 they were operating 26 agencies over a wide area of the United Kingdom, at which 350 men were employed. Although home sales were dominant after 1840, exports continued to be important, with regular consignments going to India, Australia, New Zealand, South Africa, Malaya, Gibraltar, China and North America. Their 'Arctic Ale', taken by the Admiralty on expeditions to the Arctic in 1852 and 1875, was able to withstand temperatures of over 90°F below freezing point without deteriorating—a reminder of the superb keeping qualities of Burton ale. In respect of exports, Allsopp's and Bass's operated a joint policy of price-fixing. In Jan. 1888, for example, they agreed that the 1·060 gravity ale should be exported at £19 per tun of four hogsheads, 1·055 at £18 and 1·050 at £17, a uniform discount of 10 per cent to be allowed on large orders.[39] Agencies were also used to promote overseas business, the one in Paris being especially important, while the firm also participated in international trade exhibitions in Britain and Europe.

Allsopp's policy in relation to agencies was unquestionably sound but their attitude towards tied properties was strangely hesitant and short-sighted. Restriction of licences after 1869 failed to convince the firm's Directors of the need to secure adequate retail outlets and even at the time of its incorporation in 1887 the firm owned very few tied houses. The new Company made determined but belated efforts to solve the problem by excessive purchases of tied properties in a highly competitive market and the heavy burden of fixed-interest charges on debentures, raised to support this expenditure, was to a large extent responsible for the series of financial crises through which the Company passed after 1887.[40] Purchases were concentrated particularly in Northern England, South Wales, The Potteries and London, with the result that by 1915 the Company owned 461 tied houses, 300 of which were freehold properties.[41]

The dominance of S. Allsopp & Sons Ltd. and Bass, Ratcliff & Gretton Ltd. throughout the second half of the 19th century can be appreciated by reference to the employment and output statistics for 1861 and 1888.[42] In 1861 they gave employment to almost exactly two-thirds of the 3,000 brewery workers in the town. Of the remaining 16 firms only Burton Brewery Co. with 300 employees, T.F. Salt & Co. and Worthington & Robinson, with 200 workers each, and Tooth Bros., with 80 workers, were of any real significance. By 1888 the structure of the industry had changed in certain respects. The two leading firms still dominated the industry with approximately 60 per cent of the workers and output but the number of firms had increased to 31, several of which were very important concerns. Burton Brewery Co., Charrington & Co., T.F. Salt & Co., Truman, Hanbury & Buxton and Worthington & Co. all employed 170 workers or more. As previously mentioned, four of these were branches of larger businesses based in other centres. Lack of business records prevents a detailed account of these and the many smaller concerns from being attempted but available evidence suggests that their characteristics were in no way different from those of Allsopp's and Bass's. Indeed, it is apparent that they frequently tried to emulate the activities of the two leading companies. Scale of production was, naturally, significant in determining the extent to which this emulation was feasible. Only a handful of firms were, for example, sufficiently large to provide the capital needed for the construction of private railways, laboratories and model breweries and the employment of qualified chemists and engineers. Moreover, the smaller firms were at a disadvantage in that they were unable to reap the benefits of bulk buying, tied properties, national advertising and the promotion of sales through agencies. It was disadvantages such as these which eventually led to the bankruptcies and amalgamations previously mentioned.

The development of large-scale brewing during the period was accompanied by a search for greater efficiency through the application of improved technological and scientific methods. The latter were of particular interest in that Bass's, Allsopp's and Worthington's were amongst the first breweries in the world to employ chemists and to find ways of applying their discoveries to the everyday running of the brewery. Prior to 1860 brewers possessed little knowledge of brewing chemistry; they simply followed basic rules concerning such matters as temperature control, fermentation and the regulation of strength, flavour and colour. Indeed, attempts to apply chemical knowledge were often regarded with great suspicion in case the beer might be adulterated with impure ingredients. As the scale of the industry increased, however, brewers began to search for greater efficiency through a reduction of wastage and through an extension of the brewing and malting season. In order to accomplish this it was first of all necessary to understand processes such as fermentation which had baffled scientists for so long.

Michael Combrune, a notable 18th century London brewer, attempted to describe the process of fermentation as—

> 'the sensible internal motion of the particles are gradually removed from their former situation, and after some visible separation, joined together in a different order and arrangement so as to constitute a new compound'[43]

William Black, writing 70 years later, was scarcely more explicit and his work was later described by an eminent brewery chemist as being 'worthy of a place in a museum of fatuous works on brewing'.[44] It was not until 1860, when Louis Pasteur began to publish the results of his research, that a new era in brewing science began. In 'Etudes sur le Vin', (1860) and 'Etudes sur la Bière', (1876) he explained, for the first time, the fermentation process in precise scientific terms by indentifying it with the life cycle of yeast. This eventually led to an identification of useful and harmful yeast cells and to an elucidation of the causes of bacterial defects in beer. However, although Pasteur made the initial break-through, great credit for the enormous advances made in brewing science between 1860 and 1890 must also go to Henry Bottinger, Peter Griess, Horace and Adrian Brown and Cornelius O'Sullivan, all of whom were employed by Burton breweries, as well as to E.C. Hansen of the Carlsberg Brewery in Copenhagen.

The first Burton brewery (and probably the first in the world) to appoint a chemist to its staff as scientific adviser was S. Allsopp & Sons, who engaged Dr. Henry Böttinger of Wurtemburg in this capacity in 1845. He was one of a trio of brilliant young chemists who had recently studied at the University of Giessen under the celebrated Baron von Liebig. Allsopp's decision may have been motivated by a variety of factors. In 1830 they, along with other Burton brewers, had been accused by a Scottish doctor named Booth of adulterating their ale with salt of steel, prunella, jalap, sulphate of lime and black rosin.[45] Successful legal proceedings against the publishers of Booth's treatise and a full inspection of breweries by experts had completely exonerated the brewers but the danger of similar accusations remained. Moreover, financial loss, incurred through deterioration of export ale in transit, continued to be a nagging problem. In 1835–6, for example, 135 hogsheads out of 1,543 sent by Allsopp's to Calcutta were classed as damaged or empty on arrival.[46] It was later said of the India pale ale trade that—

> 'the system was only commercially possible with high gross profits to carry such risks and all the other expenses incidental to it . . .

under such conditions great financial losses occurred at times through spoiled beer'.[47]

The initial employment of well-qualified chemists may have thus stemmed from a desire to safeguard reputations, to reduce wastage and also to qualify for a drawback on exports.

Whatever the reasons may have been it was not very long before Böttinger's abilities were fully tested. In 1852 M. Payer, a French chemist, publicly accused English brewers of using French strychnine as a substitute for hops. When statements in the national press failed to dispel public alarm the Burton breweries were again thrown open for inspection and their contents submitted for analysis by impartial and reputable scientists, such as Professor Hoffmann of the Royal College of Chemistry and Dr. Hassall of the Lancet Commission. By the end of the year Henry Allsopp, with the assistance of Dr. Böttinger, had established the integrity of Burton brewers beyond all doubt. Moreover, the opening of a 'model brewery' at Allsopp's shortly afterwards enabled Böttinger to conduct original research into fermentation, the results of which were later published in Muspratt's 'Chemistry as Applied to Arts and Manufactures'. Following his appointment as head brewer in 1860, he attempted to apply the results of some of his research to routine brewing processes. His success in this field was somewhat limited, for in 1865, at the age of 46, he decided to move to Wurzburg in Bavaria, where he established his own brewery.[48]

Shortly before his departure Peter Griess was appointed as his assistant at Allsopp's for 'experimental purposes'. Having worked for Professor Hoffmann since 1856, Griess was already well-known for his discovery of diazo-compounds. He was attracted to Burton by the excellent facilities that Henry Allsopp was willing to place at his disposal. During the ensuing years his suggested experiments in brewing processes and techniques were generally approved by the firm's Executive Committee in the belief that they would eventually lead to greater efficiency. Frequent additions were made to the model brewery and to the laboratory with the result that by the 1880's the latter contained excellent facilities and a wide range of apparatus including microscopes, polariscopes, aerometers, photo-micrography apparatus and forcing tanks. These were in regular use for controlling the quality of raw materials and products, thereby contributing to the efficiency and profitability of the brewery.

Bass & Co. were quick to follow Allsopp's example by obtaining the services of John Matthews around 1850. In 1865, by which time he had become the firm's 'chemist and principal brewer', he commented—

> 'we analyse a sample from every brewing of pale ale for export because a drawback is allowed us by the Government officers when certain conditions are complied with. We often analyse that ale which is not going to be exported, but not always.'[49]

This again suggests the main reason for Matthews' initial employment. In the following year Cornelius O'Sullivan, a highly qualified chemist and geologist from the Royal College of Chemistry, became his assistant at the Old Brewery in High Street. He proceeded to carry out a considerable amount of original research into the structure of barley and the actions of brewing sugar, starch and maltose, the results of which were published in the 'Journal of the Chemical Society' between 1872 and 1882. In 1874 he patented a process for 'The Treatment of Starch and Starchy substances and the production therefrom of a compound body capable of being used as a substitute for malt in brewing, and for other purposes'.[50] The value of his research was widely recognised; in 1884 he was awarded the Longstaff Medal and a purse of gold and in the following year was elected Fellow of the Royal Society. After 1886 he became increasingly involved in production rather than research. In this field he was equally successful and from 1894 until his retirement he served as Head Brewer at the New Brewery in Station Street. His abilities both as a chemist and a brewer enabled more beer to be produced from a given quantity of raw materials and also allowed a steady advance towards all-year brewing. The importance of the latter was stressed by Arthur Bass in 1884 when he said—

> 'I think neither you nor some others appreciate how fast our trade is becoming a running one—the question is not what you or I consider a reasonable time for beer to fine in, but what the customer interested expects it to be—i.e. 10 days or so. Practically all our pale ale now except that brewed in January and February and March may be said to be running beer—and even of this a large proportion is bottled at a very early date after brewing'.[51]

By the mid-1880's all-year brewing had been accomplished by at least the larger Burton breweries as a result of advances in brewing science.

Another eminent brewing chemist of the same period, Dr. Horace

Brown, was born at Burton in 1848 and engaged by Worthington & Co. as a junior brewer in 1866. By 1871 he had succeeded in equipping a small laboratory and had begun to try to apply the results of Pasteur's researches into fermentation. He quickly learnt to identify the various types of yeast cells and to be able to separate the pure ones from those that were detrimental to the keeping qualities of beer. One of his outstanding early achievements was his identification of 'Saccharobacillus Pastorianus' which was responsible for a large proportion of the deterioration of stocks of Burton ale.[52] In 1875 he began to use the 'forcing tray' in which beer was rapidly matured at a temperature of 80–90°F for about three weeks in order to test its keeping qualities by identifying various yeast forms under a microscope. By 1880 this valuable technique was being used regularly by all the leading breweries in the town. In 1877 Brown discovered that the secondary stage of fermentation determined the flavour of fully matured beer and that the secondary yeasts responsible were genetically unconnected with the yeasts that caused the primary fermentation. To some extent, therefore, he anticipated the discoveries of E.C. Hansen who in 1879 perfected a method of pure yeast cultivation and proved brewery yeasts to be a mixture of several distinct species. By introducing pure yeast cultivation, Brown and his talented assistant, Dr. G.H. Morris, were able to substantially reduce the amount of beer lost through adverse bacterial changes. Brown also carried out original research into wort composition, the structure of barley and the chemistry of malting which enriched knowledge of brewing science and stimulated technological improvements.[53] His contributions to the brewing industry earned him many honours and awards, including the Longstaff Medal of the Chemical Society in 1894 and the Royal Medal of the Royal Society in 1903. After leaving Worthington's in 1894 H.T. Brown helped to establish and direct the Guiness Research Laboratory in Dublin and was elected President of the Institute of Brewing in 1910.

One other Burton brewery to employ a chemist during this period was T. Salt & Co., who engaged the services of Adrian Brown in 1873. A.J. Brown, also a Burtonian and a graduate of the Royal College of Chemistry, devoted much of his time to the study of yeast cells, acetic ferments and the conversion of sugar into cellulose. He continued to work for Salt's until 1900, when he became Director of the British School of Malting and Brewing at the University of Birmingham. He was made a Fellow of the Royal Society in 1911 and elected President of the Institute of Brewing for the 1917–19 period.

During the second half of the 19th century the Burton brewers and chemists led the world in the development of brewing science. When Pasteur visited Whitbread's Brewery in London in 1871 he found that no use was made of the microscope and that the employment of chemists in breweries was regarded with great suspicion. In the same year Professor Frankland of Royal College of Chemistry drew attention to the fact that 11 of the 20 brewing students trained there since 1845 had proceeded to three of the Burton breweries. The extent of Burton's contribution was acknowledged a few years later by W.G..Valentin when he said—

> 'Our great brewers, among whom I would, without fear of encountering the reproach of flattery, single out the great brewing firms of Messrs. Bass & Co., and Messrs. Allsopp & Sons availed themselves speedily of the conquests made by pure science which promises to throw light upon their purely empirical processes, and to clear away the mist that hung over some of the chemical changes involved in brewing. Thus it has come to pass that from the heads of these firms down to the under-brewers, a chemical knowledge was considered the requisite thing, and that we see eminent scientific chemists now superintending the chemical departments of these firms.'[54]

Professor Graham of the Royal College of Chemistry, in his report to the 'Royal Commission on Technical Instruction' in 1882, also commented on the rarity of chemical laboratories in breweries outside Burton.

By the 1870's Burton had thus become the home of brewing science and the workplace of a number of eminent chemists. In 1876 they, together with several other local enthusiasts (P.B. Mason, H.E. Bridgeman, E.A.P. Forster and W. Odling), formed a scientific society known as the 'Bacterium Club'. Its meetings were held informally at members' houses for the purpose of discussing aspects of chemistry, geology, geography and natural history, in all of which H.T. Brown and C. O'Sullivan, in particular, were highly knowledgable. There were few societies to equal it and it was certainly no exaggeration to say that 'Burton-on-Trent in the seventies probably was the most active and stimulating centre in the country, the home of real bio-chemistry'.[55] Credit for the presence of so eminent a body of scientists in the town must be given to far-sighted brewery proprietors, such as Henry Allsopp and Michael Bass, who were prepared to provide them with salaries, premises and equipment. One could cynically say that they were merely enlightened entrepreneurs motivated by the prospect of greater efficiency and increased profits. The fact that most of the chemists eventually became brewers certainly adds strength to this view but, at the same time, one is left with the impression that their policies were also motivated by a genuine desire to further the cause of science in general. This opinion is substantiated by the references to the brewers' social and political activities later in the chapter.

The claim made in 1895 that advances in brewing chemistry had been of very little practical value was certainly not true as far as Burton breweries were concerned.[56] The rapid adoption of the 'Burton Union' system of fermentation, in preference to the former method of fermenting beer in trade casks, may have been a reflection of the new scientific approach. According to H.T. Brown—

> 'It was there [Burton] that the famous Union system had its origin, a system of fermentation particularly well adapted to the higher branches of the export trade of that time [the early 1860's]. Burton was then a Mecca to which brewers from all parts of the world made their pilgrimages in order to study the latest developments of English brewing'.[57]

It seems likely that the system was developed by Bass & Co. as early as 1840 and it was certainly in use at Allsopp's a year after Böttinger's arrival, for the union room there contained working and racking squares, yeast troughs and 'swan-neck' shaped overflow pipes and stillions.[58] As far as H.T. Brown was concerned 'nothing of value was ever done which does not involve both theory and practice'. His 'forcing tray' system proved to be of considerable value, while his ingenious device for recording temperatures in malt kilns was another illustration of his practical approach.[59] Greater knowledge of raw materials and processes used in brewing allowed more wort to be extracted from a given quantity of malt and various other economies to be made. The introduction of summer brewing, made possible by improved methods of cooling, enabled brewers to satisfy consumers' demands for lighter running ales in preference to the well-matured, heavily hopped, high gravity beers. This allowed the brewers to make further economies by increasing the rate of turnover and the output/labour ratio and by reducing the storage time for beer and the need for additional premises. After 1885 breweries elsewhere began to follow Burton's lead by employing chemists and establishing laboratories. The Laboratory Club, formed in 1886, symbolised the new outlook. The Institute of Brewing, which developed from it in

1890, sponsored further chemical research within the industry and it is worth noting that Burton chemists played a leading part in the establishment and organisation of both bodies. During 1889, for example, C.G. Matthews of Bass's and G.H. Morris of Worthington's served on the Committee of the Laboratory Club and 4 of the 11 papers read to members were contributed by them.[60]

Towards the end of the 19th century the scientific and technological achievements of the leading Burton breweries began to be offset by acute marketing difficulties arising out of the scarcity of retail outlets. Unlike their London counterparts, who had been extensively committed to the tied-house system for over a century, the Burton brewers had not previously required such a system. Traditionally they had been exporting brewers, while the relaxation of the licensing laws in 1830 had largely removed the need to own retail outlets for domestic sales. After 1869, however, when control of licences was again placed in the hands of local magistrates, licensed properties became increasingly scarce and expensive. Breweries that were unable to raise the capital for the purchase of sufficient tied houses at inflated prices often found themselves in danger of being absorbed by their more affluent competitors. In anticipation of these developments Bass & Co. adopted the wise policy of steadily acquiring properties after 1860. By the end of the century they owned over 500 houses in various parts of England, Wales and Ireland, with particularly large concentrations in Wales, South Lancashire and The Potteries.[61] Allsopp's occasionally co-operated with Bass & Co., as in 1865 when they jointly purchased the Charing Cross Hotel in London. In general, however, Allsopp's investments in tied properties were grossly inadequate prior to 1887. As previously noted,[62] their belated attempts to solve the problem precipitated a series of financial crises between then and the turn of the century. Advances to publicans totalled £82,000 and £96,000 in 1888 and 1890 respectively, while investments in tied properties amounting to over £138,000 were approved in Novermber, 1898.[63] By 1915, after enormous expenditure, their licensed properties totalled 461. Other large Burton breweries were forced to follow suit. The Burton Brewery Co., for example, acquired several hundred houses, including 52 in 1889 alone.[64] Undoubtedly, the increasing scarcity of retail outlets played a significant part in the spate of bankruptcies and amalgamations that occurred after 1900.

The extremely rapid expansion of the brewing industry in Burton after 1840 was accompanied by an equally sharp decline in a number of traditional occupations, such as cotton spinning and hat and hardware manufacture. By 1851 it had become a specialist brewing centre, with 10 per cent of its population directly engaged in the industry. During the next three decades growth continued at the same rate, with the result that from 1861 until the end of the century approximately 55 per cent of the town's working population were supported by a single industry. Burtonians were able to enjoy the security and prestige which this highly stable occupation offered and to boast—

> 'Look at our monster breweries, employing thousands of hands in the manufacture of our staple commodity, and sending it to almost every part of the habitable globe ... Thus Burton has already attained an eminence which perhaps no other town in the Kingdom, of similar population, has done'.[65]

Increasing scarcity of land and the advantages offered by sites adjacent to the main railway resulted in a marked change in the traditional pattern of brewing premises in High Street, Horninglow Street and Bond End. The first phase in the extension of the industrial zone, which occurred mainly between 1855 and 1865, was largely confined to the area around Station Street, where Bass & Co., Allsopp's and Ind, Coope & Co. erected four new breweries. The next zone to be affected was the area around Victoria Crescent, where, by 1875, there were four breweries in operation, belonging to Clayton & Co., W. & G.R. Clarkson, T. Cooper & Co. and F. Heap. The third zone of development was the Shobnall Road area on the western edge of the town, which, by 1880, contained the breweries of Mann, Crossman & Paulin (1874) and A.B. Walker (1877) and the very extensive malthouses of Bass & Co. (1874) and Allsopp's (1879). In addition, large malthouses, cooperages and stores were built by the leading companies in Horninglow Street, Anderstaff Lane, New Street and Moor Street. Thus, by 1880 most of the land between the River Trent and the Midland Railway, as well as several extensive areas to the west of the railway, had been laid out with brewery premises, railway sidings and workers' houses.[66]

Dominated by a single industry, whose growth was largely confined to a period of only 40 years, Burton inevitably developed a unique personality. The breweries required very extensive premises, surrounded by huge yards in which enormous mounds of casks could be stored. They needed spacious railway sidings and lines across the town's streets linking the various departments together and to the Midland Railway. They acquired considerable areas of land both within and outside the urban area in order to safeguard supplies of brewing water. Most of these developments were carried out hastily and with little thought for town planning. The occupation of the town centre by large breweries inhibited normal urban growth, while the purchase and retention of extensive water-bearing lands to the south-west of the town prevented expansion in that direction. Modern suburban growth and urban re-development have been largely unsuccessful in destroying the town's 19th century industrial character.

The rapidity of industrial growth inevitably resulted in scarcity of land, housing, public services and labour. The latter helped to give rise to a highly unusual arrangement whereby migrant workers from East Anglia were engaged for seasonal work in Burton malthouses. The origin of the system remains obscure but it is likely that it was introduced around 1860. There were basically three reasons why East Anglians became involved. Firstly, well-established connections already existed between the leading Burton breweries and merchants and farmers in the prime barley-growing districts of Norfolk and Suffolk. Secondly, the expansion of the brewing industry in Burton coincided with agricultural depression in East Anglia. Thirdly, the malting and harvesting seasons were complimentary to one another so that most of the men involved were able to obtain employment throughout the year. Workers generally arrived in Burton during the second half of September, in time for the start of the malting season, returning home in May.

Early in September each applicant received a letter from the brewery arranging for him to be interviewed at a nearby farm or village inn. He was required to supply a favourable reference and to be of sound health and physique. In view of the arduous nature of malting work men below 5ft. 6in. in height and under 11st. in weight were often rejected; in September 1890, for example, Bass & Co. engaged 125 East Anglians but rejected a further 167.[67] Workers previously employed and found to be hard-working, healthy, sober and honest were generally invited for a further season. Strict records were kept of insubordination, drunkenness, absenteeism and other forms of misconduct and the culprits given 28 days notice to quit. After the signing of a contract men were instructed to report to the nearest railway station at a stated time for free conveyance to Burton. Lodgings were obtained as near to the malthouses as possible in Grange Street, Wellington Street, Cross Street, Milton Street, Victoria Street and Anderstaff Lane.

Bass & Co. employed 126, 256 and 249 migrants during the

1890–1, 1896–7 and 1900–1 seasons respectively but it is not known to what extent other Burton firms used the system. The occasional transfer of workers from Bass & Co. to malthouses belonging to Edie's, Richards, Cherry & Yeomans, and Meakin's certainly suggests that other firms were involved. It seems likely, therefore, that by the mid-1890's there were 3–400 East Anglians at work in the town during the malting season. Although they were generally referred to as 'Norkies', at least three-quarters of them came from Suffolk villages, particularly in the neighbourhood of Woodbridge, Ipswich and Bury St. Edmunds. As time went by an increasing number of East Anglians settled permanently in Burton, so that by 1926 only one-fifth of Bass & Co's malting workers were migrants. The system was finally discontinued in 1939.[68]

In discussing the economic and social activities of the large London brewers of the 18th century, Professor Mathias said that 'to ignore this social situation—to see the business man only in his role as entrepreneur or capitalist ... is to deny an important reality'.[69] With this in mind, what can be said of the men who guided Burton's brewing industry through the 19th century? One fact that is immediately apparent is that they were very different from their predecessors, both in their business methods and in their social activities. The 18th century brewers were often men drawn from humble walks of life, who combined the functions of works manager, sales manager, accountant and general merchant. The second generation of brewers, who directed the industry during the early 19th century, inherited established businesses. Although skilled in the various aspects of brewing, they were specialists in the sense that they confined their attentions to a single industry. They devoted most of their time to the management of the brewery and to its commercial affairs and they often lived, as their fathers had, in or close to the brewery premises. The third generation of brewers were very different. They were men born into a higher stratum of society, who regarded themselves as administrators rather than as brewers in a practical sense, who employed managers to operate the various brewery departments for them, who became increasingly absorbed in local and even national political affairs and who demonstrated their enhanced social and economic status by residing on the outskirts of the town in sumptuous mansions surrounded by spacious parks and ornamental gardens.

This gradual progression was well illustrated by the Bass family. William Bass (1720–87), the founder of the business, was a self-made man who by hard-work and good fortune was able to invest the proceeds of his carrying business in a small brewery. His elder son, Michael Bass (1759–1827), inherited a share of the business ten years later. Michael used his skill as a practical brewer and his ability as a business man to good advantage, with the result that when he died his brewery was the most important in the town. He married the daughter of a local solicitor and played a prominent part in local administrative and social affairs, serving as Townmaster in 1794. Michael Thomas Bass (1799–1884), his eldest son, entered the business in 1817 after a sound education in Burton and Nottingham. He was particularly successful as a commercial traveller and became a partner in the firm in 1830. Five years later he married Eliza Jane Arden, the eldest daughter of Major Samuel Arden of Longcroft Hall. By 1840 he had become a prominent figure in local political and social affairs.

After 1840, as head of a large and rapidly expanding firm, he began to delegate responsibility to his partners and managers and to take a greater interest in national affairs. His career as a national politician began in 1848, when he successfully stood as one of the two Liberal candidates at Derby in the parliamentary elections.[70] His activities in Parliament over the next 35 years ranged far and wide; he was a strong advocate of free trade, he worked to abolish imprisonment for debt and he introduced Bills concerning street musicians and poaching. His greatest interest, however, lay in the rising status and influence of the working class and he instituted a detailed national survey into their incomes. His close association with Derby involved him in a long and bitter dispute between railwaymen and their employers over excessive hours of work. In 1871 a section of the 2,200 railwaymen employed at Derby enlisted his support. During the next few years he devoted considerable time, effort and money to their cause by applying pressure to the Directors of the Midland Railway Company, by speaking in support of the railwaymen in Parliament, by writing letters to the national press and by financing a private enquiry into working conditions on the railways.[71] Undoubtedly, the support of M.T. Bass, a politician noted for his impartiality and integrity, proved a decisive factor in securing a substantial improvement in the railwaymen's conditions of employment.

Although his political activities clashed with his business interests on more than one occasion, M.T. Bass retained his liberal sentiments to the end. Sir William Harcourt aptly summed up his qualities when he opened St. Paul's Institute in Burton in 1882—

'We are met here to-day to commemorate the munificent benefaction of Mr. Bass. He is a man advanced in years, in honour, and in wealth, which is the fruit of a life of intelligent industry. He was a Liberal in his youth, he is a Liberal in his age. Years and wealth have not brought to him selfish timidity. In his grey hairs he cherishes the generous sentiments which inspired his earlier days. He has received freely, and freely has he bestowed'.[72]

His liberal principles were applied to his own employees as well as to his constituents. He appointed a scripture reader at the brewery whose duties included visits to the sick and the organisation of medical treatment and convalescence. A workers' library was established and also a branch of the Post Office Savings Bank, interest on employees' deposits being made up to five per cent. Workers' social and sporting activities were encouraged and supported financially and Bass even held an annual ball at his country home at Rangemore especially for his tradesmen and servants.

His generosity brought great material benefits to both Derby and Burton. At Derby he provided the town with a Free Library, Museum and Art Gallery, costing over £35,000, a recreation ground, and free swimming baths and he contributed towards the establishment of the School of Art, the Infirmary, the Children's Hospital and a railway orphanage. At Burton he gave £56,000 for the construction and endowment of St. Paul's Church in 1874 and also provided St. Paul's Institute, which later became the Town Hall, St. Margaret's Church and the church, school and parsonage at Rangemore. An obituary in 'The Times' following his death in April 1884 referred to him as—

'one of the best specimens of a type, happily never rare in this country, of business men who believe that they are bound to give to charity tithe of their fortunes, and that they ought not to be indifferent to the welfare of the community in which they have prospered'.[73]

Apart from his many business and political activities he served on numerous local committees and indulged in riding, shooting and horticultural experiments. It may have been his love of an outdoor life that induced him to move from his house in High Street to Byrkley Lodge, five miles to the west of the town. From there he organised the building of Rangemore Hall, a superb mansion which he filled with works of art and surrounded with exquisite ornamental gardens.

The commercial, political and social achievements of M.T. Bass were emulated to a lesser extent by the other leading Burton brewers of the period. William Henry Worthington served as Chairman of the Board of Town Commissioners for many years following the re-organisation of local government in 1853, while many other brewers, such as Joseph Nunneley, John Gretton and George Meakin, served as commissioners. When Burton attained Municipal Borough status in 1878 W.H. Worthington was elected Mayor and five of the seven aldermen were brewers (M.A. Bass, S.C. Allsopp, S. Evershed, H. Wardle and J. Yeomans). It was mainly due to the energy and ability of men such as these that Burton was granted its Charter of Incorporation and became a County Borough in 1901. In national politics, Henry Allsopp, who succeeded his father, Samuel Allsopp, as head of S. Allsopp & Sons in 1838, represented Worcestershire in Parliament from 1874–80. He was created a Baronet in 1882 and raised to the peerage in 1886, with the title of Lord Hindlip of Hindlip and Alsop-en-le-Dale. In the same year Michael Arthur Bass, who had represented Stafford in Parliament from 1865–68 and East Staffordshire from 1868–86, became Baron Burton. During the same period Hamar Bass served as Member of Parliament for Tamworth and also for West Staffordshire, while Henry Wardle, head of the firm of T. Salt & Co. represented the South Derbyshire Division. Apart from M.T. Bass, most of the brewers allied themselves to the Conservative Party owing to the Liberals' support of the temperance movement and their proposal to introduce a Local Veto Bill giving local authorities the right to determine opening hours and to institute local prohibition.

Many brewers, apart from M.T. Bass, contributed generously towards the erection of fine public buildings. John Marston helped towards the construction of Horninglow Church in 1864, John Gretton donated nearly £20,000 for the building and endowment of Winshill Church, Sir W.A.H. Bass provided £30,000 for All Saints Church in 1903 and Lord Burton gave the parish of St. Chad's its very fine church in 1910. These and many other public buildings, many of which are still in use to-day, were provided out of brewery profits. Allsopp's Minute Books for the period show that requests from charities, sports clubs, social clubs and many other organisations for financial assistance generally received a sympathetic hearing, particularly if Bass & Co. had already contributed.

Employees of the leading breweries enjoyed working conditions and social services superior to those of many other industrial workers of the period. Despite their heavy burden of political, social and business commitments, men such as M.T. Bass, H. Allsopp and W.H. Worthington retained a genuine personal interest in the welfare of their employees. In 1865 old school buildings in Brook Street were leased by Allsopp's as a social club for their manual workers and £250 provided for improvements to the premises.[74] By 1887 the firm's employees had the use of a free library, a sick and funeral club, a cricket ground and a bowling green. Most of the breweries organised free Christmas dinners and parties for their workers and also ran annual excursions to London or coastal resorts; on 20 July 1865, for example, Salt's employees left Burton by special train at 4.30 a.m. on a trip to the Crystal Palace,[75] while Allsopp's workers shortly afterwards spent a day in Llandudno.

For their own part, the leaders of local industry invested part of their wealth in estates outside the town. Henry Allsopp left his town house in Horninglow Street around 1850 to live at Foremark Hall and later, as Lord Hindlip, at Doveridge Hall. John Gretton moved from High Street to Bladon House and then to Drakelow Hall with its deer park and ornamental gardens. H.A. Bass moved to Byrkley Lodge, M.T. Bass to Rangemore Hall, G.H. Allsopp to Foston Hall, J. Eadie to Barrow Hall, R. Ratcliff to Newton Park and W.C. Salt to Willington Hall. The houses were tastefully furnished with valuable antiques and their grounds laid out by some of the country's most eminent landscape gardeners. They symbolised the prosperity of Burton's breweries and the ambitions of the men who directed them.

Although extreme industrial specialisation had its problems and dangers, as William Molyneux was quick to point out,[76] the period from 1860–1900 was one of enormous optimism, confidence and prosperity for most Burtonians. Fortunately, their staple industry was highly stable in that it was supported by a buoyant consumer demand and localised by its high capital investment and its dependence upon a skilled labour force and an almost unique water supply. Nevertheless, the need to diversify became increasingly apparent and, ironically, the brewing industry itself began to provide the answer by developing ancillary trades, such as the manufacture of brewery equipment and the processing of brewery bi-products. Engineering firms developed in response to local demand for brewing utensils, refrigerators, steam engines and other brewery equipment, eventually catering for national and even international markets. Although the leading breweries continued to produce most of their own malt and casks, a number of specialist malting and coopering firms were established in the town, mainly with a view to supplying the smaller breweries. By 1900 there were four of the former and six of the latter in operation. The oldest and most important member of the group was the firm of Lewis and George Meakin who owned the Crown Maltings in Kimmersitch Street. The first block of malthouses, with a capacity of 290 quarters, was built in 1875, three years after the sale of Meakin's London and Burton Brewery in Abbey Street to Charrington & Co. A second block was added in 1882 and by 1887 the firm was employing three managers, six foremen and seventy maltmen.[77] The first malt-roasting firm, that of Richards & Co. of Horninglow Road, was established in 1897 in order to supply breweries with coloured malts for particular types of beer. In addition, firms using brewery bi-products, such as malt culms, spent hops and yeast, were established for the manufacture of animal feeding-stuffs and other products. By 1910 there were three such firms in the town: English Grains Ltd. of Derby Road (founded in 1892), Marmite Food Extract Co. Ltd. of Cross Street and Oxford's Patent Ltd. of Fleet Street.[78]

As the 19th century drew to a close the brewing industry itself began to experience difficulties that eventually resulted in fundamental changes within the structure of the industry. The increasing scarcity and cost of retail outlets, which caused Allsopp's so much embarrassment, has already been discussed.[79] Added to this problem was a steady decline in national beer sales, from 32 million s.b. in 1890 to 13 million s.b. per annum during the 1914–18 period, and an equally steady increase in the cost of brewery premises and equipment. As a result of these difficulties the processes of amalgamation, closure and take-over accelerated, reducing the number of brewing firms in the town to 21 by 1900 and 17 by 1911. Thomas Salt & Co. Ltd. were forced into voluntary liquidation in 1906, while the Burton Brewery Co., after ten lean years, was absorbed by Worthington & Co. Ltd. in 1914. Although the great investment in plant and equipment helped to bind the industry to its traditional centre, the town's Commercial Development Committee, set-up in 1907, was right to press for new industries. Despite the upsurge in beer sales after 1918, closures and amalgamations continued, culminating in the unions of Bass's and Worthington's in 1927 and of Ind, Coope's and Allsopp's in 1934. By 1950 the number of brewing firms in the town had declined to a mere four. Employment in the industry had been less seriously affected but subsequent technological developments, in the shape of mechanisation of many brewing and malting processes and the replacement of wooden casks by metal canisters, have eroded the industry to the extent that it now employs less than 15 per cent of the town's working population.

Although the history of Burton's brewing industry is divisible into many phases, according to its scale and organisation, three distinct periods can be identified; firstly, the pre-1740 period, when the industry was largely confined to small brewhouses that catered mainly for limited local markets; secondly, the 1740–1840 period, during which there was a marked increase in the scale of production, with external markets particularly in mind, thirdly, the post-1840 period in which access to national markets allowed large-scale production methods to be used. Until the present century the availability of a prolific water supply with ideal properties was the most important locational factor responsible for the presence of the brewing industry in Burton. Economic factors have, however, been largely responsible for determining the scale of the industry at any particular point in time. The coming of river navigation and canal and rail transport provided increased opportunities whereby the latent potential of the industry could be realised. This was inevitable in an industry in which transport costs in relation both to raw materials and finished products were always high.

References

1. A.R., S.A.L.B., Allsopp to John Hutchinson in Altona, 23 Apr. 1808.
2. Ibid, S.A. to Arthur Heywood of Liverpool, 13 Apr. 1808.
3. Ibid, S.A. to W. Lawton of Manchester, 7 Nov. 1808.
4. Ibid, S.A. to W. Lester, Poulterers' Arms, Cheapside, London, 28 Nov. 1808.
5. Ibid, S.A. to Thomas Barmby of Hull, 29 July 1809.
6. Ibid, Day Book, 1811–13.
7. Ibid, Ledger, 1822–6.
8. J.S. Bushnan, op. cit., p. 106.
9. P. Mathias, op. cit., pp. 189–90.
10. J.S. Bushnan, op. cit., p. 109. W. Molyneux, op. cit., p. 230.
11. John Bell, '*A Comparative View of the External Commerce of Bengal*', (1832–3), p. 14.
12. W. Molyneux, op. cit., p. 230.
13. Piggott & Co.'s '*Commercial Directory*', (1822).
14. D.M., 23 Mar. & 1 June 1815.
15. B.W.D., 25 Apr. 1812 & 5 July 1819.
16. Ibid, 18 Nov. 1830.
17. B.L.T.R., 1800–35. A. Barnard, op. cit., vol. 2, p. 112.
18. D.M., 2 & 16 Jan. 1806.
19. W. White, '*History, Gazetteer and Directory of Staffordshire*', (1834).

20. Parsons & Bradshaw, '*Directory of Staffordshire*', (1818). P.D., 1 Jan. 1829.

21. B.W.D., 28 July 1820. M.T.E.D., 10 Nov. 1834, 24 Nov. 1845 & 21 June 1849.

22. See Appendices. '*Burton Weekly News*', 8 Feb. & 18 July 1856.

23. D.M., 17 Mar. 1841. B.W.D., 11 Mar. 1844 & 27 Dec. 1861. B.P.C. Rate Book, 1851–2.

24. W. Molyneux, op. cit., p. 238. M.T.E.D., 25 Mar. 1848 & 21 June 1849.

25. S. Bagshaw, '*History, Gazetteer and Directory of Derbyshire*' (1846). *Burton Weekly News,* 2 June 1865. Burton upon Trent Commissioners' Map, 1855. M.T.E.D., 24 Nov. 1845.

26 W. Molyneux, op. cit., pp. 252–3. '*Burton-on-Trent Times*', 1 May, 17 Apr. & 6 Nov. 1858.

27. A. Barnard, op. cit., vol. 2, p. 118.

28. H. Lloyd Hind, '*Brewing Science and Practice*', (1938–40), vol. 1, paras 333 & 339.

29. B.D., 1863–1900.

30. M.T.E.D., 1888–1905.

31. A. Barnard, op. cit., vol. 1, pp. 56–101.

32. B.W.D., 2 Apr. 1842 & 30 July 1845.

33. A. Barnard, op. cit., vol. 1, pp. 42, 49, 73 & 88. *Burton Weekly News,* 24 Mar. 1865.

34. A.R., Inventory of Brewery Premises and Equipment, 1846. W. Molyneux, op. cit., p. 253. A. Barnard, op. cit., vol. 1. p. 101.

35. A.R. Executive Committee Minutes, 14 Nov. 1865, 9 Jan. 1866 and 11 Jan. 1876.

36. Ibid. Directors' Minute Book and Prospectus, 1887.

37. Ibid, Executive Committee Minutes, 1866–79.

38. A. Barnard, op. cit., vol. 1, pp. 121–69.

39. A.R., Executive Committee Minutes, 3 Jan. 1888.

40. J. Vaizey, '*The Brewing Industry, 1886–1951*', p. 11.

41. A.R., Register of Tied Houses, c. 1915.

42. See Appendices.

43. M. Combrune, '*The Theory and Practice of Brewing*', (1762), p. 80.

44. W. Black, 'Practical Treatise on Brewing' (1835).

45. W. Molyneux, op. cit., p. 232.

46. J. Bell, op. cit., p. 23.

47. H.T. Brown, '*Reminiscences of Fifty Years' Experience in the Application of Scientific Methods to Brewing*' Journal of the Institute of Brewing (J.I.B.), (1916), p. 284.

48. A.R., Executive Committee Minutes, 13 June & 29 Aug. 1865.

49. *Burton Weekly News,* 10 Mar. 1865.

50. H.D. O'Sullivan, 'The Life and Works of C. O'Sullivan' (1934), p. 53; English Patent No. 3909, 12 Nov. 1874.

51. Ibid, p. 55.

52. J.I.B., (1916), op. cit., pp. 285–6.

53. J.I.B., (1899), p. 338. H.T. Brown, 'A Grain of Barley', T.B.N.H.A.S., vol. 1, (1899), pp. 86–113. H. Lloyd Hind, op. cit., vol. 2, para 502.

54. *Supplement to the Brewers Journal and Hop and Malt Trades Review,* 20

Mar. 1876, p. 1. E.M. Sigsworth, 'Science and the Brewing Industry, 1850–1900'; Economic History Review, vol. 17, (1964–5).

55. J.I.B., (1916), p. 349.

56. W.T. Sykes, 'The Indebtedness of the Brewer to Mr. Pasteur'; J.I.B., (1895).

57. J.I.B., (1916), p. 268.

58. A.R., Inventory of Brewery Premises and Equipment, 1846.

59. A. Barnard, op. cit., vol. 1, pp. 424–7.

60. '*Transactions of the Laboratory Club*', vol. 1, (1889).

61. Bass & Co. 'Register of Properties'.

62. Supra, c.5.p.

63. A.R., Executive Committee Minutes, 1888–1900.

64. J. Vaizey, op. cit., p. 10.

65. *Burton Weekly News*, 9 Nov. 1860.

66. see figures.

67. Bass-Worthington Records; 'Eastern Counties Journals for the engagement of men'.

68. A vivid account of the lives of these workers is given by G. Ewart Evans in his recent book, '*Where Beards Wag All*', (1970).

69. '*Explorations in Entrepreneurial History*', vol. 5, (1953), p. 211.

70. J. Ingamells, '*Some Staffordshire Worthies*', pp. 134–44.

71. P.S. Bagwell, '*The Railwaymen. The History of the National Union of Railwaymen*', pp. 47–67.

72. J. Bickerdyke, 'The Curiosities of Ale and Beer', (1889), p. 344.

73. '*The Times*', 1 May 1884.

74. A.R. Executive Committee Minutes, 13 June 1865.

75. *Burton Weekly News*, 21 July 1865.

76. W. Molyneux, op. cit., p. 254.

77. A. Barnard, op. cit., vol. 1, pp. 451–9.

78. Burton-on-Trent Directory, 1911.

79. Supra, c.5.p.

VI

THE IRON-WORKING, HARDWARE AND ENGINEERING INDUSTRIES

Lack of the requisite raw materials has prevented Burton-on-Trent from ever becoming an outstanding centre for metallurgical industries. Nevertheless, during the 18th century it became significant for the distribution of imported bar iron and for the manufacture of iron bars, plates and rods, screws, nails, hoops, spades and other items of hardware. This development can be attributed to the establishment of Burton as the head of the Trent Navigation, the influence of the Birmingham-South Staffordshire area to the south-west, with its great metal-working industries, the local demand for hardware products, particularly from the brewing industry, and the availability of valuable water-power sites.

In promoting the Trent Navigation scheme during the 1690's the Pagets and their agents may, to some extent, have had the iron trade and industry in mind. For over a century they had been concerned with iron production on their estates in the Cannock-Rugeley area and were familiar with both the technical and the commercial aspects of the indsutry.[1] Through their connections with hardware merchants and workers in Birmingham and South Staffordshire they must have been aware of the supreme national importance of the region in iron production and metal-working. By the early 18th century the Midland counties of Staffordshire, Shropshire, Worcestershire and Warwickshire were responsible for approximately 27 per cent of the pig iron and 45 per cent of the forge iron production of the United Kingdom.[2] Moreover, they contained an army of craftsmen who manufactured nails, screws, locks, buckles, axes, spades and many other items of hardware for sale to customers throughout the United Kingdom and overseas. Owing to shortages of certain raw materials, such as charcoal, the region was incapable of producing sufficient quantities of pig iron and forge iron, with the result that both forge-owners and hardware workers were obliged to obtain supplies from other areas. Apart from this regional shortage, there was also a national deficiency which necessitated an annual import of approximately 18,000 tons of bar iron between 1710 and 1720, mainly from Swedish suppliers. The extension of the Trent Navigation to Burton in 1712 thus placed the town in an ideal position for handling this considerable traffic in iron.

The port of Hull provided a convenient point of entry for Swedish and Russian iron destined for Midland and Yorkshire forges. Richard and Joseph Sykes, the main iron importers in Hull, were in close contact with ironmasters in Sheffield and South Staffordshire and were able to take advantage of the improved river navigations.[3] Leonard Fosbrooke of Shardlow, who, together with George Hayne of Burton, controlled the Trent Navigation between Burton and Wilden Ferry, indulged in the import and transportation of Baltic iron to Burton Wharf, where it was collected by Birmingham carriers. Between 20 November and 23 December 1719, for example, nearly 119 tons of 'Sweeds iron', shipped in the 'Hannover' from Gavle, were unloaded at Hull on his behalf.[4] Documentary evidence linking this iron trade with Burton is provided by the day-book of an unknown carrier who transported a variety of goods over a wide area of the Midlands.[5] On 22 January, 1722 he enquired at Mr. Wells of Birmingham about 119 bars of iron that had been purchased from Mr. Sykes of Hull for Thomas Machin of Birmingham, while on 9 July, 1723 he bought 100 bars of iron from Mr. Leonard Fosbrooke at Burton for £17. 10s. Burton ironmongers and merchants, such as Henry Hogg, Samuel Marston, James Orme and Samuel and Thomas Seal, were also involved in the iron trade and it is probable that the early exporting brewers also participated. Daniel Defoe, who travelled through the East Midlands during the early 1720's, commented on the large traffic in bar iron and hardware that passed up and down the Trent at this time.[6] Burton Wharf thus provided a vital link in part of a complex system whereby the Birmingham area's enormous appetite for bar iron could be satisfied.

It was perhaps inevitable that the passage of large quantities of iron through the town would eventually give rise to some form of iron-working industry in Burton. Even more pertinent was the rapidly increasing scarcity of power sites and fuel in the Birmingham-South Staffordshire area. Water power was needed to operate bellows in furnaces, hammers and rollers in forges and circular cutters in slitting mills for iron rod production. During the 17th century many mills, formerly used for grinding corn or fulling cloth, had been converted for the above purposes, particularly along the Tame and Stour valleys. By 1717 there were at least 46 forges in the West Midlands, representing around 40 per cent of the national total, and by 1735 there were at least 15 forges and six slitting mills in Staffordshire alone.[7] Burton, with its ideal power sites along the Trent and the ability to supply large quantities of charcoal from its surrounding woodlands, lay under 30 miles from the centre of Birmingham and thus came within its sphere of influence.

In 1719 it was decided to convert an old fulling mill on a small island in the River Trent below Burton Bridge into a forge. Although the premises were initially leased by Lord Paget to George Hayne, the proprietor of the Navigation, and to William Woodcock, the Curate of Burton, the conversion was carried out by Thomas Seal, a Burton ironmonger. In August 1721 the new works, consisting of 'a Forge for hammering and plating of Iron', were re-let to Seal at an annual rent of £18.[8] Four years later a scheme to convert a cornmill at Clay Mills into a forge and to erect a slitting mill close to Burton Forge was proposed but defeated on the grounds that it would—

> 'so far interfere with the iron trade in general as to damage if not totally destroy the forge at Bromley and the Slitting Mills at Rudgeley, for which the Lord Paget has a Rent of £100 per annum'.[9]

Thomas and Samuel Seal retained full control of Burton Forge until 1733, when they were declared bankrupts and forced to dispose of their estates in Burton, Horninglow, Egginton and Gresley.[10] Although they continued to live and work at the forge, the business was subsequently acquired by Sampson Lloyd, an important iron-master of Birmingham, who proceeded to use the works 'for Forging and Boring Gun barrels, making of Thimbles etc.'[11]

Sampson Lloyd, a member of an influential Quaker family, had inherited a number of ironworks and other properties in the Birmingham area from his father in 1724.[12] Through his intimate knowledge of the technical and commercial aspects of the iron industry he was quick to recognise the potential of Burton Forge, with its ready supply of materials and power. Little information is available about the works during the early years of Lloyd ownership. Around 1747 it was entirely concerned with forging and plating but its activities were hindered by shortage of water during periods of dry weather, when the Navigation Company, who owned a lock adjoining the forge yard, drew off large quantitites of water to assist the passage of their boats along the river.[13] Although the forge was omitted from the Hulme Lists of 1736 and 1750, there is no reason for supposing that its operation was discontinued during this period and it is likely that its main purpose was to forge plates both for use by local hardware manufacturers and for despatch to the Lloyds' slitting mill in Birmingham.

The development of iron trading and forging in Burton during the first half of the 18th century was accompanied by the emergence of a small hardware industry. By 1740 Thomas and Francis Thornewill of Burton had established a small business on the south side of New Street at which they manufactured spades and other edge-tools.[14] In 1746 Thomas secured the use of an adjoining freehold property through his marriage to Elizabeth Astle, the widow of a wealthy feltmaker and hatter.[15] As a result of further additions to their premises and a corresponding increase in business the Thornewills next turned to iron forging. In 1753 Thomas Thornewill approached William Wyatt, the Earl of Uxbridge's steward, for permission to use Clay Mill which had been abandoned as a corn mill around 1730. It lay three miles to the north of Burton and derived its power from the River Dove. According to Wyatt, there was—

> 'nothing of any value remaining except the building and those in a very shattered and ruinous condition. I had a person with me to take the place in the conditions its now in for a Blade Mill that is a Mill for Grinding all sorts of large Edge Tools and Iron plates and for the plating of Iron'.[16]

In 1755, after satisfying himself that the scheme would not reduce the profits of his ironworks at Rugeley, the Earl of Uxbridge agreed to lease Clay Mill to Thornewill at an annual rent of ten guineas. During the same year Thornewill spent over £300 on repairs to the building and on its conversion into 'a plating Forge for hammering and plating of Iron into thin plates'.[17] Apart from 'grinding tools, its main purpose was to provide the works in Burton with a steady supply of iron plate'.

In the absence of any detailed records it must be assumed that the two Burton forges were typical of the period and would have contained a 'finery' in which pig iron was hammered into blooms by water-driven tilt hammers, weighing around 6 cwts. each, and a 'chafery' in which the blooms were reheated and beaten into bars and plates. Forges of this type normally employed two men as finers and hammermen and an apprentice to assist them; they could process up to 300 tons of iron per annum. Large quantities of charcoal were required in the 'finery' but coal could be used in the 'chafery'.[18] In comparison with later works the Burton forges were thus extremely small but they proceeded, nevertheless, to play a significant part in the evolution of the local hardware industry for the remainder of the century.

The expiry of the navigation and mill leases, following the deaths of Henry Hayne in 1758 and Samuel Seal in 1762 enabled the Lloyds to secure a much greater measure of control over Burton Forge and the water rights relating to it. In anticipation of this they spent almost £200 on improvements to the forge during the summer of 1761 and planned to invest a further £100 on the premises during the following year. Between 1762 and 1766 a syndicate, which included Sampson, Nehemiah and Charles Lloyd, systematically acquired the leases of the navigation, forge, mills, fisheries and other related properties.[19] These transactions included the lease of 'that Iron Work ... of Burton Forge, being a forge for making, manufacturing and plating of iron', for a fine of £450 and an annual rent of £9.[20] The securing of the navigation and mill leases at the same time ensured that the forge would receive an adequate supply of water at all times. From 1762 until the early years of the 19th century the Lloyds continued to operate Burton Forge as part of a group of Midland ironworks which included furnaces at Perry Barr and Melbourne, forges at Burton, Powick and Hints and a slitting mill at Digbeth. They manufactured plates, bars, rods and hoops for a wide range of hardware producers and other customers. Amongst the latter was the notable firm of Boulton & Watt of Birmingham to whom the Lloyds sold iron plates for engine construction—

> 'We had the satisfaction of supplying B. & W. with iron for several years when we were concerned in the Iron Trade in Birmingham and this iron was made at our Forge at Burton-on-Trent which we continue to work and we should be glad to be favoured with part of your orders'.[21]

In 1791 the forge was described simply as a works for 'converting bloom and scrap iron into bars, the principal manager of which is Mr. James Lynam'.[22]

It was relatively easy to convey bulky materials to and from the forge, initially via the Trent Navigation but after 1770 via the Trent & Mersey and Bond End canals. English pig iron was obtained not only from Midland furnaces but from as far afield as Cumberland; when Charles Lloyd visited the forge in June 1774, 70 tons of Seaton pigs had recently arrived from Cumberland and a further delivery was expected.[23] Sable iron from Sweden and Russia, imported through

Hull, was also regularly used. The production of one ton of bar iron generally required the use of 24 cwts. of charcoal which, as previously noted, was a scarce commodity in well established iron districts. In this respect the close association between the Lloyds and William Wyatt proved highly advantageous, for, apart from acting as Steward to the Earl of Uxbridge at Burton, Wyatt was one of the leading timber merchants in the area. Between 1764 and 1774 he organised the clearance of extensive woodlands, including over 2,000 oak trees, on estates at Hints, Catton, Kedleston, Gresley and Seany Park.[24] Accounts for the Manors of Burton and Burton Extra for the same period indicate substantial sales of timber and cordwood; during the year commencing Michaelmas 1770, when sales totalled £1,500, the purchases of Messrs. Lloyds and Thornewill amounted to £920.[25] Although charcoal was often displaced by coal after 1790, the Lloyds were still using charcoal in their forges as late as 1804—

> 'Our last process in refining our iron is by charcoal—it is all stamped under the hammer then broken and piled on cakes for the air furnace and afterwards drawn under the hammer so that our iron must have a much stronger body than when it is rolled into cakes and bars and as we often use a quantity of cast and scrap iron to mix with the stamped iron this adds to its toughness.'[26]

Coal for use in the 'chafery' was readily available from collieries at Newhall and Swadlincote, three miles to the south-east of the forge.

No precise records are available concerning the output of Burton Forge during this period. In May 1774 it produced 22 tons of blooms which suggests an annual output of 2–300 tons. In 1798, by which time the capacity of the forge may have been greater, Charles Lloyd informed Samuel Bamford, the forge manager, that an annual output of 500 tons was desirable.[27] An average annual output of around 300 tons of bars, plates and hoops would therefore seem likely, for which approximately 450 tons of pig iron and scrap, 400 tons of charcoal and 200 tons of coal would have been required. Pig, scrap and finished bars and plates were generally carried by river and canal boats and to facilitate this the Burton Boat Company operated three 33 ton barges between Burton Forge and Shobnall Wharf. In order to avoid shortages of raw materials large stocks were kept at the forge. In February 1795 this had unfortunate consequences, for an unusually severe flood swept away several hundred pounds worth of charcoal from the forge yard and the Lloyds had to employ men to recover it from the river and the surrounding meadows at the rate of 4d. per bushel.[28]

After 1780 the rapid displacement of charcoal by coal in the smelting and refining of iron and the application of steam power to rotary motion for use in forges and rolling and slitting mills resulted in profound locational changes within the iron industry.[29] Freed from its dependence upon water power and charcoal, the industry became increasingly concentrated in large integrated works located on coalfields; by 1812 there were ten such ironworks in the Birmingham area, each of which had cost over £50,000 to establish. Inevitably, outlying concerns such as Burton Forge, whose success had depended largely upon water power and local charcoal, were generally abandoned. In 1804 Burton Forge was still a thriving works, producing 'bars of prime quality at £21 per ton or good best bars at £20 per ton' as well as large quantities of hoops for local brewers. By 1809, however, the Lloyds, eager to concentrate their activities into the Birmingham and South Staffordshire area, were making arrangements to close the forge. Two years later it had fallen into disuse and in August 1812 Samuel and Charles Lloyd agreed to pay the Earl of Uxbridge £800 for the right to remove all 'wheels cast iron and machinery' and to convert the premises, if they wished, into a corn mill, providing the products were not sold within a radius of ten miles.[30] The premises were in fact converted for use as a cotton mill by Peel & Co. in 1814. Apart from retaining a number of properties in the town, the Lloyds' association with Burton came to an end.

Throughout the 18th century Burton continued to function as an important centre for the distribution of imported bar iron. In their capacity of general merchants, the Burton brewers acted as intermediaries between the Baltic exporters and the iron and hardware manufacturers and merchants of South Staffordshire. Henry Evans, Samuel and Willaim Sketchley, William Worthington and Benjamin and John Walker Wilson were all regular importers of Swedish and Russian iron bars. Between 1 September and 16 November 1763 Samuel Sketchley imported 52 tons of Russian iron via Hull, including 1,560 bars in the 'Henry' from St. Petersburg.[31] John Walker Wilson regularly received consignments of bars, valued at around £500, from Shairps, Maude & Co. of St. Petersburg, disposing of them to iron merchants and manufacturers, particularly at Wolverhampton and Birmingham. William Whitehouse, a West Bromwich nail-ironmonger, speaking about the iron trade in 1812, said,

> 'My father, who is still living (upwards of eighty years of age) bought the foreign bars at Burton upon Trent, before the Birmingham Canal was made [1770], and brought them by land carriage to Birmingham; they were manufactured into wrought iron at water mills, before the steam works were erected.'[32]

Burton must have been deprived of a certain amount of its iron trade when the Trent & Mersey and Birmingham Canals, which provided a direct waterway between Hull and Birmingham, opened in 1770. Far more damaging, however, was the increased use of coke for smelting and the rapid application of steam power in ironworks, which brought about a substantial rise in English pig iron output from 68,300 tons in 1788 to 258,200 tons in 1806. This factor, together with successive increases in the duty on imported bar iron between 1796 and 1798, deteriorating Anglo-Russian relations and the adverse influence of the war with France upon Baltic trade, discouraged iron imports. Whereas in 1786 iron imports from Sweden and Russia had amounted to 17,000 and 26,000 tons respectively, by 1804 total British iron imports had fallen to 22,000 tons.[33] In 1806 the Napoleonic blockade abruptly terminated an already dying trade and with it ended Burton's role as an iron-distributing centre.

Meanwhile, the Thornewills had considerably expanded their iron forging and spade making business. In 1760 they secured the freehold of their New Street premises for £140 and in 1764 they were able to negotiate a new sixty-year lease on Clay Mills Forge for a fine of £200.[34] By the early 1770's they had added rolling and slitting mills to the forge and built a warehouse on the bank of the nearby Trent & Mersey Canal. The latter was used for the storage of iron bars purchased from Hull merchants and Burton brewers. Wray & Hollingsworth of Hull and John Walker Wilson of Burton were both regular suppliers, the latter providing 93 tons of Russian iron between 1775–8 at a cost of £1,380.[35] Francis Thornewill managed Clay Mills Ironworks, assisted by a group of approximately ten forgemen, rollers and slitters, while Thomas ran the New Street Spadeworks, with the aid of fifteen workers. Apart from spades, small quantities of axes, scythes, hoops and nails were produced, mainly for sale to local brewers, farmers and builders. Regular consignments of spades were sent by road to London and it is likely that others went by canal and river to Hull for export; during the early 1760's William Bass, a Burton carrier, transported over 4,000 spades to London each year on behalf of the Thornewills.[36] The latter also supplied iron rods to the nearby screw manufactory and to domestic nailers and screw-makers.

The success of the Thornewills' business was indicated by their growing importance as local property-owners and by their enhanced social status. During the 1790's Francis held the offices of town constable, master and feoffee and had become a relatively wealthy man by the time of his death in 1807.[37] In the same year his nephew Thomas, who had inherited a share in the business in 1786 when his father, Thomas, had died, purchased the entire lands and premises at Clay Mills from the Earl of Uxbridge for £3,220. They included 'Cliffcroft', an estate of seven acres containing Dove Cliff House, built around 1790, with its 'gardens, plantations and pleasure grounds', Clay Mills Forge, with 'all those iron works and all the slitting mills, forges, warehouses, buildings and works', and a warehouse and tenement near to the canal.[38] Having secured control of the works he proceeded to add 'a foundry and iron-casting-house' and also to lease another forge at Wichnor.[39] Unlike Burton Forge, the Clay Mills Ironworks continued to flourish and this was undoubtedly due to the close association between Thornewill's and the Burton hardware manufacturers.

A branch of the hardware industry that was particularly important in Burton during the second half of the 18th century was screw manufacture. This may have been initiated by Samuel Seal, the lessee of Burton Forge, but by 1760 the business was being carried on by the son-in-law of William Wyatt in premises on the west side of High Street.[40] The techniques of manufacture at this time were highly laborious, and involved the forging of a screw head, followed by the cutting of the thread either by filing or by the use of dies operated by a spindle and winch.[41] Shortly after 1760 a patent for 'cutting screws of iron called wood screws' was granted to Job Wyatt of Tatenhill and William Wyatt of Burton. A few years later William and his brother Benjamin acquired an old corn mill on a small stream at Tatenhill, three miles to the south-west of Burton, and spent £1,100 on its conversion and on the installation of lathes, in order to apply the patent.[42] John Wyatt, another member of the talented Lichfield family, held a considerable reputation as a skillfull inventor of mechanical gadgets and may well have been involved in the invention of the screw-cutting lathe. Unfortunately, the Wyatts' attempts to operate the mill were largely unsuccessful and they soon leased the works to Messrs. Shorthose, Wood & Co., who carried out a number of modifications.

William Shorthose, a carpenter, George Wood, a baker, Philip Port, a feltmaker and hatter, and William Smith, a gardener, all of Burton, embarked on the screw-making business around 1765, when they opened a small manufactory on land between New Street and Pinfold Lane. They obtained iron rods and plates from the nearby Thornewill works and used them for forging screw blanks and patten rings. By perfecting the screw-cutting lathe, they operated Tatenhill Screw Mill successfully, producing 700 gross of screws per week with the help of 30 employees. When they purchased it from William Wyatt's executors in 1779 it was described as—

> 'a new erected house, with proper conveniences, at Tatenhill near Burton upon Trent aforesaid, and an Overshoot Mill in good repair, used for the manufacturing of wood screws by lathes or engines, with the mill pool about 2 acres, 2 roods, now lett at £42 per annum'.[43]

In 1786 Shorthose, Wood & Co. abandoned the mill, probably because of the inadequacy of the water supply in summer and later sold it to James Fox of Derby who used it for the manufacture of 'clock and watch engines, fluting engines for cotton rollers' and a very wide range of other metal articles.[44] At the same time they acquired a disused corn mill at Hartshorne, four miles to the east of Burton; it lay over a mile below the source of a brook and was supplied with a steady flow of water from two ponds. The mill was powered by a single water-wheel which operated 36 lathes, each capable of cutting eight or nine screws per minute.[45] In the late 1790's the mill employed 59 workers who were able to produce 1,200 gross of screws per week to the value of approximately £100.

The Screw Manufactory in Burton formed the headquarters of the business. Its main purpose was the forging of screw blanks and the production of patten rings, for which it required around £500 worth of iron wire per annum. Adjoining the works was a large warehouse in which 4,000 gross of screws could be stored ready for despatch to Hull, London and Liverpool.[46] It is likely that many consignments were exported to North America and the Continent along with numerous other items of hardware from Midland manufacturers.[47] Shorthose, Wood & Co. employed 30 men as screw forgers and patten ring makers at their manufactory. They lived in small tenements in New Street, Pinfold Lane and Bond End and in Screw Yard and Wood Yard which lay close to the works. The industry was probably semi-domestic in character, with whole families involved in a range of simple tasks; indeed, some screws may still have been made by the old method of hand-filing. By the early 19th century Shorthose, Wood & Co. had around 100 workers in their employ, four-fifths of whom were engaged in screw production and the remainder in the making of patten rings. William Shorthose, the leading partner, died in 1809, leaving properties in Burton, Hartshorne and Anslow and interest on loans totalling £500 to his wife Katherine and his son Stephen.[48]

During the same period at least fifteen families in the New Street-Pinfold Lane-Bond End district of the town were engaged in nail-making as a domestic industry. It is likely that the Thornewill Works supplied them with iron rods and may also have dealt with the collection and marketing of the finished products. Although South Staffordshire was very much the home of the nail industry at this time, most Midland towns contained groups of domestic nailers. The simple but arduous work of hammering and filing rods was particularly attractive to unskilled workers from the depressed small tenant farmer class. For a 72-hour week an adult male nailer could earn up to 16s., while women usually earned 6–8s. and children 3–5s.[49]

It is thus clear that during the second half of the 18th century Burton developed as a notable centre for iron-working and distribution and hardware manufacture. By the end of the century approximately 200 men in the town and the surrounding districts were employed in iron forging, rolling and slitting, spademaking, screw forging and milling, patten ring making, nailing and a variety of minor related tasks. Altogether, as many as 500 people may have been dependent upon this group of trades.

During the following century all branches of iron-working and hardware manufacture were profoundly affected by the progressive application of steam power and various forms of mechanisation. The use of increasingly elaborate and costly premises and equipment tended to bring about a high degree of industrial concentration. Large integrated factories began to displace collections of small workshops and domestic concerns, while areas especially suited to particular branches of manufacture expanded at the expense of outlying districts. The concentration thus possessed both organisational and spatial implications. In the iron and hardware industries the depression that followed the end of the war in France in 1815 tended to accelerate these processes by eliminating the least efficient elements.

The termination of the iron trade through Burton and the closure of Burton Forge in 1810 were two local manifestations of the approaching changes. As will be seen later in the chapter, the

Thornewills were able to overcome many problems by continually adapting their business to meet changing demand. Even Clay Mills Ironworks continued to operate, no doubt through its close association with the New Street Works. When Baltic iron was no longer available and local charcoal lost its importance, the Thornewills merely turned to Derbyshire and South Staffordshire for supplies of pig iron and coal. Otherwise, apart from the addition of a foundry and casting house, previously mentioned, the works continued to operate very much as before. In 1851 the works employed 25 men and 5 boys, most of whom lived in nearby cottages.[50] Many were members of the Corradine, Ashforth and Weaver families who had been there for at least eighty years. The proprietor, Edward Thornewill of Dove Cliff House, had inherited the works from his father in 1843. Although he sold the house in 1881, the works continued to be operated by the Thornewill family until the early 1920's, when it was sold to the Clay Mills Iron Works Co. Ltd.

The Burton and Hartshorne screw works of Shorthose, Wood & Co. were less successful in coping with technological developments. The application of steam power to screw manufacture, first used in Birmingham in 1819, soon rendered water-powered mills obsolete. Hartshorne Mill was still being used by 'Smith, Port, Wood & Co.' in 1830 but was abandoned shortly afterwards, possibly in favour of steam-operated machines at the works in Burton. In 1841 William Wood and Henry Port, the surviving partners, were still employing at least 21 screw forgers and six patten ring makers in Burton.[51] Three years later, however, after attempting to use one of the Upper Mills at Burton for screw making, they were declared bankrupt and their properties in New Street and Pinfold Lane sold to Thornewill & Co. and Worthington & Co. They were clearly the victims of a process whereby an increasing proportion of the industry was falling into the hands of a number of large Birmingham manufacturers who were employing mass-production methods. This process was accelerated after 1850 as a result of the introduction of John Nettlefold's 'worming' machines and a variety of self-acting machinery which allowed the whole process to become automatic.[52] Large-scale production allied to automation substantially reduced both the price of screws and employment opportunities. Throughout the Midlands small companies and domestic workers were forced out of business. By 1851 only nine screw forgers were continuing to work in Burton, while ten years later Samuel Ward, aged 75, of New Street and Edward Roe, aged 49, of Fleet Street were the sole survivors.

The nail industry followed very much the same pattern, with, again, Birmingham manufacturers introducing a wide range of mechanical processes after 1830. During the ensuing years thousands of Midland nailers were forced to abandon their trade and in 1865 the survivors were described as 'a hard-working population amounting to about twenty thousand ... badly fed, badly clothed, and degraded by a system which is a disgrace to England'.[53] In Burton the number of nailers remained fairly constant until the 1840's, 16 being recorded in the 1841 Census, but by 1861 the trade had almost disappeared.

The serious decline of the local screw and nail trades coupled with difficulties in the hardware industry as a whole forced Thornewill & Co. to turn increasingly towards the manufacture of iron castings. Rising demand in many parts of England for a wide range of cast iron products, such as doors, window frames, paving slabs, pipes and columns, had brought about the emergence of a specialist foundry industry during the last quarter of the 18th century. In Derbyshire and Staffordshire many foundries, capable of producing such articles and also superior castings for textile machinery and engine construction, were established during the 1780–1820 period.[54] The earliest known iron-founders in Burton were George Charlesworth (1785) and Thomas Leedham (1790) who were probably employed by Thornewill & Co. After the turn of the century spademakers gradually gave way to founders, moulders and casters as hardware manufacture was displaced by foundry work. Trade directories for 1818, 1834, and 1846 showed the firm's progression from 'spade manufacturers' to 'spade manufacturers and iron and brass founders' to 'iron and brass founders and steam engine makers'. Although they may have produced engine components since the beginning of the century, it is unlikely that they manufactured complete engines prior to 1840, by which time the industry was well-established throughout the Midlands.

It is likely that Thornewill & Co's. change to foundry work and engine production was to some extent stimulated by the needs of the local mining and brewing industries. The collieries in nearby Derbyshire and Leicestershire had been amongst the earliest to use Newcomen engines for pumping and winding during the first half of the 18th century.[55] Joseph Wilkes, the proprietor of collieries at Measham and Oakthorpe from 1767 to 1805, was a pioneer in the application of steam power and was one of the first to use a Boulton & Watt engine for winding coal.[56] The superior qualities of the Boulton & Watt engines greatly widened the scope of steam power application, so that by the early 19th century steam engines were being used in many industrial establishments not only for pumping, winding and hauling but also for the production of semi-manufactured articles. Between 1839–47 Thornewill & Co. acquired additional land around their New Street Works in order to construct large engine shops. After his uncle's death in 1843, Robert Thornewill devoted considerable energy and capital to this new venture, and in 1849 entered into partnership with John Robson Warham, an engineer from South Shields.[57]

By 1851 'Thornewill and Warham's ironfoundry and engine machine works' in New Street had become a thriving concern with 75 men and 25 boys in its employ.[58] At this time the firm was producing around 12 pumping and winding engines each year, most of which were sold to collieries in Derbyshire, Leicestershire and Warwickshire. It was probably in 1858 that Thornewill & Warham sold their first locomotive to Ibstock Colliery in Leicestershire and they provided the Burton breweries with most of their locomotives between 1860 and 1880.[59] Indicative of the firm's success was the fact that by 1861 its employees had increased to 178—a number exceeded only by the three leading breweries in the town. By 1870 it had acquired a national reputation for steam engine manufacture, supplying firms as far afield as Glasgow, London and South Wales. Encouraged by their success, the firm began to export engines, their first foreign order coming from Taskanna Colliery in Japan. After 1890 overseas orders increased substantially, with Bowes, Scott & Western of London acting as intermediaries. Collieries, cotton mills, gold mines, diamond mines and waterworks in China, Japan, India, Borneo, South Africa, Australia and South America were equipped with winding, pumping and hauling engines from Thornewill & Warham's works. Of the 329 engines traceable in their 'Engine Order Book', 202 were supplied to collieries, 66 to breweries (including 16 locomotives to Burton breweries), 12 to waterworks, 10 each to ironworks and potteries, 6 to engineering works, 5 to sewage works, 4 to railways, 3 each to gasworks and quarries, 2 to lead mines and one each to a building works, brickworks, canal company, flour mill, dock company and woodworks.

Apart from steam engine manufacture the firm also became notable for its constructional engineering. Much of the iron-work used in the large Burton breweries, opened between 1850–90, was supplied and erected by Thornewill & Warham.[60] The construction of the Ferry Bridge across the Trent at Burton in 1889 and the connecting viaduct to Bond End, at a total cost of just over £10,000, was one of the firm's major achievements.

The great success of the firm in mechanical and constructional engineering necessitated substantial extensions to its premises and a re-organisation of its administration. Several adjoining areas of land between New Street and Pinfold Lane were acquired, notably in 1876 and 1880, in order to construct new workshops. In 1868, ten years after the death of Robert Thornewill, a new partnership was formed in which Martha Hammond Thornewill, his widow, John Robson Warham and Robert Thornewill (jun.) held six, five and one-twelfth respectively of the total capital of £44,000.[61] J.R. Warham, whose great skill as an engineer had contributed substantially to the firm's success, died in 1886. Following the death of M.H. Thornewill in 1889, the business passed to her three sons Charles Francis, Arthur and Robert, the latter gaining complete control by 1893. The firm continued to thrive until the time of the First World War when business declined rapidly. In 1919 it went into voluntary liquidation and a new company, known as Thornewill & Warham Ltd., was formed. It survived until 1929 when, after almost two centuries at the New Street Works, the firm was taken-over by S. Briggs & Co. Ltd. of Burton.

In the development of Thornewill's can be seen the evolution of the British iron-working and engineering industries in general. The complete dependence of the firm upon hardware manufacture until 1800, the transition to foundry work and engineering between then and 1850 and the supreme importance of engineering afterwards, were phases through which many businesses passed. By keeping pace with technological change and fluctuations in demand the firm was able to prosper and survive. In one sense a parallel can be drawn between Thornewill's and the long-established breweries in the town. Their growth potential was very much limited by market size which, in turn, depended upon accessibility and the effectiveness of communications. As with the breweries, the opening of the railway to Birmingham and Derby in 1839 and to Leicester in 1849 enabled the firm to expand rapidly by taking advantage of increased opportunities. Unlike the breweries, however, the firm possessed no distinct locational advantages and its success was closely linked to the growth of local brewing and mining industries.

In addition to Thornewill's, a number of other metal-working and engineering firms developed in Burton during the 19th century. Thomas and William Sanders of Lichfield Street were manufacturing 'hydraulic engines' as early as 1818, apart from carrying on a business as plumbers and galziers.[62] In 1851 Samuel Sanders, their successor, owned a copper and brass foundry in Station Street, at which 13 men were employed. Philip Halbard, an ironfounder and son of a Burton locksmith, joined with Edwin Wright, an engineer, to establish the 'Britannia Foundry' in Horninglow Street around 1851.[63] They manufactured stoves, grates and other items of hardware with the aid of 15 employees. Joseph Homer, a brass finisher and ironfounder from Rowley Regis, opened a brass foundry with adjoining 'plumbing, glazing, turning and paint shops' in Station Street during the 1840's and his son was later associated with Pickering Bros. at their Union Foundry, established in Union Street in 1865, and with T.R. Shercliff at a brass, copper and iron works in Stanley Street.

After 1850 the enormous expansion of the brewing industry stimulated the development of many allied engineering businesses. Three of these, S. Briggs & Co., R. Morton & Co., and Buxton & Thornley, became nationally famous for the manufacture of brewing equipment. Samuel Briggs began work as an apprentice around 1865 for Thomas Bindley, who had established a small business as an ironmonger and coppersmith in High Street in 1840. By the early 1870's Briggs had become a partner in the firm and opened the 'Burton Copper Works' in Station Street, at which a wide range of brewery equipment in copper and brass was produced. They sold brewing coppers and many other items to all the leading Burton breweries and gradually extended their sales to other areas. In 1885 the firm, then known as S. Briggs & Co., won a prize medal, awarded for brewing machinery, at the International Inventions Exhibition held in London. By 1890 they had gained recognition as one of the leading firms in the country for the installation of brewery and distillery plant and for the manufacture of brewing coppers, hopbacks, mash-tuns, coolers, fermenting vessels, pumps, and attemperators and many other items of brewery equipment. In 1900 the firm established 'The Burton Copper and Engineering Works' in an abandoned brewery in Moor Street. It became a limited company in 1911 and by 1930 had become the largest engineering business in the town by absorbing Buxton & Thornley, T.R. Shercliff & Co. Ltd. and Thornewill & Warham Ltd.[64]

Buxton & Thornley established their 'Waterloo Works' in Waterloo Street around 1865 in order to manufacture a wide range of iron, copper and brass articles, particularly for use in breweries. Their outstanding products were an 'improved hydraulic hop press' and 'the Burton steam pump', both of which were patented and supplied to national markets. Robert Morton & Co., who established the 'Trent Works' in Derby Street around 1880, gained a world-wide reputation for the manufacture and installation of brewery equipment; their patent horizontal and vertical refrigerators were particularly successful.

Apart from the leading four, many other engineering concerns thrived in Burton during the second half of the 19th century. A large proportion of these were small in size and of short duration but a few, such as A. Elson & Co. of Horninglow Street, Orton & Son of Princess Street and Homer & Shercliff of Stanley Street, eventually became notable firms. The tendency for engineering industries to develop in response to local basic industries is well illustrated by the fact that only Thornewill & Warham's gained a national reputation for products other than brewery equipment. Employment in the industry increased rapidly from approximately 120 men in 1851 to 200 in 1861 and 600 in 1900. This conformed to the regional pattern, the number of engineering workers in Derbyshire rising from 2,900 in 1851 to 8,500 in 1891.[65] After 1900 the pattern of the industry in the town began to change as electrical and mechanical engineering assumed a greater importance and amalgamation increased the size of the unit of production.

It is thus clear that Burton's metal-working, hardware and engineering industries have evolved in four distinct phases. Prior to 1720 metal-working was unimportant and entirely domestic in character. Between 1720 and 1810 availability of water power and transport, imported iron and local charcoal stimulated the growth of iron forging and of hardware manufacture that was both domestic and factory-based. From 1810–60 the application of steam power and mechanical processes seriously curtailed both iron forging and hardware production but encouraged the development of foundry work and engineering. After 1860 engineering, closely allied to the expanding brewing industry, became the only other significant occupation in the town.

References

1. *Birmingham and its Regional Setting*, p. 147 (pub. for the British Association by the local Executive Committee, 1950). B.L.C. Johnson, 'The Midland Iron Industry in the Early Eighteenth Century'. Business History, vol. 2, No. 2, (June, 1960), p. 70.

2. W.H.B. Court, '*Rise of Midland Industries*', (1938), p. 172. A. Birch, '*The Economic History of the British Iron & Steel Industry, 1784–1879*', (1967), pp. 18–44.

3. J.A.S.L. Leighton-Boyce, '*Smiths the Bankers, 1658–1958*', (1958), pp. 202–3.

4. *Hull Port Books*, P.R.O., E. 190, 352/8.

5. This book (now in my possession) contains the name of William Dyer of Wotton-under-Edge, Glos. who may have been the carrier.

6. D. Defoe, '*A Tour Thro' the Whole Island of Great Britain*,' Vol. 3, p. 62 (6th ed. 1762).

7. E. Wyndham Hulme, '*Statistical History of the Iron Trade of England and Wales, 1717–1750*'; Transactions of the Newcomen Society, vols. 9–10, (1928–30). see also M.W. Flinn, '*The Growth of the English Iron Industry, 1660–1760*'; Economic History Review, vol. 11, (1958), p. 144. R.A. Pelham, 'The Water-Power Crisis in Birmingham in the Eighteenth Century', *University of Birmingham Historical Journal*, vol. 9, No. 1, (1963), pp. 64–91.

8. *Paget MSS.*, (S.C.R.O. D.603, unlisted), Deed of 28 Aug. 1721.

9. Ibid; Peter Walter to the Earl of Uxbridge, 2 Sept. 1725.

10. *D.M.*, 15 Mar. 1733.

11. *Paget MSS.*, William Wyatt to the Earl of Uxbridge, 27 Feb. 1762.

12. S. Lloyd, '*The Lloyds of Birmingham*', (1907).

13. *Paget MSS*, William Wyatt to the Earl of Uxbridge, 27 Feb. 1762.

14. B.P.C.R., Thomas and Francis 'Thornwell' bap. 4 Oct. 1719 and 8 July 1722.

15. *S. Briggs & Co. Deeds*, (B.D.), 2 Mar 1747 and Will of Francis Astle, 20 May 1735.

16. *Paget MSS.*, William Wyatt to the Earl of Uxbridge, 19 May 1753.

17. Ibid., 17 May 1755 and 19 Feb. 1764.

18. E. Lipson, '*The Economic History of England*', vol. 2, p. 156.

19. Supra, c. 3, p.

20. *P.D.*, 29 May 1762.

21. '*Boulton & Watt MSS*'; S. & Co. Lloyd to Matthew Boulton, 20 Nov. 1804.

22. '*Universal British Directory*', vol. 1, (1791), p. 413.

23. *Lloyd MSS.*, Charles Lloyd to Nehemiah Lloyd, 5 June 1774.

24. *D.M.*, 1764–74.

25. *Paget MSS.*, Estate Papers of William Wyatt, 1770.

26. *Boulton & Watt MSS.*, S. & C. Lloyd to Matthew Boulton, 20 Nov. 1804.

27. *Lloyd MSS.*, Charles Lloyd to Samuel Bamford, 4 Mar. 1798.

28. W. Molyneux, op. cit., p. 211.

29. see T.S. Ashton, '*Iron & Steel in the Industrial Revolution*' and A. Birch, op. cit.

30. *Paget MSS*; 'Agreement between the Earl of Uxbridge, Charles Lloyd and others', 29 Aug. 1812. see also J. Farey, '*General View of the Agriculture and Minerals of Derbyshire*', vol. 1, (1811), p. 404.

31. Hull Port Books; P.R.O.; E. 190, 374/3.

32. 'Minutes of Evidence on Petitions against The Orders in Council, 1812—taken before a Select Committee of the House of Commons, 29 April 1812'. *J. of H.C. 1812 Reports, Committees*, Vol. 3, p. 24.

33. A.D. Gayer, W.W. Rostow, and A.J. Schwartz, '*The Growth and Fluctuation of the British Economy, 1790–1850*', Vol. 1, pp. 41 & 73. See also A. Birch, op. cit., pp. 20–21. W. Smith, '*An Economic Geography of Great Britain*,' p. 117. E. Lipon, op. cit., vol. 2, pp. 160–1.

34. *D.M.*, 21 July 1758. *B.D.*, 10 Oct. 1760. *Paget MSS*; Willaim Wyatt to the Earl of Uxbridge, 19 Feb., 26 Mar. and 16 April 1764.

35. *A.R.*, Day Book of John Walker Wilson, 1775–8. Wray & Hollingsworth Letter Books, 1791 and 1795–6.
36. Bass-Worthington Records; The William Bass Book, 1762–4.
37. *B.D.*, Will of Francis Thornewill, 12 Oct. 1805.
38. *P.D.*, 3 Mar. 1807.
39. J. Farey, op. cit., vol. 1, p. 404.
40. *Paget MSS*; William Wyatt to the Earl of Uxbridge, 9 Feb. 1762.
41. Joseph Chamberlain, Manufacture of Iron and Wood Screws; *The Resources, Products and Industrial History of Birmingham and the Midland Hardware District*; ed. Samuel Timmins, (1866), p. 605.
42. Rhys Jenkins, 'Historical Notes on Some Derbyshire Industries'; *Transactions of the Newcomen Society*, vol. 14, 1933–4. S. Shaw, op. cit., vol. 1, p. 109. See also '*John Wyatt—Master Carpenter and Inventor, 1700–1766*', anon (1885).
43. *D.M.*, 9 July 1779.
44. Ibid. 18 Jan. 1787.
45. William Frazer, 'Notes on water-mills; illustrated by those on the Repton Book;' *Transactions of the Derby Archaeological Society*, vol. 63, (1942). See also *Land Tax Returns*, Hartshorne, 1785–7. S. Shaw, op. cit., vol. 1, pp. 13–14. *D.M.*, 27 Dec. 1787.
46. *D.M.*, 7 Oct. 1784.
47. 'The Weekly Entertainer,' 29 Sept. 1783. *J. of H.C., Reports, Committees; 1812*, vol. 3, p. 95.
48. *L.P.R.*, Will of William Shorthose of Burton, 4 Jan. 1805.
49. W.H.B. Court, op. cit., pp. 197 & 210.
50. Censuses of Population, 1851 & 1861; *P.R.O.*, H.O. 107, Bdl. 2012 and R.G.9, Bdls. 1964–7.
51. Census of Population, 1841; *P.R.O.*, H.O. 107, Bdl. 975. See also W. White, '*History, Gazetteer and Directory of Staffordshire*,' (1834) and S. Bagshaw, '*History, Gazetteer and Directory of Derbyshire*,' (1846).
52. S. Timmins, op. cit., pp. 606–9.
53. E. Ball, '*The Hand-Made Nail Trade*;' S. Timmins, op. cit., p. 115.
54. W.K.V. Gale, 'Early Ironfounding in the Midlands;' *Transactions of the Newcomen Society*, vol. 28, 1951–3. S.D. Chapman, '*The Early Factory Masters*', (1967), p. 148.
55. J.R. Harris, 'The Employment of Steam Power in the Eighteenth Century;' *History*, vol. 52, No. 175, (June 1967), pp. 133–48. See also A.E. Musson & E.H. Robinson, 'The Early Growth of Steam Power;' *Economic History Review*, 2nd series, vol. 11, no. 3, (1959), pp. 418–39. F. Nixon, 'The Early Steam Engine in Derbyshire'; *Transactions of the Newcomen Society*, vol. 31, (1957–9), pp. 17–18.
56. D. Wright, '*A Survey of the Industrial and Commercial Activities of Joseph Wilkes, in and around the Parish of Measham in the late 18th century*;' (B.A. Hons. Dissertation, University of Nottingham, 1968), p. 14.
57. *B.D.*, 'Indenture of Partnsership', 2 July 1849.
58. W. White, '*History, Gazetteer and Directory of Staffordshire*', (1851).
59. Briggs & Co. Records; 'Engine Order Book', c. 1855–1902. see also Bass & Co. '*A Notable Brewery Railway System*', (*1926*).
60. A. Barnard, op. cit., vol. 1, pp. 409–10.
61. *B.D.*, 'Articles of Partnership', 25 Nov. 1868.

62. Parsons & Bradshaw, op. cit., 1818 Directory.

63. Censuses of Population, 1841–61. see also Burton upon Trent Town Commissioners' Map, 1855.

64. S. Briggs & Co., Deeds and correspondence, 1870–1930.

65. D.M. Smith, '*The East Midlands Industrial Area*', vol. 2, (Ph. D. Thesis, University of Nottingham, 1961).

VII

THE TEXTILE INDUSTRIES

The history of the textile manufacture in Burton-on-Trent is of considerable interest rather more for its variety and longevity than for its importance in terms of employment and production. Textile industries, as distinct from purely subsistent domestic work, have been carried on in the town for more than seven centuries. Between 1550 and 1680, when Burton was noted for the manufacture of woollen cloth and from 1790 to 1830, when it possessed a thriving cotton spinning industry, textile workers were more numerous than those in any other manufacturing occupation in the town. There is little doubt, however, that the absence of significant locational factors and the relative isolation of the town from major textile zones have prevented this group of industries from assuming a really dominant position. Diversity has generally been an outstanding characteristic of the industries, with the manufacture of woollen, worsted, linen and cotton yarns and fabrics all being carried on during the last two hundred years. An examination of the development of these industries is valuable in that it provides an insight into national and regional trends, particularly in relation to such processes as the application of power-operated machinery to textile manufacture, the displacement of a domestic system by a factory system and the geographic concentration of the various branches of the industry.

Until the end of the 18th century the woollen cloth industry held a highly privileged position in England, being carefully protected and regulated by state legislation. The reason for this was simply that it provided more employment than any other manufacturing industry and contributed the greatest export revenue.[1] Its significance was enhanced by its universal distribution, for it was not until the 17th century that East Anglia, Kent, the West Country and the West Riding of Yorkshire began to emerge as major zones of production at the expense of other areas.[2] It was also to some extent exceptional in that its division into many different trades, within the basic sections of wool preparation, yarn spinning and cloth weaving and finishing, led, at an early date, to a capitalistic form of organisation in which workers were often domestic wage-earners who depended for their livelihood upon the resources of an entrepreneur or clothier. In the wool preparation section the raw material was graded by wool-staplers, scoured and cleansed by scribblers and then carded or combed according to the length of fibre. Long-staple combed wool in the form of worsted yarn was used for the manufacture of serges, shalloons, bombazines, callimancos, knitted goods and a variety of other fabrics. Spinning, a relatively simple operation, was often carried on in the home by women and girls, while weaving required a much higher degree of skill and was normally accomplished by men who had served a seven-year apprenticeship. The finishing processes, often carried out in a single workshop, included scouring, burling, calendering, in the case of worsted cloth, raising, shearing and dyeing. Prior to finishing, woollen cloth (as opposed to worsted) was sent to a fulling mill, where it was scoured with the aid of fullers' earth and then felted in order to prevent shrinking. This was carried out by soaking, soaping and pounding the cloth with wooden hammers operated by water power and by stretching the cloth by hand every two or three hours. Fulling mills were first introduced towards the end of the 12th century and proceeded to occupy the sites of former corn mills in many parts of the country.[4] Apart from these and an abortive attempt to introduce 'gig-mills' and 'shearing-frames' during the 16th century, the woollen cloth industry was little affected by technical innovations prior to 1700. The introduction of John Kay's 'fly-shuttle' in 1733 accelerated the weaving process without inhibiting the domestic system and it was not until after 1770 that mechanisation and factory development began to revolutionise the industry.

In the early 14th century Burton Abbey had large numbers of sheep grazing on 'divers pastures near the Trent' and their wool was sent as far afield as Florentine markets.[5] Soon afterwards, when restrictions were placed on English wool exports, a local woollen cloth industry began to emerge. The main indication of this development was the presentation of a fulling mill to the Abbey by Robert Stapenhill around 1340 and the appointment of 'William le Walkere' as the fuller. In addition, the Abbey leases contain frequent reference to weavers, tailors, mercers and dyers living in the town from the end of the 13th century, with premises in High Street and New Street. All the available evidence indicates that the woollen cloth industry thrived up to the time of the dissolution of the Abbey in 1540. At this time the 'Nether Walk Mill' was on lease to Richard Lowe of Burton who was granted—

> 'the Walk Mill House standing upon the Trent near the corn mill with the Walk Mill brook and a meadow place thereto belonging with the stream of water and course and recourse to and from the said mill with a meadow to frame and lay his timber upon'.

He paid an annual rent of £3. 10s. and was responsible for repairs to the mill and weir, with the exception of the 'great timbers'.[6]

After the dissolution Sir William Paget, the new Lord of the Manor, immediately encouraged an expansion of the woollen cloth industry. In 1555 he re-let the Nether Walk Mill to Agnes Lowe, a widow, and her two sons, William and Richard. This was renewed for a fine of £9 in 1561 by Roger, Thomas and John Lowe (fullers of Burton), who agreed to 'full and dress all cloths made in Burton before those made elsewhere'.[7] Clearly the mill served groups of clothworkers throughout the area. Meanwhile a new fulling mill, known as the 'Upper or Over Walk Mill' had been built during 1555 and 1556 in accordance with the instructions of William Caldwell, the leading Burton clothier. It was sited on an island in the Trent between Stapenhill and Bond End, and Caldwell agreed to pay Lord Paget an annual rent of 53s. for its use.[8] Further growth of the industry necessitated the construction of a third mill in 1574, when Lord Paget concluded an agreement with Thomas Graunger, a millwright of Coventry, who agreed to—

> 'builde work form and sett up workmanly and substancially one fulling mylne with two substanciall fullers to full clothe withall and a convenient house of two baies, near to the same mylne at the over fulling mylne sett and being at Burton upon Trent uppon the ryver of Trent and nowe in the occupation of William Caldwall and John Clarck of Burton afforesaid clotheirs. Mylne etc. to be ready by Michaelmas next.[9]

Paget provided all the building materials and paid Graunger £36 for his work.

The expansion of fulling was accompanied by a substantial increase in all other branches of the industry, most of which were based in workshops and tenements in High Street, Horninglow Street and Anderstaff Lane. William Caldwall and John Clark, who appear to have possessed the requisite ability and capital, emerged as the leading clothiers and co-ordinators of the industry. Their active participation in the industry made them much nearer to their Yorkshire counterparts than to the clothiers of the West of England, who were not usually skilled craftsmen themselves. John Clarke probably began his working life as a weaver; he rented a house and workshop in High Street and also a dyehouse to which all the cloth made in the town was taken. In 1582, when he became involved in a lengthy dispute with the town authorities, it was said that—

> 'beinge put out of his dyinge house was his overthrow and iii hundredth persons more which he daylye sett a worke for want of which aforesayed the towne of Burton hath bene decayed'.[10]

His lease of at least one of the fulling mills and ownership of weaving and finishing shops and a dyehouse, upon which over a quarter of the town's population depended, made him a highly influential person. His cousin, William Caldwall, whose family owned extensive lands in Rolleston, may have been more concerned with the commercial aspects of the industry than with production. William's brother, Richard Caldwall, who became a wealthy physician in London, gave generously to worthy causes in Burton and the surrounding area, including £120 to be lent for five years, interest free, to poor tradesmen in Burton 'for advancing their stocks wherein the clothyers were to have preference', John Clarke, Nicholas Clarke, William Wightman and Henry Clarke, all of whom were clothiers, were the first recipients.[11] The Burton clothworkers specialised in the manufacture of kersies which were produced in many northern and midland towns. By the early 17th century there had developed a well organised system of agents and carriers to link these towns with Blackwell Hall and the London market. Such a system may well have been in existence during the previous century.

Throughout the first half of the 17th century the woollen cloth industry continued to thrive in Burton and to give employment to more workers than any other form of manufacture, without showing any signs of further expansion.[12] The town's frequent involvement in the Civil War, however, severely damaged its properties, trade and industries. Writing during the 1650's, Sir Simon Degge commented—

> 'It was before the last wars a town much given to cloathing, their kersies being in great esteem in this country; but since the war it

> has declined in trade, having suffered much by the plunder, it being held out against the King'.[13]

It is clear from surviving Caldwall Charity Deeds, however, that the industry not only survived the war but continued to be significant. In 1657 eleven clothiers received money from the charity, while in October 1662 thirteen out of the seventeen recipients were clothiers.[14] In addition to a small number of other types of clothworkers, the names of at least 40 clothiers have been traced during the early 1660's. The need for so many of them to rely upon charity is an indication of their limited means and lack of prosperity. Most of them were probably weavers by trade who relied upon the services of a few journeymen and apprentices and nearby spinners and preparatory workers. The most outstanding clothier during this period was Solomon Clarke of Shobnall Grange, who in 1669 had five hearths taxable in Burton Extra and eight in Burton.[15] He also rented the 'Upper Walke Mill' and it is likely that some of his properties in the town contained weaving and finishing shops. Owing to shortage of small currency with which to pay his employees, Clarke issued farthing tokens inscribed with his name, occupation and a picture of the clothworkers' arms.[16] It would seem there were still approximately 300 workers engaged in woollen cloth production in Burton and the surrounding districts during the 1660's. Spinning would have been carried on in many homes both in the town and in the rural areas. Weaving would also have been highly dispersed, although larger workshops housing groups of weavers also existed. The industry was served by at least two fulling mills and one dyehouse which probably had a finishing shop attached to it.

Although the Civil War affected the woollen cloth industry adversely, profound national locational changes in the industry were far more damaging in the long term. Towards the end of the 17th century many midland towns, such as Coventry, Nottingham and Burton, suffered from the concentration of the industry into the West Riding of Yorkshire and other important manufacturing zones. By 1680 the woollen cloth industry in Burton and, indeed, the town's economy in general, had become extremely depressed. When Dr. Plot visited Burton shortly afterwards he referred only briefly to 'the clothing trade and felting, which is chiefly exercised about Tamworth, Burton-on-Trent and Newcastle-under-Lyme'.[17] Many of the surviving clothworkers were forced to secure loans from the town funds, while their sons sometimes became parish apprentices. Families who had been engaged in clothworking for over a century turned to other occupations such as brewing and hat-making.[18] By 1700 the woollen cloth industry was but a shadow of what it had been less than forty years before and those still concerned with it formed a depressed social group.

The fate of the local fulling mills was indicative of this decline. In 1721, when George Hayne leased the Upper Mills and weir for use by the Trent Navigation, they were said to be 'very ancient ... being very long for the use of a Cloth Mill ... Burton being once a Town famous for a particular sort of Strong Woollen Cloth'.[19] At the same time the 'Nether Walk Mill ... heretofore in the tenure of Peter Bunn' was converted for use as an iron forge. At some stage prior to 1676 a fourth mill had been built near to the corn mill and this continued to operate. In 1726 it was on lease to the Rev. William Woodcock but in 1735 it passed into the hands of the Gibson family who continued to work the mill until 1780.[20] During the 1750's Henry Hayne, the proprietor of the Navigation, spent over £1,000 on repairs to the fulling and corn mills, despite his complaint that—

> 'there is not nor ever will be half imploy for either, one part of the Town grinding away and the Clothiers in it very few in number and those unable to carry on any manufactures worth notice which is sure to be the case whilst that trade is subsisting in Yorkshire where they will always both in quality and price undersell them'.[21]

A half-used mill that also produced wash leather was, therefore, all that remained of a once-thriving chain of fulling mills by the early 18th century.

Accompanying the serious decline in the woollen cloth industry was a refreshing diversification of the textile industry in general. The appearance of jersey-combers, jersey-weavers and framework-knitters in the town during the early years of the 18th century was an indication of the rising worsted and hosiery trades and the tendency for 'manufacturing districts on the decline to fall back on these plain worsted fabrics'.[22] It is likely that mercers such as Richard Allsopp, John Bott and John Wakefield, who were influential men in the town, encouraged this development. The distribution of the worsted industry tended to evolve in the opposite way to that of woollen manufacturing. Prior to 1700 the former was concentrated in the Norwich area and the West Riding but afterwards became more dispersed, probably due to the increased demand for lighter fabrics. In the East Midlands woolcombers, jersey-spinners and framework-knitters often worked in close association in the production of knitted goods, under the direction of merchant hosiers. In Burton the earliest recorded worsted worker was Edward Clare, who was practising as a jersey-comber as early as 1719. The Clare family owned a workshop on the north side of New Street at which they carried-on combing, spinning and weaving. By the 1760's they were regularly sending small consignments of their products to London.

Several families of woollen clothworkers managed to survive the changes. The Brackley's, who had been important clothiers throughout the previous century, continued until 1726 when Jonathan Brackley died. In 1711 his properties consisted of—

> 'the house where I now live, the Dye house where the Kilne and the lead stands together with the said Kilne and lead, one bay of building commonly known by the name of the weaving shop, one half of the orchard . . . lying on the south side of a street in Burton called Cat Street, and commonly known as Cat Street Close.'[23]

Robert and Richard Shilton were also notable clothiers during the 1680–1720 period, the former serving as Townmaster in 1700. The family continued to work as clothiers in premises on the east side of High Street throughout the 18th century. Joseph Shilton, who inherited his father's business in 1781, was probably the last of the traditional Burton clothiers. The Astles, Crocketts and Waltons were three other families who continued to play a significant part in the industry.

The Astles were eventually able to survive by turning their attentions from woollens to worsteds. Benjamin Astle worked as a Burton clothier and as a farmer at Horninglow for many years before deciding to establish a tammy-weaving business in High Street in 1755.[24] The manufacture of tammies, which were cheap worsted gowns, was carried-on in many midland towns, ranging from Uttoxeter in the north-west to Kettering in the south-east, during the second half of the 18th century. Benjamin Astle and his two sons, Benjamin and John, appear to have initiated the industry in Burton. Following their father's death in 1761, Benjamin and John built-up a thriving business in High Street and in a number of shops and a warehouse in Horninglow Street. In 1769 the increased trade forced them to seek additional workers—

> 'Wanted at Burton upon Trent—A number of journeymen Weavers, that can work strong tammies; such men may meet with constant employ and good work. Apply Benjamin and John Astle'.[25]

Skilled workers, such as woolcombers, were often in great demand, as a further advertisement in 1793 indicated—

> 'To Woolcombers—Wanted immediately, from twenty to thirty journeymen woolcombers; such as are good workmen may meet with good work and constant employ by applying to John Astle in Burton-on-Trent'.[26]

They were, moreover, highly paid, well organised and mobile, until mechanisation of woolcombing undermined their status early in the following century. The Astle's business declined rapidly after 1800 and was discontinued in 1808 when John Astle died.

A second tammy-weaving business was operated by the Bott family, who had been concerned with the mercery trade since the 17th century. John Bott became involved in worsted manufacture around 1760 and succeeded in developing extensive premises on the east side of Anderstaff Lane, described in the following advertisement of 1785—

> 'Manufactory to be let or sold—
> The house, workshops and utensils, used in woolcombing, weaving, dressing, dyeing and hot-pressing Tammies and other stuffs, in possession of, and belonging to John Bott and Son, situated in Burton-on-Trent; where for a number of years an extensive business has been carried on. The above premises are complete and have the advantage of the river running close'.[27]

As will be seen later, the Botts were concerned in all branches of textile manufacture and were involved in the establishment of a mill at Tutbury in 1780 for the spinning of cotton and worsted yarn. The failure of early attempts such as this to mechanise the production of worsted yarn may have induced them to abandon tammy-weaving in 1785. Their former premises in Anderstaff Lane were leased by Charles Grice, who had run a small tammy business in Horninglow Street since 1770, and John Wood, a Burton dyer.[28] Although the latter continued to use the workshops for dyeing for many years it is likely that tammy-weaving was discontinued shortly after 1800.

Apart from very small concerns run by Joseph and Thomas Hind and Thomas Brelley, the tammy industry was thus concentrated in the two manufactories described above. Their location close to the river enabled them to obtain a ready supply of water for washing and dyeing. Combers, weavers and dyers worked together and were probably supplied with yarn by domestic spinners. One woolcomber could normally satisfy the requirements of ten spinners, who in turn supplied yarn to the weavers and finishing workers. Astle's request for 20–30 woolcombers in 1793 suggests a thriving industry, which, during the last quarter of the 18th century, may have provided employment for as many as 3–400 workers, including domestic spinners. The industry was also to be found in nearby Tutbury and at Uttoxeter, where Thomas Bladen employed 'woolcombers and weavers in his "manufactory"'.[29] After 1800 the tammy industry suffered severely from the growing popularity of cheap cotton fabrics and the rapid expansion of power-operated worsted manufacture in the West Riding of Yorkshire. By 1810 the industry had disappeared from the town.

As previously noted, the transition from woollen to worsted manufacture in Burton during the course of the 18th century adversely affected the fulling industry. Dyers, pressers and other finishing workers were, however, still required and these continued to work in premises at the western end of Burton Bridge. In 1733, when Henry Adams, the only dyer in the town, retired from business, these were described as—

> 'a very convenient House situate on Burton Bridge, by the River Side, and a convenient Dyehouse, containing four coppers, two Fats, and an extraordinary Callender, two hot Presses, and a good Stock of Paper and Planks, six-score yards of Tenters'.[30]

The dyehouse passed to Ralph Brittan and then, in 1742, to Samuel Shevyn and John Lawty. The latter were still in possession of the property in 1754 when it was burgled and the following articles stolen—

> 'four sale tammys, three dy'd dark drabs not tenter'd, the other white ... Also some yard wide callimancoes and country cloths, jersey and linen, jersey and woollen, and fine knit stockings, all in white, and some country tammies'.[31]

In 1772, when Samuel Shevyn moved to Atherstone, William Statham converted the premises into an alehouse. For the remainder of the century the textile workers in the town were served by Joseph Staley of Bridge Street, John Staley of High Street and Lichfield Street and John Wood of Anderstaff Lane.[32] The latter was easily the most important of the three and was mentioned in numerous local documents and in contemporary trade directories until 1818.

Two early attempts were made locally to mechanise the process of worsted spinning by the application of the roller-spinning machine. Both Tutbury and Alrewas Mills, opened during the early 1780's, were designed for the spinning of worsted and cotton yarns. The latter was described in 1789 as a 'Cotton and Jersey Mill . . . on the River Trent . . . with very compleat machinery for the purpose of spinning both cotton and jersey'.[33] As in other parts of the Midlands, the experiment was unsuccessful, mainly because the quality of the worsted yarn produced was not sufficiently high. In Yorkshire the early use of the throstle for worsted spinning produced more favourable results and helped the region to compete successfully with others.[34] Under the emerging system of factory-based workers and power-operated machinery it became impossible for small centres of production, such as Burton, to survive. Large capital investment in machines and premises became necessary for economic survival and those who persisted with the old methods soon became degraded both financially and socially. Many highly skilled trades, such as woolcombing and handloom weaving were replaced by a range of unskilled and semi-skilled activities, many of which could be performed by women and children. In Burton the woollen and worsted industries failed to meet the challenge, with the result that they scarcely existed after 1810. Small groups of traditional workers struggled for survival; in 1818 Parsons & Bradshaw's 'Directory' listed only three woolstaplers, one of whom was also a woolcomber and worsted manufacturer, four spinners, one weaver and one stocking-weaver. The most important woolstapler was Thomas Cooper, who owned 'a wool warehouse with a counting house, stable, workshops and tenements on the north side of New Street'.

Also affected by similar technological changes was the small hosiery industry that had developed in Burton in association with worsted manufacture. Burton lay outside the main East Midland hosiery zone, which was bounded by Chesterfield, Derby, Hinckley and Nottingham. By the early 18th century this region contained over 60 per cent of British knitting frames. They were located both in urban and rural areas and produced a very wide range of articles from worsted, cotton and silk yarns.[35] The industry was at that time essentially domestic in character, frames being hired out by master hosiers, who also arranged for the supply of yarn and the sale of finished products. The earliest known framework-knitters in Burton were Thomas Smith, Benjamin Brough and John Marshall, all of whom accepted parish apprentices between 1729 and 1739.[36] Their close association with jersey-weavers indicates that Burton formed a westerly extension of the Leicestershire worsted hosiery district, producing stockings, breeches, waistcoats and various other knitted garments. There was no suggestion of a link with the extremely important silk hosiery industry of nearby Derby. Small numbers of framework-knitters, stockingers and breeches-makers continued to work in Burton throughout the 18th century but records indicate that it was not until 1775 that the first hosier, Thomas Marriot, became a resident. After 1810 most of these domestic hosiery workers disappeared from the scene as the change to a factory-based industry gathered momentum throughout the region.

Another minor branch of textile manufacturing that developed in Burton and the surrounding districts during the 18th century was the production of linen yarn and cloth from imported and locally-grown flax. The cultivation of flax and the manufacture of linen were stimulated in many English counties during this period by the popularity of linen fabrics and the severe restrictions placed on the import of linen.[37] During the second half of the century the number of flax-dressers both in and around the town undoubtedly increased in response to the large quantities of undressed Baltic flax imported by the leading brewers and Trent merchants. Some of the flax-dressers, such as the Bakewells and the Wakefields, owned premises in the town, particularly in Horninglow Street, while others operated bleaching yards in nearby villages. Around 1770 there were at least three yards at Newborough, owned by William Beck, John Mills and William Arnold, and one belonging to John Hodson at Anslow.[38] These villages lay on the heavy Boulder Clay lands to the west of Burton, where flax cultivation was widespread, particularly after the introduction of a flax bounty system in 1782. The local linen industry reached its peak during the final thirty years of the century but after 1806 it declined very rapidly owing to the cutting-off of supplies of undressed Baltic flax and the need to use every possible acre of farmland for food production in order to defeat the Napoleonic blockade.

Woollen, worsted, hosiery and linen workers were thus active in Burton throughout the 18th century. All of them worked in the home or in small workshops and their products were mainly for local use. Tammy-weaving was to some extent exceptional in that it was organised on a larger scale and undoubtedly catered for external markets. With the exception of fulling, none of these branches of the textile industry used power-operated machinery and they tended therefore, to be widely dispersed. By 1820 they had all virtually disappeared from the town, as large-scale factory-based production profoundly affected their national distribution. Clothiers, jersey-combers, tammy-weavers, framework-knitters and flax-dressers thus shared the fate of the nail-makers, screw-forgers and spademakers, whose livelihoods were also destroyed by technological progress.

One branch of the textile industries evolved in a very different way, however, and gave Burton its first taste of the new factory system. This was the cotton-spinning industry, which, from 1790–1830 formed the most important manufacturing industry in the town in terms of employment. Its relatively late appearance in Burton was typical of the industry's national development. Throughout the 17th and first half of the 18th centuries it had grown steadily in South Lancashire despite repressive legislation and the hostility of powerful factions connected with the woollen industry. By 1760 a number of technological developments had set the stage for further and considerably greater, expansion. Paradoxically, the most exciting and revolutionary changes were initiated in the Midlands, following the migration to Nottingham in 1768 of James Hargreaves and Richard Arkwright, the most outstanding of the Lancashire inventors. In Nottinghamshire and Derbyshire they were able to escape the animosity of domestic cotton workers and to enjoy the moral and financial support of important hosiers, such as Samuel Need of Nottingham and Jedediah Strutt of Derby, who required increasing quantities of cotton yarn.[39] Arkwright's immediate success in applying the water-frame to cotton-spinning at Cromford set the pattern for future development throughout the region. In addition to new mills constructed, many existing buildings along rivers or streams were converted for use. By 1800 the Midland counties possessed at least 110 cotton mills, of which 39 were in Nottinghamshire, 31 along the Derwent Valley in Derbyshire, 16 in other parts of the Trent basin and 24 elsewhere.[40]

Burton lay close to the southern margin of this manufacturing zone, and its participation in the industry began in 1780 with the arrival of Robert Peel from Lancashire. The latter had been involved in textile manufacture for a period of at least thirty years, and around 1760 had joined with Jonathan Haworth of Darwen and William

Yates of Blackburn in the establishment of a textile print-works at Brookside, near Church in Lancashire. He had afterwards worked with Hargreaves in the development of carding and spinning machines, thereby incurring the displeasure of local hand-spinners. By the mid-1770's Peel owned works and warehouses in various parts of the county. His efforts to concentrate and mechanise the various processes of cotton manufacture continued, however, to arouse the opposition of domestic workers, who, in 1779, attacked his mill at Altham, threw his machines into the nearby river and threatened his life.[41] Although fifty-six years of age, Peel decided immediately to leave his native county, and in the following year he moved to Burton, where he leased two large houses in Horninglow Street.

Burton offered to him a number of distinct advantages: it was linked by waterway to Liverpool, through which raw cotton passed in large quantities; it lay within easy reach of the East Midland hosiery district, which required large quantities of cotton yarn; it possessed a number of suitable mill sites at which water power was available, and was secure from attack by domestic cotton workers. Having established himself in the town Peel immediately set about the task of constructing and equipping a number of mills, the details of which have never been satisfactorily described. The evidence provided by contemporary literature and official returns[42] is to some extent conflicting but a detailed examination of local Land Tax Returns and of documents from the Lloyd MSS has provided a satisfactory solution to the problem.

The first mill to be built by Robert Peel was located at Winshill on the site of the former fulling mill and close to the corn mill. Until 1779 the premises were leased by John Hayne from the Earl of Uxbridge and occupied by John Gibson. In the following year the mill was acquired by the Lessees of the Trent Navigation and sub-let to Robert Peel. By the end of 1781 the old premises had been demolished and a new cotton spinning mill constructed; two years later it was described as—

> 'all that Cotton Mill or Cotton Work with the appurtenances then lately erected and built upon or near the site of an ancient fulling mill upon the said River Trent and then late in the occupation of John Gibson which said Cotton Mill was then in the occupation or possession of Robert Peele and Company who had erected the same'.[43]

The second mill to be built by Peel was also referred to in the same document as--

> 'that new erected building or Mill with the appurtenances then intended for Cotton or other works situate in Bond End aforesaid in a certain close there called the Black Pool Close'.

It was constructed during 1782 and 1783 approximately 300 yards to the south of Fleet Stones, near to the end of the present Watson Street. Confirmation is provided by the Land Tax Returns for Burton Extra and by a variety of records and chance references. Thomas Dicken, a local brewer and mercer, writing to a friend in 1782 said—

> 'Another cotton mill is to be built near to the bridge in the Bond End, it is to be supply'd with water by a cutt from the Upper Weir'.[44]

To help with the construction, Peel purchased several large consignments of timber costing £66 from J.W. Wilson of Burton between March and August of the same year.[45] Between 1784–87 Peel built a third mill, later known as the Weir Mill or Upper Mill, next to the Upper Weir on the site of the old fulling mills. According to the 'Universal British Directory' of 1791 the 'three extensive cotton manufactories erected a few years since near this town by Messrs. Peel, Yates & Co., now afford employment to some hundreds of persons'. In Burton Extra were 'two spacious cotton-mills ... on the banks of the Trent', while in Winshill lay 'the other cotton mill of Messrs. Peel, Yates & Co. on an island surrounded by the Trent'.[46]

Thus, in the space of a decade, Peel had re-created an industrial complex similar to the one that he had left behind in Lancashire. In 1792 he retired to Manchester, leaving the mills in the care of several of his sons. When he died three years later, at the age of 72, he left estates valued at around £40,000. Although later described as 'a simple and hard-working countryman, caught up almost by chance in the pioneer era of the cotton industry', he was clearly an extremely active and astute businessman.[47] The bitterness that he had aroused amongst workers in his native county appears to have been absent in Burton, where the inhabitants seem to have treated him with respect and affection. Many members of his family came to join him, including his seventh son, John, who managed the Burton mills for over 20 years.[48] His third son, Robert, proved to be the most ambitious and successful member of the family. By the time of his father's death he had become the proprietor of a large and highly profitable cotton manufacturing concern and the owner of the extensive Thynne estates around Tamworth, which he had represented in Parliament since 1790. He had also established cotton and bleaching mills at Fazeley and Bonehill and calico-printing works at Tamworth, and had become a partner in several important commercial banks. By the early 19th century, Peel, Yates & Co. had become one of the largest industrial concerns in the United Kingdom, employing 15,000 workers and paying £40,000 per annum to the Government in duties on its printed goods.

Although a considerable amount has been written about the outstanding political activities of the Peel family, their industrial affairs remain shrouded in mystery. In the almost total absence of any business records one can only deduce how their mills were run by reference to similar establishments in the area. Cotton spinning became an important activity in nearby Tutbury, Alrewas and Measham and in all of these three ventures men with strong Burton connections were involved. None of these could match the Peel mills at Burton in terms of output and employment, for the latter continued to expand after the retirement of Robert Peel, the elder. Around 1795 a fourth mill, known as the 'New Building', was erected by the side of the second mill in Bond End. In 1814 Peel, Yates & Co. converted part of Burton Forge, abandoned by the Lloyds in 1811, for use as a fifth cotton mill.[49] By 1815 their Burton works thus comprised Winshill Mill, Burton Forge Mill and the three Bond End Mills. Contrary to popular belief, the surviving warehouse in Green Street was never used as a mill but was initially built as a warehouse during the late 1820's.[50]

The Measham Mills of Wilkes & Jewsbury were built during the same period as part of a large industrial complex. Joseph Wilkes, the son of an Overseal farmer, was born in 1732 and spent most of his early life working as a farmer and cheesefactor. His success in these fields, coupled with his interests in the Trent Navigation after 1762, enabled him to earn substantial profits, which he later invested in land reclamation, turnpike and canal construction, coalmining, brick-making and a variety of other industrial and commercial enterprises. His acquisition of the Parish of Measham for £56,000 in 1777 was a clear indication of his abilities. In 1783, in partnership with his brothers Thomas and John, he built the first of his cotton mills at Measham, using the River Mease to provide the power.[51] He later opened a bleaching mill at Measham and also weaving shops both there and at nearby Appleby. Finally, in 1802, in association with

Thomas Jewsbury, a former colliery manager, he built a second and larger cotton-spinning mill at Measham.[52]

In 1781 work began on the construction of a five-storey cotton and worsted-spinning mill at Tutbury, following a successful petition to the Crown from the local inhabitants. The pioneers of the scheme were John and Charles Bott, two tammy-weavers of Burton, who were able to gain the support of William Lucas, who owned a nearby cornmill, Thomas Webb of Barton under Needwood and Francis Greasley of Tutbury. The mill opened for business in 1783 under the name of Messrs. John Bott & Co.[53] Alrewas Mill, built by the side of the Trent in 1784, was also designed for both cotton and worsted-spinning. It was initiated and largely financed by Thomas Dicken, a Burton mercer and brewer. By the early 1790's, after serious financial and technical difficulties, the mill was being used successfully for cotton spinning and was giving employment to 300 workers.[54] Between 1780–5 Burton and the surrounding districts thus witnessed an industrial revolution which excited the business instincts of men drawn from many walks of life. Apart from Robert Peel, few of the new mill proprietors had previously experienced the difficulties involved in running a power-operated, factory-based enterprise with a concentrated and largely unskilled labour force.

The new mill buildings were quite unlike any previously built. They were substantially larger and more elaborate than the existing breweries and the workshops of the hardware and worsted manufacturers in the town. Considerably more capital was therefore required to construct and equip them. Most of these early mills were built according to the pattern laid down by Richard Arkwright at Cromford, where he erected multi-storied buildings with an adjoining factory village. The Tutbury Mill of John Bott & Co. was L-shaped in plan, five stories high and had internal dimensions of 186 ft. by 27 ft. Robert Peel's first mill at Burton had four stories and measured 120 ft. by 30 ft. It is likely that his three Bond End Mills were of similar size but the Forge Mill, opened in 1814, was considerably smaller. The first mill opened at Measham by Joseph Wilkes was four stories high, measured 85 ft. by 30 ft. and contained 3,000 spindles. Alrewas Mill was five stories high and measured 140 ft. by 30 ft. The cost of building an Arkwright-type mill during the 1780's was generally around £3,000, while the later steam-operated mills often cost in excess of £10,000.[55]

In addition to the main mill structure, the water-wheel and many of the interior fittings and machines were originally made on the site by skilled craftsmen, such as millwrights and clockmakers, recruited from a wide area. Each mill was powered by one or two water-wheels around 14 ft. in diameter and capable of producing 15–20 h.p. Tutbury Mill, for example, relied on two 14 ft. wheels. The machinery used inside the mills obviously varied according to their functions. Most of the mills in and around Burton were entirely or mainly concerned with cotton spinning and therefore contained carding engines, for converting raw cotton into a soft rope or sliver, and either jennies, water-frames or mules for spinning yarn. Although the latter were superior, in that they could produce fine yarn suitable for top-quality hose and lace, many midland mills continued to use the water-frame pioneered by Arkwright. In instances where cotton companies were also concerned with weaving, yarn was either let out to hand-loom weavers working at home or in workshops or the mills were equipped with various adaptations of the power loom. In 1817 the machinery at Tutbury Mill comprised 60 carding engines and 7,000 spindles, probably in the form of water-frames, while in 1815 Alrewas Mill contained—

> 'about 80 lots of Breaking and Finishing Carding Machines, with Drawing, Roving and Stretching Frames appropriate thereto, upwards of 4,000 Water or Throstle spindles—also about 800 spindles for doubling and twisting yarn for various purposes—also of 50 power Looms for weaving Calicoes, with Dressing Machines and Mules for Spinning Weft to Supply the same.'[56]

Although the Peels had been accustomed to using jennies in their early Lancashire mills, it is practically certain that water-frames were installed in their Burton mills. All available evidence suggests that their activities were confined to spinning until 1814, when the Forge Mill may very well have been opened specifically for calico production. Early directories merely described them as cotton manufacturers but a later publication referred to—

> 'Four large cotton factories, both for spinning and power-loom weaving, which have long been carried on here by Messrs. Peel & Co. and give employment to several hundreds of the inhabitants'.[57]

Wilkes & Jewsbury at Measham used separate weaving shops containing over 200 looms, while Tutbury Mill may have relied to some extent upon hand-loom weavers, as 90 of their 280 employees in 1817 were outworkers.

The difficulties experienced in water-powered mills, owing to variations in the water supply, encouraged manufacturers to quickly turn to steam power as a possible solution to their problems. In 1785 Robinson's mill at Papplewick, near Nottingham, became the first to rely entirely upon steam power. Generally, however, Midland mill owners were slow to abandon water power; by 1800, 42 of the 92 Boulton & Watt engines that had been installed in cotton mills were located in Lancashire and it has been estimated that even as late as 1835 85 per cent of Midland Mills still used water power.[58] Nevertheless, there is evidence to show that mill proprietors in the Burton area either used or contemplated the use of steam power at an early date.

Peel & Co. were amongst the first to use it, as the following extract from Robert Peel's letter of 1787 shows—

> 'I just now rec'd a line from son R. Peel with an order for you [Boulton & Watt] to make us an Engine same as that we use at Chester for fourteen Horsis to be fixed at Warrington in six months from the date'.[59]

The first steam engine used to operate a Staffordshire cotton mill was installed by Boulton & Watt in one of Peel & Co's. Bond End mills at Burton in 1792, following lengthy preparations during the previous year. The second mill built by the Peels in Burton was supplied with water from an extensive leat leading from the Trent near to the Upper Mills and it is likely that this was not altogether effective. In 1792 Boulton & Watt installed a 26 h.p. parallel motion engine in an engine house measuring 33 ft. by 30 ft. at what became known as the Steam Engine Mill.[60] The other Burton mills, however, continued to use water power. At Measham Joseph Wilkes contemplated the use of a Boulton & Watt engine as early as 1783—

> 'We want one [a steam engine] to work a cotton mill for 3,000 spindles. We beg to be informed if you are certain it will work as steady as water, as I find Mr. Arkwright was obliged to alter one he erected at Manchester to a Water Wheel and our friend Mr. Peal of Burton is in some doubts about an Ingin being smooth enough'.[61]

Wilkes eventually decided to use a 21 ft. diameter water-wheel assisted by a Newcomen engine, with a Watt condenser, which pumped water back into the mill dam. Shortly afterwards he purchased two small Boulton & Watt engines to operate a corn mill and a combined corn and carding mill at Measham but it was not until 1802 that he installed a 36 h.p. engine in a new carding and roving mill.[62] Tutbury Mill continued to rely on water wheels until 1880, when turbines were installed by Macadam's of Belfast. Alrewas Mill, although ideally placed for using water power, changed to steam at some time prior to 1815 when it contained a 'most complete Steam Engine of 45 horse power', used to drive throstles, mules, carding-machines and power-looms.[63]

The solution to the problem of whether or not to introduce steam power was often determined not so much by the inadequacy of the water supply as by the availability of coal. Mills that were sited along the floors of remote valleys, at some distance from a coalfield, generally continued to use water power whether it was entirely satsifactory or not. Conversely, proprietors such as Joseph Wilkes, whose mills lay close to collieries, were far more eager and able to turn to the new system. This was undoubtedly one of the reasons why most of the Measham mills were powered by steam, while Tutbury Mill, which lay three miles west of the Trent & Mersey Canal and seven miles by road from the nearest colliery, continued to rely on water power.

Unlike other branches of textile manufacture, the cotton industry relied entirely upon supplies of an imported fibre. Prior to 1795, when imports from North America began to increase rapidly, English manufacturers used mainly South American and West Indian varieties. Midland mills, engaged in the production of high-grade yarns for hosiery and lace manufacture, often used Pernambuco and Maranham long-staple cottons, imported into Liverpool and London from Brazil, usually via Lisbon. Demerara, Surinam, Domingo, Sea Island and New Orleans cottons were also used, the latter being of considerably lower quality. The practices of Dicken, Wilson & Co. of Alrewas Mill provide a useful insight into the workings of the system. Benjamin Wilson, the leading Burton brewer of the period and a man possessing a profound knowledge of overseas trade, became a partner in the firm in 1800 and also their chief buyer of raw cotton. In July 1800 he purchased his first consignment, comprising 50 bags of Pernambuco and 40 bags of Maranham, from Peters, Schlick, Hintze and Lindenberg of Lisbon. The cotton travelled in convoy from Lisbon to Liverpool where it was received by Joseph Greaves, a cotton broker, and despatched via the Trent & Mersey Canal to Alrewas Mill.[64] In a letter to Peters in 1806, Wilson stressed the importance of quality—

> 'I have been in the habit of importing Brazil Cottons for a cotton mill in which I am myself concerned, but lately prices with you have been such as left very little room for speculation . . . we make it a point of spinning a superior article, and nothing but superior cotton will suffice'.[65]

Wilson's connections with North American merchants began in April 1801 when he purchased 84 bales of New Orleans and 16 bales of Carolina cottons from F. Peppin & Co. of Charleston. This was followed soon afterwards by orders of 100 bales of New Orleans cotton from R. Bird & Co. of New York and 150 bales of New Orleans and 100 bales of best Sea Island from Simon Walker of Philadelphia. During the last three months of 1801 Wilson bought cotton to the value of £11,000 on behalf of Alrewas Mill.[66] In view of Wilson's affinity for speculating, he may well have disposed of some of this large quantity to other mills in the area. The close similarity between the system outlined above and that used by Strutt for his mills at Belper and Milford suggests that it was common to similar businesses throughout the region.

Midland spinning mills catered particularly for the needs of the local hosiery manufacturers and handloom weavers. Some of their products were, however, distributed throughout the United Kingdom and even overseas. Many consignments were sent to German ports and then distributed at the Hamburg, Bremen, Leipzig and Frankfurt fairs. Alrewas Mill was certainly involved in this trade, making full use of Benjamin Wilson's valuable Baltic connections. In 1803, for example, he arranged for the despatch of 2,500 bundles of cotton yarn from Manchester and 'several hundred bundles of knitting yarn and cotton twist', produced at Alrewas, to John Hutchinson in Altona. Similar consignments were also occasionally sent to merchants in Danzig and Konigsberg.[67]

The recruitment of an adequate labour force in Midland mills presented considerable problems, particularly in remote rural areas or in areas where other forms of employment were available. Skilled craftsmen, such as stonemasons, millwrights and clockmakers, were initially required to build the mill and to make and install the machinery. In Burton, Joseph Newbold, Thomas Tanner, William Walford, William Matthews (millwrights), Samuel Dickinson (cotton machine maker) and William Fosbrook (mechanic) were employed during the 1780–1800 period while the Peel mills were under construction.[68] Once in operation, the mills required mainly unskilled and semi-skilled workers; women and children were employed particularly in the carding and spinning sections, while men worked as overlookers, mechanics, clerks, spinners, weavers and dressers.

Several methods were used to overcome labour shortages, the most significant of which was the employment of child apprentices. The extent to which the system was used in the Burton area is difficult to ascertain but there is no doubt that it formed a regular characteristic of all local mills. At Tutbury Mill in 1816 there were two workers under the age of ten years and 73 between the ages of 10 and 18, out of a total labour force of 280.[69] Alrewas Mill, with its 300 employees, was equipped with a special apprentice house, and apprentices were ready for hire when the mill was offered for sale in 1815. Wilkes and Jewsbury regularly employed parish apprentices at Measham—

> 'To Overseers and Churchwardens.
> Wanted by Messrs. Thos. Jewsbury and Co. at their Cotton Manufactory, Measham, near Ashby-de-la-Zouch, a number of Healthy Boys and Girls as Apprentices to the business of Calico-Weaving.—Liberal and Humane Treatment may be relied upon, and a moderate Premium only expected'.[70]

They were accommodated in two large apprentice houses next to the mill, one of which was valued at £1,100 in 1819. The Peels employed considerable numbers of apprentices; in 1802, for example, Sir Robert had 1,000 working in his mills in Lancashire and the Midlands. By 1816 the number had fallen to 500 but he had earned for himself something of a doubtful reputation as an employer of child labour.[71] Undoubtedly, apprentices were employed in the Burton mills but there are no records affording evidence of numbers and working conditions. Child labour was generally found unsatisfactory and by 1816 children under 10 years of age formed less than five per cent of the total labour force in cotton mills.

At their Derbyshire mills, Arkwright and Strutt secured the services of many reliable workers by leasing well-built cottages at low rents to men with large families. Many other mill-owners adopted this system. At Alrewas, Dicken, Wilson & Co. constructed—

> '12 Cottages or Tenements for work people, and a pleasant convenient Messuage fit for the residence of a Principal or Superintendant of the concern'.[72]

Peel & Co. built cottages close to their mills at Winshill and also in Back Lane, Waterside and other streets near to Bond End Mills. They also provided superior houses for overlookers, superintendents and clerks. Mills were sometimes fortunate in being able to obtain workers from other depressed industries. In Burton many members of the Rice, Sollory, Fletcher and Marriott families, who for many years had been concerned with feltmaking and hat-making, turned to cotton spinning and dressing after 1810. It is also likely that many former brewing, hardware and worsted workers were forced to move into the mills, particularly after the collapse of the Baltic trading system in 1806. There is substantial evidence that the Peels also transferred reliable workers from their Lancashire mills to Burton; men such as William Haldren, Samuel Hallard, William Eagliston, James Sweatmore, Joseph Billington, John Pemberton and George Cheshire, who were employed as spinners at the Burton mills around 1800, probably came from the Manchester area.[73]

Both Tutbury and Alrewas mills employed approximately 300 workers during the early years of the 19th century and it would seem likely that at least 400 were engaged in spinning, bleaching, weaving and associated activities at Measham. In Burton the five mills operating after 1814 must have provided employment for at least 500 workers and possibly as many as 800. Such figures can be deduced only by reference to mill capacities and by using a certain amount of evidence provided by the Burton Parish Church Registers. The latter record the names of 68 male cotton spinners and 8 other male cotton workers during the 1815–19 period but, unfortunately, give no indication of female or child employees. Male workers over the age of 18 generally formed between 15 and 25 per cent of the total labour force in cotton mills at that time and knowledge of this fact gives some value to the above figures. Whatever the precise number may have been, the fact remains that the cotton industry was the most important single employer of labour in Burton between 1790 and 1830.

Owing to the great scarcity of official currency prior to 1816, the regular payment of such a large labour force posed a serious problem. Many mill-proprietors, including the Peels, found it expedient to resort to payment in kind and also to the issue of token coinage. They soon discovered that the truck system could be used to reduce the cost of labour and that token currency became acceptable over a wide area. Peel, Harding & Co. of Fazeley issued silver tokens valued at 2s. 6d., 1s. and 6d., while Peel, Yates & Co. of Burton used two types of penny tokens in 1814, showing a picture of Bond End Mill on the obverse, together with the inscription 'Payable by James Pardoe, Burton 1814'.[74] The latter was presumably a partner in the firm or a mill manager.

Little evidence is available concerning working conditions in the local mills. Prior to 1800 apprentices lived and worked in squalid surroundings in the Peel mills in Lancashire; indeed, an apidemic of fever in one of their works at Radcliffe Bridge in 1784 led to one of the first public enquiries into factory conditions. It is likely, however, that the 1802 Act resulted in a general raising of standards. Although imperfect, the Act instructed Justices of the Peace to appoint clergymen and Justices as mill visitors in specific areas. When the mills of Wilkes & Jewsbury at Measham and of Peel, Yates & Co. at Winshill were visited in 1803 everything was found to be satisfactory.[75] A report presented to a Parliamentary Committee in 1816 by Messrs. John Bott & Co. painted a rosy picture of life at Tutbury Mill. The firm had erected a gallery in the church capable to holding 200 people, children employed at the mill were given free instruction one evening per week in writing and arithmetic, while the development of the cotton industry had enabled Tutbury to 'overcome its former character of drunkenness and brutality'.[76] Biased though such reports undoubtedly were, there is no reason to believe that conditions in the mills were inferior to those outside. Indeed, workers outside often worked in poorer conditions, for longer hours and for lower wages in order to preserve some measure of individual freedom.

During the early years of the 19th century the cotton industry was of considerable importance as an employer of labour in Burton and the surrounding districts, particularly in view of the fact that its prosperity coincided with a marked decline in a number of traditional industries such as hat-making, worsted manufacture, iron-working and hardware. Unfortunately, the early impetus given to cotton manufacture in the Midlands by men such as Arkwright, Strutt and Peel was not maintained and as time went by counties such as Derbyshire and Staffordshire became relatively less important. In the former county the number of cotton mills declined from 18 per cent of the national total in 1787 to a mere five per cent by 1850. Mills in outlying districts, particularly, suffered, many being abandoned or converted for the production of sewing cotton and tape.

Alrewas Mill appears to have run into serious financial difficulties around 1810. Joseph Dicken of Highlins Park, who had become a partner in the firm in 1808, was declared bankrupt in 1815 and the mill was offered for sale on several occasions at the low price of £4,000.[77] It was abandoned shortly afterwards but later re-opened for the spinning of worsted yarn. In 1841 it was giving employment to 65 of the local inhabitants. By 1851, however, the business was closed and part of the mill was occupied by M. & W. Bond & Co. for the manufacture of tape and smallware.[78] Measham Mills suffered a similar fate; they ceased to function as cotton works around 1830 but by the 1850's were in the possession of George Hunt, who employed over 250 workers in the production of gimp, fancy cords and silk bindings.[79] Tutbury Mill, however, was far more successful. In 1823 it was purchased and improved by John Webb, who was able to employ over 300 workers in the spinning of cotton yarn. After 1870, under the control of Walter John Lyon its trade declined steadily and it was finally abandoned as a cotton works in 1888.[80]

The Burton Mills of Peel & Co. reached their peak around 1815 and as late as 1834 were still providing employment for 'several hundreds of the inhabitants'.[81] At the time of their closure in 1841 there were at least 129 cotton workers in the town, of whom 45 were listed as spinners and 44 as weavers.[82] The decision to abandon the mills was sudden and was greeted with great dismay—

> 'In the year 1841 it was an almost decided opinion that on the Cotton Mills being closed, Burton would bow down to the dust, that the glory had departed, as the trade was the mainstay of the town . . . Nothing could equal Peel's calico and Port's hats'.[83]

It was probably in the following year that Alexander Small of Whaley, Derbyshire acquired Winshill Mill and began to use it for tape manufacture. By 1851 he was in partnership with John Taverner and John Sharp, and the firm had 42 employees, many of whom lived in nearby cottages.[84] During the same period two mills, presumably in Bond End, were used by William Cooke, a smallware manufacturer employing 250 workers.[85] 'Forge Cotton Mill' was acquired by Jonathan Haythorn 'for the manufacture of small wares'. His 60 employees, many of whom were girls, included spinners, doublers, twist hands, winders and weavers.[86] Apart from Winshill Mill, which continued to produce tape until the end of the century, all of these ventures were short-lived and were abandoned before 1860.

The reasons for the decline of the Midland cotton industry during the first half of the 19th century are difficult to assess. One contributory factor was undoubtedly the way in which many mills were sited along rivers and streams remote from the urban centres and hosiery establishments that they supplied. After application of steam power to textile machinery the cost of transporting materials and products to and from such mills began to outweigh the advantage of abundant water power and cheap labour. In Lancashire cotton spinning and weaving, while showing some geographical separation, developed simultaneously within a relatively compact zone and often in urban surroundings. Lancastrian manufacturers were generally more willing and able to change to steam power and to reap the rewards. Proximity to the Liverpool Cotton Market and to the facilities required for exporting yarn and cloth must also have given them a distinct advantage over their Midland competitors. Moreover, the latter had to compete, sometimes unsuccessfully, with the hosiery and lace industries for scarce resources of labour and capital. Taking all of these factors into consideration, it would seem that once the initial impetus given to the Midland cotton industry by men such as Arkwright and Peel had subsided and water power had largely given way to steam power, the differential costs of transport, associated with an industry entirely dependent upon the import of its basic raw material and partly reliant upon the export of its products, operated in favour of the Lancastrian region.

After 1850 the textile industries ceased to occupy a significant place in Burton's industrial structure and, to-day, little remains to remind the local historian that, for two periods in the town's development, woollen cloth manufacture and cotton spinning were dominant activities. On several occasions Burton has lain outside or on the fringe of major textile zones and has ultimately suffered from the process of geographic concentration. Nevertheless, the diversity of its former textile industries and the way in which their evolution has reflected regional and national trends are of considerable interest to the economic historian.

References

1. E. Lipson, '*The Economic History of England*', vol. 2, p. 10.
2. R.B. Westerfield, 'Middlemen in English Business; particularly between 1660 and 1760', pp. 255–6; *Transactions of the Connecticut Academy of Arts and Sciences*, vol. 19, (May, 1915).
3. E. Lipson, '*A Short History of Wool and its Manufacture*', c. 4–6.
4. Sir John Clapham, '*A Concise Economic History of Britain from the earliest times to 1750*', p. 154. see also R.A. Pelham, '*Fulling Mills*', and

L.F.J. Walrond, 'Early Fulling Stocks in Gloucestershire'; *Journal of the Institute of Archaelogy*, (May 1964).

5. F.A. Hibbert, '*The Dissolution of the Monasteries*', p. 81, see also *Burton Abbey MSS*; unpublished transcriptions No's. 1167–1551 by I.H. Jeayes.

6. *Anglesey MSS*: (S.C.R.O.), D(W) 1734/2/5/1f, Deed of 13 June, 27 Henry VIII.

7. *P.D.*, 20 April 1555 and 12 Aug. 1561.

8. *Anglesey MSS*; D (W) 1734/3/1/26/f6 and 1734/2/3/11.

9. Ibid. 1734/3/4/85; Agreement of 7 Jan. 1574.

10. Ibid. D (W) 1734/2/5/15j, 22 Feb. 1582/3.

11. *P.P.R.*, Will of Richard Caldwall, 9 Aug. 1582.

12. Numerous clothworkers are recorded in *Q.S.R.(Staffs)*, 3 May 1606 and 17 Oct. 1608. see also *P.D.* 1608–9.

13. W. Molyneux, op. cit., p. 71.

14. *Caldwall Charity Deeds* (S.C.R.O.), 1642–62.

15. *H.C.S.*, (1923), The Staffordshire Hearth Tax, 1669–70.

16. *North Staffs. Journal of Field Studies*, vol. 1, (1961).

17. R. Plot, op. cit; p. 109.

18. *B.P.C.D.*, Townmasters' Accounts, 1680–1740.

19. *Paget MSS*: William Wyatt to Earl of Uxbridge, 1 Sept. 1762.

20. Ibid. 28 Aug. 1721; 22 Aug. 1726; 16 Aug. 1735.

21. Ibid. Henry Hayne to the Earl of Uxbridge, 3 Aug. 1754; Petition by John Gibson to the Earl of Uxbridge, re Fulling Mills, 1757.

22. Sir J. Clapham, op. cit. p. 242.

23. *L.P.R.*, Will of Jonathan Brackley of Burton, 28 April 1711.

24. Ibid. Will of Benjamin Astle of Burton, 18 Sept. 1755. *B.W.D.*, 25 Nov. 1755.

25. *D.M.* 17 Feb. 1769.

26. Ibid. 28 Mar. 1793.

27. Ibid. 30 June 1785.

28. Ibid. 2 Aug. 1787. see also Burton *Land Tax Return*, 1790.

29. *D.M.* 8 Mar. & 15 May 1771.

30. Ibid. 6 Sept. 1733.

31. Ibid. 29 Apr. 1754.

32. *Land Tax Returns*, Burton, 1781 & 1790. *P.D.*, 5 Nov. 1785.

33. *D.M.* 5 Mar. 1789.

34. S.D. Chapman, '*The Early Factory Masters*', pp. 12, 103 & 122. M.M. Edwards, '*The Growth of the British Cotton Trade, 1780–1815*', pp. 31–3.

35. See W. Felkin, '*A History of the Machine—Wrought Hosiery and*

Lace Manufacture', (1867) and F.A. Wells, '*The British Hosiery Trade—its History and Organisation*', (1935).

36. *B.P.C.D.*, Townmasters' Accounts, 1729–39.

37. J.C. Cox, '*Three Centuries of Derbyshire Annals*', p. 209.

38. *D.M.*, 15 Nov. 1765, 19 Apr. & 1 Nov. 1771 & 29 Oct. 1773.

39. E. Baines, '*The History of Cotton Manufacture in Great Britain*', (1835). A.P. Wadsworth & J. de L. Mann, '*The Cotton Trade and Industrial Lancashire, 1600–1700*', (1931). R.S. Fitton & A.P. Wadsworth, '*The Strutts and the Arkwrights*', (1959). S.D. Chapman, op. cit. pp. 47–8 & 147.

40. S.D. Chapman, op. cit. p. 69.

41. N. Gash, '*Mr. Secretary Peel*', p. 20. see also Sir Lawrence Peel, '*A Sketch of the Life and Character of Sir Robert Peel*', (1860).

42. S. Shaw, op. cit., vol. 1, p. 14. *House of Lords Session Papers, 1819*, 'An Account of the Cotton and Woollen Mills and Factories in the United Kingdom and a return of the names of several visitors by the Justices of the Peace'.

43. *Lloyd MSS.* Deeds of 2 Jan. 1784 & 21 Nov. 1803.

44. *John Hayne's Letter Book*; Thomas Dicken to John Hayne, 16 July 1782.

45. *A.B.*, Day Book of J.W. Wilson, 1782.

46. *Universal British Directory*, vol. 1, p. 413.

47. N. Gash, op. cit. pp. 4, 22 & 23.

48. The Burton Parish Church Registers contain 23 entries for the Peel family between 1784 and 1838.

49. *Land Tax Returns*, Burton 1810–15. *Paget MSS*; Deed of 29 Aug. 1812.

50. *Burton Pure Ice and Hops Storage Co., Deeds of 1835–98.*

51. D. Wright, op. cit. (unpublished thesis).

52. S.D. Chapman, op. cit. p. 85. *H. of L. Session Papers*, op. cit. 1819.

53. C.H. Underhill, '*History of Tutbury and Rolleston*', p. 121.

54. *U.B.D.*, vol. 1, p. 413. *D.M.* 1 Sept. 1791. W. Pitt, '*A Topographical History of Staffordshire*', (18), p. 67.

55. R.S. Fitton & A.P. Wadsworth, op. cit. p. 210. S.D. Chapman, op. cit. p. 134.

56. *D.M.* 16 Feb. 1815 & 5 Feb. 1823.

57. W. White, op. cit. (1834).

58. W. Smith, op. cit. p. 98. see also D.M. Smith, '*The East Midland Industrial Area* (unpublished thesis, 1961). J. Lord, '*Capital and Steam Power, 1750–1800*'. M.M. Edwards op. cit. pp. 204–12.

59. *Boulton & Watt MSS*; Robert Peel to Boulton & Watt, 22 Feb. 1787.

60. Ibid. correspondence and engine designs, 1791–2.

61. Ibid. Messrs. Wilkes, Overseal to Boulton & Watt, 19 Oct. 1783.

62. Ibid. correspondence of 28 June & 25 July 1786 & 1 Nov. 1787. see also J. Farey, op. cit. vol. 2, p. 492. D. Wright, op. cit. pp. 25–7.

63. *D.M.* 16 Feb. 1815.

64. *A.R.* Letter Book and Day Book of Benjamin Wilson, July 1800. see also T. Ellison, '*The Cotton Trade of Great Britain*', p. 171.

65. *A.R.* Benjamin Wilson to C.D. Peters, Lisbon, 19 Feb. 1806.

66. Ibid. correspondence, May to December, 1801.

67. Ibid. correspondence, 1803–6.

68. *B.P.C.R.* 1780–1800.

69. *Minutes of Evidence, 1816.*

70. D. Wright, op. cit. p. 31. *D.M.* 3 Dec. 1807.

71. *Minutes of Evidence, 1816.*

72. *D.M.* 16 Feb. 1815.

73. *B.P.C.R.* 1780–1805.

74. *North Staffs Journal of Field Studies*, vol. 1 (1961), pp. 19–23.

75. *House of Lords Session Papers, 1819.*

76. *Minutes of Evidence, 1816.*

77. *D.M.* 16 Feb. & 1 June 1815.

78. Censuses of 1841 and 1851. see also W. White, op. cit. 1851 Directory.

79. D. Wright, op. cit. p. 151.

80. T.L. Coxon (modern typescript article).

81. W. White, op. cit. 1834 Directory.

82. 1841 Census.

83. *Burton Weekly News*, 13 Feb. 1857.

84. 1851 Census.

85. S. Bagshaw, op. cit. 1846 Directory.

86. 1851 Census and *Burton Parish Church Rate Book, 1851–2.*

VIII

THE HAT INDUSTRY

During the 17th century the manufacture of felt hats developed as a thriving industry in London, following the incorporation of the feltmakers in 1604. Its importance was emphasised in 1667, when the feltmakers were granted a Royal Charter, and in 1672, when an Order in Council prohibited the import of foreign hats. By this time there were around 7,000 workers in London alone engaged in the industry, using a variety of imported furs and large quantitites of coney skins obtained from as far away as Yorkshire.[1] Elsewhere, the industry remained poorly developed until the following century.

The complex process of manufacture was divided into the two distinct sections of feltmaking and hat-making. The former involved the matting and adhesion, by a combination of pressure, moisture and heat, of the hair of the rabbit, hare, coypu or beaver or of various other animals. Although some hats were also made from woollen felt, true 'beaver' hats were generally produced from coney fur, with a nap of beaver in the case of superior hats. Initially, 'pullers' removed the long hairs from a fur which was then stiffened with a special solution. A feltmaker then loosely matted part of the cut fur into a triangular shape or 'bat' on a 'fur plate' by a process known as 'bowing'. The bow, six feet in length, was supported from the ceiling above the fur plate and the catgut string, vibrated by means of a wooden pin, caused the loose fur to fly into a wickerwork frame or 'basket'. The resulting 'bat' was then covered with a damp linen cloth and a hardening skin of half-tanned horsehide and pressed or baked until the layers adhered together. After the process had been repeated and the two 'bats' united by further pressing, the rough felt cone was passed to a hat-maker. In a 'battery room' the latter scalded and rolled the cone in order to toughen and shrink it. Extra fur was added to thin patches and the felt stiffened by brushing it was a solution of 'proofing'. If necessary, a nap of special fur was then added with a brush and secured by dipping and rolling. Finally, the hat was shaped, by passing it over a hat-shaped wooden block,[2] and then trimmed, dyed and packed.

A fair degree of skill was thus required in both sections of the industry and, until 1777, a seven-year apprenticeship was compulsory. Some of the preparatory processes, such as pulling, required little skill and were often accomplished by women and children. Feltmaking was normally a domestic occupation but battery work was more satisfactorily carried out in a workshop or manufactory. The division of the industry into so many processes and the relatively high value of the raw materials used tended to produce a capitalistic form of organisation, in which co-ordination might depend on a number of leading manufacturers. It also tended to concentrate manufacture into specific localities, as in London where a large proportion of the feltmakers and hatters lived in Southwark and Bermondsey. The long hours of arduous work, carried-on in a steamy atmosphere, made the occupation unattractive and one often associated with the more depressed sections of society.

The first recorded hatter in Burton was John Blundell, who issued token halfpennies for local use in 1669.[3] It is likely, however, that he was a manufacturer of woollen hats and was thus associated with the numerous woollen cloth workers in the town at that time. William Wayte (1690), Michael Downes (1699), William Denston (1704) and Francis Astle (1709) were probably the first of the true felt and hat-makers. After 1715 the numbers increased steadily and by 1730 there were over 20 feltmakers in the town, occupying cottages and workshops in Bond End, New Street and Horninglow Street. The most likely reason for this development was the inability of the Feltmakers' Company of London to cope with the rapidly rising demand for English beaver hats both at home and overseas. Towards the end of the 17th century the restrictive practices of both masters and journeymen within the Company was said to be severely limiting the growth of the industry. At the same time the collapse of the French hat industry after 1685 paved the way for an expansion of English hat exports to Spain, Portugal and other countries previously supplied by France.[4] Some London masters were prepared to ignore the Company's restrictive ordinances and to increase production but the problem was largely solved by developments outside London. The hat industry proceeded along a course similar to that of the hosiery industry, with a number of provincial centres providing a free environment in which the industry could develop, as well as the necessary supply of cheap labour. London, however, remained very much the main centre of production and continued to maintain strong links with the provinces. Other factors that may also have contributed to the growth of feltmaking in Burton during the early 18th century were the opening of the Trent Navigation as far as Burton in 1712, which greatly extended the potential market available to local manufacturers, and the pressing need for new forms of employment in the town.

The early growth of the industry in Burton was directed by Francis Astle, a man of considerable local influence. In 1709 he established a manufactory on the south side of New Street, later described as—

> 'A House and Shop standing in the New Street in Burton upon Trent, in Staffordshire, fit for a Hatter, there being conveniences and Room for the employment of twenty-four men, with all the necessary implements belonging to the said business, ready, fix'd'.[5]

He also relied upon the output of a growing number of domestic feltmakers with premises in New Street and nearby Bond End. His business appears to have been profitable, for when he died in 1736 he left extensive lands and properties to his wife, Elizabeth, and to his sister, Anne Port, and also set aside land yielding £5 per annum for the benefit of four poor boys at 'Mr. Alsop's School' in Burton.[6] Other notable families to enter the trade during the same period were the Denstons, Fitchetts, Sollery's, Harrisons and Ports. Contemporary parish records contain frequent references to feltmakers, the Townmasters' Account for 1725, for example, records the letting-out of parish apprentices to John Port, Robert Port and John Harrison, feltmakers of Bond End.

After 1730 the industry continued to expand steadily, reaching a peak between 1770 and 1810, when at least 60 men were engaged in it. Most of the workers continued to live in Bond End, where some of the cottages leased from the Earl of Uxbridge had small workshops attached to them. There were three small manufactories; one on the south side of New Street, used by the Astle and Cooper families, another at Fleet Stones in Bond End, owned by the Ports, and a third, belonging to the Denston family, on the north side of Horninglow Street. The Ports eventually became the most prosperous of the feltmakers and hatters in the town, mainly as a result of the efforts of John Port (1742–1802) and Philip Port (1756–1809). John, the son of Stephen and Esther Port of Bond End, began work as a feltmaker around 1760. In 1772 he acquired leasehold premises in Bond End, containing 'outhouses, workshops and appurtenancies ... particularly suitable for a Hatter' previously used by Thomas Port.[7] He proceeded to expand his business rapidly and by 1791 had become an important supplier of hats to the army and navy. It was no doubt the profits made from these contracts that enabled him to open the Soho Hat Factory at Bond End Wharf around 1800.[8] After his death in 1802 his son John continued to run the business for over 20 years. Philip Port inherited his grandfather's business in 1765 and by 1780 had become one of the leading hat manufacturers in the town, with freehold and leasehold premises at Fleet Stones.[9] During the same period Thomas and Godfrey Cooper owned premises in New Street, High Street and the Market Place. Judging by Godfrey's advertisement in 1777 for 'fifteen or sixteen journeymen hatters' their business must have been of some significance.[10] The only hat-making concern of note outside the New Street-Bond End district belonged to William and John Denston. It comprised four burgages on the north side of Horninglow Street, with houses fronting the street and workshops at the rear. Unlike the other Burton hatters, the Denstons were wollen and worsted hat manufacturers at the north end of the town.[11]

Supplies of coney skins for the feltmakers were no doubt obtained from the areas surrounding the town but the scarcer and more expensive furs would probably have been purchased from London dealers. It is also likely that there was a strong link between Burton and London in respect of the marketing of the finished products. Prior to 1760 feltmakers greatly outnumbered hatters in the town and the reason for this may have been that many felts were sent to London manufacturers in a semi-finished state. This could well have been a method whereby the latter increased their output of hats by making use of relatively cheap provincial labour. At the same time finished hats might also have been sold to London dealers by Burton manufacturers. Such associations were certainly in existence by the 1760's, when John Downes, William Denston, Dorothy Port and Robert Fitchett were sending regular consignments of felts and hats to George Wagner and James Oliphant in London by road carrier and receiving parcels (probably containing furs) in return. During 1763, for example, William Bass carried over eight tons of goods to London on behalf of these Burton feltmakers.[12] Burton manufacturers may also have exported their products by taking advantage of the Trent Navigation and the low outward freight charges from Hull. Felt hats were exported regularly from Hull to the Baltic countries, Holland, Southern Europe and North America: when the 'Rebecca' sailed for Lisbon and Carolina in February 1756, for example, her cargo included 44 dozen felt hats valued at £57. 18s.[13] In particular, English manufacturers supplied military hats to the armed forces in the Baltic countries and it is conceivable that John Port's later contracts with the English armed services may have originated in this way. Hat exports were certainly encouraged by legislation introduced in 1784. This required most types of hat manufacturers to take out an annual licence and placed a duty on all hats except for those exported in packages of two dozen or more.[14] Burton hatters would thus have qualified for a drawback in the same was as the exporting brewers.

The Burton hat industry continued to flourish until 1815 when the end of the war with France greatly reduced the demand for hats by the services. Far more serious, however, was a gradual change in fashion from beaver hats to those made from silk. Cheap varieties, covered with a silky material known as 'English tissue', became increasingly popular and large quantities were imported from France following the removal of trade restrictions. Many London manufacturers quickly re-organised their businesses in order to cater for the change in demand but the smaller provincial hatters responded more slowly. Parsons and Bradshaw's 'Directory' of 1818 listed 10 hat manufacturers in Burton but there were at least a further 40 workers in the industry. The most important hatters were John Port of Bond End, Benjamin Beale and Thomas Cooper of New Street and William Denston of Horninglow Street. After 1820 the industry declined steadily with the result that by 1841 only 27 hatters, half of whom were aged 60 years or over, remained in employment.[15] The old trade of feltmaking became less and less important as hatters turned to the manufacture of cheap silk and straw products. In his 'Directory' of 1851 William White observed that 'the manufacture of hats, formerly extensively carried on here, has also declined during the last thirty years'. By this time there were only 22 hatters in the town, half of whom were purely concerned with straw hats. Although small quantities of felt, silk and straw hats continued to be manufactured in Burton until the end of the century, the industry was virtually extinct by 1860. In other Midland towns, such as Atherstone and Newcastle-under-Lyme, which had also become important centres of production during the 18th century, the industry suffered the same fate. Mechanisation of the industry during the second half of the 19th century brought about an even more fundamental change in location which left the Manchester-Stockport area as the main zone of production in the United Kingdom.[16]

References

1. J.H. Hawkins, '*History of the Worshipful Company of the Art or Mistery of Feltmakers of London*', (1917), pp. 27–34.
2. Ibid, pp. 11–24.
3. North Staffs. Journal of Field Studies, vol. 1, (1961).
4. G. Unwin, '*Industrial Organisation of the Sixteenth and Seventeenth Centuries*', pp. 217–24.
5. *Paget MSS*; Deed of 26 Aug. 1709. *D.M.*, Advertisement of 11 Sept. 1735.
6. *B.D.*, Will of Francis Astle, 20 May 1735.
7. *D.M.*, 28 Aug. 1772.
8. *U.B.D.*, vol. 1, p. 413. *L.P.R.*, Will of John Port of Bond End, 24 Sept. 1798.
9. *P.D.*, 1 Aug. 1801 and 3 Dec. 1805. *L.P.R.*, Will of Philip Port of Burton, 14 Dec. 1806.
10. *D.M.*, 21 Mar. 1777. *P.D.*, 23 Sept. 1762 and 12 May 1780.
11. Bailey's '*Western Directory*', (1784), p. 489. *L.P.R.*, Will of William Denston of Burton, 21 July 1802.
12. Bass-Worthington Records; William Bass Book, 1762–4.
13. *Hull Port Books*, P.R.O., E. 190, 370/2.
14. S. Dowell, '*History of Taxation and Taxes in England*', vol. 4.
15. 1841 Census.
16. J.H. Hawkins, op. cit., p. 14.

IX

MISCELLANEOUS INDUSTRIES

In describing the staple occupations of a town it must be remembered that these normally represent only a small proportion of the total number of trades that have been practised there. Prior to the development of large-scale industrial specialisation, each town possessed an extensive range of industries capable of supplying the local community with most of its requirements. At the end of the 17th century Derby contained craftsmen belonging to 36 different trades out of a total population of 694 families.[1] In Burton, throughout the following century, there were metalworkers such as whitesmiths, braziers, pewterers, blacksmiths and locksmiths, woodworkers such as carpenters, sawyers and wheelwrights, tanners, cordwainers, fell-mongers, curriers, masons, tallow-chandlers, soap-boilers, rope-makers, millers, peruke-makers and various other craftsmen. Many of these differed from their modern counterparts in that they manufactured articles and sold them to the general public; their premises often consisted of a shop fronting the street, a workshop at the rear and living accommodation above. In small towns such as Burton it was not uncommon for men to be engaged in several minor trades; during the 1790's, for example, Charles Dodsworth was a breeches-maker, a glover, a furrier and a 'sub-distributor of stamps'.[2] Local self-sufficiency was never entirely complete, however, and there was generally a need to purchase highly specialised and luxury articles from other areas.

An industrial history would, therefore, be incomplete if it failed to examine the characteristics and development of at least a few of these less significant industries. The rope, timber, corn-milling, leather, brick and pottery industries have thus been selected for special treatment in that they have certain aspects worthy of consideration. Most of them have been carried on in the town for a considerable period of time and have therefore felt the effects of technological change in the same way as the major industries. The alabaster-carving industry, an early Burton specialism for which the town gained a national reputation, has also been selected for special consideration.

Rope-making

Until recent times most English rope was manufactured from soft hemp (cannabis sativa), produced from the stem fibres of a temperate herbaceous plant of the nettle family. The manufacture involved a number of processes which, until the end of the 18th century, were entirely carried out by hand. After preparation, the fibres were laid parallel and twisted together by a spinner in a long, narrow building or yard known as a rope-walk. This was done by fastening a group of fibres to a 'whirl' and then walking slowly backwards, feeding-in additional fibres at the same time. The hemp yarn was then stretched and, if necessary, passed through a bath of tar. The final process, known as laying the rope, involved the twisting and stretching of yarns into strands and strands into cables.[3] Prior to the end of the 18th century, when horses began to be used for this purpose, as many as 80 men might be required to assist with the laying of a large cable. Edmund Cartwright's 'Cordelier', patented in 1792, and Joseph Huddart's invention of 1793, together with a series of later modifications, greatly assisted manufacture but it was not until after 1860 that mechanised processes generally superseded hand-spinning.

Rope-making was thus a skilled occupation requiring extensive premises. Although it was no doubt practised in Burton on a small scale from an early date, it was not until the middle of the 18th century that it became significant. The import of large consignments of hemp from Russia and Poland by the exporting brewers provided the stimulus for this development. Benjamin Wilson, the leading Burton brewer of the period, began his working life as a rope-maker and for a time may have combined the two trades. By the 1780's the town contained at least eight rope-makers, of whom the most important were William Denston and John Wilson of Horninglow Street and William Trickle of High Street.[4] They used Russian, Memel and Rhine hemp imported by Benjamin, William and J.W. Wilson and may also have made use of some locally grown fibres. In 1818 the leading manufacturer was Barnabas Leedham of Horninglow Street who was listed as a 'flax-dresser, rope, twine and sacking maker'.[5] There is no indication that Burton producers catered for external markets; other local industries and agriculture no doubt provided most of the demand.

By 1851 only two rope and twine makers remained in the town, the more important being James Elson who owned a rope-walk in Anderstaff Lane and a house and shop in High Street.[6] The industry had clearly become a victim of large-scale production, whereby ports, with access to imported fibres and large markets and with important shipbuilding industries, were rapidly becoming the main centres of production. Small rope-walks continued to operate in Burton until the early years of the following century but were of little significance.

Woodworking and the Timber Trade

Following the completion of the Trent Navigation in 1712, Burton developed as an important centre for the distribution of timber purchased by Trent merchants in Hull and Gainsborough or imported by brewers from St. Petersburg, Riga and Danzig. Logs, boards and staves carried up the Trent were sold to local builders, carpenters and farmers and to merchants in Birmingham and South Staffordshire. During the 1780's John Walker Wilson, Joseph Clay & Son, William and Thomas Worthington, John Yeomans and William Kinder, all of whom were brewers, were the leading timber merchants in the town. J.W. Wilson, the most important of the group, owned a raff yard adjoining Bond End Wharf in which he often had more than £1,000 worth of timber in stock.[7] William Wyatt, Steward to the Earl of Uxbridge between 1739 and 1773, was also an important timber dealer in respect of local woodlands. He sold best oak to the Admiralty, cordwood to local forge-owners and general purpose timbers to builders and carpenters throughout the area.[8]

The collapse of the Baltic trading system in 1806 severed the connection between brewing and the timber trade, which henceforth became specialist occupations. By 1818 the main timber dealers in the town were Henry Clark, Charles and Joseph Perks and Bass & Carter. Clark's timber yard, opened around 1780, lay alongside Peel's Cut immediately to the south of Fleet Stones, while that of Perks & Son was situated nearby on the north side of the Bond End Canal.[9] The latter led to Shobnall Wharf and the Trent & Mersey Canal, along which much of the timber was carried. The Perks developed their interest in timber from their family links with William Sherratt and Charles Hill, whose families had been engaged in brewing for many years. Bass & Carter's timber yard was also conveniently sited on the bank of the Trent & Mersey Canal at Horninglow Wharf. As time went by the brewers came to rely increasingly upon the timber merchants for supplies, while the latter proceeded to develop woodworking businesses, using steam-operated wood-cutting machinery.

The rapid expansion of the brewing industry after 1840 further stimulated this development and by 1851 the number of timber and woodworking firms had increased to six: viz. Bass & Greaves of Horninglow Road, John Griggs and William Riley of Horninglow Street, Henry and Thomas Clark & Son of Fleet Stones and High Street, Joseph Outram of Common Side and Charles Perks & Sons of Bond End.[10] John Griggs owned a 'house, timber yard, sawhouse and shaving shops' in Horninglow Street Court at which he employed 15 hoop shavers, 10 sawyers, a wheelwright and an errand boy. Together, the six firms employed around 150 men.

Later in the century other important businesses developed, such as J.B. Kind of Shobnall Street (established around 1880), and Sharp Bros. & Knight of Shobnall Road (1887). Unlike their predecessors these occupied spacious sites on the western edge of the town, where they were able to take advantage both of the canal and the branch railway from Horninglow to Shobnall. By 1900 the industry had largely come under the control of J.B. Kind Ltd., Sharp Bros. & Knight, Mason & Sons of Hawkins Lane, Redfern & Mason of Wetmore Road, W. Riley & Son of Uxbridge Street and Charles Perks & Sons of Lichfield Street.[11] The latter was thus the sole survivor of the early businesses; it continued until 1921, when its premises were acquired by the Midland Joinery Works Ltd.

Corn Milling

Prior to the 19th century most towns and villages possessed at least one water-powered corn mill, the profits of which generally passed to the lord of the manor or his lessees. In mediaeval Burton the Abbey controlled four such mills at Winshill, Stapenhill, Clay Mill and Moor Mill Dam.[12] By the early 18th century, however, only those at Winshill and Clay Mill remained and these, together with a malt mill in Burton, were providing Lord Paget with an annual profit of between £150 and £250.[13] During the year ending 22 March 1705, for example, receipts for the corn and malt mills totalled £169 and £121 respectively, while the joint profit amounted to £169. Wages amounting to £75 were paid to William Bowers and Joseph Knapper at the malt mill, Joseph Norris, John Radford and Joseph Smith at Burton Corn Mill (Winshill) and Richard Newton and Thomas Redferne at Clay Mill. The latter mill closed around 1730 and the others were leased by Lord Paget to the Hayne family at an annual rent of £120. In 1763, when the mill, weir and navigation leases passed under the control of the 'Lessees of the Trent Navigation', Winshill Mill alone was used for grinding corn.[14] Henry Evans, one of the lessees, and Joseph Wilson, the miller, proceeded to run the mill until the end of the century. They extended its business by grinding not only local corn but also large quantities brought up the river from Nottinghamshire and Lincolnshire.

During the early 19th century a number of additional corn mills were built in Burton that were independent of water power. Around 1805 a steam-operated mill was built at Horninglow Wharf and leased by the Earl of Uxbridge to Francis Allen, a farmer of Wetmore, and John Sanders, a miller of Horninglow.[15] Shortly afterwards a similar mill was opened on the north side of Pinfold Lane by the Union Mill Co., 'corn millers, flour dealers and bakers', under the direction of William Kynnersley. It was four stories high and contained a 12 h.p. steam engine, an oat-meal machine, a drying kiln, a bakehouse and store-rooms.[16] By 1851, however, the premises were being used by John Staton, a cement and plaster manufacturer. Meanwhile, a third cornmill, which was wind-operated, had been opened in 1818. It stood on the south side of Derby Lane (to the rear of the present Station Hotel) and was operated until 1856 by John Stonier, 'miller at the windmill', and Thomas Buxton.[17] From then until 1891, when it was demolished, it was worked by George Read & Son, who also owned the Granville Mills at Swadlincote.

The increasing concentration of large-scale corn milling in important corn growing districts and ports during the second half of the 19th century limited the success of many small mills elsewhere. In Burton only Winshill Mill, with its cheap and effective supply of power, was able to survive this competition. It continued to be operated by the Wilson family until the 1860's when it passed into the hands of T.G. Greensmith & Co., the present owners.

The Pottery Industry

The expansion of coalmining in the neighbouring area of South Derbyshire during the second half of the 18th century was accompanied by the emergence of a small pottery industry which, for a short time, extended as far as Burton. In 1794 Sir Nigel Gresley of Drakelowe Hall and C.B. Adderley of Hams Hall established a pottery works within 50 yards of Gresley Hall and also opened 'a place at Burton'.[18] The latter probably stood on the north-east side of High Street, where William Edwards later established his works.

Although they secured the services of William Coffee, a modeller from the Derby porcelain factory, the venture met with little success and was sold to William Nadin of Brizlincote around 1800. Nadin used his influence to secure an order for a £700 dinner service from Col. Desbrow, the Chamberlain to Queen Charlotte, but was unable to produce porcelain of the required standard. Around 1805 he sold the works to a Mr. Burton of Linton, who, for a few years, produced 'ordinary Staffordshire wares' and china ornaments in the form of boots, shoes and slippers.

Around 1832 William Edwards, a Derby solicitor and the brother-in-law of William Duesbury of Derby China Works, opened a yellow-ware manufactory at the Hay in Burton. Edward Gregory, Enoch Copeland, Thomas Chapman, James Moon and other experienced potters from Derby and North Staffordshire were brought to Burton.[19] Experiments with a new form of china were unsuccessful for 'Mr. Edwards' artificial gods and goddesses, made at the Burton-on-Trent works, came out of the oven with their limbs twisted into every conceivable form'.[20] In other fields, however, the firm manufactured excellent products, mainly thanks to the skill of a painter named Samson Hancock and a modeller named Wornell. Shortly after 1840 Edwards closed the Burton factory, moved to Butt House, Woodville and opened a yellow-ware works at Ashby Holes on Gresley Common. The Burton premises were eventually incorporated into the property of the nearby Burton Brewery Company. By 1851 the only practising potter left in the town was Walter Tunnicliff of Horninglow, who had previously worked with William Edwards.

Leather-working

Prior to 1850 most towns contained groups of fellmongers, who traded in hides and skins, tanners, curriers and leather-dressers, who prepared the hides, and glovers, saddlers and shoemakers, (often known as cordwainers or corvizors), who converted leather into finished products. The most important of these craftsmen were often the tanners, whose premises and equipment tended to be the most elaborate.

After arrival at the tanyard, the hides were salted down and stacked in piles. When required, they were soaked in water pits to remove the salt and dirt and then laid in lime pits in a strong lime solution to assist hair removal and to soften and loosen the fibres of the hide. After ten days in the pits the hides were scraped and then washed in a solution to remove all traces of lime. Tanning was then accomplished by passing the hides through a series of tanks containing tanning liquor, normally prepared from oak bark. After soaking in the liquor for six weeks they were drained, dried and separated into sheets of uniform thickness by shaving, splitting and stretching. Finally, the leather was made soft and smooth by curriers or dressers who treated it with dubbin, often made from cod oil and tallow.[21]

Records suggest that during the 17th century leather-working ranked third in Burton after the woollen cloth and malting industries; of the 87 tradesmen listed in the Caldwall Charity Deeds between 1637 and 1662 ten were leather-workers. The most important family engaged in the industry were the Wakefields, who operated a tanyard on the south side of Horninglow Street at which they made saddles and other articles. By the early 18th century John Wakefield was paying an annual rent of 21s. for the property, which included a messuage with outbuildings, a tanyard and a garden 'lying below the Lime flatts or Pitts'.[22] John and his brother Francis, were two of the leading citizens of the town at this time, the latter serving as Townmaster in 1702.

During the 18th century tanning and the associated trades became steadily less important. By 1760 only one tanyard remained in the town; this stood on the south side of New Street and was used by Thomas Ward and, afterwards, by Thomas Grew.[23] Around 1770 a second tanyard was opened on the east side of High Street by William Toplis. This was later used by William Wilders and eventually became absorbed into the premises of the Burton Brewery Company.[24] As far as is known these tanyards relied upon local supplies of hides and bark and sold their leather to local finishing workers. The latter disposed of their products to farmers, brewers and a wide range of other consumers throughout the area but there is no indication that leather-working became sufficiently extensive or specialised to cater for distant markets, in the same way as it did in Stafford, Walsall and a number of other Midland towns.

As the national leather industry became increasingly concentrated and dependent upon imported hides, minor centres of production declined in importance. By 1851 Burton provided employment for only 30 boot and shoe-workers, 7 saddlers and 2 glovers and contained one tanyard.[25] The latter, situated alongside the Midland Railway in Mosley Street, was later incorporated into the property of Messrs. Roberts & Birch Ltd. Until 1921, when a boot and shoe factory was established, no attempt was made to mechanise any branch of the leather industry.

Brick-making

The construction of industrial and domestic premises in Burton prior to 1900 was largely accomplished by the use of locally-made bricks and tiles, manufactured from deposits of marls and clays at Stapenhill, Winshill, and Shobnall. Their extraction and the use of brick-kilns was carefully controlled by the Pagets, who, by the end of the 17th century, were deriving an annual revenue of around £5 per annum (representing one twentieth of the produce) from the industry. Anyone wishing to 'sett up a kilne for the burneing of Bricks and Tyles' had to apply for permission to do so.[26] Expansion of the town after 1740 led to a corresponding growth in brick-making, using clays extracted from the Winshill Wood area between Winshill and Stapenhill. The normal procedure was to dig the clay from October to April and to use the summer season for brick-making. For this reason some workers combined the jobs of malting and brick-making, as the two were seasonally complimentary to one another. A rent of 5s. to 7s. 6d. per season was charged for each kiln and common bricks were sold at 10s. 6d. to 11s. per thousand. The outstanding brickmakers of the period were the Ash family, who were particularly active at Winshill after 1770. They supplied bricks for many of the public buildings and brewery premises erected between then and 1800.[27]

During the early 19th century considerable quantities of fine clays were extracted at Stapenhill for brick manufacture. Around 1815 Thomas, William and Joseph Simnett, Thomas Lakin, Joseph Elson, Richard Dyche, Thomas Ash, John Siddals and William Bullers were employed as brickmakers at the two brick-yards operating there.[28] Each was able to produce around 8,000 bricks per week, for which he received £2. 4s. They used approximately 400 tons of coal in the kilns each season, purchased from H. & W. Nadin of Stanton and Newhall. Prices of bricks and tiles varied from 10s. per thousand for common bricks to £4 per thousand for large soughing tiles. In 1814 when Peel & Co. were reconstructing the Forge Mill they bought over 46,000 common bricks from the Stapenhill yards. During the 1814–15 seasons the Earl of Uxbridge's profits from these yards amounted to almost £370.

Exhaustion of the best clay deposits at Stapenhill led to a sharp decline in the local brick industry after 1850 and it became necessary to buy huge quantities of bricks elsewhere in order to cater for the enormous demands of the brewing industry. In 1900, however, the firms of Lowe & Sons, Chamberlain & Lowe, Hodges & Co., and

Smith & Co. were still excavating clay and producing bricks and tiles at Winshill, Stapenhill, and Shobnall.[29]

Alabaster Carving

The first industry for which Burton gained a national reputation was the manufacture of incised alabaster slabs, effigies, tomb-chests, monuments and images. This was based upon the large deposits of alabaster, a massive form of gypsum, that lie close to the surface within the Keuper Marl in the Fauld, Tutbury and Tatenhill areas immediately to the west of the town. The soft, easily cut stone proved ideal for interior decorative work.

Its use by Norman masons for part of the west doorway of Tutbury Church towards the end of the 11th century, indicates that its existence was noted at an early date but it was not until the second half of the 14th century that alabaster began to be widely used for church ornaments in preference to oak, cast bronze, freestone, marble and brass. The earliest surviving alabaster monument in England is the effigy of John de Hanbury, made around the year 1300, in Hanbury Church, seven miles to the west of Burton. It was clearly carved by a mason who failed to realise the potential offered by alabaster. The effigy of Sir John Bracebridge at Kingsbury and fragmentary remains fround at Tutbury Church and beneath the wall of Burton Abbey suggest, however, that a local workshop may have been operating by the middle of the 14th century.[30] Local quarries were certainly in existence by 1374 when John of Gaunt ordered six cartloads and two large blocks of alabaster to be sent from Tutbury to London for the construction of a tomb for his late wife.[31] This tomb, placed in Old St. Paul's, was unfortunately destroyed during the Great Fire of 1666.

Although quarried and used in the Burton area from an early date, it was the craftsmen of Nottingham and Chellaston who first gained a national reputation for the carving of alabaster. Nottingham functioned as the main centre for the industry throughout the 15th century, but it was two Chellaston workers, Robert Sutton and Thomas Prentys, who became particularly famous. The earliest known Burton alabaster workers were William le Peyntour and John le Peyntour, who worked in the town between 1340 and 1370 as 'peyntours' of tombs, monuments, panels and images that were often elaborately coloured and gilded. During the following century the numbers of such workers certainly increased, with Robert Bowes (1403), John Redying (1403), Robert Boode (1429), Robert Bysshop

(1461), John Blounte (1464) and John Pawnton (1465) employed as 'peyntours' and John Lende (1459) and Robert Wade (1460) as 'ymage makers'.[32] John Pawnton may well have been the organiser of the industry, for he owned several valuable properties in Burton and the surrounding districts and was able to bequeath a messuage in New Street and a number of other premises to the four gilds of Burton in order to provide for the maintenance of the gild priests. Twenty years later Robert Bochur and Gilbert Twyst worked as 'alabastur men' in Burton.[33]

Before the end of the 15th century Burton was beginning to surpass both Nottingham and Chellaston in the quantity and quality of its output. Henry Harpur and William Moorecock of Burton were becoming known throughout the Midlands for their excellent workmanship; surviving tombs of Sir Nicholas Montgomery at Cubley (1494), Rolleston Babington at Ashover (1509) and Henry Foljambe at Chesterfield (1510) have been attributed to them. By 1520 the Burton workshops had become the most important in the country, despatching incised slabs, effigies and images over a wide area. Not surprisingly, surviving tombs are particularly numerous in Staffordshire but are to be found as far afield as Glamorgan, Monmouthshire and Berkshire. An examination of these has shown that, although possessing certain common characteristics of style, tombs attributed to Burton alabasterers are by no means identical. This may indicate the existence in the town of a number of workshops, each with its own distinctive style, or it may signify the employment of carvers outside Burton for less complicated tasks.

When Leland visited Burton during the 1530's he commented on 'many Marbellers working in alabaster', but gave no indication of the numbers involved. The most outstanding Burton alabasterer from then until 1570 was Richard Parker, to whom have been attributed the superbly carved altar tomb at Charwelton, Northamptonshire (1556) and that of Lord Chancellor Bromley at Wroxeter, Salop (1555). Evidence suggests that Parker also exported carvings to the Continent, assisted by his mother-in-law, Margery Walker of Burton. The latter rented a shop in Bristol which may have been used not only for the sale of carvings but for the storage of alabaster 'tables' awaiting shipment. At the time of her death in 1553 debts owing to her included:

> 'Itm Laurence Clav for tables of alablast
>
> xiij/l . vis. viijd.
>
> Itm Thoms Lycett for tables of alablast
>
> ix/l . xs.'[35]

The sale of products over a wide area of England and even overseas necessitated a well organised system of distribution. In some instances provisional agreements to make an effigy or tomb were concluded well in advance of a person's death. Harry Broke of Lubenham, Leicestershire, who was probably born at Burton around 1507, decreed in his will that upon his death an alabaster slab was to be engraved in Burton with 'the pictor of me' in armour and harness and 'the Brocke under my hed'.[36] At a later date a contract was drawn up in which the alabasterer agreed to produce a tomb of a particular design, for a stated price by a fixed date. A surviving agreement made between George Shirley of Staunton Harold and Richard and Gabriel Royley of Burton in 1582, concerning the erection of a tomb at Somerton, Oxfordshire for Thomas Fermor and his wife, is no doubt typical of the period. The alabasterers agreed to—

> 'fully finish a very faire Tumbe of very faire well chosen and durable Alabaster stone ... and well p'potioned picture of a gentleman with furniture and ornamentes in armour ... and p'fect picture of a faire gentlewoman with a Frenchood ... and sett out with good and convenable oiles, golde and colours round about the edge and creste of ye said Tumbe ... that ye said George Shirley within one monthe next after request be made shall find and send to Burton convenable and sufficient waines cartes and cattle to draive leade, carye and bring all ye peeces and p'tes of ye said Tumbe, and also to cause ye foundacion of ye said Tumbe to be made by a masonne at his own charges'.[37]

Despite the iconoclasm of the Reformation and the pre-Restoration period, a surprisingly large number of major works attributed to Harpur, Moorecock, Parker and their contemporaries have fortunately survived. So too have many examples of the somewhat inferior products of the Burton school that developed after 1560. The latter displayed lack of imagination and originality, a persistence in the Gothic tradition and a complete lack of understanding of the new Renaissance styles. While London craftsmen, under the influence of highly competent Italian and Flemish carvers, were able to produce superbly carved and exact portraitures of the dead, Richard and Gabriel Royley, the leading Burton alabasterers, were content to manufacture 'lamentable shadows of works by the earlier Burton generation, degenerate both in their human types and in their would-be Italian decoration'.[38] Nevertheless, the Royleys' work was eagerly sought after throughout the Midlands and by concentrating on a limited number of designs and adopting mass-production methods they were able to manufacture cheap and accurate carvings in large quantities. They were aided by the patronage of the Littleton family of Penkridge whose coat of arms was inscribed on many of their works. So prolific was their output that a large proportion of the work must have been carried out by assistants but no records have survived to show the number employed.[39] By 1589, when Richard Royley died, the artistic standard of their workmanship had fallen to an extremely low level.

The Burton alabaster carving industry was saved from extinction by Joseph Hollemans, a talented Dutch craftsman who settled in the town around 1590. By combining the Flemish style of carving with superb workmanship and bold ideas he was able to produce some of the finest alabaster monuments ever made. His eccentric designs and lavish use of ornament have survived in the Spencer tombs of Great Brington, Northamptonshire (1586 and later) and Yarnton, Oxfordshire (1609) and in the Fermor tombs at Easton Neston, Northamptonshire (1612). The monument to Edward Moseley at Rolleston (1638) was probably one of his last works, by which time the excellent black and white marble work of the London carvers had become popular throughout the country. The havoc wreaked by the Civil War and the effects of Puritanism merely hastened the end of an industry which was already dying because of changing tastes and lack of artistic inspiration (Hollemans excepted).

Alabaster and gypsum continued to be quarried at Castle Hays and Fauld, the alabaster being used locally for gravestones, tables, paving stones, chimney pieces, salts, candlesticks, plates and dishes and the gypsum for plastering walls and floors and for pottery moulds.[40] As the Allsopp and Hawkins monuments in Burton Parish Church testify, the art of alabaster carving persisted locally for at least a further two centuries, without regaining a wide reputation. In recent times J.C. Staton's of Fauld and Tutbury have supplied alabaster blocks for ornamental work in notable buildings in Britain and the U.S.A. and have mined large quantities of gypsum for the manufacture of plasterboard and other materials.

References

1. J. Houghton, '*A Collection for the Improvement of Husbandry and Trade*', (1692–4).
2. *U.B.D.*, vol. 1, (1791), p. 418.
3. H.W. Dickinson, 'A Condensed History of Rope-making'; *Transactions of the Newcomen Society*, vol. 23, (1942–3).
4. Bailey's '*Western Directory*', 1784. *U.B.D.*, vol. 1, (1791). *B.P.C.D.*; Townmasters' Accounts, 1780, 1785 & 1791. *D.M.*, 17 Sept. 1789.
5. Parsons & Bradshaw's '*Directory*', 1818.
6. W. White's '*Directory*' 1851. *Burton Parish Church Rate Book*, 1851–2.
7. *A.R.*, Day Books of J.W. Wilson, 1778–85.
8. *Paget MSS*; Estate Accounts, 1739–73.
9. *Land Tax Returns*, Burton Extra, 1781–1830. Parsons & Bradshaw's '*Directory*', 1818. Wood's *Map of Burton*, 1837.
10. W. White's '*Directory*', 1851. *Burton Parish Church Rate Book*, 1851–2. 1851 Census.
11. '*Burton Directory*', 1900.
12. W. Molyneux, op. cit. pp. 44–5.
13. *Paget MSS*, Accounts for Buton Mills, 1704–36.
14. *P.D.*, 14 Feb. 1744 & 10 Feb. 1763.
15. Ibid., 6 Jan. 1806.
16. Parsons & Bradshaw's '*Directory*', 1818. *P.D.*, 17 Aug. 1825.
17. 1814 and 1851 Censuses. '*Burton Weekly News*', 10 Oct. 1856.
18. L. Jewitt, '*The Ceramic Art*', pp. 374–5.
19. *B.P.C.R.*, 1820–50.
20. L. Jewitt, op. cit; p. 375.
21. 'The Tanner', *Derbyshire Life and Countryside*, March 1968, pp. 34–7.
22. *Paget MSS*. Particulars of Townlands, 1710.
23. *D.M.*, 20 Nov. 1761, 8 Mar. 1771, 23 Feb. 1786, 28 Feb. 1788 & 5 Mar. 1789.
24. *Land Tax Returns*; Burton-on-Trent, 1781 & 1790.
25. 1851 Census. *Burton Parish Church Rate Book*, 1851–2.
26. *Paget MSS*; request by Thomas Knapper (brickmaker) of Winshill for permission to use a piece of waste ground at the eastern end of Burton Bridge, 23 Aug. 1709.
27. *B.P.C.D.* Townmasters' Accounts, 1739–85. *P.D.*, 2 Mar. 1772. *A.R.*, Day Books of Benjamin & J.W. Wilson, 1775–95. *L.P.R.*, Wills of Valentine Ash (sen. and jun.) of Winshill, 4 Nov. 1798 & 8 May 1804.
28. *Paget MSS*; Accounts of Stapenhill Brickyards, 1814–15.
29. '*Burton Directory*', 1900.
30. Sir Oswald Mosley and Edwin Brown, '*The Natural History of Tutbury*', (1863), p. 8. S.A. Jeavons, '*The Monumental Effigies of Staffordshire*', part 1. P.B. Chatwin, 'Monumental Effigies in the County of Warwick'; *Transactions of the Birmingham Archaelogical Society*, vol. 47, (1921), p. 50.
31. K.A. Esdaile, '*English Church Monuments, 1510–1840*, p. 51.
32. *Burton Abbey MSS*; transcriptions by I.H. Jeayes, no's. 1041–2, 1261, 1315, 1322, 1329, 1410, 1453, 1455, 1511–2, 1516–7 and 1519.
33. P.D. Chatwin, 'Three Alabaster Tables'; *Transactions of the Birmingham Archaelogical Society*, vol. 48, (1922), p. 179.

34. K.A. Esdaile, op. cit., p. 52, P.B. Chatwin, (1922), op. cit., p. 142.
35. P.B. Chatwin (1922), op. cit., p. 180; Will of Margery Walker of Burton-on-Trent, (1546) and inventory (1553).
36. *H.C.S.*; New Series, vol. 1, (1917–18), p. 312.
37. F.H. Crossley, '*English Church Monuments, A.D. 1150–1550*', pp. 32–3.
38. K.A. Esdaile, op. cit., p. 48.
39. *B.P.C.R.*, 31 Jan. 1581/2; Richard and Gabriel Cartwright (alias Royley) were present at the marriage of their apprentice, Richard Wharton, to Joyes Hamp of Winshill.
40. R. Plot, op. cit; pp. 173–4.

X

CONCLUSION

In the foregoing chapters a sectionalised treatment has been adopted in the interests of lucidity and continuity but this must not be allowed to distract attention from the close relationship that often existed between certain industries or from the evolution of industry in general. Moreover, in studying the many technological advances and the changing scale and pattern of industry during the 18th and 19th centuries one must not overlook their social implications. The industrial revolution not only made it possible to produce a wide range of commodities more quickly and cheaply than hitherto; it also completely changed the status of industry in English society and created a new manufacturing class.

At the start of the 18th century manufacturers were generally craftsmen who possessed little capital and who often relied upon landowners, merchants and professional men to provide them with premises. This is immediately apparent when one examines the ownership of industrial properties in Burton during the first twenty years of the century. The mills used for grinding corn and malt, fulling cloth and forging iron, together with the related navigation rights, were owned by the Earl of Uxbridge. Apart from the corn and malt mills, which provided him with a direct revenue, these were held on lease by George Hayne, the proprietor of the navigation, and the Rev. William Woodcock. The millers, fullers and iron-workers who used the premises were thus the employees of capitalists who could not in any sense be regarded as manufacturers. Many of the small inn breweries were held on lease from Uxbridge, who received not only an annual rent but also a toll proportionate to the quantity of malt used each season. Other industrial premises, such as hatters' workshops, weaving shops and tanyards, were also held on lease from him. Some freehold properties were used for brewing, hat-making and other manufacturing processes but in general the ownership of land, property and capital and the direction of local affairs were vested in men who were not industrialists.

As the century proceeded a different pattern began to emerge. By 1770 the mill and navigation leases were held by a syndicate with industrial and commercial interests. The forge mills at Winshill and Stretton had passed under the control of the Lloyds and the Thornewills, who had invested substantially in their improvement. A number of important breweries had developed in freehold premises, despite the fact that Uxbridge had exempted exporting brewers from payment of the malt toll. Freehold industrial premises were rising sharply in value and whereas, thirty years before, a brewery might have cost £200, it was now fetching over £1,000. Men such as Benjamin Wilson, William Worthington, Henry Evans, Samuel Sketchley and Thomas Thornewill were involved in a variety of inter-related industrial and commercial activities from which they were deriving great wealth and influence. Together they formed the rising manufacturing class who, as the scale of industry increased and a larger proportion of the population became engaged in it, began to enjoy an enhanced status in local society.

At the same time the influence of the old land-owning class waned as they gradually lost control of the means of production and distribution in the shape of mineral rights, power sites, mills and navigable waterways. The Earls of Uxbridge attempted to check this process by offering brewers and other manufacturers leasehold premises at favourable terms, by entering into a long dispute with the Grand Trunk Canal Company over the price of land and the construction of warehouses, by encouraging the construction of the Bond End Canal and by retaining ownership of the water rights and mills along the Trent. The Trent and Mersey Canal largely superseded the Trent Navigation after 1780 and as time went by many industries were able to secure their independence by substituting steam power for water power. Thus, although the Earls of Uxbridge continued to be important local property owners their control over industry and commerce and the destinies of those engaged in them was gradually relinquished. There was a substantial difference between early 18th century Burton, with its vestiges of semi-mediaeval institutions and practices, and the town in the latter part of the century with its dynamic, industrial and progressive outlook.

The new manufacturing class was composed of men drawn from widely differing backgrounds. Amongst the 18th century Burton brewers, William Worthington, Joseph Clay, Thomas Salt and John Musgrave started as coopers or maltsters in small brewhouses. Benjamin Wilson (sen.) began his working life as a ropemaker, Samuel Sketchley as a barber, William Bass as a carrier and Charles

Leeson as a chandler. Henry Evans was the son of a merchant, particularly concerned with the iron trade, and John Davies Greaves the son of a wealthy farmer. Amongst the cotton manufacturers, both Robert Peel I and Joseph Wilkes came from farming families, while John Bott and Thomas Dicken were the sons of mercers. Industrial enterprise sometimes brought together men of widely differing trades, as in the case of the Burton screw manufactory of Shorthose, Wood & Co. which was owned by a carpenter, a baker, a feltmaker and a gardener. Few of these men were outstanding for their technical abilities; their success was often based upon their skilful use of modest capital, their wise selection of raw materials and marketing of products and their efficient organisation of labour.

Of the many men concerned with Burton's economic advancement during the 18th century, the Peels and the Lloyds stand out above all others. Single-minded in their industrial activities, both families developed businesses of national importance and through politics and banking respectively became household names. Of almost equal standing was Joseph Wilkes who must surely rank as one of the outstanding entrepreneurs and community builders in the Midlands during this period. In the space of twenty years he changed Measham from a small collection of miners' and farm-workers' cottages into a thriving industrial township of 1,100 inhabitants. Through his amazing ability and energy he became the owner of extensive lands and properties, coalmines, brickworks, tanyards, corn mills, bake-houses, ironworks, cotton mills and banks, in addition to promoting the development of turnpikes and canals, both locally and regionally, and becoming an agricultural pioneer of national repute. All of his activities formed part of a well-conceived and carefully co-ordinated plan in which transport developments, extractive, manufacturing and service industries and banking were inter-woven. He displayed throughout great business acumen and innovating flair and a genuine concern for his subordinates. In Benjamin Wilson II's business one is again impressed by the extraordinary range of his knowledge and activities and his enormous enthusiasm and energy. Although a highly successful entrepreneur, however, he lacked the genius and vision, and one suspects, also, the dynamic personality of Wilkes. Wilson was an ambitious businessman who wished to amass wealth and property, while Wilkes also wished to transform the environment in which he and his fellow human beings lived.

For enterprising men such as Wilson and Wilkes there were handsome profits to be earned from modest outlays. In 1773 Wilson acquired brewery premises valued at £1,300, for which his father had paid £164 in 1742; by 1806 their value had risen to £7,000 and his share of the business amounted to almost £21,000. His brother, J.W. Wilson, paid £1,040 for his brewery in 1774 and sold it to Henry Evans in 1790 for £2,500. Henry Evans began business in 1754 in premises costing £250, while his son sold the brewery to the Worthingtons in 1819 for £8,950. The raising of mortgages for the purchase of and additions to such properties does not appear to have posed a serious problem; trade and industry were often self-financing, with established and successful entrepreneurs assisting newcomers. The provision of adequate circulating capital may have been more difficult, particularly for brewers obliged to offer lengthy periods of credit and to maintain large stocks of raw materials. In June 1782, when the brewery premises and equipment of John Walker Wilson were valued at £2,400, his brewing stock amounted to £4,635, his raff stock to £813, debtors to £7,245 and creditors to £738. In April 1806 Benjamin Wilson's stock was valued at £10,257, debtors amounted to £5,985 and creditors to £4,227. Inadequate capital resources could sometimes be overcome by maintaining a surplus of creditor balances—a relatively easy procedure for a Burton brewer holding accounts with Hull and Baltic merchants. He could obtain a large consignment of iron or timber from St. Petersburg, sell it immediately on arrival in Burton, use the proceeds to purchase barley and hops and then pay for the imported commodity with ale the following spring. During the 1770–90 period, when barley prices and freight and insurance charges were low a thrifty brewer could make a gross profit of around £2,500 on the sale of 2,000 barrels of ale and an annual outlay of £3,500 on materials and wages. He might also make half as much again from his dealings in other commodities, his share of boat profits and from interest on loans and other investments. The ability of the leading brewers to withstand the lean period from 1806 until 1815 was largely due to their success in earlier years.

It was not until the middle of the 19th century that brewers were called upon to undertake considerable capital expenditure, in the form of new breweries, maltings and stores, elaborate equipment and railway systems, by which time they had accrued substantial profits from exports to India and a marked increase in home beer sales. Prior to this they were able to finance many other local entreprises, such as commercial banks and industrial activities. J.W. Wilson, Joseph Clay and William Worthington II were particularly notable in the field of banking, while Benjamin Wilson helped to finance the development of the coalmining industry in South Derbyshire and the cotton industry in the Trent Valley. Capitalisation of the cotton industry was difficult in that the proportion of fixed capital was high. The Peel mills at Burton were financed by an established manufacturer, while those at Measham were built with profits made by Joseph Wilkes from a wide range of activities, such as farming, cheese-trading and coalmining. Between 1786 and 1791 he was able to secure loans totalling £22,000 from Isaac Hawkins, a Burton attorney, while through banking he was able to raise considerable short-term capital. As many other industrialists, such as the Peels and Lloyds, discovered, the latter was a valuable method of financing projects without having to surrender the income derived from profitable assets. In some instances it was necessary for individuals to pool their resources and, as in the case of the Trent Navigation syndicate, combinations of manufacturers, merchants and professional men were not uncommon. The fact that partners were liable for the debts incurred by a particular concern to the full extent of their private fortunes does not appear to have inhibited investment, although participation was inevitably confined to a relatively small section of the community. It was upon this willingness and ability to invest that the industrial revolution both locally and nationally, relied. During the 19th century the introduction of limited liability and the re-distribution of national income and wealth greatly widened the ranks from which investors were drawn, while the approach towards investment became national rather than local.

The pace at which the industrial revolution proceeded, both in terms of technical innovation and organisation of labour, varied from one industry to another. As far as Burton was concerned the cotton industry was, from the outset, a factory-based, power-operated activity and between 1780 and 1840 it functioned alongside semi-domestic forms of manufacture, such as hat-making and hardware production. Domestic nailers and hatters were as much a part of early 19th century Burton as were the spinners and dressers who worked in the mills. Occupations such as brewing, iron-working and fulling resembled one another in that they required the use of large specialised buildings, whereas many other branches of manufacture could be carried on in the home with very modest equipment. Brewing was a domestic industry only in so far as inns and large houses possessed their own brewhouses. The early Burton breweries were manufactories in which maltsters, coopers and other craftsmen were employed. As business increased, new premises were added, larger utensils installed and additional workers engaged, without any radical change in the basic form of the brewery. Technical innovations, such as hydrometers, steam pumps and union systems, could be used when they became available in the same premises by the same workers. The huge breweries of the late 19th century were fundamentally similar in design and layout to the very much smaller breweries of the previous century. Moreover, the activities of the workers engaged in them were unchanged in many respects and it was not until the middle of the following century that old trades such as coopering were replaced by mechanised processes. In other industries workers were often less fortunate. The local woollen, worsted, hat, iron-forging and hardware workers were only some of those who lost their livelihoods as a result of technological and locational changes, particularly during the early years of the 19th century. These inevitably produced fundamental changes in the industrial structure of the town, ranging from considerable diversity during the 1780-1810 period to extreme specialisation after 1850.

The foregoing chapters clearly indicate that the subject of industrial location is highly complex and that it is rarely possible to explain satisfactorily the processes of industrial growth and decline in precise terms. Alabaster carving, the first notable specialism to develop in Burton, could be said to have been based purely on local deposits of alabaster. This does not explain, however, why the industry was confined to the 1350–1640 period, why Nottingham and Chellaston were initially more important than Burton and why the industry declined rapidly after 1620. Such aspects can be explained only in terms of changing tastes, artistic trends and the capabilities of individual craftsmen. Local geology thus accounts for the presence of the industry but not its magnitude and timing. The existence of textile industries in the town for over six centuries can to some extent be attributed to the availability of water power but it is noticeable that the various branches remained important only for as long as the town lay within a major zone of production. The decline of the cotton industry in Burton and many other Midland centres provides a good instance of how difficult it can be to analyse locational changes. Iron-working and hardware industries developed in Burton largely because of the availability of water power and raw materials in the form of imported bar iron and local charcoal and coal. Their eventual decline and collapse was brought about not by the exhaustion of these facilities but by technological changes and economic pressures leading to geographic concentration. Brewing provides one of the few examples of an industry whose importance has been largely determined by the characteristics of the local water supply. Many towns, far better placed than Burton, developed brewing industries during the 18th century but few, if any, possessed a water supply capable of producing beer equal in flavour and keeping qualities to that of Burton. From this developed the ironical situation in which a town situated in the centre of the country catered primarily for external markets.

In practically all the industries described, the overwhelming importance of communications in determining the potential level of economic development is apparent. Transport and communications control access to markets and raw materials and often form a major part of distributional costs. For these reasons the opening of the Trent Navigation in 1712, the Trent and Mersey Canal in 1770 and the Birmingham to Derby Railway in 1839 all stimulated phases of intense economic growth. Prior to widespread urban development, links with the London market were often important. It was there that Burton ale first gained a national reputation and the lucrative connections with the Baltic and Indian merchants were initiated. The success of the Trent Navigation depended largely on the mutual interests of London and provincial merchants. London required a wide range of Midland products, such as cheese, butter, hardware, pottery, lead, ale and timber and could offer many imported and manufactured goods in return. During the 18th century Burton sent regular consignments of ale, cheese, hats, hardware and worsted products to London both by road and waterway. It was not until the following century that transport improvements and provincial urban growth permitted a wider distribution of products.

The reconstruction of industrial development in Burton has thus attempted to fulfil three broad objects: to unravel some of the mysteries and to correct some of the misconceptions relating to Burton's history, to identify certain evolutionary trends of regional and national significance, and, finally, to analyse a number of general economic processes which might, in conjunction with similar studies for other towns, assist in the formulation of basic theories on such topics as industrial location, growth and decline.

BIBLIOGRAPHY

Original Sources

1. Burton upon Trent
   (a) Public Library: Burton Parish Chest Documents – Townmasters', Constables' and Charity Accounts – 17th and 18th centuries.
   (b) Museum: John Hayne's Letter Book, *c.*1780.
   (c) Parish Church: (i) Registers of Baptisms, Marriages and Burials, 1538-1900. (ii) Vestry Book, 1699-1782. (iii) Rate Book, 1851-2.
   (d) Town Hall: Burton Abbey MSS.
   (e) Allied Breweries (U.K.) Ltd.: Allsopp Records: (i) 29 volumes of business records of the Wilson-Allsopp Brewery, 1770-1826. (ii) 4 volumes of business records of the J. W. Wilson Brewery, 1773-97. (iii) Hop Book, 1846-53. (iv) Allsopp Deeds, 1742-1934. (v) Inventory of brewery premises and equipment, 1846. (vi) Minute Books of Executive Committee, 1865-1900. (vii) Prospectus of St. Allsopp & Co. Ltd., January 1887. (viii) Agency Books, *c.*1910. (ix) Register of Tied Properties, *c.*1915.
   (f) Bass-Worthington: (i) Bass-Worthington Deeds, 1730-1927. (ii) Register of Tied Properties, 1860-1920. (iii) Eastern Counties Journals of Bass & Co., 1889-1926. (iv) The William Bass Book, 1762-4.
   (g) S. Briggs & Co. Ltd.: (i) Deeds of S. Briggs & Co. and Thornewill & Co. 1740-1900. (ii) Thornewill & Warham's Engine Order Book, 1855-1900. (iii) Plan of Thornewill & Warham's Works by T. Spooner, 1856. (iv) Correspondence and business records of S. Briggs & Co. 1875-1900.
   (h) Marston, Thompson & Evershed Ltd.: Collection of Deeds, 1680-1900.

2. Staffordshire County Record Office and The William Salt Library
   (a) The Paget Deeds, 1550-1850; (b) The Paget MSS (D.603 unlisted); estate letters and accounts, 1700-1820; (c) The Anglesey MSS (D.1734); estate letters and accounts, 1550-1800; (d) Staffordshire Deeds, 1600-1850; (e) The Talbot Deposit; (f) Land Tax Returns for Burton upon Trent and district, 1781-1835; (g) Register of Staffordshire Canal boats and river barges, 1795; (h) Books of Recognizance, Staffordshire, 1680-1800; (i) Staffordshire Quarter Sessions Rolls, 1580-1640; (j) Richard Caldwall's Charity Bonds, 1637-66.

3. Lichfield Public Library: Lichfield Probate Registry, Wills proved in the Peculiar Court of Burton, 1680-1830.

4. Derby Reference Library: (a) Derby Canal Company Minute Books, 1793-1861; (b) Derbyshire Deeds and Wills.

5. Derbyshire County Record Office: Land Tax Returns of Winshill and Hartshorne, 1780-1835.

6. Melbourne Hall: Coke or Lothian MSS.

7. Birmingham Reference Library: (a) Birmingham Reference Library Deeds; (b) Wyatt MSS.; (c) Boulton and Watt MSS.; (d) Lloyd MSS.

8. Public Record Office: (a) Hull Port Books (P.R.O., E. 190), 1680-1787; (b) Censuses of Population for Burton upon Trent and district, 1841, 1851, and 1861.

9. British Transport Commission: (a) Surveys of the River Trent, 1782 and 1793; (b) Trent Navigation Minute Books, *c*.1800; (c) Statements of Accounts of the Trent Navigation Company, 1830-90; (d) Returns of Traffic and Expenses at Burton-on-Trent Railway Station, 1872-1922.

10. Principal Probate Registry (Somerset House): various Burton Wills, 1550-1800.

11. Guildhall Library: (a) Feltmakers' Company MSS. (b) Fire Policy Registers of the Royal Exchange Assurance Company.

12. Hull Public Library: Wray & Hollingsworth Letter Books, 1791 and 1795-6.

Printed Books

T. S. Ashton — *Iron and Steel in the Industrial Revolution* (3rd ed., 1963).

P. S. Bagwell — *The Railwaymen: The History of the National Union of Railwaymen* (1963).

E. Baines — *The History of Cotton Manufacture in Great Britain* (1835).

J. L. Baker — *The Brewing Industry* (1905).

A. Barnard — *The Noted Breweries of Great Britain and Ireland* (2 vols.) (1889).

W. T. Baxter — *The House of Hancock; Business in Boston, 1724-1775* (1945).

J. Bell — *A Comparative View of the External Commerce of Bengal* (1832-7).

A. Birch — *Economic History of the British Iron and Steel Industry, 1784-1879* (1967).

W. H. Bird — *A History of the Institute of Brewing* (1955).

J. S. Bushnan — *Burton and its Bitter Beer* (1853).

J. D. Chambers — *The Vale of Trent, 1670-1800* (Econ. Hist. Rev. Supplement No. 3) and *Nottinghamshire in the Eighteenth Century* (1966).

S. D. Chapman — *The Early Factory Masters* (1967)

M. Combrune — *The Theory and Practice of Brewing* (1762).

Dr. T. Congreve — *A Scheme or Proposal for making a Navigable Communication between the Rivers of Trent and Severn, in the County of Stafford* (1716-17).

W. H. B. Court — *Rise of Midland Industries* (1938).

W. E. Crick, and J. E. Wadsworth — *A Hundred Years of Joint Stock Banking* (1936).

F. H. Crossley — *English Church Monuments, A.D. 1150-*

1550 (1921) and *English Church Craftsmenship* (1941).

D. Defoe — *A Tour Thro' the whole Island of Great Britain, Vol. III* (6th ed., 1762).

W. Dickenson — *The History and Antiquities of the Town of Newark* (1819).

M. M. Edwards — *The Growth of the British Cotton Trade, 1780-1815* (1967).

T. Ellison — *The Cotton Trade of Great Britain* (1886).

K. A. Esdaile — *English Church Monuments, 1510-1840* (1946).

J. Farey — *General View of the Agriculture and Minerals of Derbyshire* (3 vols., 1811-17).

W. Felkin — *A History of the Machine-Wrought Hosiery and Lace Manufacture* (1867).

R. S. Fitton and A. P. Wadsworth — *The Strutts and the Arkwrights* (1959).

N. Gash — *Mr. Secretary Peel* (1961).

A. D. Gayer, W. W. Rostow and A. J. Schwartz — *The Growth and Fluctuation of the British Economy, 1790-1850* (1959).

Geological Survey — *Geology of the Country between Burton upon Trent, Rugeley and Uttoxeter* (1955).

J. L. & B. Hammond — *Rise of Modern Industry* (1920).

J. H. Hawkins — *History of the Worshipful Company of the Art or Mystery of Feltmakers of London* (1971).

F. A. Hibbert — *The Dissolution of the Monasteries* (1910).

J. Houghton — *A collection for the Improvement of Husbandry and Trade* (1692-4).

J. Ingamells — *Some Staffordshire Worthies* (1905).

W. T. Jackman — *The Development of Transportation in Modern England* (1916).

S. A. Jeavons — *The Monumental Effigies of Staffordshire, Part I & II* (1955).

L. Jewitt — *The Ceramic Art* (1883).

J. A. S. L. Leighton-Boyce — *Smith's the Bankers, 1658-1958* (1958).

E. Lipson — *The Growth of English Society* (1951), *A Short History of Wool and its Manufacture* (1953), and *The Economic History of England, Vol. II* (6th ed., 1956).

S. Lloyd — *The Lloyds of Birmingham* (1907).

H. Lloyd-Hind — *Brewing Science and Practice* (2 vols., 1938-40).

J. Lord — *Capital and Steam Power, 1750-1800* (2nd ed., 1966).

D. MacPherson — *Annals of Commerce, Vols. III & IV* (1805).

P. Mantoux — *The Industrial Revolution in the Eighteenth Century* (1928).

P. Mathias — *The Brewing Industry in England 1700-1830* (1959).

W. Molyneux — *Burton-on-Trent: its History, its Waters and its Breweries* (1869).

Sir. O. Mosley and E. Brown — *The Natural History of Tutbury* (1863).

H. D. O'Sullivan — *The Life and Works of C. O'Sullivan* (1934).

Sir L. Peel — *A Sketch of the Life and Character of Sir Robert Peel* (1860).

J. Phillips — *A General History of Inland Navigation, foreign and domestic* (1795).

J. Pilkington — *The Present State of Derbyshire* (1789).

W. Pitt — *A Topographical History of Staffordshire* (1817), and *General View of the Agriculture of the County of Stafford* (1808).

R. Plot — *Natural History of Staffordshire* (1686).

S. Pollard — *The Genesis of Modern Management – A Study of the Industrial Revolution in Great Britain* (1965).

J. Richardson — *Philosophical Principles of the Science of Brewing* (1784).

H. Scrivenor — *The Iron Trade: tracing its rise and progress, with its present state* (1845).

S. Shaw — *History of Staffordshire* (2 vols., 1798).

W. Smith — *An Economic Geography of Great Britain* (1953).

C. E. Stretton — *The History of the Midland Railway* (1901).

W. Stretton — *The Stretton MSS* (1910).

S. Timmins, (Edit.) — *The Resources, Products and Industrial History of Birmingham and the Midland Hardware District* (1866). Includes *Chamberlain, J.*, 'Manufacture of Iron Wood Screws', and *Ball, E.*, 'The Hand-Made Nail Trade'.

C. H. Underhill — *History of Burton upon Trent* (1941), and *History of Tutbury and Rolleston* (1949).

G. Unwin — *Industrial Organisation in the Sixteenth and Seventeenth Centuries* (1904).

J. Vaizey — *The Brewing Industry, 1886-1951* (1960).

A. P. Wadsworth and J. de L. Mann — *The Cotton Trade and Industrial Lancashire, 1600-1780* (1931).

F. A. Wells — *British Hosiery Trade – Its History and Organisation* (1935).

T. S. Willan — *River Navigation in England, 1600-1750* (1964).

F. S. Williams — *The Midland Railway: its rise and progress* (1878).

A. C. Wood — *The History of Trade and Transport on the River Trent* (1950).
Pub. for the British Association by the local Executive Committee

Anon. — *John Wyatt-Master Carpenter and Inventor, 1700-1766* (1885).

Bass & Co.	*A notable Brewery Railway System* (1926), and *A Visit to Bass's Brewery* (*c*.1897).

Directories:

Bailey	*British Directory, Vol. II, The Western Diretory* 1784
Tunnicliff	*A Survey of the County of Stafford* 1789, and *Universal British Directory, Vol. I* 1791
Parsons and Bradshaw	*Directory of Staffordshire* 1818
Piggot & Co.	*Commercial Directory* 1822
White	*History, Gazetteer and Directory of Staffordshire* 1834
Bagshaw	*History, Gazetteer and Directory of Derbyshire* 1846
White	*History, Gazetteer and Directory of Staffordshire* 1851
White	*History, Gazetteer and Directory of Derbyshire* 1857
Wright	*Directory of South Derbyshire* 1874
Slater	*Directory of Derbyshire* 1884
	Directory of Burton-on-Trent 1900
	Directory of Burton-on-Trent 1911

Maps and Illustrations

William Wyatt's Plan of Burton-on-Trent and surrounding areas (10 sheets), 1757-60 (Stafford County Record Office).

Burdett's Map of Derbyshire, 1767 (Derby Reference Library).

Burton-on-Trent Enclosure Award Map, 1823 (Burton Museum).

Greenwood's Map of Derbyshire, 1825 (Derby Reference Library).

Wood's Map of Burton-on-Trent, 1837 (Burton Museum).

W. Wesley's Map of Burton-on-Trent, 1848 (Burton Museum).

Burton upon Trent Town Commissioners' Map, 1855 (Burton Town Hall).

T. Spooners Map of Burton-on-Trent, 1857 and 1865 (Burton Public Library).

J. A. Mason's Map of Burton-on-Trent, 1879 (Burton Public Library).

Ordnance Survey Maps (6, 2½ and 1 inch to 1 mile) of Burton-on-Trent and the surrounding area — various editions from mid-19th century.

Geological Survey Maps — modern 1 inch sheets 140 (Burton-on-Trent), and 141 (Loughborough).

Staffordshire Views Vol. II (Stafford County Record Office) — various sketches of Burton-on-Trent, 1732-1900.

Newspapers

The Derby Mercury, 1732-1870 (Derby Reference Library).

The Burton-on-Trent Times, 1855-8 (National Newspaper Library, Colindale, London).

The Burton Weekly News, 1856-69 (National Newspaper Library, Colindale, London).

The Burton Chronicle, 1867)	Burton Daily Mail Offices Burton-on-Trent.
The Burton Observer, 1898-1900)	
The Burton Daily Mail, 1948)	

Dr. Burney's Newspapers (containing extracts from various 18th century newspapers – Stafford County Record Office).

Unpublished Theses and Articles

J. Baxter 'The Organisation of the Brewing Industry' (Ph.D. Thesis, University of London, 1945).

I. S. Beckwith 'Gainsborough – some notes on the history of a small inland port' (typescript, 1965).

T. L. Coxon 'Tutbury Mill' (modern typescript).

A. Davies 'The Trade and Shipping of Hull in the seventeenth century' (Thesis, 1937 – Hull Public Library).

A. J. Halliday 'The Development, of Burton-on-Trent – A Study in Urban Geography' (M.A. Thesis, University of London, 1956).

D. M. Smith 'The East Midlands Industrial Area' (Ph.D. Thesis, University of Nottingham, 1961).

D. Wright 'A Survey of the Industrial and Commercial Activities of Joseph Wilkes, in and around the Parish of Measham in the late 18th cnetury' (B.A. Hons. Dissertation, University of Nottingham, 1968).

Parliamentary Journals, Reports and Acts

House of Commons Journals: Volumes XV, XVII.

Parliamentary Journal, 1824, Volume XVII.

Hansard – Parliamentary Debates, 3rd series, Vol. 205

Select Committee: Minutes and Reports

Minutes on the Frame-work-Knitters' Bill – The Hosiers' and Framework-Knitters' Examinations before A Committee of the Honourable House of Commons, 1780.

Minutes of Evidence Relating to the Orders in Council, 1808-12.

Minutes of Evidence on the State of Children Employed in the Manufactories of the United Kingdom, 1816.

Report of the Select Committee of the House of Commons on the State of the Police in the Metropolis and the Licences of Victuallers, 1817.

An account of the Cotton and Woollen Mills and Factories in the United Kingdom and a return of the names of several visitors appointed by the Justices of the Peace; House of Lords Session Papers, 1819.

Reports of H.M. Commission appointed to collect information concerning the employment of children in factories; Factories Inquiry Commission, 1833.

Supplementary Report of Central Board of Factories Inquiry Commission, 1834.

Acts

Trent Navigation Act, 10 & 11 William III, c.26.

Derwent Navigation Act, 6 George I, c.27.

Trent & Mersey Canal Act, 6 George III, C.96

Burton upon Trent Town Act, 19 George III, c.39.

Trent Navigation Act, 23 George III, c.41.

Burton upon Trent Town Act, 16 & 17 Victoria, c.118.

Burton-on-Trent Railway Bridges, Act, 22 & 23 Victoria, c.136.
Burton-on-Trent Railway Acts, 23 & 24 Victoria, c.65; 30 & 31 Victoria, c.71; 41 & 42 Victoria, c.67; 44 & 45 Victoria, c.59.
Burton-on-Trent London & North-Western Railways Act, 24 & 25 Victoria, c.208.
Burton-on-Trent Great Northern Railway Act, 37 & 38 Victoria, c.157.
Burton-on-Trent North Staffordshire Railway Act, 26 & 27 Victoria, 132.

Periodicals

Transactions of the Newcomen Society:

E. W. Hulme — 'Statistical History of the Iron Trade of England Wales', Vol. IX (1928-29).
R. Jenkins — 'Historical Notes on Some Derbyshire Industries', Vol. XIV (1933-4).
H. W. Dickinson — 'A Condensed History of Rope Making', Vol. XXIII (1942-3).
W. K. V. Gale — 'Early Ironfounding in the Midlands', Vol. XXVIII (1951-3).
F. Nixon — 'The Early Steam Engine in Derbyshire', Vol. XXXI (1957-9).

Economic History Review:

M. W. Flinn — 'The Growth of the English Iron Industry, 1660-1760', Vol. XI (1958-9).
A. E. Musson and E. H. Robinson — 'The Early Growth of Steam Power'.
J. Sperling — 'The International Payments Mechanism in the Seventeenth and Eighteenth Centuries', Vol. XIV (1961-2).
J. M. Price — 'Multilateralism and/or Bilateralism: The Settlement of British Trade Balances with, "The North", *c.*1700'.
E. N. Sigsworth — 'Science and the Brewing Industry, 1850-1900', Vol. XVII (1964-5).

History:

C. Wilson — 'The Entrepreneur in the Industrial Revolution in Britain', Vol. XLII (June 1957).
J. R. Harris — 'The Employment of Steam Power in the Eighteenth Century', Vol. XLII (June 1957).

Journal of Economic History:

S. Pollard — 'Fixed Capital in the Industrial Revolution in Britain', Vol. XXIV (Sept. 1964).

Business History:

B. L. C. Johnson — 'The Midland Iron Industry in the Early Eighteenth Century', Vol. II (June 1960).

Explorations in Entrepreneurial History:

P. Mathias — 'Industrial Revolution in Brewing: developments in the Brewing Industry in England, 1700-1830', Vol. 5 (1953).

Transactions of the Connecticut Academy of Arts and Sciences:
R. B. Westerfield — 'Middlemen in English Business: particularly between 1660 & 1760', Vol. 19 (May 1915).

Journal of the Institute of Archaeology:
L. F. J. Walrond — 'Early Fulling Stocks in Gloucestershire', (May 1964).

Scandinavian Economic History Review:
P. K. G. Hildebrand — 'Foreign Markets for Swedish Iron in the Eighteenth Century', Vol. VI (1958).
D. S. Astrom — 'English Navigation Laws and Baltic Trade, 1660-1700', Vol. VIII (1960).

Geography:
T. S. Willan — 'Yorkshire River Navigation, 1600-1750', (Sept. 1937).

The East Midland Geographer:
I. S. Beckwith — 'Transport in the Lower Trent Valley in the Eighteenth & Nineteenth Centuries', Vol. 4, Part 2 No. 26 (Dec. 1966).

Transactions of the Laboratory Club:
Dr. E. Hansen — 'Some Points in connection with Practical Brewing', Vol. I (1889).
A. Young — 'Practical Aspect of Fermentation', Vol. I (1889).

The Journal of the Chemical Society:
1876 and 1882

The Brewers' Almanack and Wine and Spirit Trade Annual:
1894

Supplement to the Brewers' Journal and Hop and Malt Trades Review:
1876

Transactions of the Guiness Research Laboratory:
1903

Journal of the Institute of Brewing:
1899, 1909 and
H. T. Brown — 'Reminiscences of Fifty Years Experience of The Application of Scientific Methods to Brewing', (1916).

Transactions of the Burton-on-Trent Natural History and Archaeological Society.
H. T. Brown — 'A Grain of Barley', Vol. 1 (1889).
F. E. Lott — 'Burton Waters – Drinking and Brewing', Vol. 8 (1896).

Transactions of the Derby Archaeological Society:
H. Green — 'The Southern Portion of the Notts. and Derby Coalfield and the development of Transport before 1850', Vols. 9-10 (1935-6).

H. S. Twells — 'Mr. Drewry and the Derby Wagons', Vol. 63 (1942).

W. Fraser — 'Notes of Water Mills: illustrated by those on the Repton Brook', Vol. 63 (1942).

J. L. Hobbs — 'The Sanders Family and the Descent of the Manors of Caldwell, Coton-in-the-Elms and Little Ireton', Vol. 68 (1948).

Derbyshire Miscellany:

G. H. Green — 'Agreement between Mr. L. Fosbrooke and the London Cheesemongers', Vol. 2, No. 5, (Feb. 1961).

Derbyshire Life and Countryside:

Article on 'The Tanner', (March 1968).

Transactions of the Birmingham Archaeological Society:

P. Chatwin — 'Monumental Effigies in the County of Warwick, Parts, 1 and 2', Vols. XLVII and XLVIII (1921 and 1922).

P. Chatwin — 'Three Alabaster Tables'.

University of Birmingham Historical Journal:

R. A. Pelham — 'The Water-Power Crisis in Birmingham in the Eighteenth Century', Vol. IX, No. 1 (1963).

Historical Collections, Staffordshire:

(published by the Staffordshire Record Society and the William Salt Archaeological Society) 1884, 1917-18, 1920, 1922, 1923, 1929, 1930, 1932, 1934, 1935, 1937, 1940 and 1948-9. Including:

'The Staffordshire Hearth Tax 1669-70', (1923).

A. L. Thomas — 'Geographical Aspects of the Development of Transport and Communications affecting the Pottery Industry of North Staffordshire during the Eighteenth Century', (1934).

I. H. Jeayes — 'Transcriptions of Burton Abbey MSS', (1937).

North Staffordshire Journal of Field Studies:

E. A. Watkin — 'Staffordshire Tokens and Their Place in the Coinage of England', Vol. 1 (1961)

The Railway Magazine:

G. A. Wade — 'A Town of Railways and Beer', Vol. IX (Aug. 1901).

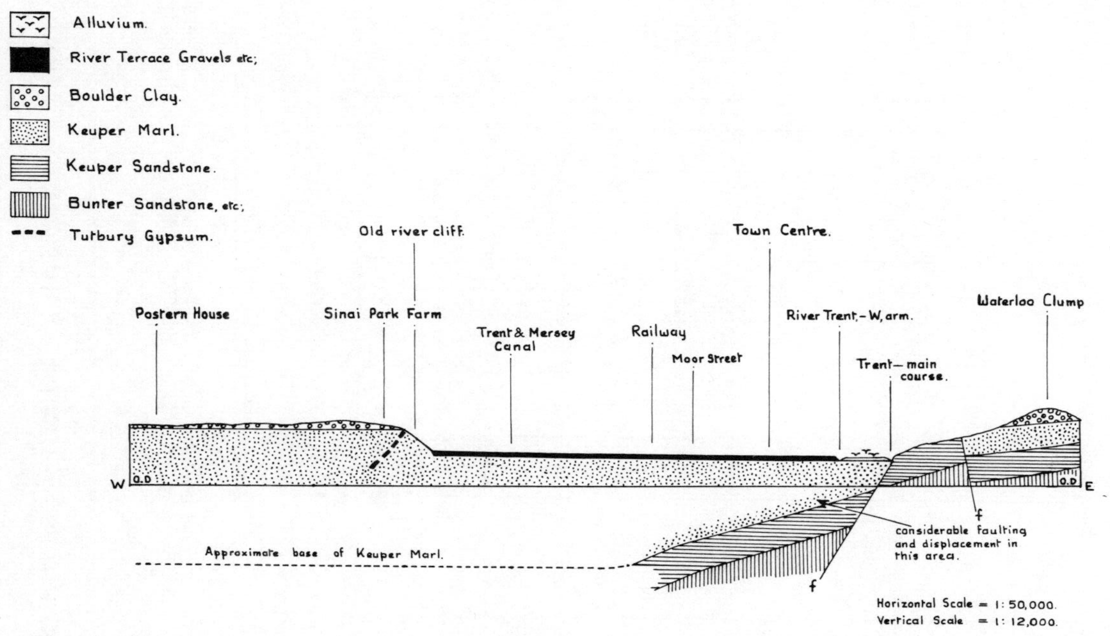

SECTION ACROSS THE TRENT VALLEY, BURTON ON TRENT.

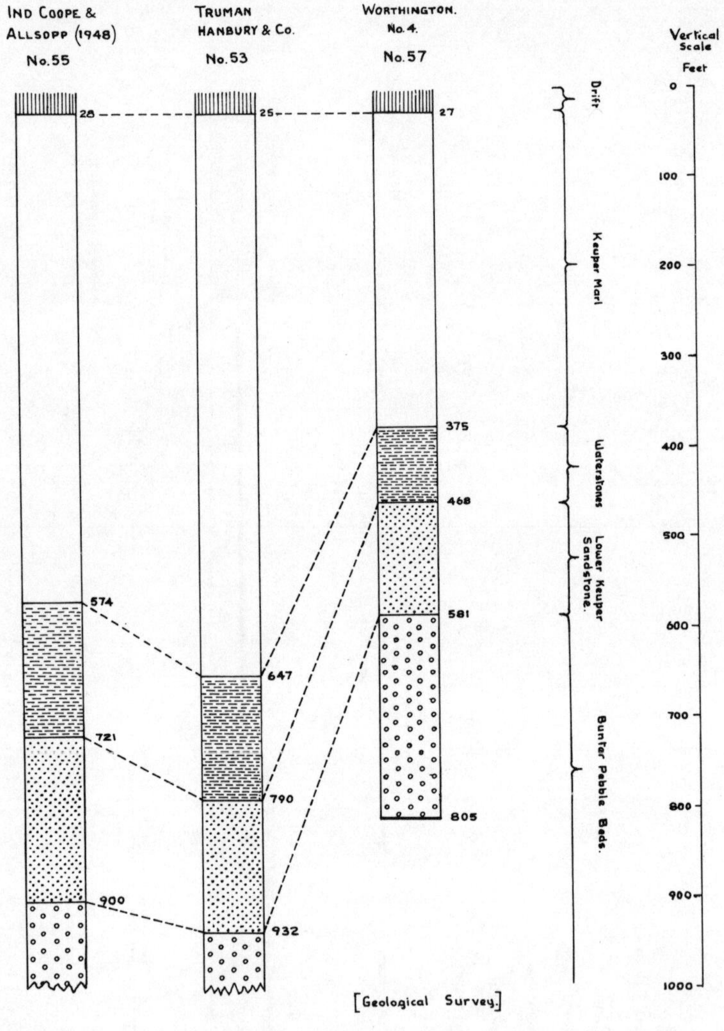

BOREHOLES UNDER BURTON ON TRENT.

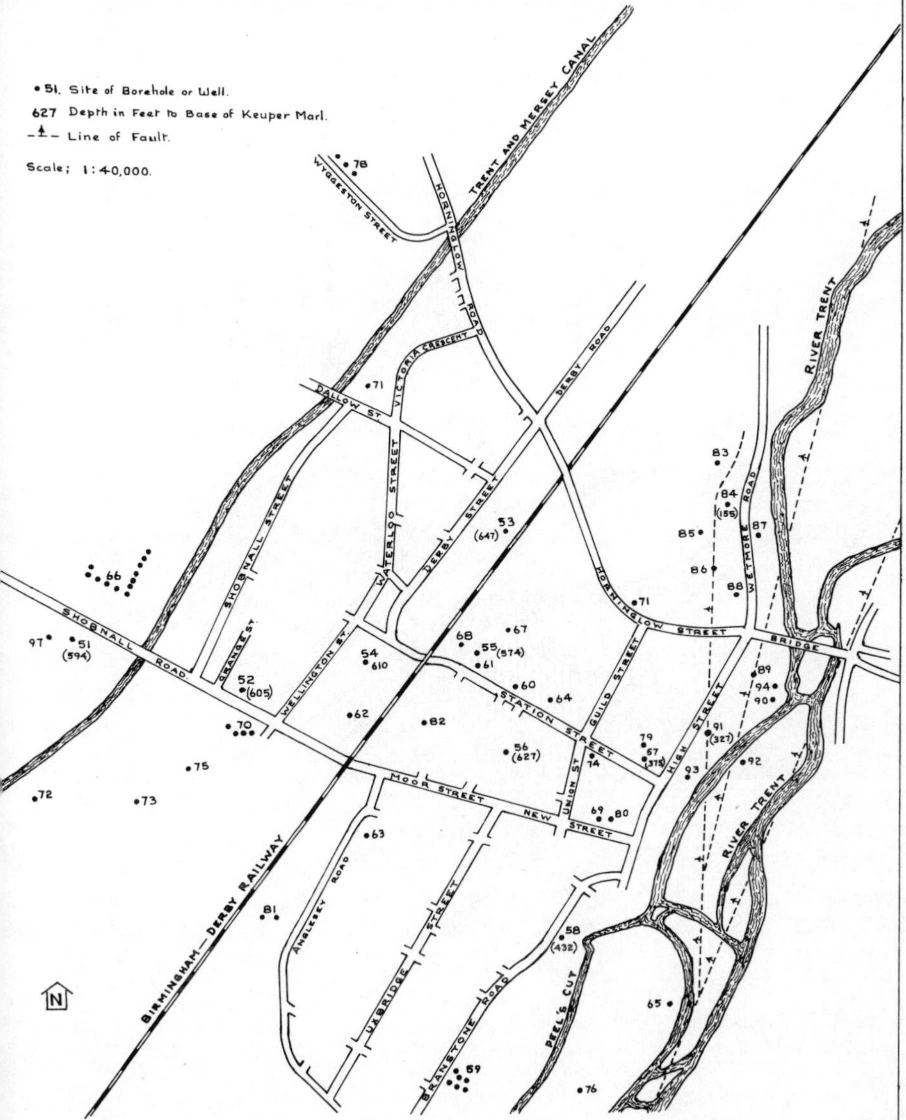

MAIN BOREHOLES AND WELLS IN BURTON.

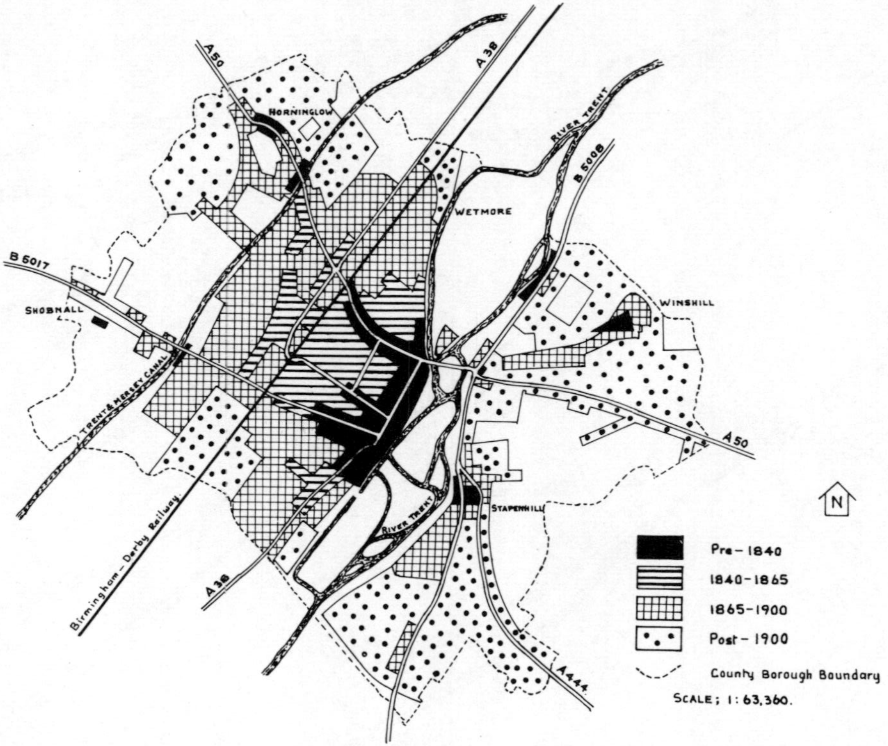

SIMPLIFIED URBAN GROWTH MAP OF BURTON ON TRENT.

(Excluding Re-development since 1950.)

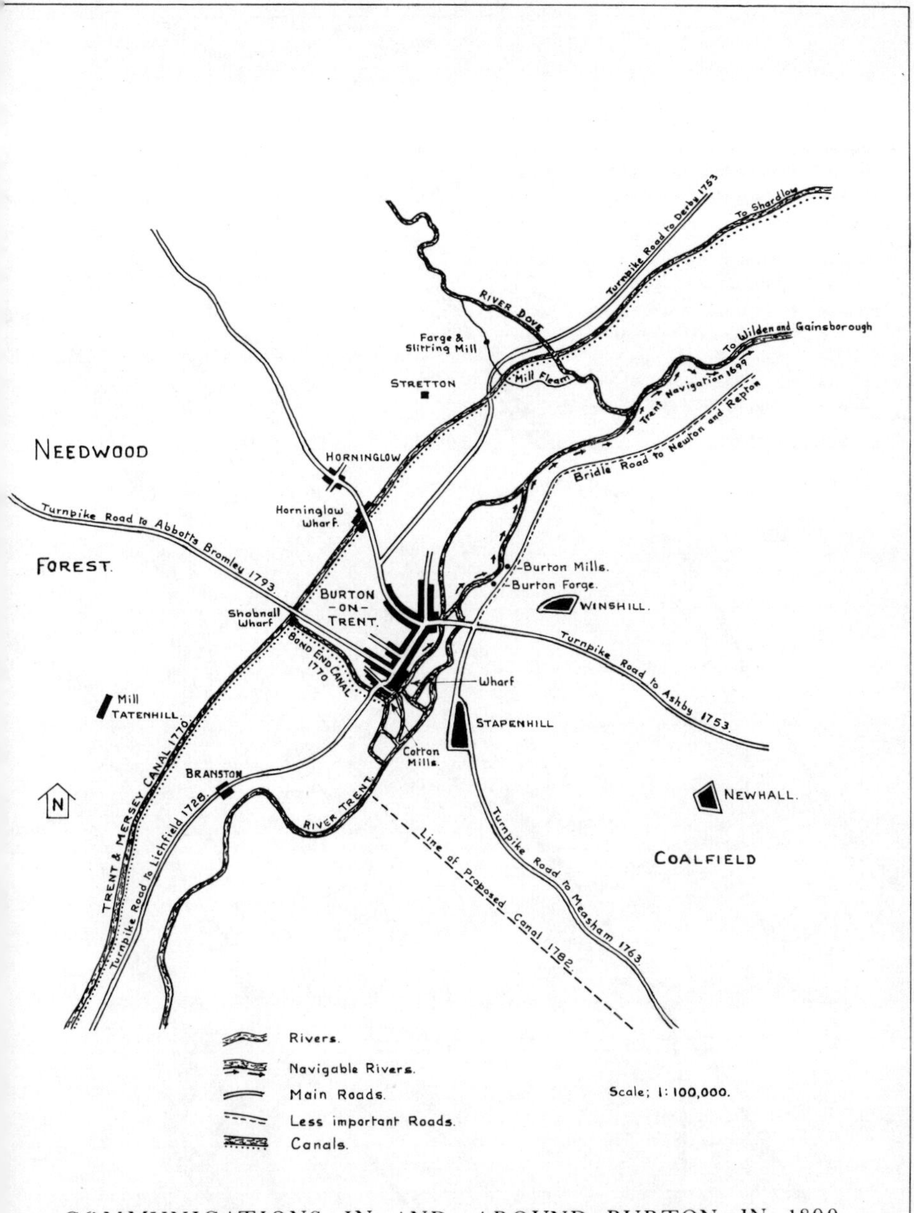

COMMUNICATIONS IN AND AROUND BURTON IN 1800.

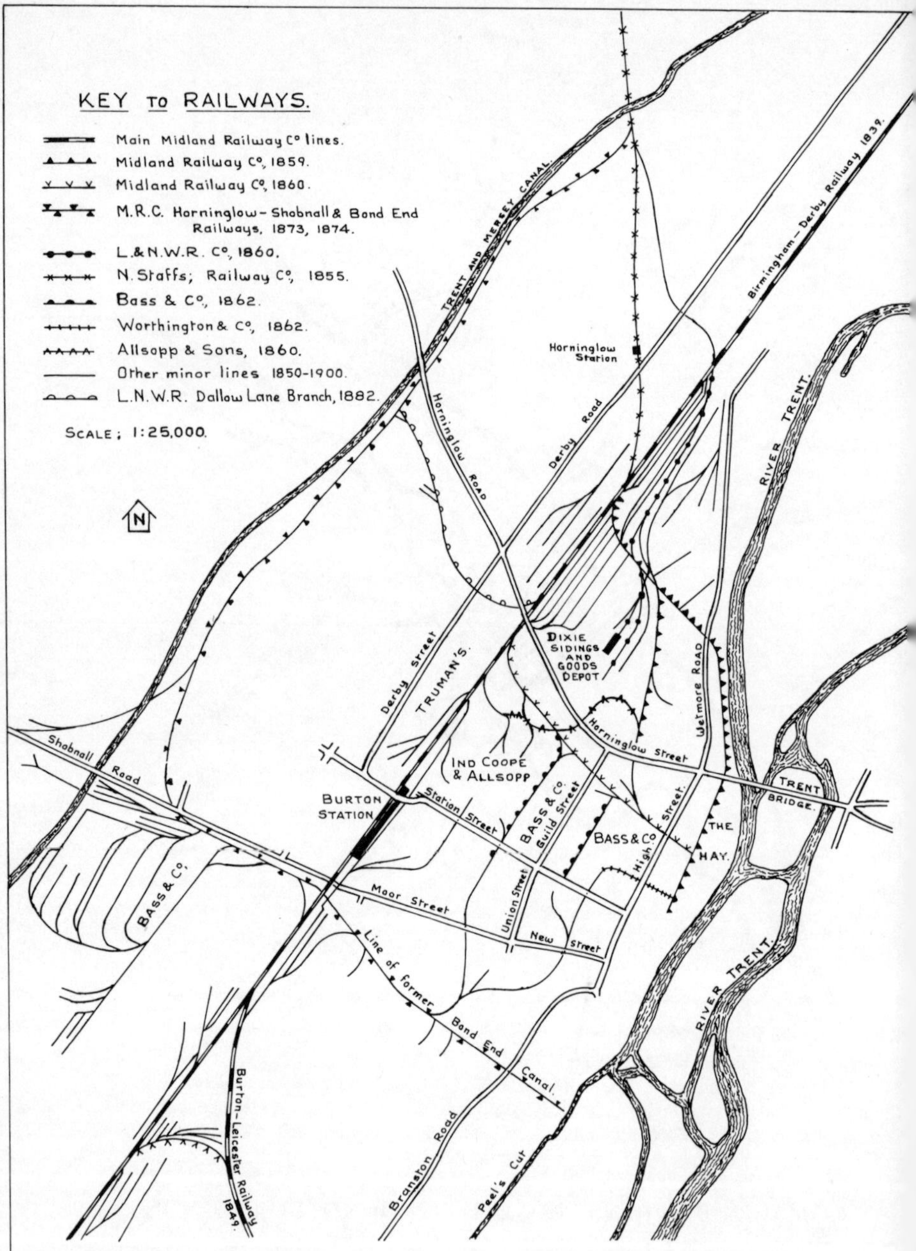

RAILWAY NETWORK. BURTON ON TRENT 1900.

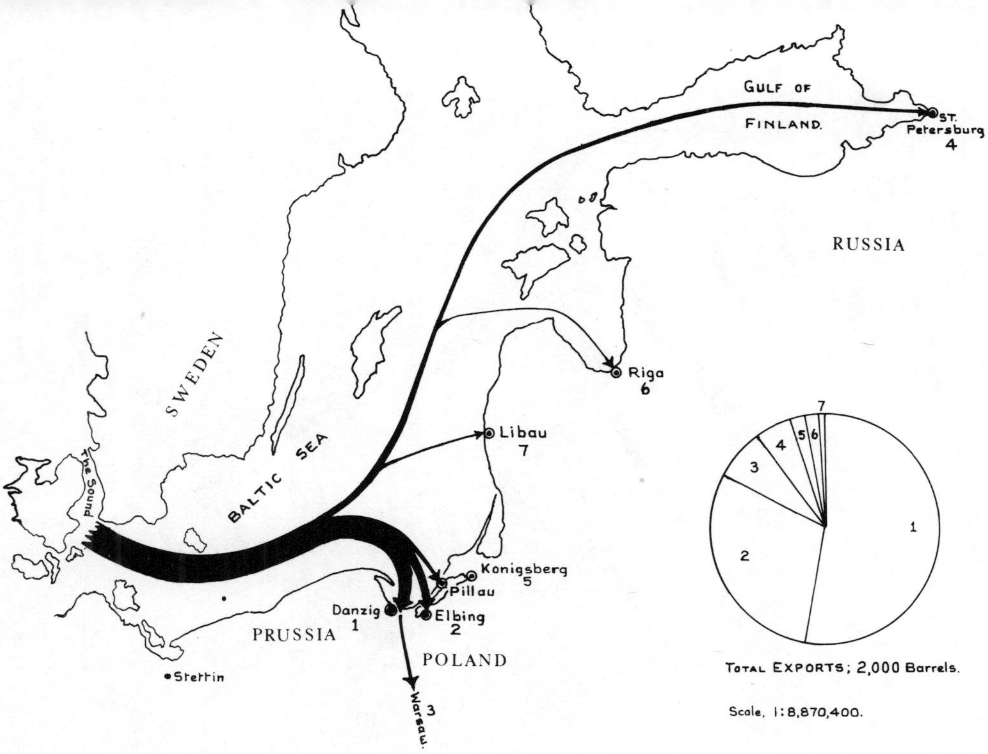

BENJAMIN WILSON'S ALE EXPORTS IN 1789.

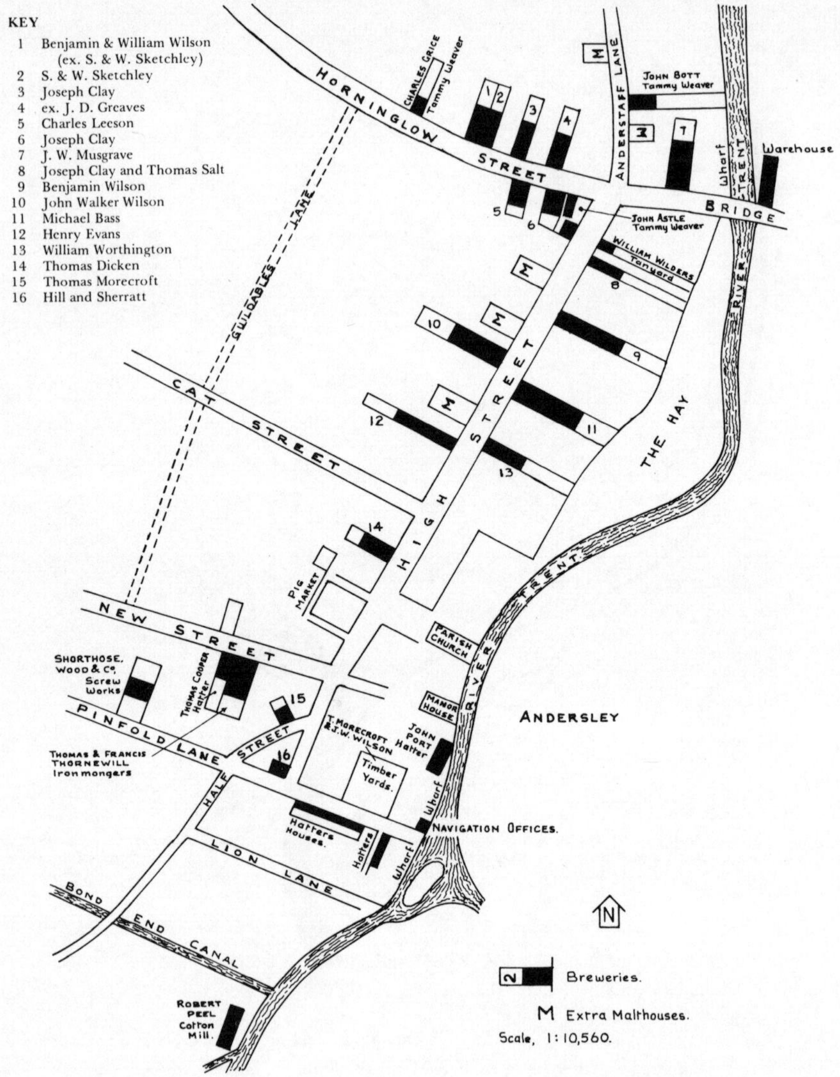

LOCATION OF INDUSTRY IN BURTON 1790.

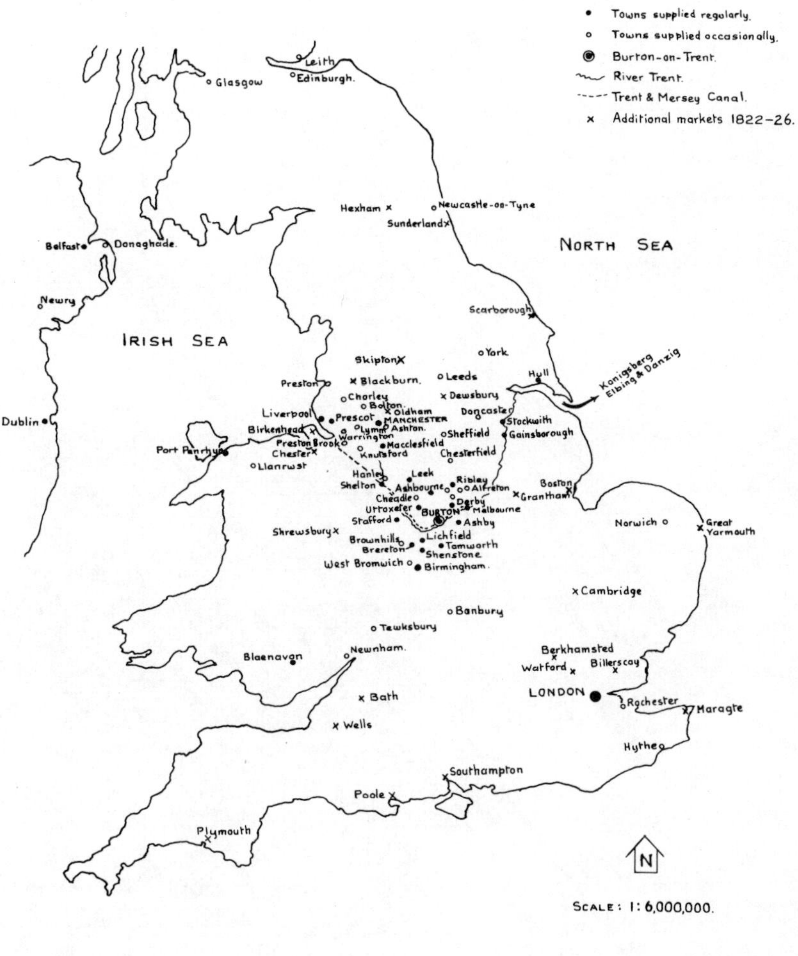

DISTRIBUTION OF ALE FROM ALLSOPP'S BREWERY 1807-11, AND 1822-26.

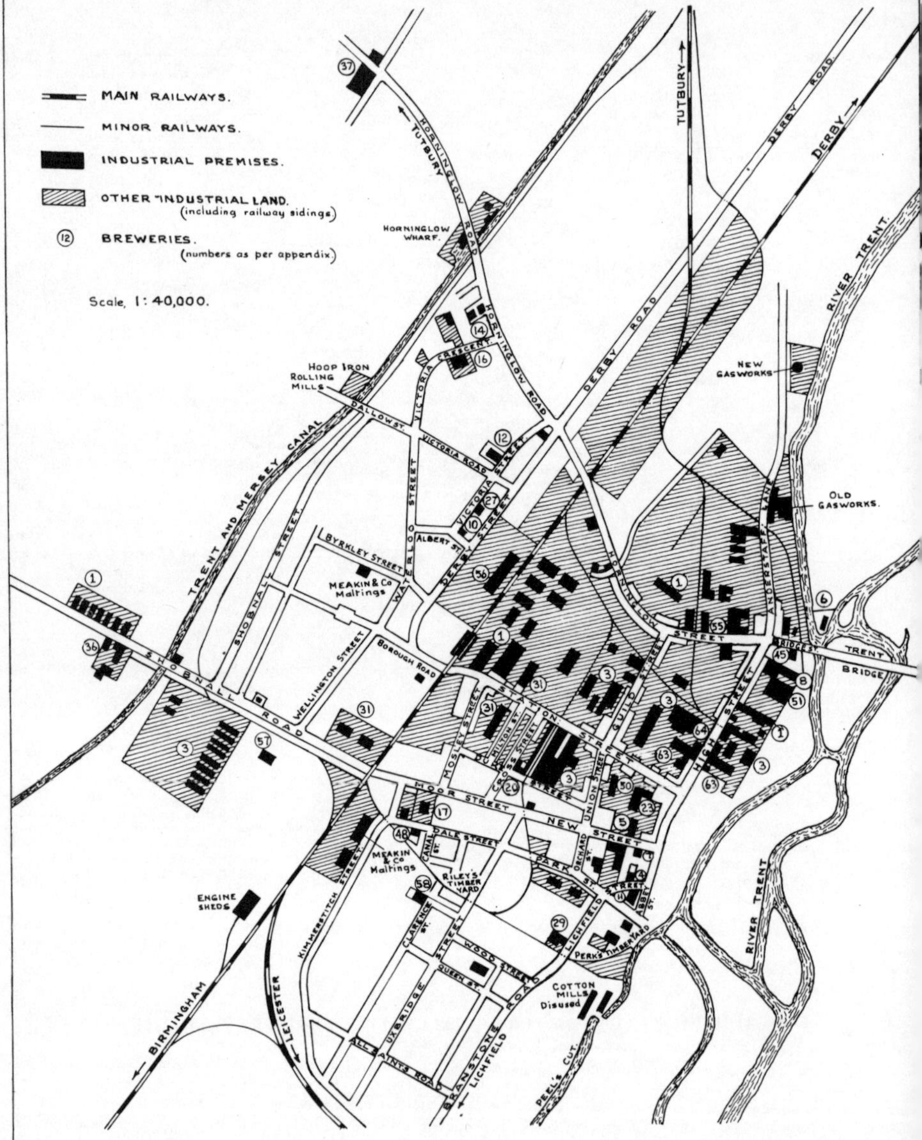

LOCATION OF INDUSTRY. BURTON - 1880

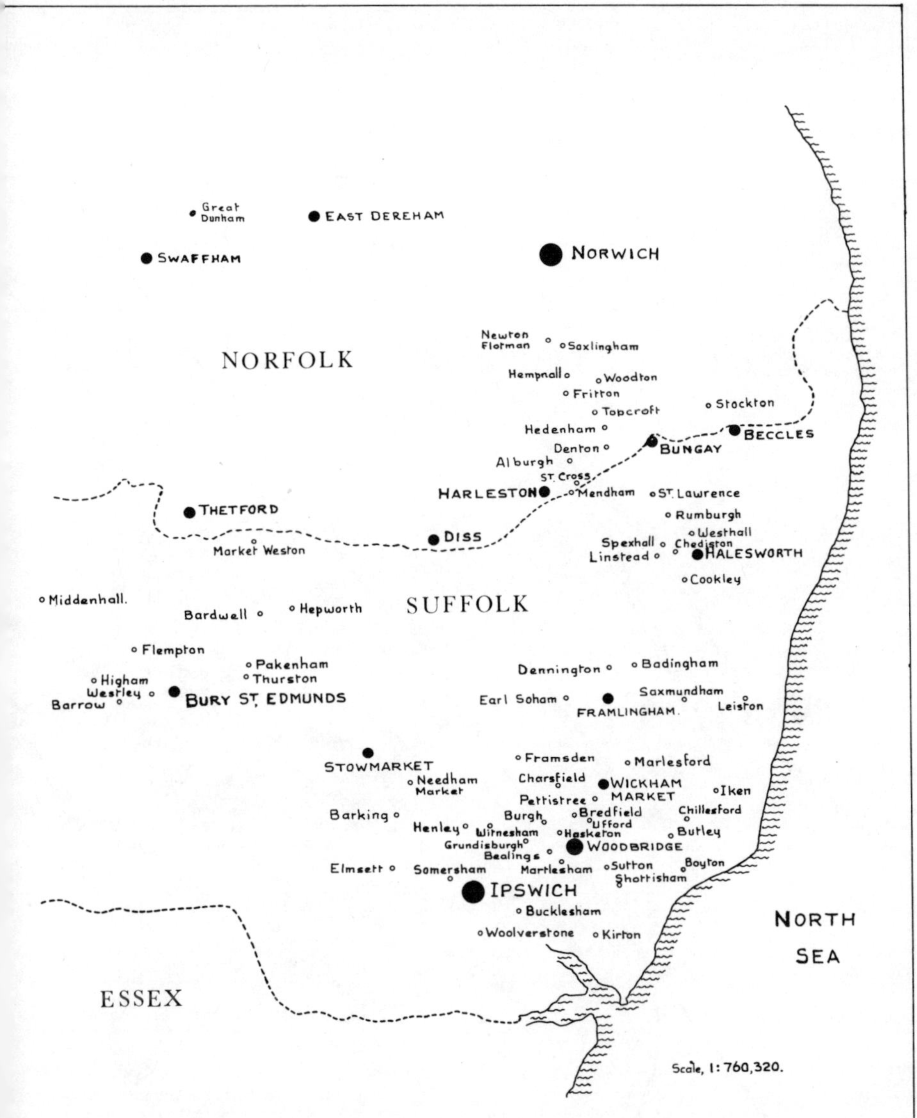

EAST ANGLIAN CENTRES SUPPLYING WORKERS TO BASS & CO 1890-91.

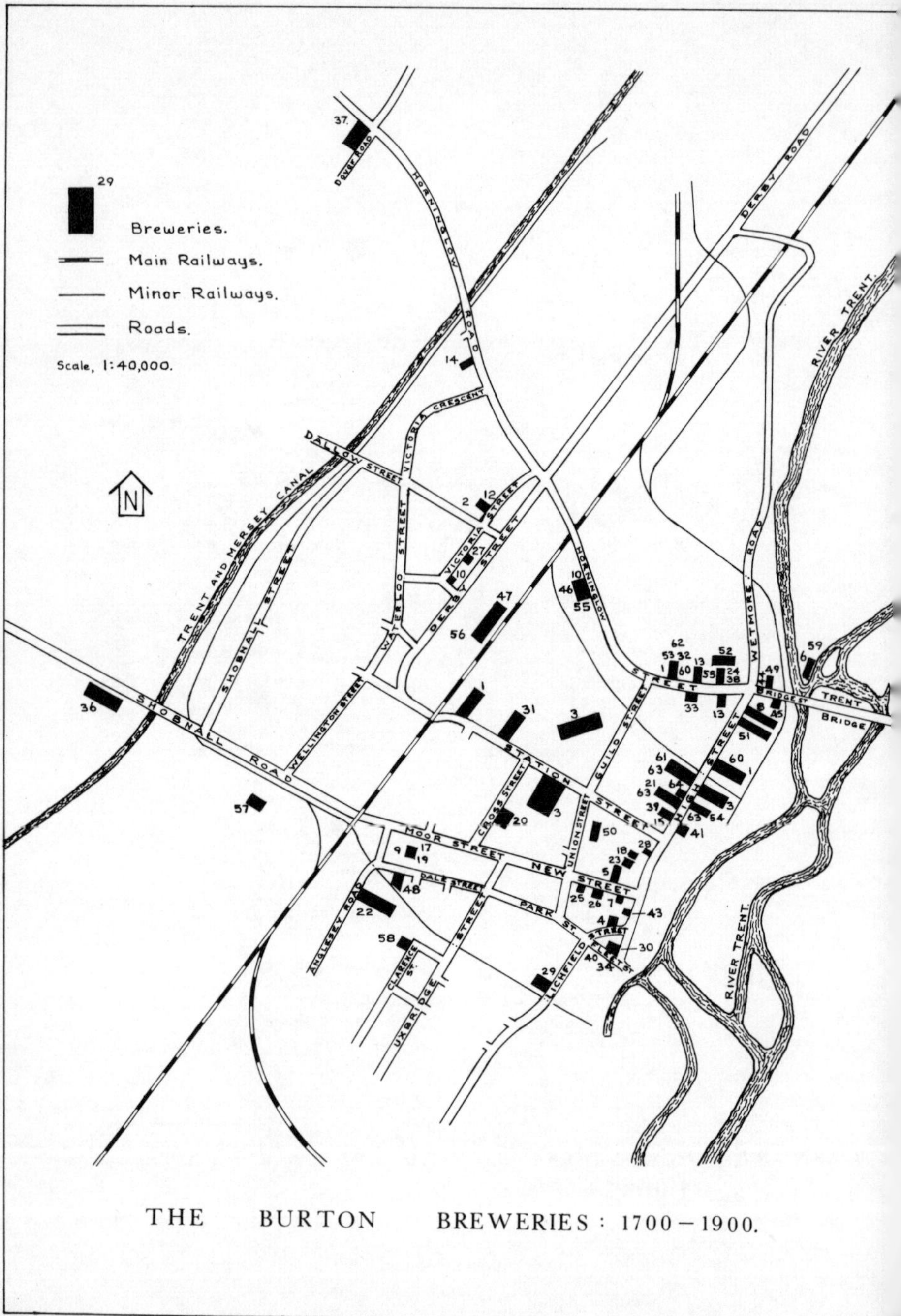

THE BURTON BREWERIES: 1700–1900.

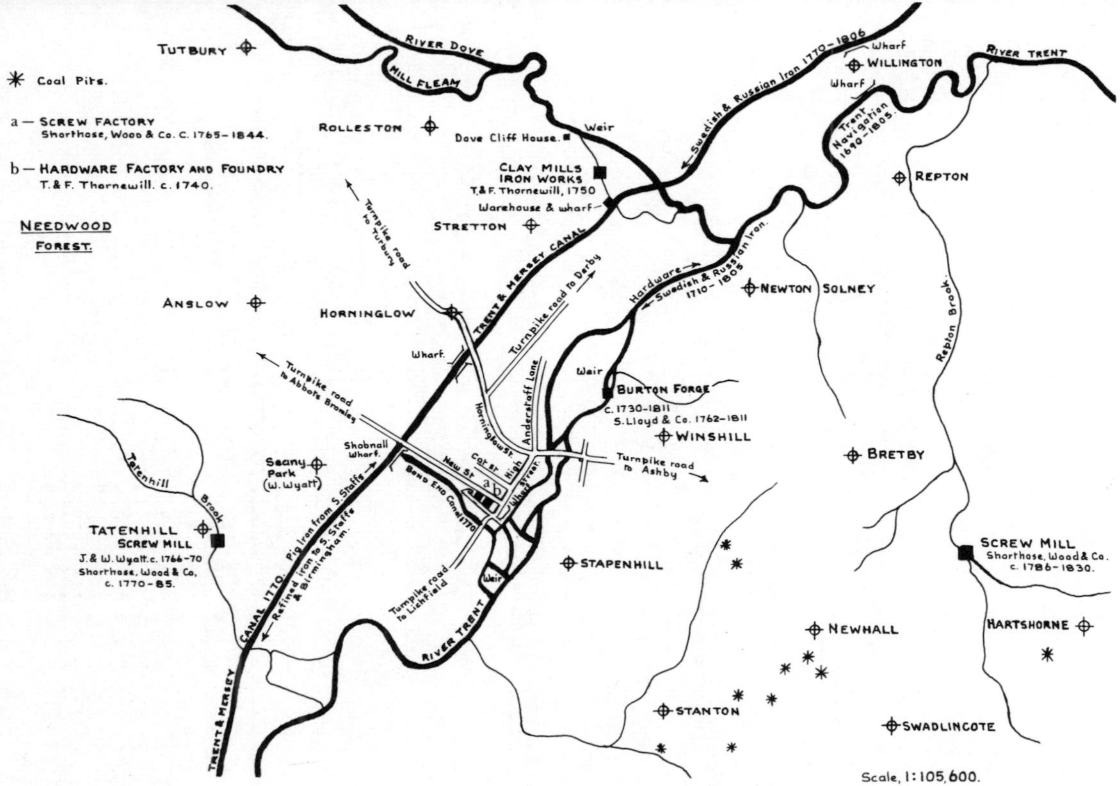

THE IRON INDUSTRY AND TRADE 1700–1850.

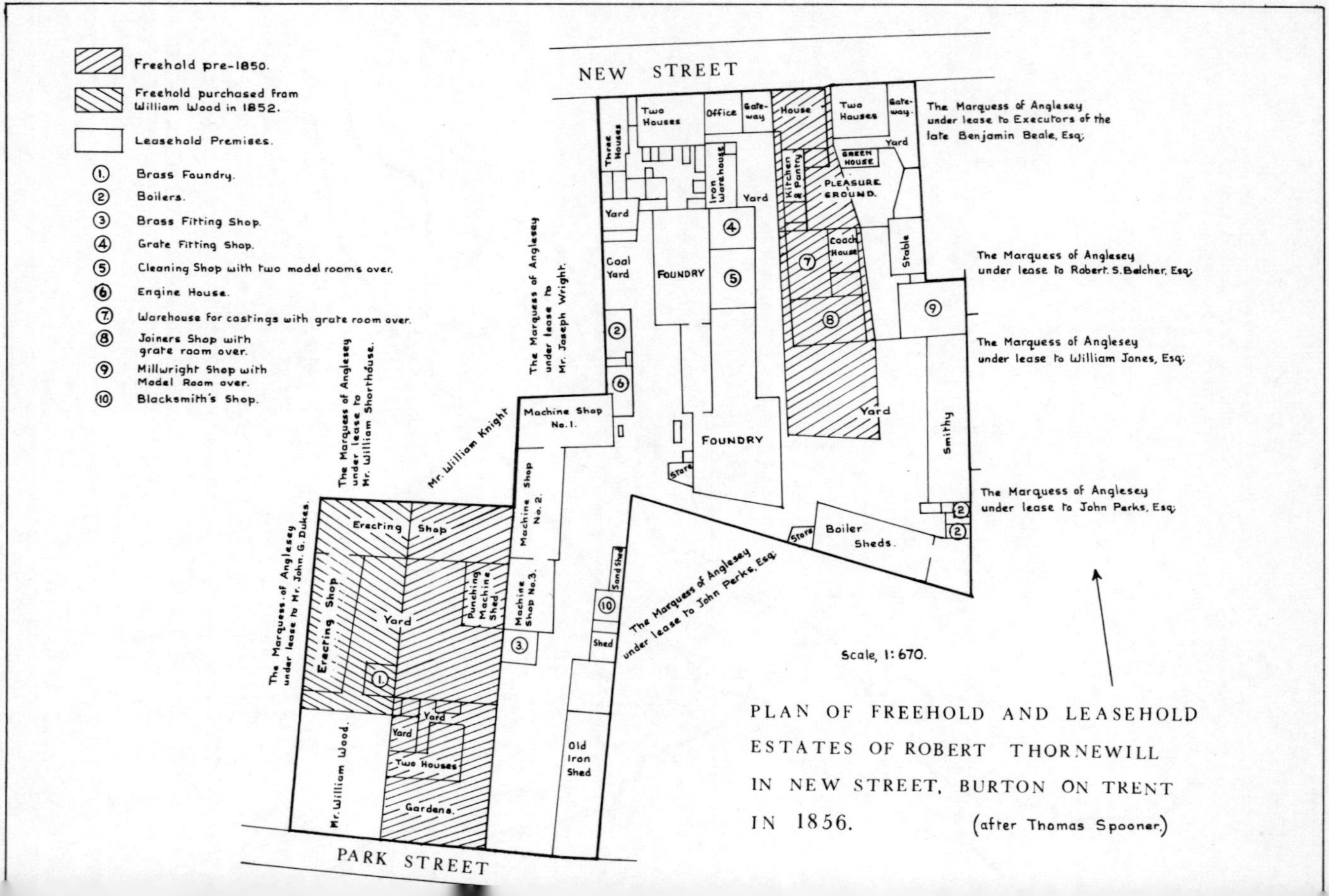

PLAN OF FREEHOLD AND LEASEHOLD ESTATES OF ROBERT THORNEWILL IN NEW STREET, BURTON ON TRENT IN 1856. (after Thomas Spooner.)

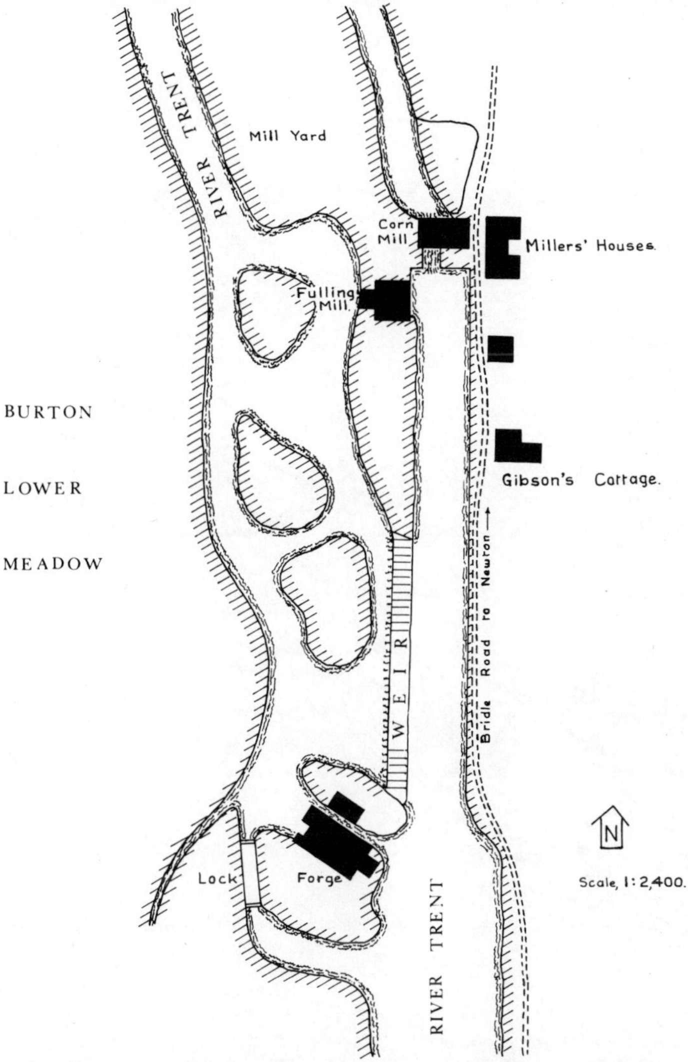

THE BURTON LOWER MILLS: 1760.

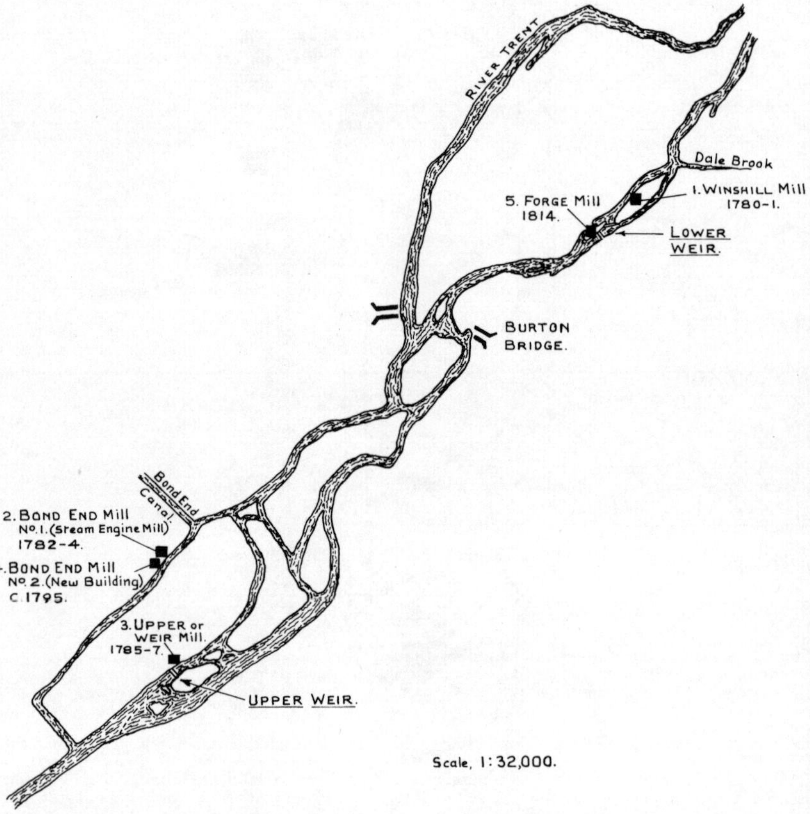

THE PEEL COTTON MILLS AT BURTON: 1820.

LIST OF APPENDICES

1 Variations in Lithology and Water Supply beneath the Valley Gravels at Burton upon Trent.
2 Deep Boreholes sunk by Brewing Companies beneath Burton upon Trent.
3 List of Principal Boreholes and Wells in Burton upon Trent (shown on figure 2).
4 Variations in the composition of Burton Brewing Waters.
5 Population of Burton upon Trent and surrounding settlements, 1801-61 and 1500-1901.
6 List of Staffordshire Canal Boats and River Barges operating on waterways in the Burton Area in 1795.
7 The Ale Exports of Hull, 1738-1787.
8 Estimated Total Output and Exports of Ale from Benjamin Wilson's Brewery, 1770-1808.
9 Barley malted during the 1785-6 season by Benjamin Wilson.
10 Malthouses used by Benjamin Wilson during the 1790-91 season.
11 Barley purchased by Benjamin Wilson, 1785-1802.
12 Transcription of letter written by Benjamin Wilson to J. D. Abegg of Elbing, 1791.
13 Exports of Ale to the Baltic by Benjamin Wilson, 1770-71 season.
14 Ale Shipments by Benjamin Wilson to the Baltic, 1788-9 season.
15 Typical Benjamin Wilson Accounts for Shipments of Ale to Baltic customers.
16 Account of typical Timber Import by Benjamin Wilson, 1783.
17 Accounts for typical Tallow Purchases by Benjamin Wilson.
18 Accounts for typical Cotton Imports by Benjamin Wilson.
19 Summary of Profits of Benjamin Wilson's Brewery, 1795-1802.
20 Profit and Loss Account for Benjamin Wilson's Brewery, 1802.
21 Account for typical Iron Purchase by John Walker Wilson.
22 Account for typical Timber Purchase by John Walker Wilson.
23 Extracts from the Ledger of John Walker Wilson.
24 Imports and Exports of Samuel Sketchley through Hull, 1758 and 1763.
25 Distribution of Ale, Stout and Porter by Samuel Allsopp, 1808-9.
26 Ale sent to the Baltic by Samuel Allsopp in the spring of 1814.
27 Some Pale Ale Exports from Samuel Allsopp's Brewery, 1824-25.
28 Ale Imports of Calcutta, 1832-33.
29 Exports of Ale to Calcutta by Bass, Allsopp and Hodgson, 1832-36.
30 Statistical Summary of Brewing in Burton, 1831-1900.

31 The Burton Breweries in 1851.
32 Burton Brewery Premises, 1851.
33 Burton Breweries in 1861.
34 Burton Breweries in 1888.
35 Hiring of East Anglian labourers by Bass, Ratcliff & Gretton Ltd., 1890-1900.
36 Output of Iron Forges in Staffordshire and Derbyshire, 1717-50.
37 Sales of Timber and Cordwood from lands in Burton and Burton Extra, 1769-1774.
38 Transcription of a letter from the Lloyd MSS concerning Burton Forge in 1774.
39 List of Workers at Clay Mills Forge in 1851.
40 Extracts from Thornewill & Warham's Engine Order Book.
41 Main Metal-working and Engineering Firms in Burton-on-Trent, 1850-1900.
42 List of Workers employed at the Tape Mill, Newton Road, Winshill, 1851.
43 Insurance Valuation of Peel, Yates & Co's Cotton Mills at Burton-on-Trent, 1795.
44 Burton Residents employed in the Burton Cotton Mills in 1841.
45 List of workers employed at the Forge Cotton Mill, Winshill, 1851.
46 Burton Hatters in 1841.
47 Summaries of Accounts for Stapenhill Brickyards, 1814-15.
48 Monumental Effigies attributed to Burton Alabaster-carvers, 1480-1638.
49 Family tree of Wilson and Allsopp.
50 Family tree of Bass.
51 Family tree of Thornewill.
52 Breweries of Burton-on-Trent, 1700-1900. (shown on figure 12).

APPENDIX 1

Variations in Lithology and Water Supply Beneath the Valley Gravels at Burton Upon Trent

Date of Boring	Company	Site of Boring	Water Obtained	Lithology
1863	Bass & Co.	New Brewery Station Street	Excellent hard water supply from 96 ft – from bed of loose sand and gravel	Valley gravels 26 ft. Keuper Marl 70 ft.+
c.1864	Bass & Co.	Middle Brewery, Station Street. 90 yds. N. of 1863 bore	Negligible – less than 1 gal. per hour	Valley gravels 26 ft. Keuper Marl 194 ft.+ (gypseous marls and hard sandstone bands)
1860/1	Allsopp & Sons	Station Street (near Station)	No useful supply	Valley gravels 28 ft. Keuper Marl 102 ft.+
1870	Robinson's	Union Street	Very large supply of hard gypseous water from 100 ft.	Valley gravels 26 ft. Keuper Marl 74 ft.+
1883	Robinson's	Union Street. 20 yds. W. of 1870 bore	None	Valley gravels 26 ft. Keuper Marl 124 ft.+
c.1870	Salt & Co.	Station Street. (near Staffordshire Knot)	Steady supply of moderately hard water from 95ft.	Valley gravels 26 ft. Keuper Marl
c.1895	Worthington & Co.	High Street	Good supply of hard gypseous water from 500 ft.	Valley gravels 25 ft. Keuper Marl & Lower Keuper Sandstone 475 ft.+
c.1897	Burton Brewery Co.	Wetmoor Road	Moderately hard saline water from 400 ft.	Valley gravels 25 ft. Keuper Marl & Lower Keuper Sandstone 255 ft. Bunter Pebble Beds 120 ft.+
c.1899	Bell & Co.	Lichfield Street West	Steady supply from 410 ft.	Valley gravels 25 ft. Keuper Marl & Lower Keuper Sandstone 500 ft.+

Information extracted mainly from: 'Burton-on-Trent: its History, its Waters, and its Breweries' – William Molyneux, 1869. and 'Burton Waters – Drinking and Brewing' – F. E. Lott – Transations of the Burton-on-Trent Natural History and Archaeological Society, 1896'.

APPENDIX 2

Deep Boreholes Sunk by Brewing Companies Beneath Burton Upon Trent

Brewing Company and Location of Borehole	Height O.D. of Bore (ft.)	Depth of Bore (ft.)	Water Level below surface (ft.)	Water Supply (Gals./Hr.)	Strata encountered Base of each bed shown in feet (except for last fig:)*
Marston, Thompson and Evershed, Shobnall Rd.	162	1,025	23	10,000	S.30; K.M.594; L.K.S.787; B.P.B.1,025
Bass & Co., Grange Pumping Station, Shobnall Rd.	159	900	Overflows	10-14,000	S.35; K.M.605; L.K.S.820; B.P.B.900
Truman, Hanbury, Buxton & Co., Derby Street.	154	1,034	43	8,000	S.25; K.M.647; L.K.S.932; B.P.B:1,034
Ind Coope Ltd., Station St. No. 1 (1939)	154	1,101	80	14,830	S.31; K.M.610; L.K.S.860; B.P.B.1,101
Ind Coope Ltd., Station St. (1948)	155	1,369	137·5	8,000	S.28; K.M.574; L.K.S.900; B.P.B.1,269
Worthington & Co., No. 4 High Street.	155	905	—	5,000	S.27; K.M.375; L.K.S.581; B.P.B.905

S. = Superficial deposits such as terrace gravels. **K.M.** = Keuper Marl. **L.K.S.** Lower Keuper Sandstone. **B.P.B.** = Bunter Pebble Beds.

* The figures for the Bunter Pebble Beds show the depth of the bore, not the base of the bed.

Source : Geological Survey.

APPENDIX 3

List of Principal Boreholes and Wells in Burton Upon Trent, Shown on Figure

No.	Name of Company	Depth in Feet	Remarks
51	Marston, Thompson and Evershed	1,025	Water Yield – 10,000 gals./hr.
52	Grange Pumping Station	900	10-14,000 gals./hr.
53	Truman, Hanbury, Buxton	1,034	8,000 gals./hr.
54	Ind Coope, Allsopp No. 1	1,101	14,830 gals./hr.
55	Ind Coope, Allsopp 1948	1,269	8,000 gals./hr.
56	Marmite Co. No. 3	998	2 Boreholes yield 25,000 gals./hr.
57	Worthington No. 4	905	5,000 gals./hr.
58	Midland Joinery Co.	525	
59	Blackpool Street	25	6 Bores to 25 ft.
60	Station Street	28	
61	Station Street (Goodhead's)	28	
62	Curzon Street	26	
63	Dale Street	23½	
64	Station Street Tubes	24	
65	Bond End	30	
66	Shobnall	17-31	13 Bores.
67	Engine House Well	30	
68	Main Buildings	40	
69	Brindleys	30	
70	English Grains Ltd.	30	3 Bores and 1 well.
71	Burton Co-operative Dairy	18	
72	Nile Well	30	24,000 gals./hr.
73	Cairo Well	31	10,000 gals./hr.
74	Staffordshire Knot	–	4 Bore Tubes yield 5,000 gals./hr.
75	No. 4 Malthouse	26	6,000 gals./hr.
76	Blackpool Well	29	2 pumps - each produce 30,000 gals./hr.
77	Plough Well	26	3,000 gals./hr.
78	Wyggeston Street	20-24	3 wells yield 5,100 gals./hr.
79	No. 1 Brewery Well	31	4,675 gals./hr.
80	Station St. Cooperage	30	5,250 gals./hr.
81	Crown Maltings	25	3,033 and 3,650 gals./hr.
82	Mosley Street Well	43	10,000 gals./hr.
83	Walsitch Well	–	6,000 gals./hr.
84	Worthington No. 2	400	6,464 gals./hr. from Pebble Beds.
85	Anderstaff Lane Well	–	10,000 gals./hr.
86	Worthington No. 3	401	5,826 gals./hr.
87	Salt's Anderstaff Lane Bore	157	
88	Wheelwright's Yard Well	28	5-7,000 gals./hr.

No.	Name of Company	Depth in Feet	Remarks
89	Salt's Brewery No. 1 & 2	100-116	2,500 and 3,000 gals./hr.
90	Hay Well	30	2 pumps – each produce 16,000 gals./hr.
91	Worthington No. 1 & 2	455-758	3,900 and 16,500 gals./hr.
92	Andressey Well	35	2 pumps each produce 20,000 gals./hr.
93	Arbor Well	27	5-7,500 gals./hr.
94	Oxhay (Hay Tubes)	24	10 Tubes
95	Marston, Thompson and Evershed	25 abt.	

Source : Geological Survey

APPENDIX 4

Variations in the Composition of Burton Brewing Waters

	Shallow Wells			Artesian Bores				
	20-32 ft. gravel beds			70-200 ft. Upper Keuper Marl			350-550 ft. Lower Keuper Sand	180-400 ft. Bunter Cong.
No. of samples av.	20	20	200	10	5	50	3	2
Total solids	below 100	above 100		above 100	under 200			
Sodium Nitrate	6.8	13.6	10.2	5.1	7.6	6.0		
Sodium Chloride	6.4	3.5	4.7	8.2	7.0	7.6	40.9	18.7
Sodium Sulphate							24.0	10.5
Magnesium Chloride	5.7	10.0	8.1	2.4	3.3	2.9		
Magnesium Sulphate	17.4	39.6	24.0	40.8	34.8	37.2	24.0	12.0
Magnesium Carbonate								0.8
Calcium Sulphate	21.8	52.4	37.4	165.2	89.1	142.1	80.2	
Calcium Carbonate	23.0	29.0	25.5	23.5	22.5	23.5	22.0	26.0
Silica, iron, aluminium	0.9	0.9	1.1	1.8	0.7	0.9	2.9	
Total Solids	82.0	140.0	111.0	247.0	165.0	220.0	194.0	68.0

All figures in parts per 100,000
(*Source* : H. Lloyd Hind, Brewing Science and Practice, Vol. I (1938), paras. 324 & 347; based mainly on the work of F. Lott.)

APPENDIX 5

Population of Burton Upon Trent and surrounding settlements, 1801–1861

	1801	1811	1821	1831	1841	1851	1861
Burton-on-Trent	3679	3972	4114	4339	4863	6374	9534
Burton Extra	716	872	910	910	1193	1289	2849
Branston	281	373	412	382	441	473	542
Horninglow	272	297	341	391	852	815	1968
Stretton	330	372	374	373	410	413	472
Stapenhill	457	447	535	572	577	635	1112
Winshill	309	317	357	344	377	405	880
TOTAL	6044	6208	6508	6797	8136	9768	17357

(*Source* : W. Molyneux, P. 123)

Population of Burton Upon Trent and surrounding settlements, 1500–1901

A. 1500–1801

Date	Population[1]
1500	1,000
1550	1,200
1580	1,900
1640	2,600
1666	2,500
1688	2,300
1710	1,800
1743	3,000
1766	3,300
1790	5,000

B. 1801–1901

Date	Population[2]
1801	6,044
1811	6,208
1821	6,508
1831	6,797
1841	8,136
1851	9,768
1861	17,357
1871	20,378[3]
1881	32,000[4]
1891	46,047
1901	50,386

1 All population figures in table A are estimates based mainly upon registrations of baptisms and burials at Burton Parish Church and upon Hearth Tax Returns.

2 Population figures in table B have been extracted from the Censuses of Population which commenced in 1801.

3 Burton and Burton Extra only.

4 Approximate figure.

APPENDIX 6

List of Staffordshire Canal Boats and River Barges Operating on Waterways in the Burton Area in 1795

Name of Proprietor	Number of Vessels. (all boats unless indicated)	Location of Proprietor	Route followed
Ball, John & Co	1	Endon	Manchester-Shardlow
Bird, John	1	Burton/Trent	Manchester-Shardlow
Briscoe, George	2	Summerhill	Stourport-Shardlow
Burton Boat Co.	3 barges	Burton/Trent	Burton Forge-Shobnall
Burton Boat Co.	8 barges	Burton/Trent	Burton-Gainsborough
Burton Boat Co.	1	Burton/Trent	Burton-Birmingham
Burton Boat Co.	7	Burton/Trent	Shardlow-Runcorn etc.
Collyer, John & Co.	1	Hanley	Shardlow-Manchester
Cope, George	1	Milton	Shardlow-Runcorn
Evans, Henry	1 barge	Burton/Trent	Burton-Gainsborough
Gilbert, John	16	Clough Hall	Shardlow-Runcorn
Granger, Thomas	8	Bilston	Burton-Stourport
Granger, William	7	Sedgeley	Burton-Stourport
Griffin, Soloman	1	Armitage	Shardlow-Froghall
Hales, Ralph & Co.	2	Cobridge	Shardlow-Manchester
Hales, Ralph & Co.	1	Cobridge	Shardlow-Froghall
Hadley, Sampson	1	Sandon	Shardlow-Runcorn
Heath, William	1	Cockshead	Shardlow-Runcorn
Henshall, Hugh & Co.	2	Stone	Shardlow-Stourport
Henshall, Hugh & Co.	1	Stone	Shardlow-Wolverhampton
Henshall, Hugh & Co.	2	Stone	Shardlow-Birmingham
Henshall, Hugh & Co.	2	Stone	Shardlow-Stourbridge
Henshall, Hugh & Co.	3	Stone	Shardlow-Manchester
Henshall, Hugh & Co.	16	Stone	Shardlow-Runcorn
Hill, Richard & Co.	1	Aston	Shardlow-Runcorn
Holloway, Jeremiah	3	Ettinghsall	Burton-Stourport
Hughes, John	1	Milford	Shardlow-Runcorn
Jervis, John	1	Deepmore Lane	Shardlow-Runcorn

Keeling, Edward	1	Hanley	Shardlow-Runcorn
Marsh, Charles	3	Colton	Shardlow-Manchester
Mellor, Thomas	1	Tunstall	Shardlow-Manchester
Richards James	1	Bilston	Burton-Stourport
Sampson & Newill	2	Stoke	Shardlow-Oxford
Shelley, Sampson	1	Oulton	Shardlow-Runcorn
Smith, Joseph & Sons	7 barges	Burton/Trent	Horninglow-Gainsborough
Smith, Joseph & Sons	7	Burton/Trent	Horninglow-Manchester, Stourport etc.
Sparrow, John & Co.	10	Cockshead	Shardlow-Froghall
Taylor & Hateley	10	Bilston	Burton-Bilston & Stourport
Tharme, Sampson	1	Stone	Manchester-Shardlow
Wedgewood, Joseph	1	Etruria	Runcorn-Shardlow
Wilkes, Richard	4	Wolverhampton	Willington-Bilston
Williamson, Robert	3	Longport	Shardlow-Manchester
TOTAL	128 boats 19 barges		

(*Source* : Original Register of boats and barges – Staffs. County Record Office.)

The Ale Exports of Hull, 1738–1787

	1738		1750		1756		1765		1771		1787	
	Amount	%	Amount	%	Amount	%	Amount	%	Amount	%	Amount	%
Northern Europe	112	59	1209	100	1959½	97	5248	90	10844	99	21016	91
Amsterdam	16		15						80		1520	
Archangel					5						8	
Bremen							72		320		160	
Danzig	13		310		495		1448		496		2800	
Dunkirk											80	
Elsinore			6									
Hamburg	13		3		10½		144				960	
Konigsburg	15		120		70		800		160		2800	
Lubeck							64				120	
Memel											1288	
Middleburg			7						48			
Norway					4							
Narva					160				116			
Ostend											304	
Pillau											120	
Rouen											80	
Riga	11		180		473		480		704		1896	
Rotterdam	9						80		616		80	
Stockholm			7									
St. Petersburg	34	18	561	46	742	37	2160	37	8304	76	8800	39
Southern Europe	78	41			20	1	560	10	120	1	1800	8
Ancona											80	
Cadiz	26											
Genoa	9										280	
Lisbon	35											

Appendix 7 (cont'd.)

Leghorn					20				40			
Naples											1280	
Oporto	8						560		80		160	
Other Regions					33½	2					120	1
Jamaica					25							
Maryland					8½							
Virginia											120	
TOTAL	190		1209		2013		5808		10964		22936	

1 Recorded in the Port Books in gallons, barrels, casks, or tons.
All amounts in the above table are in barrels. (1 barrel - 36 gallons.)
(*Source* : Hull Port Books, P.R.O., E. 190)

APPENDIX 8
Estimated Total Output and Exports of Ale from Benjamin Wilson's Brewery, 1770–1808

Season	Exports to the Baltic in Barrels[1]	Estimated Total Output in Barrels
1770–71	779	1,000
1771–72	693	1,000
1772–73	745	1,000
1773–74	720	1,000
1774–75	969	1,300
1775–76	1,095	1,400
1776–77	558	900
1777–78	1,101	1,400
1778–79	664	1,000
1779–80	647	1,000
1780–81	1,034	1,400
1782–83	1,350	1,850
1786–87	1,550	2,050
1788–89	1,950	2,500
1789–90	2,300	2,800
1790–91	2,400	3,000
1791–92	3,500	4,000
1792–93	3,300	3,900
1793–94	1,500	2,200
1794–95	1,900	2,600
1795–96	1,900	2,600
1798–99	1,800	2,500
1802–03	3,000	3,800
1803–04	2,500	3,300
1805–06	2,600	3,400
1806–07	Nil[2]	1,000
1807–08	Nil[2]	1,500

1 1 Barrel = 40 gallons.

2 Does not allow for a small export to Ireland, and the possible export of ale via London.

(*Source* : A.R., Day Books of Benjamin Wilson, 1770-1808)

APPENDIX 9

Barley Malted During the 1785–6 Season by Benjamin Wilson

A. *The New Malthouse (High Street)*

Date Received	Supplier of Barley	No. of Qtrs.	Price Per Qtrs. (s.)	Cost £	s.	d.
Oct. 20	Mr. Kirby, Ibstock	12	37	22	4	0
22	Mr. Kirby, Ibstock	12	37	22	4	0
25	Mr. Ratcliff, Stanton	12	33	19	16	0
29	Mr. Hawksworth, Stanton	10	35	17	10	0
Nov. 1	Samuel Bradley, Heather	11	35	19	5	0
9 9	Mr. Smith, Congerstone } Mr. Banter, Congerstone }	10½	36	18	18	0
9	Mr. Cawer, Hartshorne	10	34/6	17	5	0
17	Mr. Wenton, Ibstock	10	34	17	0	0
25	Mr. Otty, Ibstock	10	36	18	0	0
26	Mr. Hanson, Ticknall	10	34	17	0	0
26	Mr. Woodward, Stanton-Greasly	10	33/6	16	15	0
30	Richard Roe, Burton	12	32	19	4	0
Dec. 4	Mr. Woodward, Stanton-Greasly	3½	32/6	5	13	0
4	Mr. B. Wilson, Burton	7	36	12	12	0
4	Mr. Woodward, Stanton-Greasly	10	32	16	0	0
4	Mr. Thirby	9	32	14	8	0
21	Mr. Ordish, Burton	10	35	17	10	0
28	Mr. Ordish, Burton	10	34/6	17	5	0
30	Mr. Morley, Smisby	5¼	35	9	3	9
Jan. 4	Mr. Peach, Ibstock	10	36	18	0	0
17	Mr. Ordish, Burton	10	34/6	17	5	0
21	Mr. Peach, Ibstock	10	35	17	10	0
21	Mr. Matchett, Milton	10	35	17	10	0
21	Mr. Tyler, Mountsorrel	10	35	17	10	0

Feb. 15	Mr. Ordish, Burton	10	31	15	10	0
15	Mr. Tyler, Mountsorrel	21½	31	33	6	6
25	Mr. Stamp	20	29	29	0	0
Mar. 11	Mr. Clark, Willesley	10	28	14	0	0
13	Mr. Killingby, Walton	10	32	16	0	0
13	Mr. Shilton	12	34	20	8	0
13	John Abbot	7	32	11	4	0
	TOTAL:	324½		544	17	0

B. George Yeomans' Malthouse (High Street)

Nov. 15	Mr. Hawksworth, Stanton	9⅞½	35	17	7	9¾
25	Mr. Booth, Blackfordby	10	36	18	0	0
26	Mr. Hawksworth, Stanton	10⁴⁄₈½	35	18	9	8¾
26	Mr. Weston, Ibstock	10	34	17	0	0
29	William Abney, Esq., Measham	10	34	17	0	0
29	William Abney, Esq., Measham	10	32	16	0	0
Dec. 14	William Abney, Esq., Measham	10	32	16	0	0
14	John Smith, Packington	10	31	15	10	0
14	Mr. Lakin, Shackerston	10	32/6	16	5	0
Jan. 10	Mr. Hawksworth, Stanton	10	35	17	10	0
25	Mr. Peach, Ibstock	10	35/6	17	15	0
27	Mrs. Butler, Ibstock	10	35	17	10	0
28	Mr. Green, Normanton	10	33/6	16	15	0
Feb. 3	Mrs. Butler, Ibstock	20	35	35	0	0
23	Mr. Peach, Ibstock	10	29	14	10	0
24	Mr. Killingby, Rosliston	10	29	14	10	0
27	Mrs. Butler, Ibstock	12	32	19	4	0
27	John Smith, Packington	10	31	15	10	0
	TOTAL:	192½		319	16	6½

C. *Old Malthouse (High Street)*

Date Received	Supplier of Barley	No. of Qtrs.	Price Per Qtrs. (s.)	Cost £	s.	d.
Dec. 4	Mr. Weston, Ibstock	10	34	17	0	0
4	Mr. Woodward, Stanton-Greasly	10	32/6	16	5	0
4	Mr. Ordish, Burton	10	35	17	10	0
10	Mr. Otty, Ibstock	10	32	16	0	0
17	Mr. Otty, Ibstock	10	34	17	0	0
29	Mr. Hawksworth, Stanton	10	35	17	10	0
Jan. 9	Mr. Ley, Linton	10	36	18	0	0
9	Mrs. West, Newton	10	31	15	10	0
21	Mr. Houghton, Greasly	10	33/6	16	15	0
28	Mr. Houghton, Greasly	10	32/6	16	5	0
Feb. 2	Moses Mammott	10	33/6	16	15	0
2	Moses Mammott	10	32/6	16	5	0
10	Mrs. Butler, Ibstock	10	35	17	10	0
16	Mr. Peach, Ibstock	10	29	14	10	0
24	Mr. Pearsall, Foremark	10	30	15	0	0
27	Mr. Pearsall, Foremark	10	30	15	0	0
27	John Bradley	10	30	15	0	0
Mar. 11	Mrs. Butler, Ibstock	10	32	16	0	0
11	Mr. Woodward, Stanton-Greasly	10	28	14	0	0
11	Mr. Symonds	10	29	14	10	0
	TOTAL:	200		322	5	0
	TOTAL BARLEY PURCHASES FOR 1785–6	717¼		1,186	18	6½

AVERAGE COST PER QUARTER . . . . . . 33/– approx.

(*Source* : A.R., Malt Book of Benjamin Wilson, 1785–6)

APPENDIX 10

Malthouses used by Benjamin Wilson during the 1790–91 Season

Name of Malthouse	Location of Malthouse	Quarters of barley malted	
John Wayte's	High Street W.	421	Average price 32/– per quarter
Mr. Whitehouse		391	
New Malthouse	High Street E.	335	
Old Malthouse	High Street E.	288	
Mr. Morecroft's	Lichfield Street W.	241	
The Black Boy	High Street	212	
Mr. Sergeant's	High Street W.	90	
Charles Standley's	High Street W.	80	
Mr. Reynold's	Anderstaff Lane	40	
Mr. Greaves's	Horninglow Street N.	20	
	TOTAL	**2,118**	**£3,389 approx.**

(*Source* : A.R., Malt Book of Benjamin Wilson, 1789–1802.)

APPENDIX 11

Barley Purchased by Benjamin Wilson, 1785–1802

Season	Amount Purchased in quarters	Average Price per Qtr. (Shgs.)	Total value of Barley Purchased (approx:)
			£
1785-6	717	33	1,176
1786-7	1,307	25	1,634
1787-8	2,125	25	2,656
1788-9	1,852	23	2,130
1789-90	1,922	32	3,075
1790-1	2,118	32	3,389
1791-2	2,997	36	5,395
1792-3	1,377	40	2,754
1793-4	1,054	42	2,213
1794-5	380	42	798
1795-6	2,179	42	4,576
1796-7	1,980	38	3,762
1797-8	483	35	845
1798-9	1,395	33	2,302
1799-1800	1,091	—	—
1800-1	—	—	—
1801-2	2,423	52	6,300
1802-3	3,096	32	4,954

(*Source* : A.R., Malt Book of Benjamin Wilson, 1785–1802.)

APPENDIX 12

Letter written by Benjamin Wilson (jun.) to J. D. Abegg of Elbing, 19 February 1791

By the annexed invoice and bill of loading you will perceive that I have sent you on the Phoenix (Capt. Leonard) 125½ and 25¼ casks of Burton Ale shipped therein, which I wish safe to hand and to your perfect content. The remaining half of your order goes in the Porter (Capt. Mentrup) which ship takes the remaining part of my Elbing Friends' orders. I have taken great care of your interest Mr. Abegg in the execution of your order, as the excellent quality of the ale in question will testify, and I shall ever persevere the same endeavours for your satisfaction and my credit. Everything goes against the Brewer this year. The price of barley is not only high in the extreme, but the late new duty of malt is a great drawback on my profit. It is thought to be so burdensome and appressive to the subjects of the country that Petitions are sent up to the Minister to take it off – but I despair of such an event. Pipe staves are also so extremely high from their scarcity that I am under the necessity of laying on 6 casks in addition. Mr. Hay has taken great pains for some cause or other to interest himself in favour of the Traveller (Capt. Harwood) but such was his hurry to get away and to avail himself of a fine westerly wind, that he would not wait for two little lots which were appointed to him, and which were bona fide on their way to Hull, ordered particularly for him. He talks of visiting you and the rest of my friends to engross the transport of the ale another year, but if he succeeds therein his ship must inevitably wait till this period before he can depart, for it is not in my power to furnish a quantity of ale for any ship sooner, except I brew it sooner, which is really dangerous for the Quality and also for its ultimate preservation. I am the best judge what weather to brew it in, and when to send it off from Burton, and knowing also that my credit and your interest is inseparable you cannot better promote both than by leaving the business to me altogether.

I am etc. B.W.

(*Source* : Allsopp Records, Letter Book of Benjamin Wilson.)

APPENDIX 13

Exports of Ale to the Baltic by Benjamin Wilson, 1770–71 Season

Destination	Name of Customer	Amount in Barrels
Hull	John & Simon Horner	160
	Mr. Thorley	51
	Wilberforce & Smith	58
	Samuel Watson	90
	George Storer	40
	Mr. Richard Terry	30
	Williamson & Waller	40
	Mr. Best	200
	TOTAL	669
London	Mr. Raikes	60
Riga	Mr. Heinrich Grote	50
	TOTAL	779

APPENDIX 14

Ale Shipments by Benjamin Wilson to the Baltic, 1788–89 Season

Destination	Customer	Value of Ale £	s.	d.	Amount of Ale in Barrels
Dantzig	Frederick Muckle	295	5	4	90
	Carl Zimmerman	727	13	8	210
	J. H. Blume	114	13	8	35
	Barstow & Elliott	266	11	3	80
	Mr. Ropell	34	0	11	10
	Mr. Teitz	67	12	5	20
	J. Freemants & Co.	67	10	11	20
	J. C. Walter	151	15	3	45
	O. F. Schmidt	71	8	0	21
	F. W. von Ankum	434	5	6	125
	J. C. Mackensen	217	14	5	65
	J. C. Sontag	133	13	3	40
	Guillaume du Bois	436	15	11	130
	G. Martinstein	66	11	6	20
	Bartell & Strebelow	99	19	9	30
	John Paleske & Son	66	6	3	20
	TOTAL	3,151	18	0	951
Elbing (via Pillau)	M. Frome	150	7	2½	45
	J. Hingelberg	335	14	10	100
	J. D. Abegg	802	1	1	240
	J. J. Roskampff & Co.	503	15	1½	150

Appendix 14 (cont'd.)

	Messrs. Koustrup	270	6	11½	80
	J. D. Darchow	67	7	3	20
	TOTAL	**2,129**	**12**	**5½**	**635**
St. Petersburg	I. Kusoff	337	11	7	100
Liebau	R. King	30	8	8	10
Warsaw	J. C. Tauber	490	6	7	150
	TOTAL	**858**	**6**	**10**	**260**
Hull*	Wilberforce & Smith	111	5	0	30
	Terry & Wright	112	1	6	30
	C. Thorley	74	6	4	20
	TOTAL	**297**	**12**	**10**	**80**
	GRAND TOTAL	**6,437**	**10**	**1½**	**1,926**

*Probably sent by the Hull merchants to the Baltic – maybe to Riga.

APPENDIX 15

Typical Benjamin Wilson Accounts for Shipments of Ale to Baltic Customers

	Burton		27th April 1795
	J. D. Abegg at Elbing.		
	Pr. the 'Traveller', Capt. Horwood for Pillau.		
XX	140 half casks Ale cont.	5,575 gallons	
	20 Quarter casks Ale cont.	355 gallons	
		5,930 Gal: at 19d.	469 9 2
A	12 casks Porter + cont.	432 Gal: at 15d.	27 0 0
	140 casks @ 14/6; 20 @ 9/- 12 @ 13/- + Cartage		119 14 8
	Terry & Wright charges		30 3 6
			646 7 4
	Drawback on 6362 gals; @ 8/- pr. 34 gal.		74 14 0
			571 13 4
	Insurance on £640 @ 10½% =	£67 4 0	
	Commission	3 11 0	70 15 0
			£642 8 4

(+ Purchased a few days previously by Wilson from Goodwin, Skinner & Thornton of London.
XX & A = cask marks.)

	Burton		February 1799
	Fred. Muhl & Son at Dantzig.		
	Pr. the 'Humber', Capt. Wright.		
F M & S	100 Half casks Ale cont.	4,131 galls.	
	5 Whole casks Ale cont.	420 galls.	
	12 Qtr. casks Ale cont.	211 galls.	
		4,762 galls. at 18d.	357 3 0
	100 casks @ 14/6; 5 Whole @ 26/-; 12 Qtr. @ 9/6 + cartage		85 14 4
	Government for Convoy — ½ per cent on £450		2 5 0
			£445 2 4

Thos. Barmby Charges £21 5 2 Drawback £56.

(F M & S = cask mark.)

(*Source* : A.R., Journal of Benjamin Wilson, 1795 & 1799.)

APPENDIX 16

Account for Typical Timber Import by Benjamin Wilson

1783

Invoice of Staves from Messrs. Paleske & Sons, Dantzig, by the 'Sally', Benjamin Metcalfe.

60 shock Crown Pipe Staves at	56	3360 - 0	
10 shock Brack Pipe Staves at	46	460 - 0	
70 shock		3820 - 0	
	Charges		
Sound dues 11 - 27 Kings Duty	37 - 24		
Towns duty	45 - 15		
Certificate of 2 bills of loading etc.	7 - 18		
	90 - 27		
Prussian duty at charges	52 - 18	143 - 15	
		3963 - 15	
Commission at 3%		118 - 26	
		4082 - 11	
Exchange at £ per 24½			£166 12 3

(*Source* : A.R., Journal of Benjamin Wilson, 1783.)

APPENDIX 17

Accounts for Typical Tallow Purchases by Benjamin Wilson

		£	s	d
21st June 1799				
Bt. of John & Stephen Catley of London				
16 casks Archangel Tallow near	119-2-26 at 58/-	346	19	3
21 casks St. Petersbury Tallow	156-0- 1 at 58/-	452	8	6
7 casks Tallow	55-1-10 at 58/-	160	9	6
4 hogsheads Country Tallow	48-0-12 at 58/-	139	10	2
		£1,099	7	5
Bt. of Jos. Hardcastle at London				
65 casks Russia Tallow neat	490-1-21 at 59/-	1,446	15	3
Bt. Hopkins & Lincoln				
60 casks White Candle Tallow	452-3-15 at 60/-	1,358	13	0

(*Source* : A.R., Journal of Benjamin Wilson, 1799.)

APPENDIX 18

Accounts for Typical Cotton Imports by Benjamin Wilson

1st August 1800

Cotton Acct. to De. Visme & Co. Lisbon. Cr.				
for 50 bags Pernambuco Cotton shipped by the 'Aecalus',				
Capt. Wm. Youngford to Liverpool.				
Amounting to R^{s}.	2593/585.			
for 50 bags Maranham Cotton by the 'Mediator',				
Capt. Johnstone for Liverpool	3674/250			
for sundry petty expenses	5/400			
Brokerage on draft	7/865			
R^{s}.	6281/100.	£1,684	8	11

24th November 1801

F. & T. Dicken & Co. to Cotton Account.						
For 109 Bales long staple Sea Island Cotton						
pr. the 'Thomas' Capt. Higgins from						
Charlestown to Liverpool						
Neat 32,280 lbs. at 25½				£3,429	15	0
Charges in Charlestown for						
mending Bags Canvas etc.	£ 5	9	0			
Wharfage, Storage etc.	9	19	10			
Bill Lading & Certificate	2	10	0			
Commission at 5%	172	7	8	190	6	6
				3,620	1	6
for £3,270 – Insurance & Duty				119	6	9
Charges in Liverpool						
Freight on 30,959 lbs.	386	19	9			
Primage 5%	19	7	0			
Entry, Town Dues & Land Waits	2	4	4			
Cartage, Porterage & Canvas etc.	7	3	11			
Commission	10	18	0	426	13	0
				£4,166	1	3

(*Source* : A.R., Journal of Benjamin Wilson, 1800.)

APPENDIX 19

Summary of the Profits of Benjamin Wilson's Brewery 1795–1802

Date Year ending 30 April	Brewing Profits £	s.	d.	Net Profit transferred to Stock Account £	s.	d.
1795	506	15	4	411	5	1½
1796	2,762	3	0	3,655	9	11½
1797	2,944	7	1	3,049	13	3½
1798*	—	—	—	—	—	—
1799	3,075	3	7¾	3,135	4	8¼
1800	1,439	1	0¼	2,836	9	7¾
1801	3,000	15	11¼	7,603	18	2¾
1802	2,636	19	11¾	3,953	6	10

* Not available

(*Source* : A.R., Journal of Benjamin Wilson, 1795–1802.)

APPENDIX 20

Profit and Loss Account for Benjamin Wilson's Brewery (Year ending 30 April 1802)

Burton, April 1802

Sundries Drs. to Profit & Loss for Sundry Profits	£	s.	d.	Profit & Loss Drs. to Sundries for Sundry Losses	£	s.	d.
By Brewing for this year's profit	2,636	19	11½	To Ale under S. Allsopp loss on 6½ casks ale	19	8	0
By Barley pr. Leck, a Profit being over Insured . . .	61	5	2	To Wm. Burrow Loss on the Exchange	29	1	7
By Cheese Trade with T. Cartwright a Profit of . . .	371	5	8½	To Barley pr. Schmidt for an insurance risk	200	0	0
By Interest Account for a Profit	1,058	14	8	To Edw. Pheasant a Bankrupt	61	8	0
By Smith Millner & Co. for a statement			9	To Proper Expence for my Expenses	1,332	9	0
By Ship the 'Humber' the balance of this acc . . .	41	9	0	To Reimer Heirs write off	2	4	7
By Wheat Account Profit thereon . . .	432	8	4	To Housekeeping for my Expenses in Houskp.	294	2	0
By Twist Trade with F. & T. Dicken for one Year's Profit to 30 June 1801	2,451	0	0	To Adventure in Wheat with F. & T. Dicken for my half of share loss	10	13	4
By Underwriting Account with F. W. Plummer Profit . . .	165	15	11	To Speculation in Wheat for own Account – loss	850	2	4
By Exchequer Bills for a Profit . . .	88	12	11	To Ale under G. F. Keist loss on 6½ casks ale	14	8	6
By E. Eagle & Son for a statement . . .			10				
	7,307	14	3¼		2,813	17	4

(*Source* : A.R., Journal of Benjamin Wilson, 1802.)

APPENDIX 21

Account for a Typical Purchase of Iron by John Walker Wilson

17th August, 1778

Bought of A. H. Sutherland & Co., St. Petersburg.

658 bars Demidoffs Iron	Rb.	918 - 54
Less Agio	Rb.	9 - 10
		909 - 44
Customs		43 - 51
Receiving, weighing & shipping		17 - 01
Lighterage at Gronstadt (Kronstadt)		9 - 85
Port Charges		6 - 66
Brokerage		4 - 59
Commission		24 - 77
	Rb.	1015 - 83

Rb. 1015 - 83 – Exchange at 46¾	£197	17	6
Brokerage & Portage	1	17	7
Duty at Hull	45	15	2
Freight	18	0	0
Port Charges		9	0
Primage		3	3½
Dock dues		15	0
Town dues	2	17	2
Commission		18	0
Insurance	5	5	0
	£270	18	8½

(*Source* : A.R., Day Book of J. W. Wilson, 1778.)

APPENDIX 22

Account for a Typical Purchase of Timber by John Walker Wilson

28th August, 1778

Bot. of Mathw. Wm. Fischer & Co., Riga.

148 pieces Sq. Timber	Rbls.	364 - 46
Duties & charges		66 - 23
Proper Port charges and River money		28 - 72
Commission at 4%		18 - 34
	Rb.	477 - 85

Rb. 477 - 85 at 4/10 per Rb.	£115	9	7
Duty at Hull	18	6	11
Entry Fees & Corporation Dues	1	16	6
Freight	128	3	6
Port Charges, Primage & Dock dues	11	2	2
Landwaiters fees, 12 doz. staples, postage	1	6	0
Commission at 2%	3	4	3
	£279	8	11

(*Source* : A.R., Day Book of J. W. Wilson, 1778.)

APPENDIX 23

Extracts from the Ledger of John Walker Wilson, Brewer – A/c with J. Broadley Esq. (Merchant of Hull)

Dr.		£	s.	d.
1773				
Dec. 29	To a bill as pr. Bill Book	234	4	0
1774				
Jan. 22	To Do.	38	13	0
		272	17	0
Feb. 16	To 20 Casks Ale; 675 gals at 16d.	45	0	0
	20 Casks at 10/- ea.	10	0	0
	Cartage		3	4
Mar. 30	To 10 Casks Ale: 340 gals at 16d.	22	13	4
	To 10 Casks 10/- e. & Cartage	5	1	8
Dec. 27	To 5 Bls. Ale; 181 gals at 17d.	12	16	5
	5 Bls. 10/- ea. & Cartage	2	10	10
		98	5	7
	To Cash balancing this Acct.		12	2
		98	17	9

Cr.		£	s.	d.
1773				
Dec. 15	By 10 Bales Petersburg Clean Hemp Wt. 193: 0: 19 at £24 5s. p. ton	234	4	4
Dec. 20	By 6 Bales Cordelian Wt. 49: 3:14 at 15/6.	38	13	0
		272	17	4
1774				
Jan. 26	By Bill of Staves. 19:3:6 at 60/-	59	8	0
	Labourage		6	8
April 21	By Bill of Hd. Crown Staves 9:1: 12 at 46/-	21	10	1
	Labourage		3	0
April 25	By Bill of Brack Pipes 5:0:0: at £3 Labourage 1/8d.	15	1	8
	By Cash pd. Jos. & A. Smith Freight of Do.		8	4
		96	17	9

Account of Robt. Chr. Thorley (Merchants of Hull)

Dr.		£	s.	d.	Cr.		£	s.	d.
1785					1785				
Jan. 27	To 50 Bls. Ale T	182	14	0	Sept. 12	By 20 Bobbins Flax 21:3:21 at 36 per C.	40	0	8
May 5	To 12 Bls. Ale	46	15	3	Oct. 12	By 70 Bobbins Flax 75:1:26 at 38 per C.	143	8	3
	To Overcharge in 70 Bobbins Flax	5	13	3	1786				
July 8	To Balance carrd. to Cos. Ledger Fol.		2	5	Mar. 10	By Cash	51	16	0
		235	4	11			235	4	11

Account of Matthew & William Fischer of Riga

Dr.		£	s.	d.	Cr.		£	s.	d.
1777					1777				
Mar. 12	To 50 Bls. Ale —1581 gals at 17d.	111	19	9	March 24	By Debenture & Bounty	20	18	0
	50 Bls. at 10/- ea. Cartage 2d.	25	8	4	June 12	By My Draft on J. Wm. Anderson	100	0	0
Mar. 24	To charges on Do. to Hull 6-1-7 My Postage 1-0½	6	2	7½	Oct. 6	By your Dft on Capt. Thos. Middleton	3	13	9
	To Sale of 16 Casks of Ale per McFarland	41	12	5		By discount of 2½%	3	1	3½
	To Balance due to Contra	7	10	4½	Sept. 13	By Logs per the 'Caroline'	63	12	1½
						By Postage	1	8	4
		192	13	6			192	13	6

APPENDIX 24

Imports and Exports of Samuel Sketchley through Hull, 1758

Exports

Date	Destination	Ship	Commodity	Quantity
March 30	Danzig	Elizabeth and Ann	Lead	100 half pigs
April 1	Danzig	Elizabeth and Ann	Lead	2 cwt. 1 qr. 14 lbs.
April 1	Danzig	Elizabeth and Ann	Ale	100 casks of 20 tons.

Imports

Date	Destination	Ship	Commodity	Quantity
July 22	Riga	Elizabeth and Ann	Fir timber	40 loads
July 26	Riga	Elizabeth and Ann	Fir timber	60 loads
July 28	Riga	Elizabeth and Ann	Fir timber	30 loads
July 28	Riga	Elizabeth and Ann	Deals & lathwood	10 loads
August 2	Riga	Elizabeth and Ann	Fir timber	100 loads
August 5	Riga	Elizabeth and Ann	Fir timber	30 loads
August 12	Riga	Elizabeth and Ann	Fir timber	14 loads
Nov. 20	Konigsburg	Perrott	Undressed flax	54 matts.

(*Source* : Hull Port Books; P.R.O., E. 190. 371/1.)

Imports by Samuel Sketchley through Hull, 1763

Date	Origin	Ship	Commodity	Quantity
July 6	Amsterdam	Vigilantia	Wainscott boards	1014
July 20	Riga	Rebecca	Undressed flax	40 matts – 70 cwts
July 26	Riga	Rebecca	Undressed flax	40 matts
August 22	Konigsburg	Nancy	Linen yarns	5400 lbs.
August 22	Konigsburg	Nancy	Undressed flax	48 matts
August 29	Konigsburg	Nancy	Hogs' bristles	263 doz. lbs.
August 30	Petersburgh	Elizabeth	Rough hemp	8 bundls. – 120 cwt
August 30	Petersburgh	Elizabeth	Undressed flax	60 bundls. – 42 cwt
Sept. 1	Petersburgh	Elizabeth	Iron bars	420 bars – 8 tons
Oct. 29	Petersburgh	Henry	Russia iron	1560 bars – 40 tons
Oct. 29	Petersburgh	Henry	Deals	3 loads
Nov. 4	Petersburgh	Henry	Timber & iron	?
Nov. 16	Petersburgh	Henry	Russia iron	4 tons
Dec. 17	Konigsburg	Nancy	Rough hemp	4 bundles
Dec. 22	Konigsburg	Nancy	Rough hemp	?
Jan. 2	Petersburgh	Kepple	Hogs' bristles	14 doz. lbs.

(*Source* : Hull Port Books; P.R.O., E. 190, 374/3.)

APPENDIX 25

Distribution of Ale, Stout and Porter by Samuel Allsopp, 1808–9

1 November 1808 – 30 April 1809

Location of Customers	Ale sent (in barrels)
Burton and places within 10 miles of the brewery	372
Derby and district	268
Other Midland areas	97
Liverpool	319
Manchester	362
Other towns in Lancashire and Cheshire	35
Ireland	39*
London	152
Hull	12
Other areas in England, Scotland and Wales	54
TOTAL SALES	1,710

* Some of the Ale sent to Liverpool and to Port Penrhyn near Bangor was probably exported to Ireland.

(*Source* : Allsopp Records; Day Book 1807–14.)

APPENDIX 26

Ale sent to the Baltic by Samuel Allsopp in the Spring of 1814

Name of Customer	Location	Quantity of Ale in barrels	Value of Ale in £	s.	d.
Howesens & Co.	Danzig	20	124	8	6
J. G. Schultz & Son		35	234	9	0
Thomas Allsopp		50	306	4	6
A. L. Muhl & Co.		45	299	10	0
Jacob Kabrun		20	123	12	7
J. Freemant & Sons		10	62	3	6
TOTAL		180	1,150	8	1
J. J. Roskampff & Co.	Elbing	60	370	14	6
Ferdinand Huckein	Braumberg	15	92	11	0
TOTAL		75	463	5	6
Heinrich Heibel	Berlin	12	80	10	6
J. F. Wesenberg		16	106	11	0
TOTAL		28	187	1	6
Richard Rennard	Hull	40	246	7	6
GRAND TOTALS		323	2,047	2	7

(*Source* : Allsopp Recrds; Day Book, 1801–14.)

APPENDIX 27

Some Pale Ale Exports from Samuel Allsopp's Brewery, 1824–25

Date Sent	Customer	Location	Quantity of Ale (barrels)*	Final destination (where known)
22/ 2/1824	Petrie, Chapman & Co.	London	28	
21/ 2/1824	Captain Edwards	London	40	
28/ 2/1824	R. Gladstone & Co.	Liverpool	238	Calcutta
1824	Charles Jones	London	115	
8/11/1824	Daniel Willink	Liverpool	40	
8/11/1824	J. Gladstone, Grant & Wilson	Liverpool	194	Calcutta
3/12/1824	J. Gladstone, Grant & Wilson	Liverpool	100	Bombay
7/12/1824	Plummer & Wilson	London	40	
23/12/1824	Cropper & Benson	Liverpool	60	
1824	Lewin & Lassells	Liverpool	36	
1824	Edward Grimmer	London	38	
24/ 1/1825	Rev. F. I. Moore	Kings Bromley	40	Buenos Aires
5/ 3/1825	Captain Probyn	London	40	
6/ 5/1825	Captain Beadle	London	40	
6/ 5/1825	Captain Chapman	London	200	
13/ 5/1825	John Lord	Calcutta	40	Calcutta
6/ 6/1825	Taylor, Potter & Co.	Liverpool	100	
13/12/1825	Adams, Robinson & Co.	Jamaica	10	Kingston, Jamaica

* Allsopp usually sent the Ale in hogsheads containing around 80 gallons.

(*Sources* : J. S. Bushnan and Allsopp Records; Day Book 1822–26.)

APPENDIX 28
Ale Imports of Calcutta, 1832–33

Supplier	Butts	Hogsheads Good	Hogsheads Dam. & Emp.	Dozens	Value sa. Rupees
Bass	52	3,358	258	28	1,60,006
Hodgson	151	2,122	38		1,40,958
Allsopp	31	874	60		65,077
Barclay & Perkins	2	203	4		7,585
Dunbar		294	22		13,479
Ashby	16	62	3		4,391
Ind & Smith		280	25		13,568
Abbot		29	2		1,112
Aberdeen Ale		66	24		2,564
Watts		27			850
Hibbert		89		40	2,400
Tennant		35			700
Surplus Stores		26	7	1,672	7,907
Porter		8		553	2,903
Cape Beer		25	70		664
TOTAL	252	7,498	513	2,293	4,24,834

(*Source* : John Bell 'A Comparative View of the External Commerce of Bengal' (1832–3), p. 14.)

APPENDIX 29

Exports of Ale to Calcutta by Bass, Allsopp and Hodgson, 1832–36

Brewery	1832-3	1833-4	1834-5	1835-6	
Bass Hodgson Allsopp	5193 3636 1404	2901 3375 2514	3519 1599 2862	3264 450 2136	All figures in barrels (36 gals.)
TOTAL	12003	11064	9615	6780	

(*Source* : John Bell, (1832-6).)

APPENDIX 30

Statistical Summary of Brewing in Burton, 1831–1900

Date	No. of Breweries	Output (barrels)	Employees	Average Output per Brewery (barrels)
1831	9	50,000	200	5,550
1851	17	300,000	956[1]	17,650
1861	20	971,000	3,086[1]	48,550
1868	26	1,755,252	5,074	67,510
1888	31	3,025,000	8,215	96,940
1900[2]	21	3,500,000	8,000	166,670

1 Not including clerical staff.

2 Approximate figures.

APPENDIX 31

The Burton Breweries in 1851 – (extracts from the Census of Population)

Name of Brewery[3]	Name of Brewer	Age	Birthplace	Brewery Location	Employees[1] M[4]	B[5]	Total
Allsopp & Son	Thomas Poyser	48	Mickelover	High St. E. Horninglow St. N.	292	12	304
Bass, Ratcliff & Gretton	Samuel Ratcliff	70	Burton	High St. E.	338	29	367
Burton Brewery Co.	John Proudman			High St. E.	33		33
Hicklin's	Benjamin Hicklin	64	Brailsford	High St. W.	4		4
Hill's	John Hill	35	Derby	Lichfield St. S.	19		19
Marston's	John Marston	29	Burton	Horninglow	8		8[2]
G. & F. Meakin's	George Meakin	37	Wolverhampton	Water Road	26		26
	Francis Meakin	32	Burton Extra				
J. & T. Meakin's	Jonathan Meakin	59		High St. W.	7		7
	Thomas Meakin	26					
Middleton's	William Middleton	40	Shoreditch	High St. E.	18	2	20
Nunneley's	Joseph Nunneley	38	Leicester	Bridge St. S.	11	1	12
Perks'	John Perks	40	Burton Extra	Horninglow St. S.	21	2	23
Salt's	Thomas F. Salt	43	Burton	High St. E.	45	8	53
Thompson's	John Thompson	69	Brinklow, War:	Horninglow St. N.	14		14
	Francis Thompson	28	Burton				
Worthington & Robinson's	Thomas Robinson			High St. E. & W.	51	9	60
Yeomans'	Mary Yeomans	56		High St. W.	6		6
				TOTALS	893	63	956

1 Not including managers and clerical staff
2 An estimate based upon employees in 1861 Census.
3 Very small inn brewhouses of William Gretton New Street and Sarah Measom, High Street, omitted.
4 Men
5 Boys.

(*Source* : P.R.O., H.O. 107, Bdl. 2012.)

APPENDIX 32
Burton Brewery Premises, 1851

Name of Firm[1]	Short Description of Premises	Annual value of Premises £	s.	d.
Allsopp & Sons	Brewery in High St., steam engine houses, cooperage, malthouses for 612 qrs., stores, offices and houses in High St., Horninglow St., and Anderstaff Lane.	1,200	7	6
Bass, Ratcliff & Gretton	Brewery in High St., steam engine houses, cooperage, malthouses for 1,289 qrs., stores, yards, stables, offices, houses etc. in High St., Bridge St., Horninglow St., and Anderstaff Lane.	2,028	10	10
Burton Brewery Company	Brewery in High St., steam engine house, cooperage, malthouses for 20 qrs., stores, offices, stables and houses in High St., and Anderstaff Lane.	262	16	0
Benjamin Hicklin	Crown Inn & 8 qr. malthouse in High St.	43	0	0
Messrs. Meakin & Ginder	Brewery in High St., malthouses for 16 qrs., stores and house in High St. and Anderstaff Lane.	97	14	0
Wm. Middleton	Brewery, stores and house in High St.	38	3	4
Joseph Nunneley	Brewery in Bridge St., cooperage, malthouses for 32 qrs., stores, offices and stables in Bridge St. and Anderstaff Lane.	229	5	0
John Perks	Brewery, cooperage, malthouses for 16 qrs. office and stables in Horninglow St.	132	8	0
Thos. Fosbrook Salt	Brewery in High St., steam engine houses, cooperage, malthouses for 63 qrs., stores, offices etc. in High St., Horninglow St., Brook St., Lichfield St., Bridge St., and Anderstaff Lane.	447	18	0
Messrs. Thompson & Son	Brewery and Bear Inn in Horninglow St., cooperage, malthouses for 33 qrs., house, stores, stables and excise office in Horninglow St., Anderstaff Lane and Brook Lane.	246	11	9

Messrs. Worthington & Robinson	Brewery, malthouses for 145 qrs., stores, offices and houses etc. in High St.	444	3	8
Mary Yeomans & Son	Blue Posts Inn in High St., malthouses for 20½ qrs. in High St. and Station St.	96	2	0
Sarah Measom	Star Inn Brewhouse, malthouse for 5 qr. and stables in High St.	52	0	0
William Gretton	Carpenters Arms Inn in New St.	25	0	0

1. Firms in Burton Extra not included.

(*Source* : Burton Parish Church Rate Book, 1851-2.)

APPENDIX 33

Burton Breweries in 1861

Brewery[4]	Location of Brewery	No. of Employees[1]	Output[2]
S. Allsopp & Son	Station St., High St., Horninglow St.	889	270
Bass, Ratcliff & Gretton	High St., Station St.	1,167	350
J. Bell	Lichfield St.	15	5
T. Berry	High St.	8	2.5
Burton Brewery Co.	High St.	297	90
T. M. Carter	Horninglow St.	30	10
J. Eadie	Cross St.	15	5
S. Evershed	Bank Square	18	5.5
Charles Hill & Son	Lichfield St.	30	10
Ind, Coope & Co.	Station St.	50	6
London & Burton Brewery Co.[3]	Abbey St.	35	11
J. Marston	Horninglow Road N.	10	3
J. Nunneley	Bridge St.	16	5
T. F. Salt & Co.	High St.	194	60
J. & F. Thompson	Horninglow St.	35	11
Tooth Bros. (London & Colonial)	Victoria Crescent	80	25
Worthington & Robinson	High St.	191	60
M. & J. Yeomans	High St.	6	2
	TOTAL	3,086	971

1 Generally do not include clerical staff.

2 Estimated output in thousands of barrels per annum.

3 G. & F. Meakin until 1860.

4 Star Inn Brewery (High St.) and Green Man Brewery (New St.) omitted.

(*Source* : Most of employment statistics taken from Census of Population Burton-on-Trent, 1861; P.R.O., R.G.9. Bdls. 1964–7.)

APPENDIX 34

Burton Breweries in 1888

Brewery	Location of Brewery	No. of Employees	Output[1]
S. Allsopp & Sons Ltd.	Station St., High St.	1,750	460
Bass, Ratcliff & Gretton Ltd	High St., Station St.	2,760	980
J. Bell	Lichfield St.	50	20
T. Bindley & Co.	New St.	70	30
H. Boddington[2]	Trent Bridge		
J. & T. Bowler	New St.	20	7
Burton Brewery Co.	High St.	350	130
Carter & Scattergood	Victoria St.	70	30
Charrington & Co.	Abbey St.	190	80
W. & G. R. Clarkson	Victoria St.	50	20
Clayton & Co.	Norninglow Rd. S.	40	15
T. Cooper & Co.	Victoria Crescent	100	40
Dawson & Co.	Moor St.	80	35
Everard & Co.	Trent Bridge	50	20
J. Eadie & Co.	Cross St.	80	35
S. Evershed	Bank Square	50	20
F. Heap	Victoria St.	30	10
C. Hill & Son	Lichfield St.	40	15
Ind, Coope & Co.	Station St.	450	200
Mann, Crossman & Paulin	Shobnall Rd.	365	150
J. Marston	Horninglow Rd. N.	50	20
J. Nunneley	Bridge St.	30	10
J. Porter & Son	Dale St.	30	10
T. Robinson & Co.	Union St.	170	65
T. F. Salt & Co.	High St.	400	180
Sykes & Co.	Wood St.	50	20
F. Thompson & Son	Horninglow St.	50	20
Truman, Hanbury & Buxton	Derby St.	200	100
A. B. Walker	Shobnall Rd.	80	35
P. Walker	Clarence St.	100	45
Worthington & Co.	High St.	470	220
J. Yeomans	High St.	10	3
	TOTAL	8,215	3,025

1 Estimated output in thousands of barrels.

2 May have closed *c.*1885. Everard & Co. used Boddington's Brewery before moving to the Trent Brewery, Anglesey Road, in 1898.

(Information drawn from many sources, but especially A. Barnard, 'Noted Breweries of Great Britain and Ireland', 1889.)

APPENDIX 35

Hiring of East Anglian labourers by Bass, Ratcliff, & Gretton Ltd., for work in the Malthouses in Burton-on-Trent, 1890–1900

Area of Recruitment	1890-91	1896-97	1900-01
Woodbridge	29	40	25
Bury St. Edmunds	17	30	23
Ipswich	31	40	27
Halesworth	8	11	13
Framlingham	3	9	18
Bungay	3	14	6
Mildenhall	1		
Beccles	2	1	
Saxmundham	1	5	
Wickham Market	4	7	2
Needham Market		1	1
Newmarket		3	4
SUFFOLK TOTAL	99	161	119
Harleston	13	4	7
Swaffham	2	3	1
Norwich	9	7	9
Thetford	1	5	7
Diss	1		13
East Dereham		1	4
NORFOLK TOTAL	26	20	41
Mistley		1	1
Manningtree			6
ESSEX TOTAL		1	7
Burton-on-Trent[1]	1	74	82
GRAND TOTAL	**126**	**256**	**249**

1 Former East Anglian men who were living permanently in Burton.

(*Source* : Bass & Co., — 'Eastern Counties Journals for the engagement of men', 1890–1901.)

APPENDIX 36

Output of Iron Forges in Staffordshire and Derbyshire, 1717-50

(Extracts from 'Statistical History of the Iron Trade of England and Wales, 1717-1750' – E. Wyndham Hulme (Transactions of the Newcomen Society-Vols. 9-10, 1928-30).)

	A. 1717	B. 1736 Past	B. 1736 Present	C. 1750
Derbyshire				
Staveley	80[1]	120	120	120
Pleasley	100	150	–	150
Barton Fields	100	120	80	120
New Mills	120	250	120	250
Staffordshire				
Consall	150	200	150	300
Oakamore	200	250	–	
Chartley	150	200	–	
Bromley	200	200	200	
Hints	200	250	160	250
Cannock	100	100	–	180
Bromwich	80	200	180	300
Little Aston	100	100	50	100
Congrave	120	120	–	120
Brewood (2)	100	300	100	100
Heath	100	160	160	200
Withington	200	250	250	300
Swinnerton		100	100	140

1 All output figures in tons.

(Compiled from – A – MSS of John Fuller and his son, gunfounders of Heathfield, Sussex, 1717.

– B – Anonymous pamphlet of 1736.

– C – 'The State of the Trade and Manufactory of Iron in Great Britain considered, 1750'.)

APPENDIX 37

Sales of timber and cordwood from lands in Burton and Burton Extra 1769–1774

Date	Total Sales £	s.	d.	Sales to Messrs. Lloyds £	s.	d.	Sales to Thomas Thornewill £	s.	d.
1769–70	895	18	3	380	8	0	259	14	2
1770–71	1508	7	5	351	13	0	569	14	0
1771–72	1363	7	10				230	0	0
1772–73	724	7	10	211	15	0	40	0	0
1773–74	324	0	0	73	17	0	76	6	0

(*Source* : Paget MSS (S.C.R.O., D.603 unlisted); Estate Accounts for Burton and Burton Extra prepared by William and Samuel Wyatt, Stewards to the Earl of Uxbridge, Michaelmas 1769 to Michaelmas 1774.)

APPENDIX 38

Transcription of an unsigned letter from the Lloyd MSS concerning Burton Forge in 1774

Hints Forge 5th June, 1774.

Sir,

I was at Burton Forge last tuesday, they had made 22 tons of Blooms last month, they seem to make very good Iron at that time, they had had many Seaton Piggs in last month, but not all the parcel, they had not had many Charcoals brought in last month, the Coals from Graisley were very much better than I expected from wood that had stood so long – The two Houses will be finished in a fortnight – I met with Joseph Shaw at Burton Forge, they were out of Coak Piggs at Burton, ordered 4 tons from Burton Forge there; I was last Wednesday with Emery at Brewood to know why he did not take the Piggs from Calf Heath to Horninglow according to orders, Emery himself was not at home, his wife told me that her husband had been in Partnership with York and Berisford, but that the Partnership was dissolved that her husband had two Boats of his own and that she thought he did not intend going to Burton any more, that they had imploy for those two Boats to carry his own timber and to bring coals into their own neighbourhood. I went from there to a wharf at a place called Cross Green, where I found Emery's Boat unloading coal, the men told me that their master had ordered them to Galy Locks as yesterday and load twenty ton of piggs and take them to Horninglow, which they promised me should be done and should be at Horninglow next tuesday evening (if no misfortune happen). I wrote to James Lynam not to send more from Burton Forge than what would supply them till those arrived. They made 13 tons of blooms last month at Burton Forge had 8 Dozen of Charcoals from Senea Park and 19 dozen from Bradeley. John Dugmore told me he had taken up about 30 cords of wood at Bradeley that had been cut more than a year, his chief complaint was that it was a scattering parcel. We made 27 tons of Blooms here last month, had 79 doz. coals brought in and 18 ton of Coak Piggs. Sent 16 tons 6 cwt. Barrs to Weeford Mills and 15 tons 15 cwt to Birmingham. Saml. Beach delivered 14 tons of Rods. Our Finery bellows are quite worn out should be glad to know if I may order Colbern to make a new pair, the Finers were 47 cwt. – 2 – 13 out of yield the two last months, making 58 tons of Blooms, the only excuse they have is the want of Blast, bothe to yield and quantity, Stokes is not pleased with Lambert's manner of working. Teams got £33 – 1 – 7½ last month.

(*Source* : Lloyd MSS. A letter probably written to Sampson, Charles or Nehemiah Lloyd by one of their managers. Copy taken by Humphrey Lloyd, 1967.)

APPENDIX 39

List of Workers at Clay Mills Forge in 1851

Owner of Ironworks: Edward Thornewill of Dove Cliff, aged 50, born at Stretton – employer of 25 men and 5 boys

Name	Age	Place of birth
Thomas Ashforth	42	Stretton
William Ashforth	38	Stretton
George Ashforth	35	Stretton
George Ashforth	63	Stretton
John Ashley	15	Lichfield, Staffs.
James Camp[1]	37	Findern, Derbys.
John Corradine	71	Stretton
John Corradine	40	Stretton
Benjamin Corradine	30	Stretton
Joseph Head	36	Stretton
John Head	77	Stretton
William Page	32	Stretton
John Page	20	Stretton
James Street	29	Stretton
James Weaver	73	Burton
James Weaver	33	Stretton
George Weaver	27	Stretton

1 Millman at forge (all others listed as forgemen).

(*Source* : P.R.O., H.O. 107, Bdl. 2012)

(Census of Population, Stretton & Clay Mills, 1851.)

APPENDIX 40

Extracts from Thornewill & Warham's Engine Order Book

Engine No.	Date[1] Ordered	Type of Engine	Works Supplied	Location of Customer
115	c.1855	Winding	Colliery	Shipley
116		Pumping	Brewery	Hicklin's Burton
117		Pumping	Colliery	Staveley
118		Vertical	Colliery	Moira
121	c.1856	Winding	Colliery	Gilt Brook
122		Winding	Colliery	Swannington
124		Winding	Colliery	Wharncliffe
126		Horizontal	Colliery	Swanwick, Nr. Alfreton
128		Vertical	Brewery	Griffiths, Lichfield
134	c.1857	Horizontal	Colliery	Measham
125		Winding	Colliery	Wyken, Nr. Coventry
144	c.1858	Winding	Ironstone Wks.	Babbington
146		Winding & Pumping	Colliery	Bretby
148		Tank Locomotive	Colliery	Ibstock
151		Winding	Colliery	Marehay & Whitley
154	c.1858	Pumping	Lead Mine	Nr. Matlock
158		Horizontal	Colliery	Swadlincote
159		Vertical	Colliery	Kimberley
162		Locomotive	Coal & Iron Co.	Silverdale
164		Pumping	Colliery	Moira
167		Horizontal	Brewery	Meakin's, Burton
168		Pumping	Lead Mine	Cromford
173	c.1860	Winding	Colliery	Granville
175		Winding	Colliery	Cannock Chase
176		Pumping	Brewery	Allsopp & Sons, Burton
184		Sawing	Brewery	Salt & Co., Burton

Engine No.	Date[1] Ordered	Type of Engine	Works Supplied	Location of Customer
193	*c*.1861	Locomotive	Colliery	Snibstone
196		Winding	Colliery	Hucknall
212		Winding	Railway	Midland Railway Co.
223	1863	Locomotive	Brewery	Allsopp & Sons, Burton
224	1863	Locomotive	Brewery	Bass & Co., Burton
227		Horizontal	Gold Mine	Wales
234	*c*.1864	Horizontal	Pottery Works	Knowles, Woodville
236		Horizontal	Brewery	Worthington & Co., Burton
250	*c*.1865	Horizontal	Brewery	Philips', Burton
313	*c*.1868	Sawing	Brewery	Nunneley & Co., Burton
317		Horizontal	Brewery	Bell & Co., Burton
339-41	*c*.1871	Hauling, Winding & Pumping	Colliery	Taskanna Colliery, Japan
392	*c*.1875	Horizontal	Brewery	Trumans', Burton
470	*c*.1880	Exhibited at the Royal Agricultural Society	Show	
472		Driving Hoists	Brewery	Burton Brewery Co.
511		Vertical	Brewery	Bowler's, Anchor Brewery, Burton
543-4	*c*.1885	Pumping	Sanitary Works	Buenos Aires, Argentina
597-8	1889	Pumping and Winding	Colliery	Taeping Colliery Co., China
630	7-7-92	Winding	Colliery	Dundee Coal Co., Natal, S.A.
635	31-8-92	For driving Machinery	Cotton Mill	Bowes, Scott, & Western – for Peru
636	29-12-92	Winding	Colliery	B.S.W., for Mysore, India.
640	2-3-93	Horizontal Driving	Brewery	John Bell & Co., Burton
695	27-4-95	Horizontal	Gold Mine	B.S.W., for Coolgardie, W. Australia.
698	20-7-95	Haulage	Gold Mine	B.S.W., for Murchison C. C., N. Australia
780	1897	Winding	Colliery	South African Collieries Ltd.
783	25-9-97	Pumping	Gold Mine	Gold Quartz Syndicate, Brit. Guiana.
835	27-1-1900	Horizontal		B.S.W., London
843	21-1-00	Horizontal	Laundry	Spiers & Bond, London.

Engine No.	Date[1] Ordered	Type of Engine	Works Supplied	Location of Customer
844	1900	Haulage	Colliery	Powell Duffryn Steam Coal Co. South Wales
845		Haulage		Wm. Black, Airdrie
846	1900	Haulage		Messrs. London, Port Glasgow.
847	30-3-00	Haulage		B.S.W., London
848	1900	Haulage	Colliery	Haunchwood
849	1900	Haulage		New Russia Co.
850	1900	Haulage		New Russia Co.
851	16-4-00	Winding	Colliery	China
852	27-4-00	Compound	Colliery	Glamorgan
853	25-5-00	Horizontal	Colliery	B.S.W.
854	14-6-00	Horizontal	Timber Works	Lyons & Co., Abbots Bromley
855	10-8-00	Horizontal	Colliery	Palmer Morewood, Alfreton
856	1-10-00	Haulage		London & Co., Port Glasgow.
857	12-12-00	Horizontal	Colliery	Clydach Vale, S. Wales
893	8-5-02	Winding		B.S.W., for Rajah of Sarawak, Borneo
901	29-10-02	Hoisting	Colliery	Wankie Coal Co., Rhodesia.

1 Before 1892 very few dates were recorded in the 'Engine Order Book'; dates given before this time are therefore only approximate.

APPENDIX 41

Main Metal-Working and Engineering Firms in Burton-on-Trent, 1850–1900

Name of Firm	Location of Premises	Products Manufactured	Date Established	Date Closed	Further Information
Bindley & Briggs	High St. & Station St.	Iron, Brass & Copperware; particularly brewing equipment.	1840	*c.*1890	Continued after 1880 as T. Bindley, Ironmongers, High St. & S. Briggs & Co., Station St.
S. Briggs & Co.	Station St. moved to Moor St. in 1900	Mainly brewery equipment until 1929.	*c.*1890	still in existence	Absorbed Buxton & Thornley in 1912 and T. R. Shercliff & Co. Ltd. & Thornewill & Warham in 1929.
Buxton & Thornley	Waterloo Works, Waterloo St.	Iron, Brass & copperware: particularly brewing equipment.	*c.*1865	1912	Absorbed by S. Briggs & Co. Ltd.
A. Elson & Co.	Horninglow St.	Cooper & Brass equipment for breweries.	1873	still in existence	
Glovers	Byrkley St.	Brass & cooper goods	*c.*1885	*c.*1910	This firm may have developed from business of John Borwell, an iron-founder in Byrkley St. in 1874.
Halbard & Wright	Britannia Foundry, Horninglow St.	Stoves, grates & other iron-ware.	*c.*1851	*c.*1890	
Homer & Shercliff	Stanley St.	Brass & copper equipment for breweries.	*c.*1890	1929	Joseph Homer associated with Pickering Bros. of Union St. in 1884. Absorbed by S. Briggs & Co. Ltd. in 1929.

Appendix 41 (cont'd.)

Robert Morton & Co.	Trent Works Derby St.	Brewery equipment particularly refrigerators	*c.*1880	still in existence	
Orton & Son.	Princess St.	Carriage builders	*c.*1890	still in existence	Geo: Orton, Sons & Spooner Ltd. formed 1934; manufacturers of fairground equipment etc. Moved to Victoria Crescent.
Pickering Bros.	Union Foundry, Union St.	Brass & cooper equipment especially for breweries	1865	*c.*1890	Joseph Homer also associated with the firm in 1884.
Thornewill & Warham	New St.	Iron, brass & cooperware, steamengines, including locomotives.	*c.*1740	1929	Mainly a hardware firm prior to 1840. Absorbed by S. Briggs & Co. Ltd., in 1929.

N.B. At least 20 small businesses existed at various times in addition to those listed above.

APPENDIX 42

List of Workers employed at the Tape Mill, Newton Road, Winshill, 1851

Proprietor: Alexander Small aged, 60, of Whaley, Derbyshire – a tape manufacturer employing 42 hands.

Mechanic: James Bainbridge, aged 31 of Derby.

Tape workers, makers and weavers:

Name	Age	Place of Residence	Place of Birth
Maria Atkin	16	Horninglow Street	
Caroline Bradbury	22	Winshill	Stapenhill, Derbys.
Elen Bradbury	15	Winshill	Winshill, Derbys.
Elizabeth Brearly	17	Anderstaff Lane	Burton
Emma Brearly	15	Anderstaff Lane	Burton
Mary Chambers	15	Back Lane	Burton Extra
Hannah Dakin	12	Station Street	Fradley, Staffs.
Harriet Dicken	16	Brook Street	Burton
Ann Fellows	51	Pinfold Lane	Stretton-in-the-Field, Leics.
Jane Fletcher	37	Lichfield Street	Burton Extra
Sarah Harrad	14	Station Street	Burton
Catherine Hikenson	16	Brook Street	Burton
Elizabeth Hikenson	18	Brook Street	Burton
Sarah Lakin	17	Anderstaff Lane	Burton
Eliza Leedham	16	Lichfield Street	Burton
Elizabeth Malbon	11	Forge Mills	Yoxall, Staffs.
Emma Malbon	13	Forge Mills	Yoxall, Staffs.
Hannah Malbon	15	Forge Mills	Cheadle, Staffs.
Harriet Malbon	20	Forge Mills	Rosliston, Derbys.
George Moore	13	Winshill	Winshill, Derbys.
Harriet Oliver	19	Anderstaff Lane	Burton
Catherine Sharp	35	Burton Road, Winshill	Whaley, Derbys.
Sarah Siddels	43	Lichfield Street	Burton Extra
John Taverner	32	Burton Road, Winshill	Appleby, Derbys.
Ann Taylor	16	Back Lane	Appleby, Derbys.
Elizabeth Welsh	16	Anderstaff Lane	Burton
Susannah Welsh	21	Anderstaff Lane	Burton
Mary Whotley	20	Anderstaff Lane	Burton

(*Source* : P.R.O., H.O. 107, Bdl. 2012 (*Census of Population*, 1851).)

APPENDIX 43

Insurance Valuation of Peel, Yates & Co's Cotton Mills at Burton-on-Trent, 1795

Values in £'s	Building	Machinery	Mill wright's work	Steam Engine	Stock	Total
Weir Mill	1254	1590	244	–	126	3,214
Winshill Mill	1000	1280	256	–	150	2,686
Bond End Mill	2118	2762	570	1,500	300	7,250

(*Source* : Sun Fire Office Insurance Registers, O.S. 7/640034, 21/674492, 21/676405; Royal Exchange Co. Registers, 30/144536.

(per Dr. S. D. Chapman, 'The Peels in the Early English Cotton Industry'.)

APPENDIX 44

Burton Residents employed in the Burton Cotton Mills in 1841

Cotton Spinners	45			
Cotton Weavers	44			
Cotton Mill Hands and Workers	26			
Cotton Dressers	4			
Cotton Carders	4			
Mechanics at Cotton Mill	2			
Calico Printers	2			
Cotton Dyers	1			
Cotton Winders	1			
TOTAL	129[1]			
	No.	No.	%	%
Males under 16 years	3	44	2	36
Males over 16 years	41		34	
Females under 16 years	22	85	17	64
Females over 16 years	63		49	
TOTALS	129	129	100	100

1 Census also indicates names, ages and places of residence of all workers.

(*Source* : Census of Population, 1841; P.R.O., H.O., 107, Bdls. 191 & 975.)

APPENDIX 45

List of Workers employed at the Forge Cotton Mill, Winshill, 1851

Proprietor: Johnathan W. Haythorne
Manager: Robert Parker, aged 28, of Balderstone, Notts. – agent for a cotton doubler, employing 60 hands.

Name	Age	Work[1]	Place of Residence	Place of Birth
Maria Allsopp	16	W	High St.	Burton
Anne Allsopp	21	D	Forge Mills	Kegworth, Leics.
Mary Aston	16	F	Screw Yard	Burton
Eliza Bainbridge	28	D	Forge Mills	Radford, Notts.
Mary Baxter	12	F	Burton Rd. Winshill	Measham, Leics.
Eliza Beesby	16	T	Anderstaff Lane	Burton
Elizabeth Best	14	F	New St.	Burton
Rosemary Bradby	22	D	Forge Mills	Burton
Mary Brenan	12	F	Screw Yard	Roscommon, Ireland.
Mary Brenan	14	F	Screw Yard	Roscommon, Ireland.
Mary Bridges	12	F	Common Side	Burton
Elizabeth Brighton	12	F	New St.	York
Emma Chambers	15	F	Swine Market	Burton
Elizabeth Coates	12	D	Anderstaff Lane	Burton
Mary Dakin	23	W	Station St.	Fradley, Staffs.
Maria Dolman	29	W	Horninglow St.	Burton
Ellen Dooley	14	F	Lichfield St.	Burton
Fanny Felthouse	16	F	New St.	Burton
Harriet Felthouse	17	F	New St.	Burton
Irene Felthouse	14	F	New St.	Burton
Mary Gilbert	53	W	New St.	Burton
Ann Gold	16	F	Burton Rd. Winshill	Buckage, Leics.
Thomas Gold	14	F	Burton Rd. Winshill	Burton
Samuel Gough	69	Dr	Branston Rd.	Tamworth, Staffs.
Stephen Grindley	37	O	Forge Mills	Manchester, Lancs.
Hannah Heath	18	F	Marriott's Yard	Burton
Elizabeth Huse	13	F	Burton Rd. Winshill	Burton
Mary Huse	17	F	Burton Rd. Winshill	Duffield, Derbys.
Hannah James	22	D	Forge Mills	Mayfield, Staffs.
Elizabeth Oldham	15	F	Pinfold Lane	Sawley, Derbys.

Name	Age	Work[1]	Place of Residence	Place of Birth
Margaret Smith	24	W	Burton Extra	France
Mary Statham	14	Wi	Lichfield St.	Burton
Harriet Vincent	17	T	Horninglow St.	Burton
Joseph Winfield	33	O	Burton Rd, Winshill	Wilne, Derbys.
Elizabeth Wilkins	19	S	New St.	Burton

1 W = Weaver
D = Doubler
F = Cotton factory worker
Dr = Dresser
O = Overlooker
Wi = Winder
T = Twist hand
S = Spinner

(*Source* : P.R.O., H.O., 107, Bdl. 2012; *Census of Population*, 1851.)

APPENDIX 46

Burton Hatters in 1841

Name	Age	Location of Premises
John Akers	35	Back Lane, Bond End
William Akers	60	Back Lane, Bond End
Edwin Beale	32	High Street
James Butler	60	New Street
John Butler	60	Lichfield Street
William Butler	20	Little Burton
George Chesher	65	New Street
Francis Dalton	25	Back Lane, Bond End
William Geary	25	New Street
George Howard	30	Fleet Stones, Bond End
James Howard	40	New Street
James Marriott	30	Lichfield Street
William Marriott	65	Back Lane, Bond End
Edward Page	60	Pinfold Lane
Alonzo Port	25	High Street
Stephen Port	60	New Street
William Port	55	Fleet Stones, Bond End
John Rice	25	Fleet Stones, Bond End
Joseph Rice	46	Shobnall
William Rice	30	High Street
William Rice	60	Fleet Stones, Bond End
Robert Richards	70	Pinfold Lane
Stephen Rogers	60	Back Lane, Bond End
James Smithard	60	New Street
Samuel Sollory	60	New Street
Thomas Sollory	45	Half Street, Bond End
James Thompson	37	Lichfield Street

(Census of Population, Burton-on-Trent, 1841; P.R.O., H.O. 107, Bdl. 975.)

APPENDIX 47

Summaries of Accounts for Stapenhill Brickyards, 1814–15

Expenses	1814 £	s.	d.	1815 £	s.	d.
Pd. Thomas Ash and John Wilson at sundry times for making bricks.	376	15	9	464	6	8
Pd. Duty on bricks	151	17	9	158	1	6
Pd. H. & W. Nadin for coals	130	15	4	116	0	0
Pd. Workmen for building hovels & kilns	92	0	0	91	12	11
Pd. W. Cooke and John Wood for carriage of coals	61	10	0	67	11	0
Total Expenses	**812**	**18**	**10**	**897**	**15**	**1**

	£	s.	d.
Total expenses at the brickyards in 1814 and 1815	1710	13	11
Total receipts from the sale of bricks and tiles	2080	8	2
To Balance being 2 years profit	369	14	3

(*Source* : *Paget MSS*; Stapenhill Brickyards' Accounts, 1814–15.)

APPENDIX 48

Monumental Effigies attributed to Burton Alabaster-carvers, 1480–1638

Names of persons depicted by effigies	Site of tomb	County[2]	Date	Likely carvers
——	Kinlet	Sh	*c.*1480	
Earl of Wiltshire	Lowick	N	1492	
Member of	Norbury	D	1493	
Fitzherbert family	Stanford-on-Teme	Wo	1493	
Sir Nicholas Montgomery	Cubley	D	1493	Henry Harpur & Wm. Moorecock
John Curzon	Kedleston	D	*c.*1500	
Thomas Kinardesley	Uttoxeter	S	*c.*1500	
Sir John Strelley	Strelley	No	*c.*1500	
Babington monument	Ashover	D	1509	Harpur & Moorecock
Richard Herbert	Abergavenny	M	1510	
Henry Foljamb	Chesterfield	D	1510	Harpur & Moorecock
Sir John Ferrers and wife	Tamworth	S	1512	
Agarde monument	Scropton	D	1515	
Richard Vernon	Tong	S	1517	
Sir Simon Digby and wife	Coleshill	W	1519	
Randolph Egerton and wife	Madeley	S	1522	
Sir Randle Brereton	Malpas	C	1522	
Lady of Kindardesley family	Uttoxeter	S	1523	
Sir John Aston and wife	Church Leigh	S	1523	
Sir Wm. Smythe and wives	Elford	S	1525	
Sir William Matthews	Llandaff	G	1525	
Nicholas Hyde	Standon	S	1526	
Robert Hazelrig	Castle Donington	L	1529	
Richard Astley and wife	Patshull	S	1532	
Sir Richard Knightley	Fawsley	N	1534	Richard Parker
John Blount	Kinlet	Sh	*c.*1535	Parker
Sir Roger Mynors	Duffield	D	1536	
Robert Sherebourne, Bishop of Chichester	Rolleston	S	1536	
Sir Walter Devereux & wives	Stowe-by-Chartley	S	1537	
Nethermyl tomb	Coventry	W	1539	
William Feilding	Monk's Kirby	W	1539	
Swillington monument	Coventry	W	*c.*1540	

Names of persons depicted by effigies	Site of tomb	County[2]	Date	Likely carvers
Sir George Forster	Aldermaston	B	*c.*1540	
Sir George Manners	Windsor	B	*c.*1540	
1st Earl of Rutland	Bottesford	L	1543	Parker
Sir John Vernon and wife	Clifton Campville	S	1545	
	Bristol	G[1]	*c.*1545	
Henry Sacheverell	Radcliffe-on-Soar	L	1554	Richard & Gabriel Royley
Lord Chief Justice Bromley	Wroxeter	Sh	1555	Parker
Thomas Andrews	Charwelton	N	1556	Parker
Sir John Gifford and wives	Brewood	S	1556	Royley
Sir Edward Littleton & sisters	Coleshill	S	1558	Royley
John Digby	Coleshill	W	1558	Royley
Sir Phillip Draycott & wife	Draycott-le-Moors	S	1559	Royley
Thomas Grey and wife	Enville	S	1559	Royley
An unknown knight	Burton (Museum)	S	*c.*1560	Royley
Sir Thomas Gifford & wives	Brewood	S	1560	
Godfrey Foljambe & wife	Checkley	S	1560	Royley
Sir Edward Aston	Stafford	S	1562	
Gervase Clifton	Clifton	D	1564	Royley
Humphrey Wells & wife	Yoxall	S	1565	Royley
An unknown knight	Tamworth	S	*c.*1565	Royley
Sir George Cornewall	Eye	H	1566	
Sir Richard Newport	Wroxeter	Sh	1570	
Sir Wm. Sneade & wife	Wolstanton	S	1571	
John and Frances Shirley	Breedon	L	1571	Royley
Sir Edward Littleton & wife	Penkridge	S	1574	Royley
John Leveson & wife	Wolverhampton	S	1575	Royley
Thomas Fisher	Warwick	S	1577	Royley
John & Elizabeth Wrottesley	Tettenhall	S	1580	Royley
Basil Fielding	Monk's Kirby	W	1580	
Thomas Fermour	Somerton	O	1582	
Thomas Lane & wife	Wolverhampton	S	1582	
Sir Edward Boughton	Newbold-on-Avon	W	1584	
Humphrey Peyto	Chesterton	S	1585	Royley
John Shirley	Breedon	L	1585	Royley
The Spencer monument	Great Brington	N	*c.*1586	
Sir John & Lady Fleetwood	Ellastone	S	1590	Royley
Walter Vernon & wife	Marchington	S	1592	Royley
William Clopton	Stratford-on-Avon	W	1592	Royley
William Bowyer & wife	Seighford	S	1593	Royley
Ralph Adderley	Hanbury	S	1595	

Name of persons depicted by effigies	Site of tomb	County[2]	Date	Likely carvers
Sir Richard Bagot & wife	Blithfield	S	1596	
Thomas Caldwall & family	Rolleston	S	*c.*1600	Joseph Hollemans
Robert Dudley	Warwick	W	*c.*1600	Hollemans
Sampson Erdeswicke[1]	Sandon	S	1601	Hollemans
Robert Burdett	Seckington	W	1603	Hollemans
Welby family	Gedney	Li	1605	Hollemans
Lady Elizabeth Seymour	Norton	N	1605	Hollemans
Sir William Spencer	Yarnton	O	1609	Hollemans
Bishop Overton	Eccleshall	S	1609	Hollemans
Ralph Egerton	Betley	S	1610	Hollemans
Sir George Fermor	Easton Neston	N	1612	Hollemans
William Sneade & wife	Keele	S	*c.*1613	
The Gerard monument	Ashley	S	1617	Hollemans
The Little monument	Penkridge	S	*c.*1620	Hollemans
Richard Parkes	Wednesbury	S	1618	Hollemans
The Meverell monument	Ilam	S	1620	Hollemans
Edward Mosley	Rolleston	S	1638	Hollemans

(*Sources* : Mainly compiled from P.B. Chatwin, Monumental Effigies in the County of Warwick; *Transactions of the Birmingham Archaeological Society*, Vols. 47 & 48 (1921–2) and S.A. Jeavons, The Monumental Effigies of Staffordshire, Parts I-III (1955) – reprint from *Transactions of the Birmingham Archaeological Society*, Vols. 69-71.)

1 Stone effigy (not alabaster).

2 Sh = Shropshire
N = Northamptonshire
D = Derbyshire
Wo = Worcestershire
S = Staffordshire
M = Monmouthshire
No = Nottinghamshire
W = Warwickshire
C = Cheshire
G = Glamorgan
L = Leicestershire
B = Berkshire
Gl = Gloucestershire
H = Herefordshire
O = Oxfordshire
Li = Lincolnshire.

APPENDIX 49

WILSON and ALLSOPP

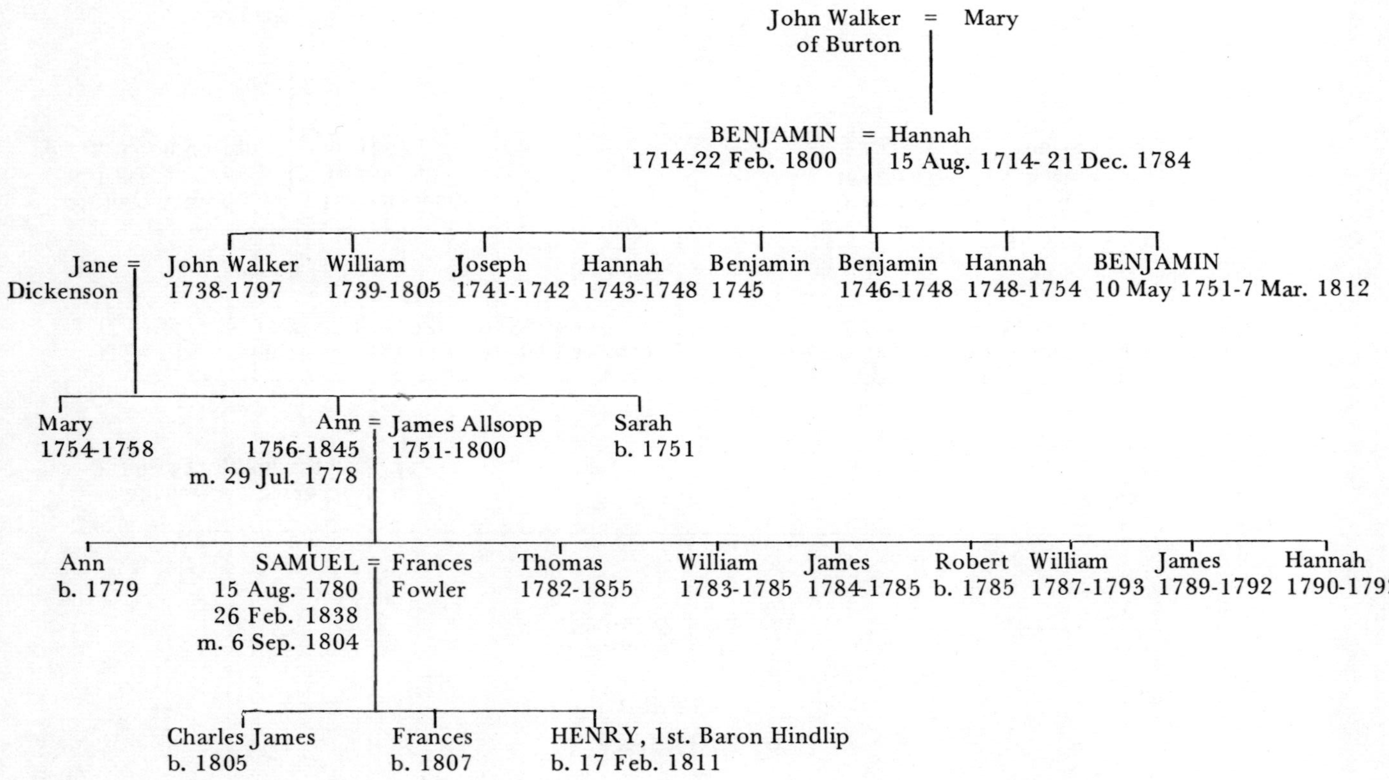

APPENDIX 50
BASS

WILLIAM = Mary
1720-1787 Gibbons

Michael = Sarah Hoskins
1759-1827 m. 2 Jan. 1794

William
b. 1763

Mary
b. 1795

Sarah
b. 1797

Frances
b. 1798

Michael Thomas = Eliza Jane
1799-1884 Arden

William
b. 1802

Abraham
b. 1804

Roger = Ann
Worthington

Michael Arthur = Harriet Georgina
b. 1837 Thornewill
1st. Baron Burton m. 1869

No male children

Hamar Alfred = Hon. Louisa
1842-1898 Bagot
m. 1879

THORNEWILL

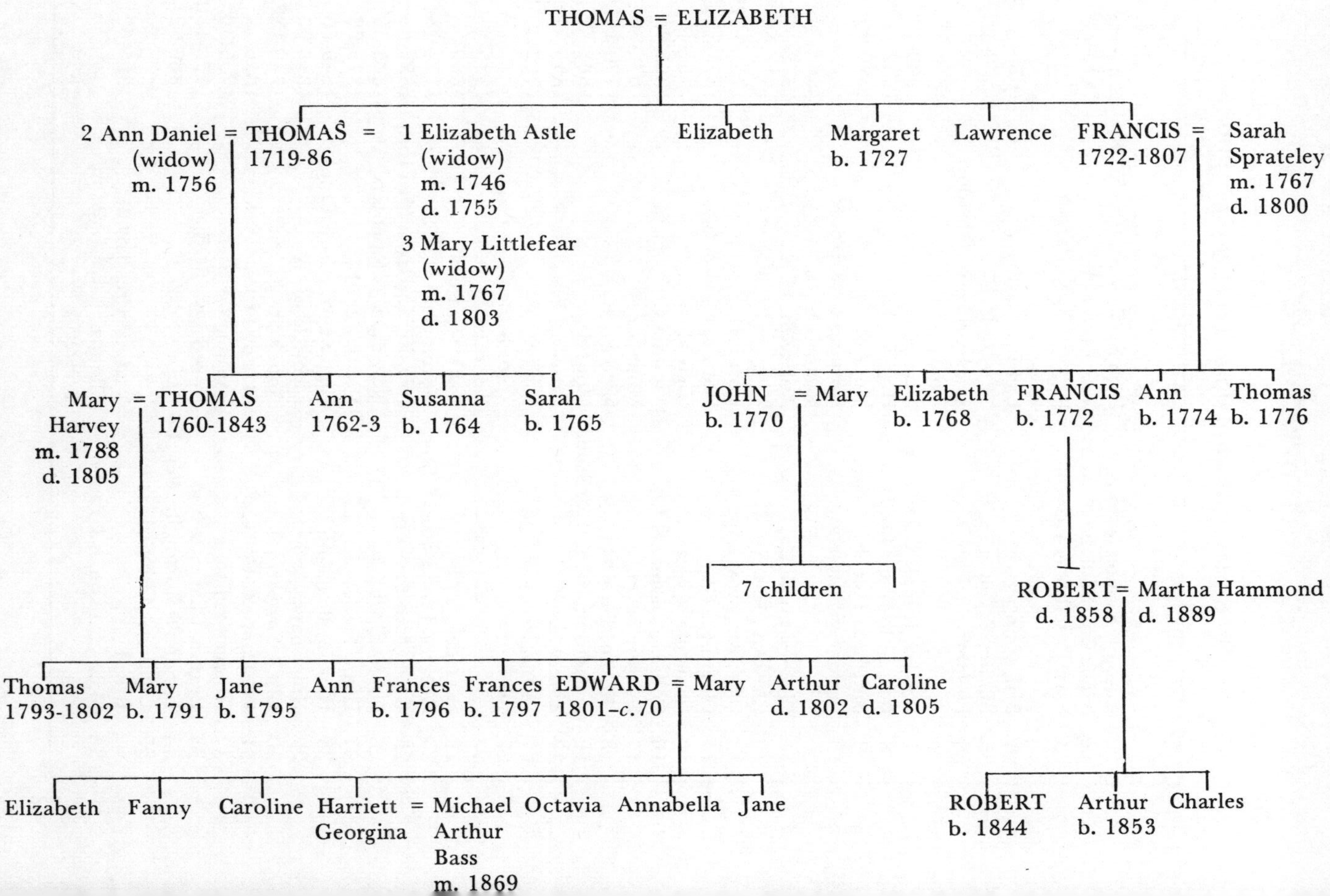
THOMAS = ELIZABETH
2 Ann Daniel (widow) m. 1756
THOMAS 1719-86
1 Elizabeth Astle (widow) m. 1746 d. 1755
3 Mary Littlefear (widow) m. 1767 d. 1803
Elizabeth
Margaret b. 1727
Lawrence
FRANCIS 1722-1807
Sarah Sprateley m. 1767 d. 1800
Mary Harvey m. 1788 d. 1805
THOMAS 1760-1843
Ann 1762-3
Susanna b. 1764
Sarah b. 1765
JOHN b. 1770
Mary
Elizabeth b. 1768
FRANCIS b. 1772
Ann b. 1774
Thomas b. 1776
7 children
ROBERT d. 1858
Martha Hammond d. 1889
Thomas 1793-1802
Mary b. 1791
Jane b. 1795
Ann
Frances b. 1796
Frances b. 1797
EDWARD 1801–c.70
Mary
Arthur d. 1802
Caroline d. 1805
Elizabeth
Fanny
Caroline
Harriett Georgina
Michael Arthur Bass m. 1869
Octavia
Annabella
Jane
ROBERT b. 1844
Arthur b. 1853
Charles

APPENDIX 52

Breweries of Burton upon Trent, 1700–1900

No.[1]	Name	Location	Date[2]
1	Allsopp, Samuel & Sons	High St. E. & Station St. N.	1807- —[3]
2	Ball & Co. (Midland Brewery)	Victoria St. W.	1870-75
3	Bass, Ratcliffe & Gretton	High St. E. & Station St. N. & S.	1777- —
4	Bell, John	Lichfield St. W.	1855- —
5	Bindley & Co.	New St. N.	1870- —
6	Boddington, Henry	Trent Bridge N. (Meadow Lane	1870-85
7	Bowler, Joseph & Thomas	New St. S.	1860-90
8	Burton Brewery Co. (Wilders)	High St. E.	1842
9	Burton & Lincoln Brewery	Moor St. S.	1890-99
10	Carter & Scattergood	Horninglow Rd. S. & Victoria St. E.	1860- —
11	Charrington & Co.	Abbey St. W.	1872- —
12	Clarkson, W. & G. R.	Victoria St. W.	1875-95
13	Clay, Joseph & Sons	Horninglow St. S. & N.	1751-1820
14	Clayton & Co.	Horninglow Rd. S.	1875-95
15	Clements & Berry	High St. W.	1855-75
16	Cooper, Thomas & Co.	Victoria Crescent E.	1865- —
17	Dawson & Co.	Moor St. S.	1872-90
18	Dicken, Thomas	High St. W.	1770-1800
19	Dickenson, Nicholls & Stone	Moor St. S.	1863-72
20	Eadie, James	Cross St. E.	1855- —
21	Evans, Henry & Son	High St. W.	1754-1819
22	Everard & Co.	Trent Bridge N. & Anglesey Rd. E.	1885- —
23	Evershed, Sydney	Bank Square W.	1860- —
24	Greaves, John Davies & Son	Horninglow St. N.	1774-1815
25	Green Man Brewery	New St. S. (Green Man Inn)	1855-69
26	Gretton, William	New St. S. (Carpenters' Arms)	1845-60
27	Heap, Frederick	Victoria St. E.	1875-90
28	Hicklin, Benjamin	High St. W. (Crown Inn)	1845-60
29	Hill, Charles & Son	Lichfield St. W.	1830-90
30	Hill & Sherratt	Abbey St. W.	1740-1825
31	Ind Coope & Co.	Station St. N.	1856- —
32	Kinder, William	Horninglow St. N.	1755-80
33	Leeson, Charles & Son	Horninglow St. S.	1753-1800
34	London & Burton Brewery Co.	Abbey St. W.	1860-72
35	London & Colonial (Tooth Bros.)	Victoria Crescent E.	1855-69
36	Mann, Crossman & Paulin	Shobnall Rd. S. (Albion Brewery)	1874- —

No.[1]	Name	Location	Date[2]
37	Marston, John & Son	Horninglow (Dover Rd.)	1835- —
38	Mason, John & Co. (& Gilbertson)	Horninglow St. N.	1825-45
39	Meakin, Jonathan (& Ginder)	High St. W.	1830-60
40	Meakin, Lewis & Co.	Abbey St. W.	1832-72
41	Measom, Sarah	High St. E. (Star Inn)	1845-70
42	Middleton, William	High St. E.	1846-60
43	Morecroft, Thomas	Lichfield St. W.	1770-90
44	Musgrave, John & Sons	Bridge St. N.	1729-1803
45	Nunneley, Joseph	Bridge St. S.	1845-90
46	Perks, W. S. & J.	Horninglow Rd. S.	1846-65
47	Phillips, Bros.	Derby St. E.	1860-73
48	Porter, James & Son	Dale St. E.	1875-95
49	Printon, Benjamin	Bridge St. N.	1708-29
50	Robinson, Thomas & Co.	Union St. E.	1863- —
51	Salt & Co.	High St. E.	1800- —
52	Saunders, William	Horninglow St. N.	1835-65
53	Sketchley, S. & W.	Horninglow St. N.	1741-90
54	Smith, Joseph	High St. E.	1710-40
55	Thompson, Francis & Son	Horninglow St. N. & S.	1840-98
56	Truman, Hanbury & Buxton	Derby St. E.	1873- —
57	Walker, A. B.	Shobnall Rd. S.	1877- —
58	Walker, Peter	Clarence St. W.	1880- —
59	Whitehead, Henry	Trent Bridge N. (Meadow Lane)	1865-75
60	Wilson, Benjamin & Son	High St. E & Horninglow St. N.	1742-1807
61	Wilson, John Walker	High St. W.	1773-90
62	Wilson, William	Horninglow St. N.	1773-1800
63	Worthington, William	High St. E. & W.	1760- —
64	Yeomans, John	High St. W. (Blue Posts)	1830-80

1 Numbers used in figures . . . .
2 Approximate dates indicated in some instances
3 — = continued after 1900

INDEX

App. = Appendix

Abbey Street:
- Hill and Sherratt Brewery: 63–4.
- London and Burton Brewery: 82,103.
- J. Sherratt Brewery: 78.

Abegg, J. D. Elbing: App., 12, 15.
Adams, Henry, dyer: 135.
Adderley, C. B., Hams Hall: 165–6.
Agencies, Brewery:
- Allsopp's: 73, 87.
- Bass's: 85.

Alabaster:
- carving trade: 169–172, 180.
- effigies: App. 48.
  - Burton Parish Church, Allsopp and Hawkins monuments: 172.
  - Rolleston: 172.
  - Tutbury Church: 169.
- geology: 2.

Albion Brewery: 82–3.
Ale:
- adulteration: 89–90.
- Arctic: 87.
- Burton's production (1780): 65; (1831–1900): App. 30; (1840s): 79; (1850–80): 80.
- exports: 65, 73, App. 7, 26.
  - Baltic: 32–40, 43–9, 53–4, 57–8, 61, 64–5, 67, 72–5, App. 7, 12–5, 24, 26.
  - India: 75–6, 89–90, 181, App. 27–9.
- home markets: 53, App. 25.
- India pale ale: 75–7, App. 28–9.
- pale ale: 75–8, 91, App. 27.
- prices: 40, 73, 75, 87.

Alice and Elizabeth, ship: 36.
All Saints' Church: 101.
Allen, Francis, Wetmore: 165.
Allsopp family: App. 49.
- Ann (Wilson): 52.
- *Collection* (Records): 53.
- G. H.: 102.
- Henry: 77, 85, 90, 93, 102.
  - Baronet (1882): 101.
  - Lord Hindlip: 101–2.
- James: 52.
- *Minute Books*: 101.
- Richard, mercer: 101.
- S. C., brewer: 101.
- Samuel, brewer: 52, 72–7, 101.
- Thomas: 52, 75.

Allsopp, Samuel and Co., brewers: 77.
Allsopp, Samuel and Sons, brewers: 3, 77, 79–90, 93–6, 101–3, App. 25–9, 32–4.
- Agencies: 73, 87.
- amalgamation, 1934: 103.
- Arctic ale: 87.
- Burton union system: 94.
- chemists: 89–90, 93.
- exports: 87, App. 26–7.
- incorporation, 1887: 86.
- India pale ale: 75–7, App. 27, 29.
- model brewery: 90.
- price-fixing: 87.
- private railways: 86.
- steam power: 84.
- tied properties: 87, 95.

Alluvial deposits: 3.
Almonde, Richard: 4.
Alrewas cotton and worsted spinning mill: 50–1, 55, 66, 136, 141–3, 145–50.
Alsop's school: 157.
Amity, ship: 44.
Amsterdam, finance houses: 47–8.
Anderson, J. W. and Co.: 47, 48.
Anderstaff Lane:
- Bass and Co., malthouses: 83–4.
- Botts, worsted manufacture: 134.
- brewery premises (1859);23;(1880): 96.
- Burton Brewery Co.: 80.
- J. Elson, ropemaker: 163.
- fulling industry: 129.
- J. D. Greaves, malthouses: 60.
- C. Leeson, brewing premises: 59.
- malthouses (1800): 39.
- J. Mason, malthouses: 78, 83–4.
- migrant workers' lodgings: 97.
- W. Musgrave, malthouses (1784): 59.
- W. Wilson, properties (1805): 55.
- Wood, dyer: 136.
- W. Wyatt's map (1760): 8.

Angel inn, High Street: 63.
Anglesey, Marquesses of: 9–10.
Anglesey coal seam: 4.
Anslow: 116–7.
- bleaching yards: 137
- Keuper Marl: 2.

Appleby:
- J. Wilkes, weaving shops: 141.

Apprentices:
- child: 147.
- parish: 9, 157.

Arctic ale: 87.
Arden, Eliza Jane: 99.
Major Samuel: 99.
Argo, ship: 44.
Arkwright, Richard, Cromford: 138, 142-4, 147, 149, 151.
Arnold, William, Newborough: 137.
Ash family, brickmakers: 168.
Thomas, brickmaker: 168.
Ashby-Burton railway: 4.
Ashby Canal: 22.
Act, 1794: 20.
Ashby Holes: 166.
Ashby Lane tollgate: 21.
Ashforth family, ironworkers: 118.
G. and Winrow, barley merchants, Newark: 42.
Astle family, clothiers: 133; feltmakers and hatters: 157.
Benjamin (d. 1761), clothier: 133.
Benjamin (2), tammy manufacturer: 133-4.
Elizabeth: 110, 157.
Francis, hatter: 156-7.
John. Tammy manufacturer: 133-5.
Atherstone: 20.

Babington, Rolleston, alabaster tomb, Ashover: 170.
Back Lane, mill workers' cottages: 148.
Bacterium Club: 93.
Bailton and Hodson, merchants, Calcutta: 76.
Bakewell family, flax-dressers: 137.
Ball and Co., brewers: App. 52.
Baltic trade:
ale exports: 32-40, 43-9, 53-4, 57-8, 61, 64-5, 67, 72-5, 181, App. 12-15, 24, 26.
Allsopp's: 72-5, App. 26.
Barley imports: 55.
Bass and Co.: 57.
book-keeping barter: 48-9, 54, 178.
commodity imports: 45, 66-7.
cotton exports: 51, 146.
Danzig (Gdansk); 36, 45-51, 54, 61, 75, App. 14, 24, 26.
decline: 10, 52, 59, 67, 78, 148.
East Country: 36.
Elbing (Elblag): 39, 45-7, 75, App. 14, 26.
Elsinore (Helsingor): 61.
end, 1825: 75.
exports: 36, 45, 51.
felt exports: 158.
financial arrangements: 47-8.
flax imports: 50, 54-5, 59, 61, 66, 137.
hat exports: 159.
hemp imports: 50, 54-5, 59, 61, 66, 162.

Baltic trade—continued—
iron imports: 43, 45, 48, 50, 54-5, 59, 61-2, 66, 113-4.
Kabrun, Jacob: 75.
Konigsburg (Kaliningrad); 36, 51, 61, 72, 75, 146.
lead exports: 61.
Musgrave's: 59.
Napoleonic Wars and blockade: 43, 47, 67, 72, 114.
Narva: 36.
Poland: 43, 46.
Prussia: 46, 73.
Riga: 36, 48-9, 54, 61, App. 13.
Russia: 36-7, 43, 45-6, 55, 58, 62, 67, 73, 75.
rye imports: 55.
St. Petersburg (Leningrad): 36, 38, 45-6, 48-50, 54, 61, 113, App. 14.
ships: 44-5, 51.
Sketchley's: 61-2, App. 24.
standstill, 1806-7: 47.
Stettin (Szczecinek): 74.
Sweden: 62.
tallow imports: 50, App. 17.
timber imports: 43, 45, 48-50, 54, 59, 61, 66, 74, 163, App. 16, 22, 24.
von Ankum, F. W.: 45, 48.
Wilson, Benjamin, snr.: 37.
jnr.: 36, 38-40, 43-52, App. 14.
J. W.: 53-5.
Zimmerman, C.: 46.
Baltimore, ship: 36.
Bamford, Samuel, Burton forge-manager: 112.
Bank Square: 83.
Banks and banking: 9, 55, 60, 66, 178.
Bannister, Maria: 33.
Bargates, Sketchley's warehouse, 1758: 61.
Barges, river: App. 6.
Barley: 31.
Allsopp's stores: 86.
Bass's suppliers: 84.
brewing: 40-2.
East Anglia growers: 97.
prices: 51-2, 64.
'water': 42, 53.
B. Wilson, jnr.: App. 9, 11.
J. W. Wilson's suppliers: 53.
costs: 74.
Barmby, Thomas, Hull: 44, 74, App. 15.
Barnard, Alfred, *Noted breweries of Great Britain and Ireland* (1889); 81, 83.
Barrow Hall: 102.
Barstow and Elliott, Danzig: 48-9.

Barter, Baltic trade: 48-9, 54, 178.
Barton-under-Needwood: 142.
Bass family: 59, App. 50.
  Arthur, brewer: 91.
  Hamar Alfred: 101-2.
  Mary: 56.
  Michael (1759-1827): 57, 66, 72, 76-7, 99.
  Sir Michael Arthur, brewer: 101.
  Michael Thomas (1799-1884), brewer: 77, 93, 99-102.
  Sir W. A. H.: 101.
  William (1720-1787), carrier and brewer: 35, 56-7, 64-6, 98-9, 114, 158, 176.
  William (2): 57.
Bass and Carter, timber dealers: 163.
Bass and Co., brewers (Bass, Ratcliff and Gretton): 83-6, 88.
  Agencies: 85.
  Bass and Ratcliff (1796): 57, 77.
  Burton Union system of fermentation: 94.
  chemists: 88, 90-1, 93.
  East Anglia workers: 97-8, App. 35.
  employment figures (1850-1900): 83; (1861): 87, App. 33; (1882): 87-8; (1888): App. 34.
  expansion, 1851-65: 80.
  India pale ale: 76, 83, App. 28-9.
  largest brewing company in the world: 81-2.
  malthouses (1874): 96.
  Middle Brewery, Station Street (1853): 84.
  New Brewery, Station Street (1864): 84.
  Old Brewery: 84.
  premises, 1851: App. 32.
  price-fixing, 1888: 87.
  production (1840): 79; (1840-50): 79; (1850-1900): 83; (1861): App. 33; (1888): App. 34.
  rail traffic, 1865: 23.
  tied houses: 95.
  well sinking, 1860s: 3.
Bass and Greaves, timber firm: 164.
Bass and Ratcliff (1796): 57, 77.
Bass, Ratcliff and Gretton, brewers, *see* Bass and Co.
Beale, Benjamin, hatter: 159.
Bear inn, Horninglow Street: 63, 79-80.
Bearwood Hill toll gate: 21.
Beaver hats: 155-6.
Beck, William, Newborough: 137.
Bell, Adam: 56.
Bell, J., brewer: App. 33-4.
Benedictine Abbey, brewing: 30.
Berry, T., brewers: App. 33.
Bewick, Joseph, Worcester: 55.
Billington, Joseph, spinner: 148.
Bindley, T., brewers: App. 34.
  Thomas, ironmonger and coppersmith: 122.
Bindley and Briggs, metalworks: App. 41.
Birmingham Canal (1770): 114.
Birmingham-Derby Junction Railway opening through to Burton, 1839: 10, 23, 77, 79, 121, 181,
Black, William, *Practical treatise on brewing* (1835): 89.
Black Pool Close: 140.
Bladon House: 102.
Blayden, *Mssrs.*. Hull: 37.
Bleaching mills: 141.
Blounte, John, alabaster worker: 170.
Blue Posts inn, high Street: 63, 79.
Blue Stoops inn, High Street: 34, 36.
Blundell, John, hatter: 156.
Bochur, Robert, alabaster worker: 170.
Boddington, Henry, brewer: 82, App. 34.
Bolland and Prestwidge, hop merchants, London: 43.
Bombay, ale imports: App. 27.
Bond, M. and W. and Co., tape and smallware manufacturers: 150.
Bond End: 10.
  brewing premises: 96.
  Burton Boat Company: 19.
  cotton spinning mills: 55, 140-4, 148-50.
  feltmakers and hatters: 156-8.
  nailmaking: 117.
  C. Perks and Sons, timber firm: 164.
  Ports, hatters: 157.
  screw forgers: 116.
  J. and W. Sherratt: 63.
  viaduct: 120.
  warehouse (1775): 17.
  J. W. Wilson, timberyard: 53.
  Wyatt's map (1760): 8.
Bond End Canal (1770): 10, 18-20, 78, 111, 163, 176.
Bond End Wharf: 17, 65, 158, 163.
Bond Street: 80.
Bonehill: 141.
Boode, Robert, alabaster worker: 169.
Book-keeping barter, Baltic trade: 48-9, 54, 178.
Boot and shoe makers: 167.
Booth, *Dr.*: 89.
Boreholes: App. 1-4;
Bott family, mercers: 134.
  Charles: 142.
  John, mercer: 132, 134, 142.
  John, textile manufacturer: 142, 147.
Bott, John and Co. (1783), Tutbury cotton mill: 134, 142, 149.
Bottinger, Henry, brewery chemist: 89-90.
Boulder clay: 3.

Boulton and Watt, Birmingham: 111.
steam engines: 29, 119, 144-5.
Bowers, William, cooper (1740): 35.
William, miller (1709): 32, 164.
Bowes, Robert, alabaster worker: 169.
Bowler, J. and T., brewers: App. 34.
Bracebridge, *Sir* John, alabaster effigy: 169.
Brackley family, clothiers: 135.
Jonathan (d. 1726), clothier: 133.
Bradley, Anthony and Co., Ashbourne: 55.
Branston: 1, 6.
population: App. 5.
Brearley, William, coal merchants, Newhall: 44.
Breeches-makers: 137.
Brelley, Thomas, tammy manufacturer: 135.
Bremen, ale imports: 61.
Brewers and breweries, *see also* Brewing industry (1700-1900): App. 52; (1851): App. 31-2; (1861): App. 33; (1888): App. 34.
Brewhouses (inns and domestic): 29-35, 38, 56-7, 59-61, 63-4, 175, 179.
Blue Stoops inn: 34, 36.
brewing vicuallers: 30.
Burton Abbey: 30.
Burton Extra: 31.
Burton-on-Trent (1604): 30-1.
Derby: 32, 35.
development into breweries, *c.* 1740: 34-5, 64.
inns: 31, 33-4, 63.
Lamb inn: 34, 60.
W. Newton, Horninglow Street: 34, 59.
Lord Paget: 30-1.
B. Printon, Horninglow Street: 33.
S. Sketchley, Nottingham: 61.
J. Smith, High Street: 33-4.
D. Watson, Abbey Street: 63.
Brewhouses (brewery):
W. Bass, High Street: 56.
J. Clay, Horninglow Street: 60.
H. Evans, High Street: 57.
C. Leeson, Horninglow Street: 59.
W. Musgrave: 58.
B. Wilson, jnr.: 38.
Worthington, High Street: 56.
Brewing: 28-9, 39-40.
adulteration: 89-90.
all-year: 91.
Burton, first record: 30.
Burton Union system of fermentation: 94, 180.
chemists: 88-95.
coal and coke: 43-4, 53, 84, 86.
fermentation: 88-90, 92.
machinery and equipment: 122-3.
Brewing—continued—
science: 89-95.
steam power: 29, 84.
water: 2-4, 29, 35, 66, 82, 84, 86, 97, 104, 181, App. 1-4.
wells: 3-4, 84, 86, App. 1-4.
yeasts: 92.
Brewing industry: 3-4, 10, 16, 22-3, 177-81.
prior to 1807: 28-71.
19th century: 72-106.
Brick clay: 2, 168.
Brick making: 168-9, App. 47.
Bridge Street:
J. Nunneley, brewers: 80, 83.
J. Staley, textiles: 136.
Bridgeman, H. E.: 93.
Briggs, S. and Co., brewery engineers: 82, 121-2, App. 41.
Brindley, James, canal engineer: 17.
Britannia Foundry, Horninglow Street: 122.
Brittan, Ralph: 135.
'Brizencote': 51.
Brizlincote:
coal pits: 4.
Brook: 2.
W. Nadin: 4, 166.
Broadley, Charles and Isaac, Hull: 44.
Broke, Harry, Lubenham: 171.
Bromley, *Lord Chancellor,* alabaster altar tomb, Wroxeter: 170.
Brook Street: 80, 102.
Brooks, Joseph, London: 40.
Brough, Benjamin, framework-knitter: 137.
Brown, Adrian J., brewery chemist: 89, 92.
Horace T., brewery chemist: 89, 91-4.
Browne, Thomas, maltster: 31.
Building stone: 3.
Bullers, William, brickmaker: 168.
Bullivant family: 4.
J., colliery owner: 4.
Bullivant and Co., coal merchants, Swadlincote: 44.
Bunne, Peter, brewer: 31, 132.
Bunter pebble beds: 3-4.
Burton, *Baron* (Michael Arthur Bass): 101.
Burton, *Mr.,* pottery manufacturer, Linton: 166.
Burton (16th-c.): 7; (17th-c.): 8; (18th-c.): 8-9; (19th-c.): 10-11.
banks: 9, 55, 60, 66, 178.
borough status: 6.
bridge: 6-8, 21, 32, 34, 109, 135.
new: 11, 23.
burgesses: 8-9.
Civil war: 31, 130-1.

Burton—continued—
Commercial Development Committee: 103.
feoffees: 8-10, 66.
physical environment: 1-5.
population: 1, 7-11, 65, App. 5.
railway stations: 23, 81.
situation: 1.
town management: 8-9, 11, 101.
Burton Abbey: 6.
alabaster: 169.
brewing: 30.
dissolution: 6, 128-9.
fulling mill: 128.
sheep: 128.
Burton and Lincoln Brewery Co.: 82.
Burton Boat Co.: 16, App. 6.
Burton Boat Co. (1762-3): 17-20, 57, 59.
Burton Brewery Co. (1842): 80, 87-8, 95, 166-7, App. 32-4.
taken over (1914): 103.
Burton Copper and Engineering Works, Moor Street: 122.
Burton Copper Works, Station Street: 122.
Burton corn mill (Winshill): 6, 8, 31, 57, 139, 164-5.
Burton Extra: 31, 57, 131,
cotton mills: 140.
Manor: 112.
population: App. 5.
Burton Forge: 19, 109, 111-3, 115, 176, App. 38.
closure (1810): 117.
conversion to cotton mill (1814): 113, 141, 168.
Lloyds: 109, 111, 113.
output (1774 and 1798): 112.
T. and S. Seal: 109.
Burton Forge Mill (textiles): 141-3, 150, 168, App. 45.
calico manufacture: 143.
Burton Lower Meadow: 57.
Burton Manor: 4, 6, 7.
house: 31.
timber sales: 112.
Burton steam pump: 122.
Burton Union system: 94, 180.
Burton Wharf: 35, 108.
Burton-on-Trent Times, May 1858: 80-1.
Butt House, Woodville: 166.
Butterfield, James, woollen-draper: 35.
Buxton, Thomas: 165.
Buxton and Dale, hop merchants, Nottingham: 53.
Buxton and Thornley, engineers: 122, App. 41.
Byrkley Lodge: 100, 102.
Bysshop, Robert, alabaster worker: 169.
Calcutta, ale imports: App. 27-9.
Caldwall, Richard, physician, London: 130.
William, clothier: 129-30.
Caldwall charity: 130-1.
deeds: 31, 131, 167.
Caldwell Hall: 58.
Calico: 51, 150.
weaving: 143, 147.
Canals: 74, 77.
Ashby: 22.
Grand Trunk: 17-8, 65.
Loughborough-Swannington: 22.
Staffordshire boats (1795): App. 6.
Trent and Mersey: 9, 18-20, 111, 114, 145-6, 176, 181.
Carboniferous rocks: 2, 4.
Carding engines, cotton spinning: 143.
Carlill, Gilder, Kirkbridge and Co., shipping agents, Hull: 44, 54.
Carlsberg Brewery, Copenhagen: 89.
Carson and Co.: 50.
Cater and Scattergood, brewers: App. 34.
Carter, T. M., brewers: App. 33.
Cartmeal, *Mr.*, canal guard: 74.
Casks: 43, 47, 49, 72, 103.
hoops: 43, 48, 55, 113.
Castle Hay gypsum bed: 2.
Castle Hays: 172.
Cat Street: 8-10, 53, 58, 133, *see also* Catte Street.
Cat Street Close: 133.
Catherine, Empress of Russia, and Burton ale: 32.
Catte Street: 30.
Catton: 112.
Catway, Thomas, barley merchants, Ibstock: 53.
Cavendish Boat Co., Shardlow: 20.
Cement and plaster manufacture: 165.
Census (1801): 8.
Chamberlain, John, Birmingham: 54.
Chamberlain and Lowe, brickworks: 168.
Chapman, Thomas, potter: 166.
Charcoal, iron manufacture: 112-3, 118.
Charing Cross hotel: 95.
Charlesworth, George, ironfounder: 119.
Charming Harriott, ship: 44.
Charrington and Co., brewers: 88, App. 34.
purchase of London and Burton Brewery: 82, 103.
Charwelton, alabaster altar tomb: 170.
Cheese, transport on Trent Navigation: 14-5, 181.
Chellaston, alabaster industry: 180.
Cherry and Yeomans, malthouses: 98.
Cheshire, George, spinner: 148.
Child apprentices: 9.

Child apprentices—continued—
feltmakers: 157.
Textile industry: 147.
Church Croft, timber yard: 86.
Churches:
building (1850-80): 11.
churchwardens' duties: 9.
St. Chad's: 101.
St. Margaret's: 100.
St. Paul's: 100.
Churchwardens: 9, 66.
Civil War: 31, 130-1.
'Clarck', John, clothier: 129.
Clare, Edward, jersey-comber: 133.
Clarence Street Brewery: 82.
Clark, Henry, timber dealer: 163.
Henry and Thomas and Son, timber firm: 164.
Clarke, Henry, clothier: 130.
John, clothier: 129-30.
Nicholas, clothier: 130.
Solomon, clothier: 131.
Clarkson, W. and G. R., brewers: 96, App. 34.
Clay, Henry: 60, 77.
Joseph (1) (d. 1800), brewer: 34-5, 59-60, 64-6, 176, 178;
timber importer: 163.
Joseph (2); 60, 77.
Joseph Spender, brewer: 77.
Clay Brewery: 78.
Clay Mill, cornmill: 110, 164.
conversion to forge: 109.
Clay Mills: 6, 115.
Clay Mills forge, Stretton: 48, 50, 110, 114-5, 118, 176, App. 39.
Clay Mills Ironworks Co., Ltd.: 118.
Clayton and Co., brewers: 96, App. 34.
Clements and Berry, brewers: App. 52.
Cliffcroft estate: 115.
Clockmakers: 142, 146.
Clothiers: 128-31, 133, 138.
Clothworking industry: 31, 127-33.
Clover seed, imports: 50.
Coal:
brewing: 43-4, 53, 84, 86.
ironmaking: 112-3, 118.
Coal measures: 2.
Coalfields:
Leicestershire: 1, 20, 22.
South Derbyshire: 1, 20.
Coalmining: 4-5, 66.
Coats and Co., brewers, Horninglow: 78.
Coffee, William, porcelain modeller: 166.
Coke:
brewing: 43-4, 53, 84, 86.
Collegiate church: 7.
Combrune, Michael, brewer, London: 88-9.
Commercial Development Committee: 103.
Commings, Richard, Repton: 56.
Common Side: 164.
Communications: 13-25; *see also* Canals, Railroads, Railways, River Transport, Roads, Trent Navigation.
Coney skins: 158.
Congreve, Thomas, Wolverhampton: 17.
Cooke, William, Smallware manufacturer: 150.
Cooper family, feltmakers and hatters: 157.
Godfray, hatter: 158.
Thomas, hatter: 158-9.
Thomas, woolstapler: 136.
Cooper, T. and Co., brewers: 96, App. 34.
Cooperages: 57, 60, 81, 84, 86, 96.
Coopers and coopering: 31, 34, 43, 55, 102-3, 179.
Copeland, Enoch, potter: 166.
Corn mills and milling: 164-5, 175-7.
Water-powered:
Clay Mill: 110, 164.
Hartshorne: 116.
Moor Mill Dam: 164.
Stapenhill: 164.
Tatenhill: 115.
Winshill (Burton Corn Mill): 6, 8, 31, 57, 139, 164-5.
Steam-powered: 145, 165.
Coroner (18th-c.): 8.
Corradine family, ironworkers, Clay Mills forge: 118.
Cotton:
exports: 51, 146.
imports: 145-6, App. 18.
Cotton spinning industry: 8, 23, 95, 138-151, 179-80.
Cotton spinning mills: 9, 138, 142-5. 149-50, App. 44.
Alrewas: 50-1, 55, 66, 136, 141-3, 145-50.
Bond End: 55, 140-4, 148-50.
Bond End New Building: 141.
Burton Forge: 141-3, 150, 168, App. 45.
construction: 146-7.
Measham: 141-5, 147-50, 177.
Tutbury: 136, 141-5, 147-50.
Weir (or Upper): 140.
Winshill: 139-43, 148-50.
Court baron: 9.
Court leet: 9.
Coventry, brewers: 29-30.
Creswell, Robert, barley suppliers, Ravenstone: 53.
Crispe, Hugh, 'couper': 30.
Crockett family, clothiers: 133.
Cromford, Derbyshire: 138, 142.
Cross Street: 97, 103.
Crown inn, High Street: 79.

Crown Maltings, Kimmersitch Street: 103.

Dale Brook: 2.
Dalrymple, Daniel, attorney and banker: 9, 55.
Danzig (Gdansk):
  exports:
    timber: 49, 54, 163.
    wheat: 50.
  imports: 36.
    ale: 36, 45-9, 54, 61, 75, App. 14, 24, 26.
    cotton: 51, 146.
    lead: 61, App. 24.
    B. Wilson, jnr.: 49.
  staves: 43, 49, 54, 63, App. 16.
Darbie ale: 31.
Darwin, Erasmus: 29.
Dawson, Edwin, Leeds: 82.
  Nathaniel: 56.
Dawson and Co., brewers: App. 34.
De Visme and Co., Lisbon: 51, App. 18.
Defoe, Daniel: 108.
Degge, John, hatter: 158.
  Sir Simon: 130-1.
Denston family, hatters: 157.
  William, hatter: 156, 158-9.
  William, ropemaker (1780s): 162.
Denton, P. and J., barley suppliers, King's Lynn: 42.
Derby:
  alehouses:32.
    keepers (1693): 30.
  brewing industry: 35.
  malthouses: 32, 35.
  Town Hall cellars: 78.
Derby Lane: 165.
  Road: 103.
  Street: 82, 122.
Derby Mercury: 35, 58.
Derwent, River: 13.
Desbrow, *Colonel*: 166.
Deuro, ship: 44.
Dickens, Francis: 50, 66, App. 18.
  Joseph, Alrewas Mill: 150.
  Thomas, mercer, brewer and textile manufacturer: 50, 63-6, 142, 177.
Dicken, Wilson and Co., Alrewas Mill: 145, 147.
Dickenson, John, Wolverhampton: 82.
Dickenson, Nicholls and Stone, brewers: App. 52.
Dickinson, Samuel, cotton machine maker: 146.
Dilke, William: 33.
Dodsworth, Charles: 161.
Dove Cliff House: 115, 118.
Doveridge Hall: 102.
Dowding, hop suppliers, Worcester: 53.
Downes, John, hatter: 158.
  Michael, hatter: 156.
Drakelow Hall: 102, 165.
Du Bois, Guillaume, timber nerchant, Danzig: 49.
Dupper and Co., Amsterdam: 48.
Dyche, Richard, brickmaker: 168.
Dyeing, textiles: 134-5.

Eadie, J., brewers: 102, App. 33, 34.
Eagliston, William, spinner: 148.
East Anglian migrant labour: 97-8, App. 35.
East Country: 36.
Edie's malthouses: 98.
Edwards, William, pottery manufacturer: 165-6.
Edys, William, Abbot of Burton: 6.
Effigies, alabaster: 169-72, App. 48.
Egginton, Seal estates: 109.
Elbing (Elblag), ale imports: 39, 45-7, 75, App. 14, 26.
Elsinore (Helsingor), ale imports: 61.
Elson, A. and Co., engineers: 123, App. 41.
  James, ropemaker: 163.
  Joseph, brickmaker: 168.
Enclosures: 9.
Engineering industry: 107-123, App. 41.
English Grains, Ltd.: 103.
Etherington, George, Hull: 44.
  Henry, Hull: 37.
Eureka coal seam: 4.
Evans, Henry, brewer: 16-7, 22, 34-5, 54, 56-8, 62, 64-7, 178.
    corn milling: 165.
    iron importer: 113.
  John: 58.
  Martha (1): 58.
  Martha (2); 56, 58.
  Rebecca: 58.
  Sarah: 56, 58.
  Thomas: 57.
Evans Brewery: 77.
Everard and Co., brewers: 82, App. 34.
Evershed, S., brewer: 83, 101, App. 33-4.

Faule:
  alabaster deposits: 169, 172.
  gypsum deposits: 2.
Fazeley, cotton and bleaching mills: 141.
Fell-mongers: 166.
Feltmakers' Company: 155-6.
Feltmaking: 148, 155-7, *see also* Hat manufacture.
Feoffees: 8-10, 66.
Fermor, Thomas, alabaster tomb, Somerton, Oxon: 171.
Ferry Bridge: 120.

Fiennes, Celia: 32.
Finance houses, Baltic trade: 48.
Finlay, James, brewer: 85.
Fischer, Matthew and William, Riga: 48-9, 54, App. 22-3.
Fitchett family, hatters: 157.
Robert: 158.
Flax:
home-grown: 137.
imported: 50, 60-1, 137, App. 24.
Flax dressers: 50, 137-8.
Fleet Stones: 140.
T. Clark and Sons: 164.
hatmaking: 157-8.
Fleet Street: 103, 118.
Fletcher family: 148.
Fletcher and Co., coal merchants: Ripley: 44.
Floaters: 24, 81.
Florence, wool imports: 128.
Flower, Ellis and Co., hop merchants, Ollerton: 42, 53.
Foljambe, Henry, alabaster tomb, Chesterfield: 170.
Foremark Hall: 102.
Forge Mill: *see* Burton Forge *and* Burton Forge Mill.
Forges: 109-115, 132, 175-6, App. 36.
Forster, E. A. P.: 93.
Fosbrook, William, mechanic: 147.
Fosbrooke family, Shardlow: 13-4.
Leonard, Shardlow: 14-5, 33, 108.
Foston Hall: 102.
Foundries: 121-2.
Fowler, James Nettlethorpe: 52.
Fox, James, metal manufacturer, Derby: 116.
Framework knitters: 132, 136-8.
Frankland, *Professor*: 93.
Fulling industry: 135, 138, 179.
mills: 109, 128-32, 139, 175.
Gainsborough:
ale exports: 32.
Burton Boat Company: 19.
H. Evans' barge: 57.
Jessop river survey: 19.
Sketchley, iron bars: 62.
Smith and Mosley: 60.
Trent Navigation: 13, 16, 19.
B. Wilson:
agents: 37.
ale exports: 44.
timber stores: 43, 50.
Gainsborough Boat Company: 20.
Gavle: 108.
Gay-Lussac, J. L.: 29.
Geology: 1-3.
George inn, High Street: 63.
Gibson family: 132.
John: 139.
Gilbertson, Robert, brewer: 78.
Gilds: 170.
Glen, William and Co., St. Petersburg: 46, 49.
Glovers, engineers: App. 41.
Glovers: 167.
Goodhead, Job, brewer: 76.
Goodwyn, H.: 29.
Goose Moor: 10.
Graham, *Professor,* Royal College of Chemistry: 93.
Grand Trunk Canal: 17-8, 65.
Grand Trunk Canal Company: 20, 176.
Grange Street: 97.
Granville Mills, Swadlincote: 165.
Graunger, Thomas, millwright, Coventry: 129.
Gravels: 3-4.
Greasley, Francis, Tutbury: 142.
Great Haywood, Trent and Mersey Canal: 18.
Greaves, Elizabeth: 61.
John, brewer: 59, 61, 77.
John Davies, brewer: 35, 59-61, 64, 66, 177.
Joseph, cotton broker, Liverpool: 145-6.
Robert Charles, Ingleby: 61, 77.
William, farmer, Ingleby: 35, 60.
Greaves Brewery: 39, 78.
Green Man Brewery: App. 33.
Green Street, Peel's warehouse: 141.
Greenlandmen, ships: 51.
Greensmith, T. G. and Co., corn millers: 165.
Gregory, Edward, potter: 166.
Gresley, *Sir* Nigel, Drakelow Hall: 165-6.
Gresley:
Common: 166.
Seal estates: 109.
woodlands: 112.
Worthington properties: 56.
Gretton, John, brewer: 63, 77, 101.
William, brewer: App. 32.
Grew, Thomas, tanner: 167.
Grice, Charles, tammy manufacturer: 134.
Griess, Peter, brewery chemist: 89-90.
Griggs, John, timber firm: 164.
Guild Hall: 9.
Guildables Close: 53.
Guilds: 170.
Gun barrels, Borton Forge: 109.
Gypsum: 2.
products: 2, 172.

Hacket, Mary: 60.
Thomas, brewer: 60, 63.
Halbard, Philip, ironfounder: 122.
Halbard and Wright, hardware manufacture: App. 41.

Haldren, William, spinner: 148.
Hallard, Samuel, spinner: 148.
Hamburg:
  cotton imports: 51.
  finance houses: 47-8.
Hampton Junction: 23.
Hams Hall: 165.
Hanbury Church: 169.
Hancock, Samson, pottery painter: 166.
Handley, William, Newark: 62.
Handloom weaving: 136, 143, 146.
Hannover, ship: 108.
Hanover, ale imports: 54.
Hansen, E. C., Carlsberg Brewery: 89, 92.
Harcourt, *Sir* William: 99-100.
Hardware industry: 8, 23, 96, 107-23, 148-9, 179-81.
Hargreaves, James: 138-9.
Harpur, Henry, alabaster worker: 170.
Harris, Richard, London: 50.
Harrison family, hatters: 157.
  John, feltmaker: 157.
Hartshorne:
  coal mines: 4, 51.
  corn mill: 116.
  screw manufactory: 116, 118.
  W. Shorthose property: 117.
  W. Worthington property: 55.
Harwood, *Capt.*, *Traveller*: 44, App. 12, 15.
Hassall, *Dr.*: 90.
Hat manufacture: 8, 23, 95, 148-9, 155-9, 175, 179-80.
  exports: 158-9.
  trade with London: 158, 181.
Hatters: App. 46.
Hawkins, Isaac, attorney: 17, 179.
Hawkins Lane: 164.
Haworth, Jonathan, Darwen: 138.
Hay, The: 166.
Hayne family, Trent Navigation: 35.
  George (d. 1724): 14-6, 33, 108-9, 132, 175.
  Henry: 16-7, 111, 132.
  John: 17, 139.
Haythorn, Jonathan, textile manufacturer: 150, App. 45.
Heap, F., brewer: 96, App. 34.
Helmsing, Lorentz, Riga: 54.
Hemp, imports: 37, 50, 162.
Henderson, James, Wolverhampton: 54.
Henry, ship: 113.
Henshall and Co., canal carriers: 19-20, 44, App. 6.
Hepworth, *Rev.* John: 56.
Heywood, A., Liverpool: 73.
Hicklin, Benjamin, brewer: 79-80, App. 31-2.
High bailiff: 8.
High Street:
  Allsop's: 77, 86.
  Angel inn: 63.
  Astles, clothiers: 133.
  M. T. Bass: 100.
  W. Bass: 56-7, 64.
  Bass and Co.: 77, 83, 91.
  Blue Posts inn: 63, 79.
  Blue Stoops inn: 34, 36.
  breweries (17th-c.): 65; (1780): 58; (18th-c.): 63; (19th-c.): 96.
  Burton Brewery Co.: 80.
  H. and T. Clark and Son: 164.
  J. Clarke, clothier: 130.
  J. Clay: 60.
  clothiers: 129.
  Crown inn: 79.
  T. Dicken: 63-4.
  H. Evans: 34, 67.
  T. Evans: 57, 64, 77.
  George inn: 63.
  J. Gretton: 102.
  hat makers: 158.
  Hicklins: 78.
  inn brewhouses: 31, 33.
  C. Leeson: 59.
  J. Meakin: 78-9.
  W. Middleton: 80.
  Midland Railway branch line: 23.
  T. Pearsall, cooper: 34, 57.
  pottery works: 165.
  rope makers: 162-3.
  Salt's: 60, 77, 80.
  screw manufactory: 115.
  Shilton family, clothiers: 133.
  S. Sketchley: 61.
  J. Smith: 33-4, 55-6.
  J. Staley: 136.
  tanyard: 80, 167.
  White Hart inn: 63.
  Wilson, B., snr.: 34, 36-7.
    B., jnr.: 38, 52, 64.
    J. W.: 53, 64.
  Woollen cloth manufacture: 128.
  W. Worthington: 56, 64, 83.
  W. Wyatt, map (1760): 8.
  J. Yeomans: 78-9.
Highlins Park: 150.
Hill, Charles, brewers: 78, 163, App. 33-4.
  John, brewer: App. 31.
Hill and Sherratt, brewers: 39, 63-4, 66, 163.
Hind, Joseph and Thomas, tammy manufacturers: 135.
Hindlip, *Lord* (Henry Allsopp): 101.
Hints: 112.
Hodges and Co., brickworks: 168.
Hodgson, Mark, brewers, London: 76, App. 28-9.
Hodson, John, bleaching yard, Anslow; 137.
Hoffman, *Professor*: 90.

Hogg, Henry, ironmonger: 108.
Hollemans, Joseph, alabaster worker: 172.
Holloway, William, maltster: 59.
Holst, J., Riga: 54.
Homer, Joseph, brass finisher and ironfounder: 122.
Homer and Shercliff, engineers: 123, App. 41.
Hoops, cask: 43, 48, 55, 113.
Hopkin, John maltster: 41.
Hops: 3.
  Bass and Co.: 84.
  hydraulic press: 122.
  B. Wilson, jnr.: 42-3.
  J. W. Wilson: 53.
Horner (Mornby), John and William, Gainsborough: 37.
Horninglow: 1.
  B. Astle, farmer: 133.
  Coats and Co., brewers: 78.
  gypsum mining: 2.
  in 1900: 10.
  population: App. 5.
  T. and S. Seal estates: 109.
  toll gate: 21.
  Trent and Mersey Canal: 18.
  W. Tunnicliff: 166.
Horninglow Brewery: 83.
  Moor: 10.
  Road:
    Bass and Greaves: 164.
    Richard and Co.: 103.
Horninglow Street:
  S. Allsopp: 52, 77, 86.
  Astles, tammy manufacturers: 133.
  Bear inn: 63, 80.
  breweries (1780): 58; (18th-c.): 63, 65; (19th-c.): 10, 96.
  bridge; 9.
  Britannia Foundry: 122.
  J. Clay: 59-60, 64, 78.
  clothiers: 129.
  A. Elson: 123.
  felt makers: 156-7.
  flax dressers: 137.
  J. D. Greaves: 60, 64, 77-8.
  Grice, tammy manufacturer: 134.
  Griggs, timber firm: 164.
  T. and M. Hacket: 60, 63.
  hatters: 158.
  inn brewhouses: 31.
  Lamb inn: 33-4, 60.
  C. Leeson: 59, 64, 78.
  J. Mason: 77-8.
  W. Musgrave: 58, 64, 78.
  W. Newton: 34.
  R. Peel: 139.
  J. Perks: 80.
  Printon's Brewery: 33.
  W. Riley, timber firm: 164.
Horninglow Street—continued—
  ropemakers: 162.
  T. Salt: 77.
  W. Saunders: 80.
  S. Sketchley: 35, 38, 55, 58, 61-2, 64.
  tanyard: 167.
  J. Thompson: 80, 83.
  Three Queens inn: 33, 59.
  Vine inn: 33, 63.
  B. Wilson, snr.: 37.
  B. Wilson, jnr.: 38, 52, 55.
  W. Wilson: 55.
  Wood's map (1837): 10.
  Wyatt's map (1760): 8.
  Street Court: 164.
  Wharf: 18, 163, 165.
Hosiery industry: 132, 136-8, 146.
Hoskins, Abraham, solicitor: 17.
  Richard: 51.
Hoskins and Hand, Manchester: 51.
Hubbernett, Christian, Riga: 54.
Hull: 13.
  Ale exports: 34, 58, 65, 72, App. 7.
  Allsopp's: 73.
  Baltic trade: 36, 45, 67, 72, 74-5, 178, App. 7.
  felt hat exports: 158-9;
  iron imports: 108, 112-3.
  S. Sketchley: 61, 113, App. 24.
  Spade exports: 114.
  Wilson, Benjamin, jnr.:
    ale exports: 44-5, 47, App. 13.
    flax and hemp imports: 50.
    merchants: 37, 44.
    shipping agents: 44.
    ships: 44, 51.
    timber stores: 50.
  J. W. Wilson:
    ale exports: 54.
    home market: 53.
Hull Port Books: 36, 65.
Hulme lists: 109.
Hulme, E. W., *Statistical history of the iron trade of England and Wales, 1717-1750*: 109, App. 36.
Humber, ship: 44, 51, App. 15.
Hunt, George, textile manufacturer: 150.
Hutchinson, John, Altona: 146.

Ibstock, barley growing: 41.
  colliery: 120.
Ind Coope and Co., brewers: 80-1, 96, App. 33-4.
  amalgamation, 1934: 103.
India pale ale: 75-6, 89-90; App. 28-9; *see also* Pale ale.
Inn breweries: 175, 179; *see also* Brewhouses (Inns and Domestic).
Inns: 31, 49.
  Angel, High Street: 63.

Inns—continued—
Bear, Horninglow Street: 63, 79-80.
Blue Posts, High Street: 63, 79.
Blue Stoops, High Street: 34, 36.
Crown, High Street: 79.
George, High Street: 63.
Lamb, Horninglow Street: 33-4, 60.
Old Crown,: 54.
Three Queens, Horninglow Street: 33-4, 59.
Vine, Horninglow Street: 33, 63.
White Hart, High Street: 63.
Institute of Brewing: 94-5.
Iron:
castings: 119.
forges: 109-15, 132, 175-6, App. 36.
foundries: 119.
imports: 48, 50, 55, 62, 67, 108, 111-4, 118, App. 21.
Iron-working industry: 107-23, 149, 179-80.

Jackson, J., barley suppliers, Newark: 42.
Jennies, cotton spinning: 143.
Jersey-combers: 132, 138.
Jersey-weavers: 132.
Jessop, William, canal engineer: 19-20.
Jewsbury, Thomas: 142.
John de Hanbury, alabaster effigy: 169.
John of Gaunt, wife's alabaster tomb in Old St. Paul's: 169.
Jordan, William, cooper: 57.
Juliana Catherina, ship: 74.

Kabrun, Jacob, Danzig: 50, 75, App. 26.
Kay, John, fly shuttle: 128.
Kedleston woodlands: 112.
Kenworthy, W. M. Danzig: 54.
Kersies: 130.
Keuper beds: 2-4.
Kimmersitch Street: 103.
Kind, J. B., timber firm: 164.
Kinder, William, timber merchant and brewer: 63, 163, App. 52.
King, Gregory: 29.
King's Mills, canal locks: 15-7.
Kingsbury Church: 169.
Kish and Co., Konisberg: 72.
Knapper, Joseph, male mill loader: 32, 164.
Konigsburg (Kaliningrad):
exports: 61, App. 24.
imports:
ale: 61, 72, 75.
cotton: 51, 146.
Kusoff, Ivan, St. Petersburg: 46, 49.
Wasily, St. Petersburg: 54.
Kynnersley, Willian, corn miller: 165.

Laboratory Club: 94-5.
Lakin, Thomas, brickmaker: 168.
Lamb inn, Horninglow Street: 33-4, 60.
Lambe, Edward, maltster: 31.
Lavoisier, A. L.: 29.
Law, Henry and Co., London: 48.
Lawton, W., Manchester: 73.
William: 15.
Lawty, John: 135.
Le Peyntour, William and John, alabaster workers: 169.
Le Walkere, William, fuller: 128.
Lead exports, Danzig: App. 24.
Leather-working industry: 166-7.
Leedham, Barnabas, ropemaker: 162.
Thomas, ironfounder: 119.
Leeson, Charles, brewer (d. 1794): 34, 39, 59-60, 64-6, 176-7.
Leeson Breweries: 78.
Leicester Railway line: 23, 121.
Leigh, Henry Blundell: 85.
Leland, John: 170.
Lende, John, alabaster worker: 170.
Leonard, *Capt.*, *Pheonix*: 44, App. 12.
Licensed premises: 82.
Licensed victuallers: 30-1, 34.
Lichfield Street:
C. Hill, brewery: 78.
T. Morecroft brewery: 63-4.
C. Perks and Sons: 164.
T. and W. Sanders: 121.
J. Staley, textiles: 136.
Liebig, *Baron* von: 89.
Lime: 22.
Limestone: 2.
Lin Brook: 1.
Linen industry: 137-8.
Lithology: App. 1-2.
Littlefear, brewer: 65.
Littlefere, Gervas, innkeeper: 33.
Littleton family, Penkridge: 172.
Lloyd family: 177, 179.
Birmingham mills: 110.
Burton Forge: 43, 109-113, 141, 176, App. 38.
Trent Navigation: 57, 111.
Lloyd, Charles: 17, 111-3.
Nehemiah: 17, 111.
Sampson, snr. and jnr.: 16, 17, 109, 111.
Samuel: 113.
Lloyd MSS.: 139.
London and Burton Brewery, Abbey Street: 82, App. 33.
London and Colonial (Tooth Bros.), brewers: App. 52.
Loughborough-Swannington Canal: 22.
Lovatt, brewer: 65.
Lowe, Agnes: 129.
John, fuller: 129.
Richard (1); 129.

Lowe—continued—
Richard (2): 129.
Roger, fuller: 129.
Thomas, fuller: 129.
William: 129.
Lowe and Sons, brickworks: 168.
Lucas, William: 142.
Lynam, James, manager, Burton Forge: 111.
Lyon, Charles Walter, brewer: 77.
Walter John, Tutbury Mill: 150.
Maldon, J. W. Wilson estate: 55.
Mallison, *Capt., Amity*: 44.
Malt:
Bass and Co.: 84.
Allsopp and Co.: 86.
B. Wilson: 41-2, 51.
Malt houses: 9, 39, 81, 96, 102-3, App. 9, 10.
Abbey: 30.
Allsopp: 86, 96.
Bass and Co.: 84, 96.
Anderstaff Lane: 83.
Shobnall Road: 84.
W. Bass: 56.
J. Clay: 60.
coke: 43.
Derby: 32, 35.
T. Dicken: 63.
H. Evans: 57.
J. D. Greaves, Anderstaff Lane: 60.
C. Leeson: 59-60.
Market Place: 30.
J. Mason, Anderstaff Lane: 78.
L. and G. Meakin: 103.
migrant labour: 97-8.
W. Musgrave: 58.
W. Newton, Horninglow Street: 34.
S. Sketchley: 61.
J. Thompson: 80.
B. Wilson, jnr.: 38, 41, App. 9, 10.
Anderstaff Lane: 39.
J. W. Wilson: 54.
Yeomans, High Street: 63.
Malt mill, Burton Market Place: 31-2, 66, 164, 175.
Malt roasting: 103.
Malt toll: 31-2, 65-6, 175-6.
Malt stores: 86.
Malting floors, Allsopp's, Shobnall: 86.
Maltsters: 31, 34, 179.
Meakin, Lewis and George: 103.
Mann, Crossman and Paulin, brewers: 82-3, 96, App. 34.
Manor: 4, 6-7.
house: 31.
lord: 8.
timber sales: 112.
Maps:
Wyatt (1760): 8.
Wood (1837): 10.
Market Place:
hat makers: 158.
malt houses: 30.
malt mill: 31-2, 66, 164, 175.
Marmite Food Extract Co., Ltd.: 103.
Marriott family, hatters: 148, App. 46.
Marriott, Thomas, hosier: 137.
Marshall, John, framework knitter: 137.
Marston family, brewers: 78.
John, brewer: 83, 101, App. 31.
Samuel, ironmonger: 108.
Marston, J. and Son, Ltd., brewers: 80, App. 33-4.
J., Thompson and Son, Ltd.: 83.
Thompson and Evershed, Ltd.: 83.
Marston Bridge, Ashby Canal: 20.
Mary, Queen of Scots: 30.
Mary Ann, ship: 36.
Mason, John: 83-4.
Jonathan (d. 1845), brewer: 77-8.
P. B.: 93.
Mason and Gilbertson, brewers: 78-9.
Mason and Sons, timber firm: 164.
Matthews, C. G., brewery chemist: 95.
John, brewery chemist: 90-1.
William millwright: 146.
Meakin, Francis, brewer: App. 31.
George, brewer: 101, App. 31.
Jonathan, brewer: 78-9, App. 31.
Lewis: 78.
Thomas, brewer: App. 31.
Meakin and Ginder, brewers: App. 32.
Meakin, Lewis and George, maltsters: 98, 103.
Meakin's London and Burton Brewery: 82, 103.
Mease, River: 141.
Measham:
bleaching mill: 141.
carding and roving mills: 145.
colliery: 119.
corn mill: 145.
cotton spinning mills: 141-5, 147-50, 177.
weaving shops: 141, 143.
J. Wilkes, purchase of parish: 141.
Measom, Sarah, brewer: 79, App. 32.
Melbourne, *Abbott*: 6.
Melburne, William, maltster: 31.
Melvill and Wolff, Amsterdam: 48.
Memel oak casks: 86.
Mentrup, *Capt., Porter*: 44, App. 12.
Mercia, Earl of, Wulfric Spott: 6.
Metal-working industries: 107-23, App. 41.
Metcalf, *Capt., Sally*: 44, App. 16.
Metcalf, Benjamin, Hull: 44.
Middleton, William, brewer: 80, App. 31-2.
Midland Joinery Works, Ltd.: 164.
Midland Railway Company: 23, 85, 99.

Migrant labour, East Anglian: 97-8, App. 35.
Mills, John, linen bleacher, Newborough: 137.
Millstone grit: 2.
Millwrights: 142, 146.
Milton Street: 97.
Mining equipment: 5.
Moira colliery: 20.
Molyneux, William, *Burton-on-Trent* (1869): 102.
Montgomery, *Sir* Nicholas, alabaster tomb at Cubley: 170.
Monumental effigies, alabaster: 169-72, App. 48.
Moon, James, potter: 166.
Moor Mill Dam: 86, 164.
Moor Street: 96, 122.
Moor Street Brewery: 82.
Moorecock, William, alabaster worker: 170.
Morecroft, Thomas, brewer: 39, 63-4.
Mornby (*sic*), John and William, Gainsborough: 37.
Morris, G. H., brewery chemist: 92, 95.
  William, brewer: 63.
Morton, Robert and Co., brewery engineers: 122, App. 41.
Mosley Street: 167.
Muilman and Sons, Amsterdam: 48.
Musgrave, James Wood (d. 1803): 59, 66.
  John, brewer: 34, 58, 64, 176.
  Henry: 59.
  William (d. 1784): 58-9, 61, 64-5.
Musgrave Breweries: 58-9, 78.
Musgreave, *see* Musgrave.
Musgrove, *see* Musgrave.
Muspratt *Chemistry as applied to arts and manufactures*: 90.

Nadin family: 4.
  H. and W.: 168, App. 47.
  William, colliery owner, Stanton: 44, 51, 66, 166.
Nail manufacture: 117-9, 138, 179.
Napoleonic wars and blockade: 43, 47, 67, 72, 114.
Narva: 36.
Need, Samuel, hosier, Nottingham: 138.
Needwood:
  Forest: 1.
  Plateau: 1, 3.
Nether Walk Mill, fulling: 128-9, 132.
Nettlefold, John, worming machine: 118.
New Mills Cotton Mills, Ashbourne: 55.
New Street: 8, 10, 170.
  brewery business: 96.
  T. Cooper, woolstapler: 136.
  feltmakers: 156.
  hat makers: 157-8.
New Street—continued—
  nailmaking: 117.
  screwmaking premises: 116, 118.
  tanyard: 167.
  Thornewill's: 110, 114, 118, 120-1.
  woollen cloth manufacture: 128.
  worsted manufacture: 133.
Newark:
  barley supplies: 41.
  breweries: 65.
  Sketchley's: 62.
Newbold, Joseph, millwright: 146.
Newborough, bleaching yards: 137.
Newhall collieries: 1, 4, 22, 51, 53, 66, 112.
Newspapers: 11.
Newton Richard, corn miller: 164.
  William, brewer: 34, 59.
Newton Park: 102.
Newton Solney, stone quarries: 3.
Nicholas, *Abbot*: 6.
Nicholls, William, brewer: 82.
Noble, Ann: 52.
  Edward More: 52.
Nock, Thomas, Walsall: 54.
Norkies: 98.
Norris, Joseph, corn miller: 164.
Nottingham Boat Company: 16.
Nunneley, Joseph, brewer: 80, 83, 101, App. 31-4.

Oakthorpe colliery: 119.
Oates, Robert: 73.
Odling, W.: 93.
Old Crown inn: 54.
Oliphant, James, London: 158.
Olive Tree ship: 44.
Opman, M. H. and Co., Hamburg: 48.
Orme, James, ironmonger: 108.
Orton and Son, engineers: 123, App. 41.
O'Sullivan, Cornelius, brewery chemist: 89, 91, 93.
Outram, Joseph, timber firm: 164.
Overseal: 141.
Overseers: 9.
Owen, William, Birmingham: 54.
Oxford Patent, Ltd.: 103.
Paget family: 8-9.
  1st *Sir* William (d. 1563): 7, 30-1, 129.
  3rd *Lord* Thomas (d. 1589): 129.
  4th *Lord* William (d. 1629): 4, 7.
  5th *Lord* William (d. 1678): 7.
  6th *Lord* William (d. 1712): 14, 20, 32, 107, 109, 164, 168.
Paget, Thomas, Ibstock: 53.
Pale ale: 75-8, 91, App. 27; *see also* India pale ale.
Paleske, John, Danzig: 49, App. 16.
Palmer, Robert, cheesefactor: 17.
Pardoe, James: 149.

Parish apprentices: 9, 157.
Parish registers: 148.
Parker, Richard, alabaster worker: 170.
Robert, Forge Cotton Mill manager App. 45.
Parnell, J. barley supplier, Newark: 42.
Parsons and Bradshaw's Directory, 1818: 136, 159.
Pasteur, Louis: 29, 89, 92-3.
Patten ring manufacture: 116-8;
Pawnton, John, alabaster worker: 170.
Payer, Monsieur, chemist: 90.
'Peal, Mr.': 144.
Pearsall, Thomas, cooper: 34, 57.
Peart, John, barley supplier, Newark: 53.
Peat beds: 3.
Peel, John: 140.
Robert (d. 1795); 54-5, 138-142, 144, 149, 151, 177, 179.
Sir Robert: 140-1, 147.
Peel, Harding and Co., Fazeley: 149.
Peel, Yates and Co.: 113, 139-44, 146-50, 168, 179.
mills: App. 43.
Bond End: 55, 140-4, 148-50.
Bond End New Building: 141.
construction: 146-7.
Forge: 141-3, 150, 168, App. 45.
Steam Engine: 144.
steam-power: 144.
Weir (or Upper): 140.
Winshill: 139-43, 148-50.
Peel's Cut: 163.
Pemberton, John, spinner: 148.
Perks, Charles and Joseph, timber dealers: 163.
Charles and Sons, timber firm: 164.
John, brewer: 80, App. 31-2.
Peter the Great and Burton ale: 32.
Peters, C. D., Lisbon: 51.
Petersson, C. A., London: 48.
Pettifors, brewers, Anstey: 83.
Pheasant and Manton, barley suppliers, Grantham: 42.
Phillips Bros., brewers: 82.
Phoenix, ship: 44, App. 12.
Pickering Bros., Union Foundry: 122, App. 41.
Pig iron: 111-2, 118.
Pillau (Baltiysk): 45.
Pinfold Lane:
screw manufacture: 116-8.
Thornewill's premises: 121.
Union Mill Co., corn mill: 165.
Plasterboard manufacture: 172.
Plot, R.: 32, 131.
Poland, *see also* Danzig, Warsaw:
ale imports: 46.
timber exports: 43.
Population: 1, 7-11, 65, App. 5.
Port family: 157, App. 46.
Port family—continued—
Anne (Astle): 157.
Dorothy: 158.
Esther: 157.
Henry, screw manufacturer: 118.
John (1), feltmaker: 157.
John (2) (1742-1802), feltmaker and hatter: 157-9.
John (3), hatter: 158-9.
Phillip: 115-6, 157-8.
Robert, feltmaker: 157.
Stephen: 157.
Thomas, hatter: 158.
Porter, James and Son, brewers: App. 34.
Porter: 73.
Porter, ship: 44, 51.
Pottery industry: 165-6.
Poyser, Thomas, brewer: 85, App. 31.
Prest, *Mr.*: 50.
Princess Street: 123.
Printon, Benjamin, brewer: 33-4, 58, 64.
Elizabeth: 34.
Maria (Bannister): 33.
Private railways, brewery: 24, 81, 85-6, 96.
Proudman, John, brewer: App. 31.
Prussia, ale imports: 46, 73.
Public houses, *see* Inns.
Pye, Rich and Co., Amsterdam: 48.
Pyecroft, Thomas, Overseal: 9.
William, Overseal: 9.

Radford, John, corn miller: 164.
Raff yard: 63.
Raikes, W. and T., London: 48.
Railroads, horse-drawn: 22.
Railways: 22-3, 78-9, 85.
Birmingham and Derby Junction: 10, 23, 77, 79, 121, 181.
Horninglow to Shobnall: 164.
Leicester line: 23, 121.
locomotives: 85-6, 120.
Midland Railway Company: 23, 85, 99.
private brewery lines: 24, 81, 85-6, 96.
Swannington: 23.
Ramm, Herman, Riga: 49, 54.
Rangemore: 100.
Hall: 100-2.
Ratcliff, John, brewer: 57, 63.
R., 102.
Samuel, brewer: 77. App. 31.
Read, George and Co., corn millers: 165.
Rebecca, ship: 158-9.
Redfern and Mason, timber firm: 164.
Redferne, Thomas, corn miller: 164.
Redying, John, alabaster worker: 169.
Repton, building stone quarries: 3.
Repton Brook: 2.

Reynolds, brewers: 39.
Rhaetic beds: 2.
Rice family, hatters: 148, App. 46.
Richards and Co., malt roasters: 98, 103.
Riga:
 exports: 61.
  flax: App. 24.
  timber: 48-9, 54, 61, 163, App. 24.
 imports: 36.
  ale: 49, 54, App. 13.
Riley, William, timber firm: 164.
 W. and Son, timber firm: 164.
River transport: 13, 77, App. 6; *see also* Trent Navigation.
Roads and road transport: 9, 13, 20-2, 56.
Robarts and Co., London: 51.
Roberts and Birch, Ltd.: 167.
Robinson, Thomas, brewer: 63, App. 31, 34.
Roe, Edward, screwforger: 118.
Rolleston: 130.
Rope walks: 163.
Rope manufacture: 37, 50, 162-3.
Roskampff, J. J., Elbing: 39, App. 26.
Rosler and Hurtig, Warsaw: 48.
Rotterdam, ale imports: 61.
Row bank (Coton-in-the-Clay), gypsum mines: 2.
Royley, Richard and Cabriel, alabaster workers: 171-2.
Russia, *see also* St. Petersburg.
 exports: 45, 55.
  flax: 55.
  grain: 55.
  hemp: 37, 55.
  iron: 55, 62.
  timber: 43.
 imports: 36, 45.
  ale: 36, 58, 67, 73, 75.
 trade hostility: 45-6.

Sable iron, imported: 111.
Saccharobacillus pastorianus: 92.
Saddlers: 167.
St. Chad's Church: 101.
St. Margaret's Church: 100.
St. Paul's Church: 100.
 Institute: 100.
St. Petersburg (Leningrad):
 exports: 45-6, 61, App. 24.
  iron: 48, 50, 113.
  tallow: 50, App. 17.
  timber: 49, 54, 163.
 imports: 36, 45.
  ale: 38, 45-6, 48, 54, 61.
Sally, ship: 44, App. 16.
Salt, Thomas, brewer: 60-1, 72, 76-7, 176.
Salt, Thomas F., brewer: App. 31.
 W. C.: 102.
Salt, T. F. and Co., brewers: 60, 77, 80-1, 87-8, 92, 101-3, App. 32-4.
Salt, transport on Trent Navigation: 15.
Sanders, John, miller, Horninglow: 165.
 R. J., hops supplier, Birmingham: 53.
 Samuel, barley supplier, Newark: 40, 42.
 Samuel, foundry owner: 121.
 Thomas and William, engineers: 121.
Sanderson, *Sir* James, Roxby and Co., hops suppliers, London: 42, 53.
Saunders, William, brewer: 80.
Screw manufacture: 115-9, 138.
Screw Yard: 116.
Seal, Samuel (d. 1762), ironmonger: 108-9, 111, 115.
 Thomas, ironmonger: 108-9.
Seany Park: 8, 112.
Seaton, Cumberland, pig-iron: 111.
Sergeant, brewer: 39.
Sewers, culverted: 9.
Shairps, Maude and Co., St. Petersburg: 46, 50, 113.
Sharp, John, tape manufacturer: 150.
Sharp Bros. and Knight, timber firm: 164.
Shaw, Stebbing, *History of Staffordshire*: 33.
Shercliffe, T. R. and Co., Ltd., engineers: 122.
Sherratt, John, brewer: 63, 77-8.
 William, brewer: 63, 163.
Shevyn, Samuel, dyer: 135-6.
Shilton, Joseph, clothier: 133.
 Richard, clothier: 133.
 Robert, clothier: 133.
Shirley, George, Staunton Harold: 171.
Shobnall: 1-2, 6, 10, 18, 20, 86.
 clay extraction: 168-9.
 Grange: 131.
 railway: 164.
 Wharf: 19, 112, 163.
Shobnall Road: 82-4, 96, 164.
Shobnall Street: 164.
Shorthose, Katherine: 117.
 Stephen: 117.
 Thomas: 73.
 William: 115-7.
Shorthose, Wood and Co., screw manufacturers: 115-8, 177.
Shorthouse, Henry, innkeeper: 33.
Siddals, John, brickmaker: 168.
Simnett, Joseph, brickmaker: 168.
 Thomas, brickmaker: 168.
 William, brickmaker: 168.
 William, maltster: 59.
Sinai Park: 8.
Sketchley:
 Elizabeth: 61.

Sketchley—continued—
Mary: 63.
Samuel (d. 1775), brewer: 35, 58, 61-3, 66, 113, 176, App. 24.
Samuel (2), brewer: 49, 62, 64, 66-7, 113.
William, brewer: 62, 64, 66-7, 113.
Sketchley Brewery: 38-40, 55, 63-5.
Slitting mills: 109.
Small, Alexander, tape manufacturer, Winshill Mill: 150, App. 42.
Smallware manufacture: 150.
Smeaton, John, canal engineer: 17.
Smisby, barley growing: 41.
Smisby Lane tollgate: 21.
Smith:
Ann: 34.
Ann (2): 34.
John, Gainsborough: 44.
Joseph (1) (d. 1727), innkeeper and brewer: 33-4, 64.
Joseph (2), brewer: 34, 55-6.
Joseph (3), corn miller: 164.
Thomas, framework knitter: 137.
William, screw manufacturer: 116.
Smith and Co., brickworks; 169.
Smith and Mosley, Gainsborough: 60.
Smith and Mousley, hop merchants, Worcester: 53.
Smith, Port, Wood and Co., screw manufacturers: 118.
Smith, Wienholt and Co., London: 48.
Soar, River: 13.
Soho Hat Factory, Bone End Wharf: 158.
Sollory family: 148, 157, App. 46.
Solly, Isaac, London: 48.
South Derbyshire plateau: 2.
South Staffordshire Waterworks reservoirs: 4.
Spade manufacture: 110, 114, 119, 138.
Spinning cotton: 134-6.
Spott, Wulfric, Earl of Mercia: 6.
Stage coaches: 21.
Staley, John, dyer: 136.
Joseph, dyer: 136.
Standley, brewer: 39.
Stanhope, coal seams: 4.
Stanhope Bretby collieries: 4.
Staniforth and Co.: 50.
Stanley Street: 122-3.
Stanton collieries: 1, 66.
Stapenhill, Robert: 128.
Stapenhill: 1, 6, 9, 11, 51.
brickyards: App. 47.
clay extraction: 2, 168-9.
collieries: 4, 51.
corn mill: 164.
population: App. 5.
Star inn Brewery: App. 33.
Statham, William, innkeeper: 136.
Station hotel: 165.
Station Street:
Bass and Co.: 84.
breweries: 96.
Burton Brewery Co.: 80.
Burton Copper Works: 122.
J. Homer, brass foundry: 122.
S. Sanders, foundry: 121.
Staton, J. C., alabaster and gypsum works: 172.
Joseph, cement and plaster manufacturer: 165.
Staves: 49-50, 53-4, 63, 81.
barrel: 63, 81.
brack: 49.
Danzig: 43, App. 16.
Danzig crown pipe: 49, 54.
'Dantzick' crown pipe: 63.
Hambro crown pipe: 54.
hogshead: 63.
St. Petersburg red deal: 49.
Stettin: 43, 49, 54, 74.
'Stretteen' pipe: 63.
Steam Engine Mill: 144.
Steam power: 176.
cotton mills: 144-5.
Robinson's mill, Papplewick, Notts.: 144.
Stenson, William, colliery owner: 22-3.
Stephenson, George and Robert, railway engineers: 23.
Stephenson, *Sir* William, hop suppliers: 42.
Stettin (Szczecinek):
staves: 43, 49, 54, 63, 74.
Steward of the Manor: 8.
Stockingers: 137.
Stockings coal seam: 4.
Stockwith: 13, 32.
Stone, Samuel, Knighton, Leics.: 82.
Stonemasons, millbuilding: 146.
Stonier, John, corn miller: 165.
Storey, George and Co.: 37.
Street lighting: 9.
Streets, re-paving: 9.
Stretton: 1, 6.
Clay Mills forge: 48, 50, 110, 114-5, 118, 176, App. 39.
population: App. 5.
Strutt, Jedediah, cotton mill owner: 138, 146-7, 149.
Strychnine, alleged hop substitute: 90.
Sutherland and Co., St. Petersburg: 48.
Swadlincote:
collieries: 4, 22, 112.
Granville Mills: 165.
Swannington:
canal: 22.
collieries: 4.
railway: 23.

Swarbourn stream: 1.
Sweatmore, James, spinner: 148.
Sweden, iron exports: 62.
Sykes, Richard and Joseph, iron importers, Hull: 108.
Sykes and Co., brewers: App. 34.

Tallow, imports: 50, App. 17.
Tammy weaving: 133-5, 138, 142.
Tamworth:
  Peel's calico printing works: 141.
  Peel's Thynne estates: 141.
Tanner, Thomas, millwright: 146.
Tanning trade: 166-7.
Tanyards: 80, 166-7, 175.
Tape manufacture: 150, App. 42.
Tarratt, Ann: 55-6.
Tatenhill: 2.
  alabaster deposits: 169.
  corn mill: 115.
  screw mill: 115-6.
Taverner, John, tape manufacturer: 150.
Taylor, Thomas: 57.
Tea-green marl: 2.
Terry and Wright, Hull: 44.
Textile manufacture: 127-51, 180.
Thimble manufacture, Burton Forge: 109.
Thompson, *Capt., Olive Tree*: 44.
  Francis, brewer: App. 31.
  James, Hull: 44.
  John, innkeeper and brewer: 79-80, App. 31.
  Thomas, Hull: 67.
Thompson, J. and F. (Thompson and Son), brewers: 80, 83, App. 31-4.
Thorley, Christopher, Hull: 44, App. 23.
Thornewill family: App. 51.
  Arthur: 121.
  Charles Francis: 121.
  Edward: 118, App. 39.
  Elizabeth (Astle): 110.
  Francis: 110, 114-5.
  Martha (Hammond): 121.
  Robert (d. 1858): 120-1.
  Robert (2): 121.
  Thomas (d. 1786): 110, 114-5, 176.
  Thomas (2): 115.
Thornewill and Warham (1849): 120-1, 123, App. 40-1.
  brewery locomotives: 85-6, 120.
  Ferry Bridge: 120.
  steam engines: 120.
Thornewill and Warham, Ltd. (1919): 121-2.
Thornewill Engineering Company: 114-20.
  Clay Mill Forge: 114, 176.
  iron castings: 119.
  iron bar imports: 50, 55.
Thornewill Engineering Co.—continued—
  iron hoop production: 43, 48, 55.
  New Street Spadeworks: 114, 118, 120.
  steam engines: 119-20.
  timber purchase: 112.
Three Queens inn, Horninglow Street: 33-4, 59.
Thynne estates: 141.
Ticknall, barley growing: 41.
Tied public houses: 73, 85, 88, 95.
Tile-making: 168-9.
Timber: App. 37.
  building: 2.
  charcoal: 2, 112.
  imports: 43, 48-9, 54, 61, 67, 74, 163, App. 16, 22, 24.
Tokens: 131, 148-9, 156.
Toll gates: 21.
Tooth Bros., brewers: 87, App. 33.
Toplis, William, tanner: 167.
Town commissioners: 9, 101.
Town hall: 9, 100.
Town masters: 9.
  account, 1725: 157.
  Michael Bass: 66.
  J. Clay: 66.
  J. W. Musgrave: 66.
  R. Shilton: 133.
  W. Sketchley: 62, 66.
  F. Wakefield: 167.
Townshend, Henry, brewer: 85.
Transport: 13-25, 181; *see also* Canals, Railways, River transport, Roads, Trent Navigation.
Traveller, ship: 44, App. 15.
Trent, River: 17-20, 22, 32-3, 47, 60, 67; *see also* Trent Navigation.
Trent and Mersey Canal: 9, 18-20, 111, 114, 145-6, 176, 181.
  timber trade: 163.
Trent and Mersey Canal Act, 1766: 18.
Trent Bridge Brewery: 82.
Trent Meadows: 10.
Trent Navigation: 9, 13-9, 22-3, 35, 181.
  Act, 1699: 8.
  Act, 1783: 19.
  ale trade: 33-4, 65.
  Bill, 1714: 15.
  bar iron imports: 15.
  Bond End Canal: 18.
  Burton Boat Company: 16.
  Burton Boat Company (1762-3): 17-9.
  Burton Wharf: 35.
  Cavendish Boat Company: 20.
  cheese trade: 15.
  closure above Wilden: 20.
  H. Evans: 22, 57, 62, 66.
  extension to Burton: 14-6, 32, 108.

Trent Navigation—continued—
- extension to Wilden Ferry: 13.
- felt exports: 157-8.
- flint trade: 15.
- L. Fosbrooke, Wilden Ferry: 14-5, 33.
- frost, 1791: 41.
- Gainsborough Boat Company: 20.
- Grand Trunk Company: 17-8, 20.
- George Hayne: 14-6, 33, 35, 132, 175.
- Henry Hayne: 16-7, 111.
- John Hayne: 17.
- Henshall and Co., Stone: 19.
- A. Hoskins: 17.
- iron trade: 107, 111.
- W. Jessop: 19.
- Kings Mills: 16-7.
- leases: 176.
- Lloyds: 111.
- Nottingham Boat Company: 16.
- Paget family: 107.
- salt trade: 15.
- S. Sketchley: 62, 66.
- syndicate: 176, 179.
- timber trade: 54, 163.
- trade (1720): 15-6.
- Trent and Mersey Canal: 18, 176.
- Upper Mills: 132.
- Uxbridge, Earl of: 17-8, 175.
- J. Wilkes: 22, 141.
- B. Wilson, snr.: 37.
- Winshill corn mill: 165.
- Winshill fulling mill: 139.
- Wyatt: 17.

Trent valley, geology: 3.
Trent Works, Derby Street: 122.
Triassic beds: 2.
Trickle, William, ropemaker: 162.
Truck system: 148-9.
Truman, Hanbury and Buxton, brewers: 82, 88, App. 34.
Tunnicliff, Walter, potter: 166.
Turnpikes: 9, 13, 20-2.
Tutbury:
- alabaster deposits: 169.
- Church, alabaster carving: 169.
- cotton and worsted spinning mill: 136, 141-5, 147-50.
- flax dressers: 50.
- gymsum: 2.
- rope makers: 50.

Twinemakers: 162-3.
Twyst, Gilbert, alabaster worker: 170.
Tyler, Richard, innkeeper: 33.

Umpler Green: 59.
Union Foundry: 122.
Union Mill Co., corn millers: 165.
Union Street: 122.
Union system: 94, 180.
Universal British Directory, 1791: 140.
Upper (or Over) Walk Mill, fulling: 129, 131-2, 140, 144.
Upper (or Weir) Mill, cotton spinning: 140.
Upper Weir: 140.
Uxbridge, Earls of: 9-10.
- *First creation, 1714*:
  - Henry, 1st earl (d. 1743): 175.
  - Henry, 2nd earl (d. 1769): 17-8, 62, 110.
- *Second creation, 1784*:
  - Henry, 1st earl (d. 1812): 115, 165.
  - Henry William, 2nd earl (Marquess) of Anglesey, 1815) (d. 1854): 168.

Uxbridge area: 10.
Uxbridge Street: 164.

Valentin, W. G.: 93.
van Bruiven, W. and Sons, Amsterdam: 48.
van der Schaaf, J. W. and M. Amsterdam: 48.
Victoria area: 10.
Victoria Crescent: 96.
- Street: 97.

Victuallers, licensed: 30-1, 34.
Vine inn, Horninglow Street: 33, 63.
von Ankum, Frederick William, Danzig: 45, 49.
Wade, Robert, alabaster worker: 170.
Wagner, George, London: 158.
Wagons, road transport: 21.
Wakefield family, flax dressers: 137.
- Francis, leather worker: 167.
- John, mercer: 132.
- John (2), leather worker: 167.

Walford, William, millwright: 146.
Walk Mill Brook: 129.
Walk Mill House: 129.
Walker, A. B., brewer: 82, 96, App. 34.
- Anne, innkeeper: 33.
- Hannah (Wilson): 36.
- John, innkeeper: 34.
- Margery: 170.
- Mary: 36.
- Peter, brewer: 82, App. 34.

Walker, John and Randle, Woverhampton: 54.
Walkere, William le, fuller: 128.
Walter, J. G., Stettin: 74.
Walton family, clothiers: 133.
Ward, Samuel, screwforger: 118.
- Thomas, tanner: 167.

Wardle, Henry, brewer: 101.
Warham, John Robson, engineer: 120-1.
Warsaw, ale imports: 48.
Wash leather manufacture: 132.

Water:
brewing: 2-4, 29, 35, 66, 82, 84, 86, 97, 104, 181, App. 1-4.
'Water' barley: 42, 53.
Water frames, cotton spinning: 143.
Water-power, cotton mills: 144-5.
Waterloo:
Mount: 2.
Street: 122.
Waterloo Works: 122.
Waterside, millworkers' cottages: 148.
Watson, David, barrister and brewer: 31, 63.
Samuel, Hull: 37.
Watson Street: 140.
Wayte, brewer: 39.
William, felt and hat maker: 156.
Weaver family: 118.
Weaver, River: 17.
Weaving industry: 135-6, 141, 143, 150, 175.
Weaving, handloom: 136, 143, 146.
Webb, John, Tutbury Mill: 150.
Thomas, Barton-under-Needwood: 142.
Weir (or Upper) Mill, cotton spinning: 140.
Wellington Street, malthouse workers: 97.
Wells: 3-4, 84, 86, App. 1-4.
Weston and Fife, hop merchants, London: 53.
Wetmore: 6, 10, 165.
Wetmore Road: 164.
Weyland, B. D., London: 48.
Wheat, imports: 50, 55.
Whitbread, S., brewers, London: 29, 93.
White, William, *Directory, 1851*: 159.
White Hart inn, High Street: 63.
Whitehead, Henry, brewer: App. 52.
John, maltster: 59.
Whitehouse, William, nail-ironmonger, West Bromwich: 113-4.
Whitehurst, brewer: 39.
Whitwick colliery: 22-3.
Whitworth, Robert, canal surveyor: 20.
Wichnor forge: 115.
Wightman, William, clothier: 130.
Wilberforce, Robert and William, Hull: 37.
Wilden Ferry: 17.
Trent and Mersey Canal: 18-9.
Trent Navigation: 13-5, 20, 33, 108.
Wilders, Henry, brewer: 80.
John, innkeeper and brewer: 33-4.
Thomas, brewer: 80.
William, innkeeper: 33.
William (2): 167.
Wilders, brewers: 39.
Wilkes family: 22.
John: 17, 141.
Joseph (b. 1732); 16, 20, 141-2, 144-5, 177, 179.
banker: 9, 179.
Burton Boat Company: 17.
colliery owner: 119.
Measham Mills: 141-2, 144-5, 179.
Thomas: 141.
Wilkes and Jewsbury, textile manufacturers: 141-3, 147, 149.
Willington:
Hall, W. C. Sale: 102.
Nottingham Boat Company: 16.
Trent Navigation: 15.
Wharf: 60.
Wilmore, Thomas, innkeeper: 33.
Wilson family: App. 49.
Ann: 52.
Benjamin, senior, brewer: 34-7, 64-6 162, 176.
Benjamin, junior, brewer (d. 1812): 36-52, 55-6, 60, 63-6, 79, 177-9, App. 8-20.
cotton exports: 146.
imports: 145-6, App. 18.
hemp imports: 162.
iron imports: 113.
tallow imports: 50, App. 17.
timber imports: App. 16.
Benjamin (3): 52.
Jane: 52.
John, ropemaker: 162.
John Walker (d. 1797), brewer: 37, 52-6, 57, 64-6, 178, App. 23.
Burton Bank: 9, 55, 66, 178.
hemp imports: 162.
iron imports: 55, 113-4, App. 21.
timber merchant: 54-5, 67, 140, 163, App. 22.
Joseph, Winshill Mill: 165.
Thomas: 52.
William, brewer: 37, 55.
hemp imports: 162.
Wilson-Allsopp Brewery: 72-5;
Winn, James, Wolverhampton: 54.
Winshill: 1, 6, 9, 11, 37.
brick clay extraction: 2, 168-9.
Burton Forge: 19, 109, 111-3, 115, 176, App. 38.
Church: 101.
corn mill: 6, 8, 31, 57, 139, 164-5.
cotton spinning mill: 139-43, 148-50, App. 45.
fulling mill: 139.
population: App. 5.
Tape Mill: App. 42.
Winshill Heath, colleries: 4.
Winshill Wood:
brick clay extraction: 168.
collieries: 4.
Wolston, John, brewer: 30.

Wood, George, baker: 115.
John, dyer: 134, 136.
William, screw manufacturer: 118.
Wood's map, 1837: 10.
Wood Yard, screw forgers' tenements: 116.
Woodcock, Benjamin, Tamworth: 54.
Rev. William: 109, 132, 175.
Woodworking industry: 163-4.
Woolcombers: 134-6.
Woollen cloth industry: 7, 127-33, 136-8, 156, 158, 167, 180.
Woolstaplers: 136;
Wornell, pottery modeller: 166.
Worsted industry: 8, 132-8, 142, 148-50, 158, 180-1.
Worthington, Ann (Tarratt): 55.
Thomas: 56.
William (1), brewer: 34-5, 54-6, 63-6, 176.
iron imports: 113.
timber merchant: 163.
William (2): 56, 178.
William (3), barley supplier, Tamworth: 53.
William Henry, brewer: 101-2.
Worthington and Co., brewers: 76-7, 81, 83, 87-8, 92, 103, 118, 178,
Worthington and Co.—continued—App. 32-4.
Wray and Hollingsworth, Hull: 114.
Wright, Edwin, engineer: 122.
Capt. J., *Humber*: 44, App. 15.
Wright's Crown Brewery Co., Market Drayton: 83.
Wyatt, Benjamin: 115.
Job, Tatenhill: 115.
John: 115.
William: 8, 17, 66, 110, 112, 116.
map, 1760: 8.
screw manufacturer: 115.
timber merchant: 163, App. 37.

Yates, William, Blackburn: 139.
Yeats and Brown, hop merchants: 42.
Yellow-ware manufacture: 166.
Yeomans, Brewer: 39, 63.
J., alderman, 1878: 101.
J., brewers, 1888: App. 34.
John, brewer: 78-9.
Mary, brewer: 79, App. 31-3.
William, brewer: 57.

Zimmerman, Carl, Danzig: 46.
Zulun, ship: 74.